Preserving the
Constitution

Copyright © 2006 Fordham University Press

All rights reserved. No part of this publication may be reproduced, stored in a retrieval system, or transmitted in any form or by any means—electronic, mechanical, photocopy, recording, or any other—except for brief quotations in printed reviews, without the prior permission of the publisher.

Reconstructing America Series, No. 11
ISSN 1523-4606

Library of Congress Cataloging-in-Publication Data

Benedict, Michael Les.
  Preserving the Constitution : essays on politics and the Constitution in the reconstruction era.—1st ed.
    p. cm.—(Reconstructing America (series) ; no. 11)
  Includes bibliographical references and index.
  ISBN-13: 978-0-8232-2553-8 (cloth : alk. paper)
  ISBN-13: 978-0-8232-2554-5 (pbk. : alk. paper)
  ISBN-10: 0-8232-2553-4 (cloth : alk. paper)
  ISBN-10: 0-8232-2554-2 (pbk. : alk. paper)
  1. Constitutional history—United States. 2. Reconstruction (U.S. history, 1865–1877) I. Title. II. Series.
  KF4541.B445 2006
  342.7302′9—dc22

                                            2006007878

08 07 06   5 4 3 2 1
First edition.

Contents

Introduction: Constitutional Politics and Reconstruction ix

I POLITICS, THE CONSTITUTION, AND RECONSTRUCTION

1. Preserving the Constitution: The Conservative Basis of Radical Reconstruction | 3
2. The Rout of Radicalism: Republicans and the Elections of 1867 | 23
3. A New Look at the Impeachment of Andrew Johnson | 32

II PARTIES AND FACTIONS IN CIVIL WAR–ERA POLITICS

4. The Party, Going Strong: Congress and Elections in the Mid-Nineteenth Century | 47
5. Factionalism and Representation: Some Insight from the Nineteenth-Century United States | 67

III POLITICS, THE CONSTITUTION, AND THE RETREAT FROM RECONSTRUCTION

6. The Politics of Reconstruction | 93
7. Salmon P. Chase and Constitutional Politics | 129
8. The Problem of Constitutionalism and Constitutional Liberty in the Reconstruction South | 152
9. Reform Republicans and the Retreat from Reconstruction | 168

10 Southern Democrats in the Crisis of 1876–77: A Reconsideration of *Reunion and Reaction* | 186

Notes 211
Index 303

Preserving the Constitution

Introduction: Constitutional Politics and Reconstruction

Henry Ward Beecher, the nation's best-known clergyman, a spellbinding orator, was delivering the keynote address at the second meeting of the American Equal Rights Association. His audience of abolitionists and woman suffragists knew that they were living through a revolution. For decades, they had fought to change the nation's course. They had witnessed the ratification of a constitutional amendment that buried the slaveholding republic that they had fought all their lives, and Americans were in the process of ratifying another that would transform it into one of equal rights for all men. As part of their Reconstruction program, Republicans had mandated that every loyal man, black or white, vote in the South. "We seem to be on the very eve of all that the friends of freedom have ever asked of this nation," Wendell Phillips marveled.[1] Even securing the vote for women seemed possible. "We are in the favored hour," Henry Ward Beecher exhorted the delegates, "and if you have great principles to make known, this is the time to advance those principles."[2]

Both historians and legal scholars have recognized that the years immediately following the end of the Civil War constituted a great era of constitution-making—an era of "constitutional politics" in which political contests were thoroughly entwined with fundamental ideas about citizenship, civil and political rights, and the relationship between state and federal government. But their approaches differ. Academics affiliated with law faculties tend to be concerned primarily with constitutional law. They tend to see law as essentially different from politics: politics is about the exercise of power, while law is about the application of rules.[3] American legal academics rarely speak of "constitutional politics." When they utilize the concept (if not the language), they tend to think of it in terms of the contest that led to the framing of the Constitution itself and the political context in which Americans have adopted constitutional amendments. On occasion, they have used the term to describe using litigation to achieve political goals.[4] From this point of view, once the political process has established a constitutional provision, interpreting it is a matter of law to be articulated by judges. They have studied the Reconstruction era primarily to discern how judges should interpret the constitutional amendments that are its greatest legal legacy, focusing especially on what they meant to contemporaries—the "original understanding" or "intent" with which they were framed and ratified.⁵

Academic historians do not study history for legal purposes. For us, the main goal is to understand why things happened the way they did and how they contributed to the world in which we now live.⁶ We have a broader view of "constitutional politics." Most of us see the framing and ratification of the Thirteenth, Fourteenth, and Fifteenth Amendments as part of a longer, broader, and essentially political process in which Americans have developed fundamental principles of governance. Judges and courts play only a part in that larger process. We see the constitutional system as larger than constitutional law. Even the histories of the Reconstruction era that attend most closely to constitutional issues do not try to tease out exact understandings and intentions.⁷

In recent years, political scientists and law faculty–affiliated legal historians have self-consciously begun to close the gap between the historical and the legal approaches to constitutional history. They are attending more closely to the role the people and representative institutions have played in determining the course of American constitutional development.⁸ Constitutional theorists are at work trying to describe a broader concept of "constitutional politics" and what it means for constitutional theory.⁹ Going beyond Bruce Ackerman's stress on the public role in "transformative moments," they see a constant engagement between the political process and the constitutional system. "Constitutional politics in the United States extends beyond the practice of judges enforcing fundamental norms made in the past or creating new ones," they observe. "It is also a function of commitments and actions within the polity at large. Creating and maintaining constitutional meaning and authority are ongoing and normal processes."¹⁰ Yet legal academics still seem to posit a dichotomy between what they are beginning to call "popular constitutionalism" and the doctrines that are promulgated by courts.¹¹ It seems particularly difficult for them to devise an understanding that integrates the people, political branches of government, and the courts in the development of constitutional policy.

Decades of overattention to the role of courts, especially the U.S. Supreme Court, have forced present-day legal theorists to work to reincorporate political realities into American constitutional theory, but no such heritage blinded Americans in the Civil War era. To the contrary, neither state nor federal courts were perceived as the primary protectors of civil liberties. Except for the protection of a few property rights, Americans relied for their day-to-day freedom on the actions and self-restraint of their legislative representatives.¹² Great constitutional issues had always been at the heart of national politics. In the "revolution" of 1800, Jeffersonian Republicans had sustained "the principles of

'98"—the repudiation of Federalist broad constructions of national power and the Alien and Sedition Acts. As a leading historian of the era explains, Republicans "saw themselves as having saved republicanism, the Constitution, and the republic."[13]

Nor had the great controversy over the nature of the federal system that culminated in the Civil War been played out in the courts. By supporting the state rights–oriented Democratic Party in the 1830s and 1840s, Americans had rendered virtually irrelevant the nationalistic decisions promulgated by the Supreme Court during John Marshall's term as chief justice. Indeed, the Democratic Party had organized in large part to save the Constitution from those misguided decisions, just as the Republican Party promised to save the Constitution from the proslavery decisions of Marshall's successor, Roger B. Taney.[14]

All knew that most state courts had done little to protect the rights of African Americans and that the Supreme Court had explicitly repudiated the idea that they had any rights to protect.[15] Therefore, it should come as no surprise that when the father of the Fourteenth Amendment, Ohio representative John A. Bingham, first proposed to empower the federal government to protect basic rights, he hardly thought of the courts at all. The initial version of the Fourteenth Amendment that he brought to the House of Representatives on behalf of the Joint Committee on Reconstruction read simply, "Congress shall have power to make all laws which shall be necessary and proper to secure to the citizens of each State all the privileges and immunities of citizens in the several States, and to all persons in the several States equal protection in the rights of life, liberty, and property."[16] The language was patterned on Article I, section 8, which specified the powers of Congress. Only later did Bingham realize that it should be patterned on Article I, section 10, which explicitly limited the power of the states, to assure that the courts as well as Congress would enforce it.[17]

In fashioning legislation and constitutional amendments to empower the federal government to protect civil and political rights, Republicans were responding to public opinion. But public opinion at all times limited what they could do. Although powerful individuals and interests had more influence than ordinary individuals, they had far less clout than they do today. Politicians' careers depended upon turning out voters, and though money helped to do it, it was not yet the fuel that powered the engines of politics. Thus politicians and parties were closely attuned to how voters seemed to be reacting to political initiatives.

The people may have "care[d] little for Constitutional hair splitting," as ex-general and future congressman Stephen A. Hurlbut wrote Thaddeus Stevens from downstate Illinois,[18] but they cared deeply about fundamentals. Looking at diaries and letters of Civil War soldiers, historian James McPherson found evidence of widespread discussion and argument over ideological and constitutional issues. Brigade and regimental debating societies addressed such questions as whether Congress alone should determine the status of states in rebellion and whether the rebel states should be treated as conquered territories. An observer of such activities remarked on the "outbursts of untutored eloquence." Officers reported "spirited, I may call them hot, controversies about slavery, the Emancipation Edict and kindred subjects."[19] Insisting that the United States was "a white man's country," for example, may have lacked sophistication, but it certainly was a good approximation of the Supreme Court's holding in the *Dred Scott* case, which had articulated the constitutional underpinnings of the slaveholding republic.[20]

Ordinary people influenced political outcomes through the political process. At the same time, elites attempted to influence voters, as competing political aspirants tried to frame issues and spin results to their advantage. Urban and even rural newspapers published long excerpts from the *Congressional Globe*, after 1873 the *Congressional Record*. Congressmen read formal speeches into the *Globe* and *Record*, published them as pamphlets, and circulated them to voters in their districts and states. Ambitious politicians like Charles Sumner made their careers by connecting to the larger public through what one of his biographers has called "a perpetual speech."[21]

Politicians, journalists (writing for newspapers that in those days were openly partisan), and intellectuals articulated both sophisticated and simple articulations of constitutional positions—in controversial literature appearing in newspapers, pamphlets, posters, slogans, and even songs; in congressional debates and well-publicized addresses at public meetings; in campaign literature; in vigorous and festive campaigning that included parades, public appearances by political celebrities, and combative public debates that often took on the character of spectator sports. The extraordinary voter turnout during the Civil War era attests to both their success and the salience of the issues.[22]

These essays are about the constitutional politics of the Reconstruction era. They are concerned with how Republicans tried to replace the slaveholding republic with a nation dedicated to freedom and equality of basic legal and political rights and how their own constitutional commitments and popular attitudes toward constitutional fundamentals limited what they could do. All of the essays have been published previously, but they have been revised and updated to reflect new scholarship. Some of them have had a significant impact on the historiography of Reconstruction. Others appeared in venues that limited their audience, and one reason I have been anxious to republish them is that I think they have something to offer a wider scholarly and student readership.

INTRODUCTION

Historians generally agree that Reconstruction fell short of its promise. My purpose in all these essays has been to explore the reasons for that sad result. For many historians the answer has been simple: White America has always been deeply affected, or perhaps it would be better to say *infected*, by racism. In the view of these historians, the struggle against slavery had little to do with sympathy for the black slave. They conclude that the Civil War was fought essentially to save the Union; interest in black freedom and equal civil and political rights was incidental and quickly faded. But my exploration of the original sources of the time suggest a much more complex story, in which pervasive racism warred with equally pervasive commitments to freedom and equal rights, in which profound events worked profound changes in people's attitudes. Among northerners, and especially Republicans, the alchemy of war in some cases changed attitudes toward race itself; in even more cases it changed ideas about how a nation newly rededicated to freedom should deal with race, even if underlying ideas of racial superiority and inferiority persisted. The potential for a racially just society that these changes engendered was not realized, but these essays argue that the reasons went beyond a simple reversion to racist attitudes. The problem was how to force change on an entire region in a nation dedicated to local democracy (gendered though it was), due process of law, and a federal system of divided government authority. Adding to the difficulty was the context of a hotly contested two-party political system, in which the defection of even a small proportion of a party's supporters was likely to lead to defeat at the polls.

Americans' ideas about constitutional liberty played a crucial role in the history of Reconstruction. They provided the basis for the Republican program of equal rights; ironically, they also set the limits to that program and reduced the prospects for its success. Americans were as concerned with preserving the Constitution as they were with changing it to protect liberty and equal rights. These two commitments were in profound tension. The question was how one could change the constitutional system to fulfill the promise of the Declaration of Independence—to entrench a republic dedicated to liberty instead of slavery—and yet preserve the essentials of federalism and local democracy. Nearly a century and a half later, we still struggle with these problems. Perhaps knowing more about how we dealt with them in the past will prepare us to deal with them better in the future.

I

Politics, the
Constitution, and
Reconstruction

1

Preserving the Constitution: The Conservative Basis of Radical Reconstruction

The Civil War and Reconstruction precipitated a profound constitutional transformation in the United States. In the seventy years following the ratification of the Constitution, the fundamental law had been interpreted more and more to accommodate slavery. Its connection to the spirit of the nation's founding document, the Declaration of Independence, had become ever more attenuated. The United States had become, in the words of the late Don E. Fehrenbacher, a slaveholding republic.[1]

The proslavery interpretation of the Constitution that sustained the slaveholding republic did more than fasten the slaves' shackles ever more firmly. In the slaveholding republic, color was associated with slavery. Therefore, proslavery constitutionalism encouraged a policy of racial restrictions even in the North. It helped create a virulent northern racism, especially among artisans and workers, who were driven to distinguish their status as white laborers from the degraded position of black slaves.[2] In the slaveholding republic, it was perfectly logical to deny that African Americans were American citizens, as the Supreme Court did in the *Dred Scott* case.[3] Although some northern states did recognize their black residents as citizens, in a slaveholding republic it was a state's recognition of black people as citizens that was anomalous, not their exclusion.

Thus, the Republican Party's rise to dominance in the northern states and its victory in the presidential election of 1860 portended a constitutional revolution—an effort to transform the slaveholding republic to one consistent with the Declaration's promise of liberty and equality. Southerners were fully aware of the significance of the change. They seceded from a Union whose constitution promised to be radically transformed from the one they had known.[4] The Civil War both speeded the process and made it even more radical than it would have been had southerners resisted within the system. No longer accommodating slavery, with the Thirteenth Amendment the Constitution became a document of freedom. Not content simply to reinterpret its existing language in light of this transformation, Republicans explicitly incorporated the change

---

The original version of this essay was published in the *Journal of American History* 61 (June 1974): 65–90.

into the document itself through the Fourteenth and Fifteenth Amendments. It was a profound transformation that changed the nature of the republic.⁵

Yet African Americans were denied the equal rights of citizenship for another century, and other racial disparities persist to this day. Historians have wondered what went wrong. What emerged from the Civil War era was not racial justice, much less racial equality. The subtitle of Eric Foner's standard account of Reconstruction reflects our sober judgment: *America's Unfinished Revolution*.⁶

Historians offer two not inconsistent explanations for the failure to carry the transformation to its logical fruition: (1) persistent racism in the North undermined commitment to a new racially egalitarian order, and (2) a conservative reaction against northern working-class militancy undermined support for black workers and their political representatives in the South.⁷ But while these factors were important, historians of Reconstruction have tended to slight another crucial element. This factor was a persistent concern with federalism—maintaining a proper balance between the responsibilities of the state and federal governments—and a corresponding reluctance to arm the federal government with the powers necessary to protect the rights now guaranteed to all.⁸

Legal and constitutional historians have paid more attention to this factor than other historians have, but they have attributed this concern with federalism primarily to the justices of the Supreme Court, whose perverse commitment to state rights, if not to white supremacy, subverted the radical constitutional transformation Republicans had tried to bring about. It was, as one has written, the most "striking instance in American constitutional history of outright judicial disregard for congressional intent."⁹

This understanding is based on a conviction that Republican Reconstruction legislation reflected a popular, or at least congressional, commitment to a transformation of federalism as part of the longer transformation from a slaveholding to a free republic. "Revolutionary constitutionalism," legal historian Robert J. Kaczorowski has called it, a determination "to begin the nation anew."¹⁰ But while Republicans knew that abolition had radically altered the constitutional system by rededicating the nation to freedom, they were deeply ambivalent about the implications of what they had done and were plainly worried about outrunning public opinion. Having transformed American constitutionalism—and indeed American society—they wanted to retain the essentials of the federal system. Their problem was how to do so and at the same time protect the rights of the people they had freed from slavery.

Facing this dilemma, Republicans opted to expand national power to protect rights whenever events forced them to. But they did so reluctantly and still attempting to preserve the traditional constitutional order of federalism as much as possible. Their rhetoric indicates that they understood the political danger of doing otherwise. They were not merely acting on their own preferences, but the preferences of the people they represented. No matter how radical it was culturally and socially, from a constitutional perspective, Negro suffrage was conservative.

Persisting commitment to federalism helps explain why Reconstruction failed to achieve its goals and why so many Republicans appeared so quickly to abandon the struggle after 1869.

Republicans' constitutional justification for their Reconstruction program indicates that it is an oversimplification to accuse them of abandoning Reconstruction. The reluctance of many Republicans to interfere in the South was manifest in their program itself. They insisted on guarantees for the security of loyal whites and blacks; they passed laws and constitutional amendments that delegated power to the national government to secure basic rights. But most Republicans did not want to displace state and local governments as the primary protectors of the ordinary rights of their citizens.[11] Coping with a revolutionary situation, Republicans framed the most limited Reconstruction they could and still secure meaningful freedom in the South. Until 1868, Republicans adhered to the position that their legislation was merely a temporary aberration in the federal system. They hoped to alter both southern politics and federal law in such a way as to minimize the need for continued federal action to protect rights. When persistent violence forced Republicans to advocate long-term federal action to protect rights, most still tried to limit its scope, and some refused to make this new departure at all.

Suggesting that Republicans were concerned with maintaining the traditional federal system is controversial, because the understanding of those who framed the Reconstruction-era constitutional amendments and civil rights legislation has implications for present-day constitutional law. The understanding or intention with which Americans framed and ratified constitutional amendments and the intent of legislators when they enact statutes is a significant source of legal authority for their interpretation. Indeed, some constitutional theorists argue that original intent is determinative.[12] Suggesting that Republicans were less than fully committed to transferring the primary responsibility for protecting rights to the federal government provides ammunition for those trying to limit the federal role today.

Because of the legal implications, a number of legal analysts researching Reconstruction have done so primarily to divine the original intent or understanding of the Fourteenth Amendment.[13] Of course, they have reached widely disparate conclusions. Academic historians are hardly surprised. Historical actors are rarely as clear about their own intentions and understandings as legal analysts would like, and historical evidence does not lend itself to interpretative certainty. Historians take complexity and ambiguity as the norm; they expect legal interpretations of legislation to be contested and resolved over time. Interrogating history for the purpose of discovering an "original intent" or "original understanding" requires the investigator to reduce complexity and arrive at a best answer. This purpose can significantly influence research methods, making them quite different from those of academic historians.[14]

Playing for high present-day stakes, legal analysts who stress the radicalism of Reconstruction-era civil rights legislation tend to concentrate on the logical implications of the Civil War constitutional transformation, often ignoring Republicans' efforts to reassure their constituents of their moderation.[15] Measured against the antebellum, proslavery Constitution, the Republican effort to reshape southern society and protect the rights of American citizens—indeed recognizing African Americans as citizens at all—*was* radical, and everyone knew it. The question was, how far would the old landmarks be obliterated? Engaged in a great constitutional transformation, Republicans sought to reassure their constituents of their continued commitment to constitutionalism and the federal system. Legal scholar Pamela Brandwein makes the point well: Republicans and their constituents knew that they were changing the prewar federal system by expanding national power to protect civil rights. "But if the 'traditional federal system' refers to a general notion of limited government, then Republicans wanted to keep this system."[16] Attempting to do so, they established the context in which Americans judged further Reconstruction legislation in the 1870s and, significantly, the context in which the justices of the Supreme Court would interpret the extent of the change.

Historians' assessments of the constitutional aspects of Reconstruction date back to the seminal studies of William A. Dunning and John W. Burgess at the turn of the twentieth century.[17] Scholars have abandoned the prejudicial conclusion of historians writing from the 1930s through the 1950s—that "For the Constitution itself . . . [Republicans] had little respect."[18] But while legal scholars have argued over Republicans' constitutional intentions and understandings, few of the historians who revolutionized our understanding of Reconstruction rethought its constitutional basis. The exceptions—brief dicta by McKitrick and William R. Brock and a longer comment by constitutional historian Alfred H. Kelly—suggested a fundamental revision. They—especially Kelly—suggested that Republicans were fundamentally conservative in their attitudes toward the United States Constitution and the federal system it delineated. Kelly argued that the Reconstruction program, so long believed by historians to have been a radical departure from traditional constitutional forms, violative of the principles of American federalism, actually was framed by constitutional conservatives who envisioned little real alteration in national-state relations.[19]

McKitrick, Brock, and Kelly presented insights of fundamental importance into the constitutional nature of Reconstruction legislation, but they either repeated older formulations or did not offer detailed analysis of the theoretical framework within which Republicans developed their program. It was primarily the students of constitutional historian and Civil War–era specialist Harold M. Hyman who, rejecting their mentor's early stress on the profoundness of the constitutional change, pointed to its limitations.[20]

They pointed out that even as Republicans exerted broad, new powers, they justified wartime measures in such a way as to preserve the old balance of the Constitution. Rather than admit that the war had precipitated a fundamental alteration in the federal system, they argued it merely had forced a suspension of peacetime constitutional provisions. Unionists reached this conclusion by different routes. Francis Lieber, the leading student of government in mid-nineteenth-century America, espoused the first interpretation: "The whole Rebellion is beyond the Constitution," he insisted. "The Constitution was not made for such a state of things. . . . The life of a nation is the first substantial thing and far above the formulas [for government] which . . . have been adopted." The Constitution had been intended to serve a nation forged by a common heritage and experience before and during the War for Independence. That nation had to be preserved even if the Constitution was violated.[21] A second school argued that the Constitution itself incorporated virtually unlimited war powers through the clause vesting in Congress the power to prosecute war (Art. 1, sec. 8). These powers were as much a part of the Constitution as its peacetime provisions, but in a state of war the war powers naturally became more prominent while other provisions receded into the background.[22]

By justifying the massive wartime expansion of the national government's power in this way, Republicans believed they had preserved the Constitution from contamination. With war's end, the occasion for using the war powers would cease. The limitations of the peacetime fundamental law would regain their sway.

The desire to preserve the federal system's prewar balance weighed heavily on the minds of leading Republicans. As early as 1861, a worried Republican Senator James W. Grimes wrote fellow Senator Lyman Trumbull, "We are gradually surrendering all the rights of the states & functions & shall soon be incapable of resuming them." Five years later, as one of the respected members of the prestigious Joint Committee of Fifteen on Reconstruction, Grimes was insisting that "During the prevalence of the war we drew to ourselves here as the Federal Government authority which had been considered doubtful by all and denied by many of the statesmen of this country. That time, it seems to me, has ceased and ought to cease. Let us go back to the original condition of things, and allow the States to take care of themselves as they have been in the habit of taking care of themselves."[23]

This kind of constitutional conservatism left Republicans ill prepared to cope with the complex problems of Reconstruction, which so clearly called at minimum for long-term national protection of citizens' rights. By 1865 Republicans had become so committed to the proposition that the national government's power would shrink to prewar dimensions at war's end that an immediate recognition of continued southern statehood upon the surrender of the rebel armies would have restored prewar state rights virtually intact, rendering the national government powerless to secure any guarantees of loyalty from the South. Because during the war Republicans had refused to acquiesce in a permanent expansion of national power at the expense of the states, in 1865 and 1866 they were forced to deny that the southern political organizations were as yet entitled to the rights of states. Therefore, the great controversy between President Andrew Johnson and his supporters and the Republican Party centered on the constitutional issue of the status of the former southern states.

Johnson held that the southern states had never legally left the Union and therefore retained their normal status in the Union. But since the southern authorities themselves had rebelled, there was no one to run the machinery of government. It was the president's obligation as commander-in-chief to restore functioning governments. Once he completed this process, the southern states automatically resumed their old places in the nation.

Thaddeus Stevens, the grimly stern Republican who combined the roles we would now call majority leader and whip in the House of Representatives, was the leading proponent of the "conquered province" theory. In his view, southerners had succeeded *de facto* in gaining the status of belligerents under international law. Once conquered, the former southern states were no different from any other territory acquired by the United States and were completely subject to the authority of the national government.

In his "state suicide" theory, the influential Republican senator Charles Sumner postulated that by rebelling the southern states had voluntarily destroyed their character as states in the Union. It was up to the national government to reconstitute them. The similar "forfeit rights" theory held that by attempting to secede the southern states had voluntarily relinquished their *rights* as states in the Union. However, they had no authority to throw off their *obligations* without the permission of the government to which those obligations were owed. At war's end, therefore, the defeated states owed allegiance to the Union even though they had sacrificed the rights and privileges that usually went with it.[24]

Each of these theories was designed to fix the status of the former southern states and the degree of national power over them. All but the southern theory maintained that the southern states were either out of the Union de facto or had ceased to exist at all.[25] Only if southern state organizations remained out of normal federal relations could Republicans exercise power over the South in Reconstruction consistently with their wartime constitutional conservatism. Thus, Republicans clearly acknowledged that once the government recognized the restoration of the southern states they would enjoy the same relations with the national government as existed before the war. It was this consideration that forced even conservative Republicans to break with Johnson in 1866, when he insisted that the southern states be restored to the Union before Congress enacted measures to protect loyal whites and blacks there. Given the limited powers that Congress had over states' domestic affairs, such a policy would have made real protection for loyalists impossible. Because Republicans did not envision permanent expansion of national power, they had to oppose their President's policy. "The time is to come when each southern state is to take its own local affairs into its own hands," Republicans recognized, "and the only security we can have that it will then move on in a loyal orbit is to be found in the permanent forces we shall have previously implanted in it."[26]

Having defined the status of the rebel states in a way that denied them immediate restoration to prewar rights, Republicans turned to three sources of national power over them. Stevens enunciated one alternative, suggesting that "as there are no symptoms that the people of these provinces will be prepared to participate in constitutional government for some years, I know of no arrangement so proper for them as territorial governments."[27] "They would be held in a territorial condition until they are fit to form State Constitutions, republican in fact not in form only, and ask admission into the Union as new States," he suggested.[28]

In a certain sense, Congress's power over the South would indeed expand if Stevens's scheme were adopted. Congress had absolute control over territorial property of the United States subject only to the few general prohibitions the Constitution imposed on congressional power. In the 1860s Congress generally allowed territories to govern themselves through territorial legislatures, but their powers were derived from and subject directly to that of Congress. And territorial governors were appointed by the president with the advice and consent of the Senate. But this power over the South would not be permanent; it would cease with statehood. In fact, it was precisely because Congress would lose its power once these territories were readmitted as states that it would have to take special care to see that they had learned their lessons: "If Congress approve their Constitutions, and think they have done works meet for repentance they would be admitted as new states," Stevens suggested. "If their Constitutions are not approved of, they would be sent back, until they have become wise enough so to purge their old laws as to eradicate every despotic and revolutionary principle." Nor could Congress force permanent changes on an unwilling people. The sole hope for a permanent rearrangement of the southern political, economic, and social order lay in southerners' voluntarily agreeing to such changes in return for statehood. "If they are to be admitted as new States they must form their own constitutions; and no enabling act could dictate its terms," Stevens insisted.[29]

Although many radicals preferred Stevens's territorial policy to establish congressional control over the South, his program met with such a negative response from more centrist Republicans that when he presented a Reconstruction bill to the House in 1867 it bore no resemblance to his earlier suggestion.[30]

Republicans discerned a second source of congressional power over Reconstruction in Congress's war powers. Building consciously on the legal-constitutional justifications for expanded national power developed during the war, these Republicans suggested that although peace would indeed restore the sway of peacetime constitutional limitations, it was up to the government to decide precisely when peace had arrived. In this case, the government might demand that the rebel states meet certain conditions in return for recognition that peace was restored.[31] This view was popularized by the conservative Richard Henry Dana in a speech delivered in Boston's Faneuil Hall on June 21, 1865: "The conquering party may hold the other in the grasp of war until it has secured whatever it has a right to acquire," he maintained.[32] This theory was received with favor in Boston. Ohio's new governor, Jacob D. Cox; House speaker Schuyler Colfax; William Pitt Fessenden, Republican leader in the Senate and the chairman of the Joint Committee on Reconstruction; Representative George S. Boutwell, also named to the Reconstruction Committee; Representative William Lawrence of the House Judiciary Committee, and the influential German Republican leader Carl Schurz all expressed views similar to Dana's.[33]

Like the theory of temporarily expanded national power in time of war from which it sprang, the grasp-of-war doctrine was designed to protect the federal system from fundamental, permanent change as a result of crisis. The federal system, Dana warned, "is held together by a balance of powers—centripetal and centrifugal forces. Let not their balance be destroyed." By simply continuing military occupation, this danger could be avoided. "If we should undertake to exercise sovereign civil jurisdiction over those States, it would be as great a peril to our system as it would be a hardship upon them."[34]

So, like Stevens's territorial scheme, the grasp-of-war policy gave no permanent power to Congress. Dana's friend John Bigelow, American minister to France, recognized the weakness of the theory immediately: There was nothing to prevent a southern state from reneging on its agreements once restored to normal relations in the Union. Dana acknowledged the danger but believed it was the best the North could do.[35] Dana had proposed a consciously conservative program. As he wrote to Charles Francis Adams Jr. immediately after his speech, "It would be an irreparable mischief for Congress to assume civil and political authority in state matters, but it is not an irreparable mischief for the general government to continue the exercise of such war powers as are necessary until the people of those States do what we in conscience think necessary for the reasonable security of the republic."[36]

Not only did Congress gain no power under Dana's doctrine, but even while the South remained in the "grasp of war," Congress's prerogatives were also strictly limited. The people of the southern states themselves were "voluntarily" to give guarantees of security through their own legislation. This might be done under the pressure of continued exclusion from the Union, but the guarantees were to be achieved through state rather than national legislation. Thus, both Stevens's and Dana's proposals not only left ultimate power to protect citizens' rights with the states, but even during the period of Reconstruction maintained a fiction of voluntarism. Even during the crisis Congress could not presume to dictate state action.

Republicans found a third source of congressional power in the duty the Constitution imposed on the national government to guarantee republican forms of government to the states. Republicans who argued that the southern states had ceased to exist during the war particularly favored this theory. If there were no state governments at all in the South, then "manifestly, the first step after the war ended was for someone to establish a local government there." And this duty the Guarantee Clause placed on the national government.[37]

This was the only constitutional basis for Reconstruction that could promise the national government permanent power after the rebel states were restored to normal relations. Some Republicans felt it assumed a standard of republicanism and gave the national government power to enforce that standard whenever a state—any state—fell short of it.[38] But few Republicans endorsed such a radical expansion of national power. In 1867 the House of Representatives agreed to a resolution instructing the Judiciary Committee to investigate "whether the States of Kentucky, Maryland, and Delaware now have State governments republican in form." Such resolutions normally passed without Republican opposition as they embodied no actual legislation, but on this occasion twenty-two Republicans joined Democrats in opposition. The committee took testimony and evidence but let the matter die.[39] Several Republicans proposed bills based on the Guarantee Clause in efforts to extend universal male suffrage and protect its exercise throughout the Union, but none passed or even won endorsement by a committee.[40]

Although Republicans regularly pointed to the Guarantee Clause as somehow sanctioning their Reconstruction policy in campaign speeches, they were reluctant to base their actual legislation on it. Instead they referred to the clause as setting a standard that southern states had to meet to be released from the grasp of war.[41] Most Republicans relied on the grasp-of-war doctrine to justify their Reconstruction legislation, and in so doing they employed the narrowest, most conservative theory of the three available—the one that virtually sanctified "the federal system as it was."

Republicans twice formulated conditions for the southern states to meet before Congress would recognize their restoration. Each time they conditioned restoration on the voluntary passage of state legislation, stolidly preserving the states as the primary authors of legislation, firmly refusing to force compliance through exercise of national power. And southern reaction demonstrated that this "voluntarism" was more than illusory.

The first conditions were the propositions embraced in the Fourteenth Amendment to the Constitution, framed in 1866. Holding that "the conquered rebels were at the mercy of the conquerors," the Joint Committee on Reconstruction offered the amendment under "a most perfect right to exact indemnity for injuries done and security against the recurrence of such outrages in the future."[42] Written by Fessenden, the committee's report closely paralleled Dana's views. The report emphasized the temporary nature of the exclusion of the southern states and conceded the "distracting and demoralizing" tendency of such a state of affairs.[43] The dangerous situation would end, the committee implied, when the southern states signified their agreement to the conditions embodied in the Fourteenth Amendment by ratifying it.

More than the mere method of proposing the Fourteenth Amendment manifested Republicans' fundamental constitutional conservatism. By the very terms of the Fourteenth Amendment, Republicans once again demonstrated their overriding desire to preserve for the states the primary responsibility for the protection of citizens' rights. An earlier version, which had explicitly authorized Congress directly to protect the rights of citizens, had met a hail of criticism from Republicans as well as Democrats. John A. Bingham, its chastened author, reworked the language to do more clearly what he originally intended—require the states to honor their obligation to protect citizens' rights equally.⁴⁴ His proposal became the amendment's initial section, which for the first time defined American citizenship and guaranteed citizens' rights. But it did not itself expand the national government's jurisdiction in areas traditionally left to the states. Its language recognized implicitly that states continued to be the primary source of the legislation that regulated citizens' rights and duties. The amendment limited states' alternatives in framing and possibly administering laws involving these rights; it did not transfer to the national government the power to frame all laws touching on them. No longer could states pass laws that denied or abridged the privileges and immunities of U.S. citizens, or that deprived any person of life, liberty, or property without due process of law, or that denied equality before the law. Possibly, states could not informally administer laws unequally. But this interpretation trod upon the farthest limit of the amendment. As a Boston newspaper reported the amendment's purpose, "The great object . . . was to compel the States to observe these guarantees."⁴⁵ So long as the states did so, the national government had no more power in areas of traditional state jurisdiction than it had before the war. "The political system of this Republic rests upon the right of the people to control their local concerns in their several states . . . ," Schurz affirmed in a speech defending the amendment. "This system was not to be changed in the work of re-construction."⁴⁶ Republicans turned ratification into a referendum on the states' obligation to protect the equal civil rights of all, eschewing discussion of specifics and what the amendment authorized Congress to do if they refused.⁴⁷

Republicans understood the dangers inherent in their first, conservative Reconstruction plan. Many of them feared that, without political power, blacks might be victimized by restored governments in the hands of former rebels. Given the political situation in spring 1866, however, Republicans felt they could not retain power if they presented more extreme conditions for restoration.⁴⁸ In an effort to minimize the danger, they passed two bills that appeared to mark radical changes in the relations between the states and the national government.

The Freedmen's Bureau bill and the Civil Rights bill both seemed to place the rights of the newly freed slaves under the protection of the national government. Yet, even with the prospect of restored, white, former rebel-dominated state governments facing them, Republicans refused to offer blacks the permanent protection they realized was needed. Offered by Lyman Trumbull, whose constitutional conservatism would become more and more pronounced,⁴⁹ the Freedmen's Bureau bill was avowedly a temporary measure, based primarily on Congress's war powers, a measure the authority for which would cease soon after the southern states were restored to the Union, the very time the freedmen would need its protection most.⁵⁰ Despite this conservatism, Republican Senate leader Fessenden barely could bring himself to support the measure, acquiescing in its passage only after personal discussions with Trumbull.[51]

The Civil Rights bill promised to stir even more doubts. It was manifestly a peacetime measure, to be passed by virtue of Congress's power under the second section of the Thirteenth Amendment to enforce emancipation by appropriate legislation. As originally presented, the bill declared the inhabitants of every state and territory entitled to certain fundamental rights without regard to color or previous status and made it a crime for anyone to deny them under the cover of law. All violations of the bill were to be tried in U.S. district courts. Most important, those who could not secure the rights guaranteed under the bill in state or local courts could transfer their cases to the federal courts in their localities. Other sections of the bill outlined enforcement procedures. Later Trumbull added a provision conferring citizenship on all persons of African descent born in the United States.[52]

On its face, the Civil Rights bill radically expanded national power. For the first time the national government accepted the responsibility for protecting the rights of its citizens. Under the bill, national courts might try cases of every description, civil and criminal, wherever state and local courts did not grant all citizens equal protection in the rights guaranteed by the bill. This broad, apparently radical bill was patently inconsistent with Trumbull's political conservatism on Reconstruction matters and his constitutional conservatism generally.[53] But in fact Trumbull had found a way to preserve rather than alter the old federal system. Although Trumbull's bill appeared vastly to expand the duties of the national government, the change would not be nearly so radical in practice. The bill threatened national assumption of jurisdiction over civil rights in order to force states to provide equal protection for those rights themselves. Court jurisdiction was the key to the bill's real purpose. Jurisdiction would be taken from the state courts only so long as they enforced state laws or court procedures that discriminated in the rights guaranteed by its first section. Once the states enforced these rights equally, there could be no removal of jurisdiction from state to national courts. The measure would apply great pressure on states to change their laws in order to regain their old spheres of jurisdiction. There would be no point in resisting. Retain unequal laws or procedures, and blacks would simply take their cases into the federal courts.

Trumbull's purpose was to force the states themselves to alter their discriminatory laws. Once they did, they would regain jurisdiction over all their citizens, and the balance of power between the state and national governments would remain unchanged. Trumbull emphasized this in his defense of the measure: "[The bill] may be assailed as drawing to the Federal Government powers that properly belong to 'States'; but I apprehend, rightly considered, it is not obnoxious to that objection. It will have no operation in any State where the laws are equal, where all persons have the same civil rights without regard to color or race."[54]

The goal of the first Republican program of Reconstruction was to protect freed people's rights in the South with the minimum possible coercion of white southerners and by encouraging the states themselves to protect their citizens' rights. Despite its manifest conservatism, southerners rejected this first offer of conditions precedent to restoration; only Tennessee chose to ratify the proposed constitutional amendment, and Republicans quickly responded by recognizing the state's return to normal rights and privileges in the Union.

Faced with southern intransigence and growing public impatience in the North, Republicans framed a second plan of Reconstruction in February 1867. In 1866 the Reconstruction Committee had been willing to restore the rebel-dominated state organizations erected under the guidance of President Johnson in return for ratification of the constitutional amendment. In the Military Government bill, which the committee reported to Congress in 1867, the Johnson governments were expressly disavowed and the southern people remanded to the direct control of the military authorities (who could utilize existing civil tribunals and officers if they wished, however). The plan seemed to justify Stevens's conquered province theory of southern status, but in fact it was proposed by two conservative Republicans, Senator George H. Williams and Representative Roscoe Conkling.[55] Stevens fought for this bill so tenaciously that possibly he saw it as an opening wedge for his views on "territorialization," but other Republicans believed, with Representative Augustus Brandegee, that it simply "holds those revolted communities in the grasp of war until the rebellion shall have laid down its spirit, as two years ago it formally laid down its arms," until, in John A. Bingham's words, "those people return to their loyalty and fealty in such a manner as shall satisfy the people of the United States, . . . represented in Congress, of their fitness to be restored to their full constitutional relations"[56]

Fearing that the Military Government bill might lead to a long period of exclusion, conservative Republicans in the House, led by Bingham and James G. Blaine, offered an amendment "to notify [southern whites] in the most solemn form . . . that . . . all they have to do, in order to get rid of military rule and military government, is to present to the Congress of the United States a constitutional form of State government in accord with the letter and spirit of the Constitution and laws of the United States, together with a ratification of the pending constitutional amendment."[57] Defeated in the House, the so-called Blaine amendment succeeded in the Senate where it was offered by the conservative Republican Senator John Sherman. The bill as finally passed promised restoration on four conditions: The people of each southern state had to frame a new constitution at a convention elected by universal male suffrage; the constitution had to be ratified in a second election; the new constitution had to provide for equal male suffrage; and the state legislature elected under the new constitution had to ratify the Fourteenth Amendment.[58]

Dana happily recognized in this bill the vindication of his doctrine of Reconstruction. "[I]t is on the principle which I had the honor to he the first to lay down in my Faneuil Hall speech of June, 1865,—what my flattering friends call my 'Grasp-of-war Speech,'" he wrote proudly.[59] Hardly a constitutional defense of the bill was made that did not justify it on these grounds.[60] Like the first Reconstruction plan, the Reconstruction Act called for voluntary state action under the threat of continued exclusion and military government if the state refused. As Garfield put it, "Congress shall place civil Governments before these people of the rebel States, and a cordon of bayonets behind them."[61]

The major conditions that Congress demanded the southern states meet before being released from the "grasp of war" were the ratification of the Fourteenth Amendment and the enfranchisement of their male black citizens. Because the Reconstruction Act required black suffrage, historians have stressed not only its social but also its constitutional radicalism. By imposing Negro suffrage on recalcitrant southerners, they point out, radical Republicans demonstrated their willingness to disregard traditional lines of state and national authority. But in fact by 1867 the argument for black suffrage was distinctly conservative. Republicans were unwilling to leave black Americans at the mercy of former rebels; they were equally unwilling permanently to extend the power of the national government to protect them. As Edwin L. Godkin, editor of the *Nation*, explained, "Our Government owes to those who can get it no other way that one thing for which all governments exist . . . security for person and property. This . . . we can supply either by the provision of a good police or by the admission of the blacks to such a share in the management of state affairs that they can provide a police for themselves. The former of these courses is not strictly in accordance with the spirit of our institutions; the latter is."[62]

The enfranchisement of black men in the southern states, then, was the one measure that would provide security for the Union and its loyal southern supporters and yet allow Reconstruction to continue on a conservative constitutional basis. "Far from desiring centralization repulsive to the genius of this country, it is in the distinct interest of local self-government and legitimate State rights that we urge these propositions," wrote Schurz, "and nothing can be more certain than that this is the only way in which a dangerous centralization of power in the hands of our general government can be prevented."[63] As the *Nation* pointed out, Negro suffrage "though brought forward as a radical remedy . . . is anything but radical."[64]

Only as the Reconstruction process neared completion did many Republicans finally realize its essential weakness. As southerners met Congress's conditions and pressed for restoration in 1868, Republicans suspected that their compliance with the Reconstruction Acts was more apparent than real. "You are hastening back States where rebelism is pervading them from end to end," complained an outspoken radical.[65] The grasp-of-war theory had worked too well, perhaps. In many states southerners had met the conditions set forth in the Reconstruction acts not out of reawakened loyalty or a new commitment to racial justice but out of a simple desire to be rid of the national presence. Radicals who recognized the weakness of the loyal forces in the South urged delay in restoration. In reality, "there are not ten men in this Senate who believe it is a safe thing to do at this time," Timothy Otis Howe warned.[66] Other radical Republicans agreed, but political necessities required readmission.

Realizing the futility of trying to delay restoration, many Republicans finally decided on an effort to guarantee permanence to the new political order in the South. As a new fundamental condition, Republicans insisted southern states agree never to alter the basis of suffrage in their new constitutions, moving to insert the requirement in the legislation restoring most of the southern states to normal relations. This time they eschewed the constraining grasp-of-war theory as a justification. Hoping to establish a basis for ongoing federal power to fasten black suffrage on the South, some turned to the Guarantee Clause for constitutional authority. The power to guarantee republican forms of government to the states was "plenary and absolute," insisted Senator George F. Edmunds. Therefore Congress clearly had the authority "to put that government in such a form that it shall 'stay put.'"[67] But the Guarantee Clause justification implied a sweeping alteration in national-state relations. Illinois Senator Richard Yates made clear just how sweeping when he argued that it made Congress the final arbiter of voting qualifications:

> When the question arises whether a constitution is republican in form, who decides it? Congress. May not Congress say that no constitution is republican in form which excludes any large class of people from voting ... ?
>
> If New York excludes any portion of her citizens who bear arms and pay taxes from the right of suffrage, hers is not, according to our republican theory, a government republican in form. Congress, not the States, decide that question.[68]

Worried that Democrats would charge Republicans with intending to impose black suffrage on the North, most Republicans recoiled from so radical a proposition. William M. Stewart, the second-ranking Republican on the Senate

Judiciary Committee, drew a parallel between the restoration of the southern states and the admission of new states. Congress had regularly exacted concessions from petitioning territories in return for grants of statehood, he pointed out. But would Congress be authorized to take action if a state repudiated such a condition? In the end, even Stewart had to concede that it would not. "I do not pretend to say that the insertion of this declaration in the bill [to restore the southern states] will alter either the constitution of the State or of the General Government." It was merely "a declaration of principle, which has generally been respected."[69]

This timorous attempt to provide permanent national power to protect rights precipitated the first of the series of intra-Republican confrontations on constitutional questions that would mark Reconstruction legislation of the post-1868 era. Conservative constitutionalists in the Republican Party, including Fessenden, Trumbull, and Conkling, the very architects of congressional Reconstruction, were unprepared to cooperate in this new attempt to limit state prerogatives. "The States have the right to alter or amend their Constitutions at pleasure," they insisted. Once restored to the Union, a southern state "will have the same power to regulate the question of suffrage that the State of New York has, unquestionably."[70] A motion to eliminate the "fundamental conditions" from the resolution restoring Arkansas to the Union failed by only one vote in the Senate, despite the Republicans' overwhelming Republican majority in the chamber.[71]

Republicans continued their career of constitutional conservatism in framing the final triumph of the Reconstruction era, the Fifteenth Amendment. Here, too, Republicans opted for the narrowest of the proposals congressmen offered. Framed, like the Fourteenth Amendment, in the negative as a limit on state authority, the suffrage amendment was designed to preserve jurisdiction over voting requirements in the states. The *New York Tribune*, the nation's most important Republican newspaper, observed that "the amendment . . . confers no power whatever on Congress, but only limits the power of the States."[72] The statement was exaggerated; the amendment authorized Congress to enforce the prohibition. But the *Tribune*'s statement indicates how Republicans thought it most politic to present their work to the public. Although several Republicans proposed constitutional amendments transferring jurisdiction over suffrage qualifications to Congress, none won much support.[73]

Republicans also protected state jurisdiction by narrowing the Fifteenth Amendment's scope. Over radicals' objections, they refused to bar property or literacy requirements, and they rejected proposals to forbid discrimination in office-holding requirements. By now, the more radical Republicans had become aware of the limitations Republicans' constitutional conservatism had set on Republican Reconstruction policy, but they were unable to overcome conservatives' constitutional scruples. The Fifteenth Amendment, so easily and so long circumvented by southern state governments, was the culmination of a Republican Reconstruction policy designed to preserve the states' primary jurisdiction over civil and political rights. A disappointed southern Republican Senator sadly referred to it as "the Dead Sea fruit which we are to gather from the plantings of a hundred years."[74]

With the passage of the Fifteenth Amendment, the formative period of Reconstruction ended. The Republican policy that restored all but three of the southern states to the Union by 1869 created the context in which later efforts to protect the fruits of victory took place. To the pessimistic Henry Adams, it might seem that "the powers originally reserved by the Constitution to the States are in future to be held by them only on good behavior" and that "the first decisive, though irrevocable step towards substituting a new form of government . . . [had] now been taken," but the more perceptive eye of James Parton discerned that although "the strict-constructionists are reduced to a feeble cohort . . . , yet Congress adheres to the tradition of their doctrines."[75]

Naturally, most Republicans believed the requirement of black suffrage from the southern states and the passage of the Fifteenth Amendment meant an end to the issue of Reconstruction. The restoration in 1868 of all but three of the insurgent states eliminated the constitutional base on which Republicans had predicated their Reconstruction legislation. Grant's famous phrase, "Let us have peace," uttered in the election campaign of 1868, was more than a political slogan; it was also a call with profound constitutional implications. The restoration of "peace" meant an end to justifications for congressional action based on the war power. Republicans offered that peace, as Carl Schurz emphasized to campaign audiences, "upon the basis of a restored Union, of results already accomplished and of a state of things already existing." New York's Governor Reuben Fenton echoed Schurz: "The Republican party accepts the Southern States with their present [reconstructed] governments as members of the Union, and in good faith would give them all the benefits of the Constitution."[76]

Neither the election of 1868, nor the acquiescence of the South in black suffrage in 1867 and 1868, nor the ratification of the Fifteenth Amendment brought peace. The forces that Republicans had implanted in the southern states proved calamitously inadequate for protecting the rights of loyal blacks and whites there. As their Reconstruction program careened toward disaster, most Republicans came to support legislation that entailed a far larger expansion of national authority than they had envisioned earlier. Demanding that the still unreconstructed states meet yet more conditions to be released from the grasp of war, they turned to the Fourteenth and Fifteenth Amendments to find permanent national power to protect the rights of citizens in the states already restored. For some Republicans this new departure marked too great an abandonment of older notions of federalism. The most dissatisfied, among them Fenton, Schurz, Dana, and Trumbull, soon openly opposed continued national interference in areas traditionally under state jurisdiction, finally joining the Liberal Republican revolt of 1872. But even regular Republicans moved only with great reluctance.

In January 1870, proposals to add permanent conditions to the resolution restoring Virginia to normal relations in the Union passed the Senate only after a difficult struggle and only by one- and two-vote margins. Joining Trumbull and Fenton (now in the Senate) in opposition were the architects of pre-1868 Reconstruction legislation, Conkling, Williams, and Sherman. In the House of Representatives, a motion by Bingham to eliminate the conditions failed by only three votes.[77] Three months later the same senators, joined now by other leading Republicans, including Schurz, stubbornly resisted efforts to use national authority to succor the radical Republican government of Rufus Bullock in Georgia. This time they succeeded in defeating the radical proposals. In the House, conservative Republicans, again led by Bingham, did the same.[78]

Republicans never shook off their state-centeredness. In passing the Force Act of 1871—constitutionally far more radical than previous legislation—they progressed to the position that Congress could step in to protect citizens' rights when states failed to do so as well as when states positively discriminated. But Republicans would not agree to the proposition that Congress had acquired direct and primary authority to protect citizens' rights through the Fourteenth Amendment. Republicans were circumscribed not only by their continuing reluctance to alter the balance of federalism, but also by their past conservatism. They remembered how carefully they had framed the constitutional amendments to preserve old areas of state jurisdiction. When Bingham was finally driven to new ground by southern intransigence and argued for the broadest interpretation of congressional powers under the Fourteenth Amendment, James A. Garfield gently reminded him, "My colleague can make but not unmake history."[79]

The limits on congressional power had been set by Republicans' earlier conservatism. Those limits could not be undone. Even Radical Charles Sumner, struggling to pass his new, broad Civil Rights bill from 1870 until his death in 1874, had to argue that the discrimination he sought to eliminate in inns, theaters, carriers, and cemeteries was somehow sanctioned by state law.[80] Given this continuing conservatism, Republicans' final decision in 1877 to abandon efforts to protect citizens' rights in the South through direct federal intervention may more aptly be characterized as a consequence than a betrayal of their principles of 1865–1868.[81]

Except for a last gasp in 1890, Congress ceased efforts to pass laws to protect southern citizens, unwilling any longer to exert powers Republicans had tried to avoid before 1868. The federal courts followed suit. Judges and justices, most of whom as Republicans remembered well the circumstances surrounding the passage and ratification of the constitutional amendments, carefully preserved the state jurisdiction upon which Republicans had been so reluctant to encroach. Accepting the Republican position that the national government could protect citizens deprive of equal protection of the laws either through state action or failure to act, the Supreme Court rigorously scrutinized congressional legislation to make certain it stayed within those boundaries. And when the loosely worded Force Act of 1871 and Civil Rights Act of 1875 came before them, the Court found both to exceed the constitutional limits with which their framers had intended to comply.[82] Even today, those who oppose expansive federal protection of civil liberty can still cite the language of the Fourteenth Amendment and the circumstances of its framing and ratification to bolster a narrow reading of federal authority to protect civil liberty.

Surveying the wreckage of Republican Reconstruction policy in the late 1870s, ex-President Ulysses S. Grant concluded that, after all, "the wisest thing would have been to continue for some time the military rule" over the South. "I am clear now it would have been better for the North to have postponed suffrage, reconstruction, State governments, for ten years and held the South in a territorial condition." But despite radicals' advocacy of that course, it had never really been an option. "Our people did not like it. It was not in accord with our institutions." Quoting Grant's insight, historian Brooks Simpson points out the immutable fact: Republicans were limited by "Americans' commitment to civil government and federalism." "For many people, 'reconstruction' was primarily the restoration of loyal civil government, pure and simple. However much one wants to debate the extent to which congressional proposals were conservative or revolutionary, they all looked to this end, one way or another. In turn, that restricted what one could do to protect black rights."[83]

Yet the constitutional conservatism of Republican Reconstruction should not be overstated. Whatever their desire to maintain the contours of the traditional federal system, Republican civil right legislation and the Fourteenth and Fifteenth Amendments made clear that the Constitution created a republic dedicated to freedom, not slavery. Republicans undermined their own efforts by their dedication to federalism, and the Supreme Court went even further in doing so. But it was these decisions that ultimately proved anomalous in a freedom-loving republic. It took nearly a century, but present-day advocates of broad national power to protect rights may exaggerate the degree to which Republicans were committed to a "revolutionary constitutionalism," but they are right that the bolder steps that radical Republicans advocated would have been consistent with the constitutional transformation of the Civil War era—more consistent than those actually undertaken. And that may be the true lesson for Americans today.

2

The Rout of Radicalism: Republicans and the Elections of 1867

When Howard K. Beale entitled his great analysis of Reconstruction politics *The Critical Year*,[1] he referred to 1866, when Andrew Johnson and the Republican Congress opened their bitter warfare over Reconstruction policy, a year that culminated in congressional elections in which northern voters endorsed Congress's position that the South was not yet entitled to full restoration of rights and privileges in the Union. The elections of this "critical year" decided the issue between the President and the majority in Congress and set the stage for congressional Reconstruction. But until the original version of this article appeared in 1972, historians generally had underestimated the importance of the elections of 1867 held in nearly every northern state to fill various state and local offices. If the elections of 1866 decided the issue between president and Congress, the elections of 1867 decided a similar issue between more radical and more conservative Republicans. The stakes of the elections of 1866 had been high: whether the nation that replaced the slaveholding republic would be fully committed to freedom—whether African Americans would be recognized as citizens of the United States, whether they would secure equal civil rights (and, as it turned out, political rights as well) with white southerners, and whether those rights would be protected by federal law. The stakes of the election of 1867 were nearly as important: whether the program embodied in the Reconstruction Act of 1867 would set the limit of postwar reform in the South, or whether Republicans would go further yet in changing southern political, economic, and social institutions. Not only Democrats saw the apparent march of Republican radicalism as threatening the Constitution itself.[2]

Historians had begun to describe the essential moderation of the initial Republican Reconstruction program with the publication of Eric L. McKitrick's *Andrew Johnson and Reconstruction* in 1960.[3] But most treated the Reconstruction Act of 1867 as the triumph of radical Republicanism. The Reconstruction Act required that southerners ratify the Fourteenth Amendment to the Constitution and agree to impartial suffrage for blacks and whites as conditions for

---

The original version of this essay was published in *Civil War History* 18 (December 1972): 334–44.

restoration to the Union. McKitrick, David Donald, and William R. Brock recognized that this law was the result of compromise between radicals and conservatives, but only Larry G. Kincaid, in an unpublished dissertation, clearly asserted that the Reconstruction Act was far more satisfactory to conservative and centrist Republicans, among them William Pitt Fessenden, John Sherman, James G. Blaine, and John A. Bingham, than it was to radicals such as Thaddeus Stevens, Benjamin F. Wade, and Charles Sumner. My own research led me to agree with Kincaid.[4] The original version of this essay was the result. It proved influential, and its insights are incorporated into Eric Foner's standard synthesis of Reconstruction, as well as into recent textbooks.[5]

When Congress adjourned in March 1867, and as the Democratic and Republican parties girded for the elections to be held in northern states from July through November, radical Republicans immediately began agitating for further Reconstruction measures beyond the Reconstruction Act. Sumner urged passage of a national law (as distinguished from a constitutional amendment) to require racially nondiscriminatory voting qualifications within all states. Not only would this enfranchise blacks in northern states, but it would also enfranchise them in the border states of Maryland, Delaware, and Kentucky, where hundreds of thousands of freed slaves were not protected by military authorities acting under the Reconstruction laws. Moreover, it would guard against the possibility that southern states might repeal impartial suffrage laws once they were restored to normal relations in the Union.[6] Sumner also demanded that southern states be required to offer free public schooling to children of both races. (He was noncommittal about whether these schools must be integrated, but years earlier he had argued that segregated schools were inconsistent with constitutional requirements of equal rights in Massachusetts.)[7] As Sumner pressed for a national impartial suffrage law and free public schools for all in the South, Stevens, Benjamin F. Butler, and other radicals began for the first time since the war to exert vigorous pressure for confiscation and land redistribution in the former rebel states. Many radicals also demanded the complete dispersal of the southern state governments erected by presidential authority in 1865, governments the Reconstruction Act recognized as provisional. Like Stevens, most radicals wished loyal, radical governments to replace them, to govern the southern "states" as territories for an indefinite time. Wendell Phillips articulated the program many radicals favored at the annual meeting of the American Anti-Slavery Society in New York City early in May. Antislavery men, he said, "will believe the negro safe when we see him with 40 acres under his feet, a school-house behind him, a ballot in his right hand, the sceptre of the Federal Government over his head, and no State Government to interfere with him, until more than one-half of the white men of the Southern States are in their graves."⁸

Another issue closely related to Reconstruction emerged during the spring and summer of 1867. An interpretation of the Reconstruction Acts delivered on June 12 by President Johnson's conservative attorney general, Henry Stanbery, so emasculated the powers of the military commanders to whom enforcement of the law had been entrusted that Republicans were forced to return to Washington in July to pass a new law to remedy the destruction. Arguing that Johnson could never be trusted fairly and fully to enforce the Reconstruction laws, radicals urged the president's impeachment and removal. Their more conservative Republican allies, who passed floor rules prohibiting debate on the question, outmaneuvered them. But by the time the July session adjourned, the impeachment issue had become completely entwined with the 1867 campaigns in the states, Democrats pointing to it as an example of Republican extremism.⁹

Conservative Republicans were not very sympathetic to the new radical demands. They had already scuttled Stevens's hopes for long-term military control of the South once, when they passed the Reconstruction Act.¹⁰ They had joined Democrats to defeat Sumner's southern education proposals. Lyman Trumbull, the conservative chairman of the Senate Judiciary committee, through which any national suffrage legislation would have to pass, publicly proclaimed during the campaign that Sumner's suffrage proposition was unconstitutional.¹¹ As late as 1868, the Republican national platform would assure northerners that blacks could be enfranchised by law only in the South.¹² Nor were the implications of confiscation and land redistribution lost upon conservative Republicans. When Butler complained of a landed aristocracy in the South, the moderate *Boston Daily Advertiser* asked, "Why a *landed* aristocracy? This mode of argument is two-edged. For there are socialists who hold that *any* aristocracy is 'fatal to the advance of the cause of liberty and equal rights'—socialists who would not hesitate to say that General Butler's large income places him in the ranks of an aristocracy. . . . It is dangerous to prove too much." The conservative *Cincinnati Commercial* began to refer to Stevens and Butler as "The Red Rads."¹³

Moreover, conservative Republicans feared the impact of the confiscation issue on southern politics. They hoped to build a southern Republican Party around the issue of accepting restoration under the Reconstruction Acts, requiring only ratification of the Fourteenth Amendment and impartial suffrage. Many Republicans believed that white southerners who were tired of the political limbo in which they were placed, who had lost faith in President Johnson's ability to protect them from Republican legislation, might join newly enfranchised African Americans in organizing new state governments in conformity with Reconstruction legislation in order finally to win readmission to the Union. If conservative southerners opposed their efforts, these whites would have no alternative but to ally with the Republican Party. Already many Republicans believed they saw this happening. Henry Wilson, who acted with conservative Republicans during 1867, sent glowingly enthusiastic letters from the South. Horace Greeley echoed him. "The harvest is white," exulted the *Boston Journal*, "and we trust that our sagacious men will see that it is not neglected."[14]

Radical agitation for confiscation and land reform could only alienate these budding converts. "The ultraists . . . are determined to build up a party in the Southern States fully in accord with themselves," the conservative Republican *New York Times* charged. "Their plan is to consolidate the negro vote with that of the 'original Union men' of the South. . . . And they rely upon confiscation to secure this result."[15] Confirming conservatives' fears, radicals opened a bitter campaign against their own conservative allies, accusing them of selling out the principles of the party. "For every broken heart and desolate home in the South, for every murdered black there, we hold Fessenden, Wilson . . . and their clan, responsible," the editors of the *Anti-Slavery Standard* railed.[16]

Intimately connected with these substantive issues dividing radicals from conservatives in the Republican Party was the problem of selecting a presidential candidate for 1868. Although many important Republicans were occasionally mentioned in 1867 as possible candidates, there were only three leading contenders. One was Benjamin F. Wade, the radical senator from Ohio and president pro tempore of the Senate. Salmon Portland Chase, also an Ohioan and Chief Justice of the United States, was a second. Most political observers considered both Chase and Wade to represent the radical wing of the Republican Party (although within Ohio politics, Wade was clearly the more radical). As of spring 1867, it had appeared that one or the other would be the Republican presidential candidate in 1868. When conservative Republicans desperately looked for a candidate to oppose them, they could find only one with the national following that would make victory possible—Lieutenant General of the Army Ulysses S. Grant.

Before the elections of 1867, radicals were by no means reconciled to Grant's nomination. The general had not even declared himself a Republican by summer 1867, and his past politics led radicals to view him with suspicion. Before the war he had been apolitical, and many considered him apolitical yet. In 1864 Republicans had feared the Democrats might nominate him for president. From 1862 until late in 1864 radicals regarded his rising fortunes with misgivings.[17] Grant reinforced their suspicions by his conduct during the Reconstruction controversy. An optimistic report he delivered in 1865 regarding conditions in the South had provided Democrats and President Johnson with their most authoritative evidence of southern good intentions at that time. During the 1866 election campaign the general had accompanied Johnson on his ill-fated "Swing 'Round the Circle," allowing himself to be used on an obviously political junket. Grant avoided making his position clear, but he gave the impression that he generally supported Johnson's policies at least through 1866. And there is no doubt as to the position of his staff. Adam Badeau and John A. Rawlins, his intimate friends and aides, both endorsed Johnson.[18] Finally, when President Johnson suspended Secretary of War Edwin M. Stanton in August 1867, renewing Republican fears that Johnson would obstruct enforcement of the Reconstruction laws, the President named Grant as Stanton's interim replacement, using the general's popularity to deflect criticism. "General Grant . . . appears to have become a cat's paw for the President," worried the editor of the radical *Independent*.[19]

But Radicals found most ominous the men who were advocating Grant's candidacy. In Pennsylvania, conservative former governor Andrew J. Curtin, defeated for the Senate by a coalition of pro-Stevens and Simon Cameron radicals, led the Grant movement. In New York, where the Grant boom progressed most rapidly, it was sponsored by the conservative Seward-Weed faction of the Republican Party, abetted by their organ, the *New York Times*. At the same time the independent Democratic paper, the *New York Herald*, urged Democrats to join conservative Republicans in supporting Grant. "There will be a tremendous struggle in the republican camp for the Convention of 1868, between the radical Chase faction . . . and the republican conservatives supporting General Grant," it prophesied. "The result, in all probability, will be a split of the republican party into two distinct parties for the succession. In this event the Northern democracy will hold the balance of power, and by casting their weight into the scale of the Grant. or anti-radical party, they will carry the election."[20] The leader of the anti-Seward and Weed forces in New York, Horace Greeley, complained privately to radical Senator Zachariah Chandler, "All that is fishy and mercenary in the Republican ranks combines with everything copperhead to escort Grant as the man destined to curb Radicalism and restore conservatives to power."[21]

So before the election of 1867, most radicals were at best lukewarm to the Grant candidacy.[22] Nonetheless, many despaired of being able to withstand the conservative onslaught. John W. Forney, owner of the *Washington Chronicle* and *Philadelphia Press*, expressed these fears in a letter to Sumner. "I shudder at the idea of another doubtful man in that post," he wrote. "I cannot tell you how this . . . has depressed me. If Genl Grant wants the nomination I presume with such agencies and his great military strength he will secure it. I fear his administration. God help us! Are we never to have the right man in that place?"[23]

Under these circumstances, the elections of 1867 took on immense importance. To a large extent, they would decide a struggle between radicals and conservatives for control of the Republican Party. They would test the political viability of radicalism for the first time.[24] If the Republicans succeeded in an election in which radicals had taken such a prominent part, radicals would argue that the people were ready for more thorough measures of reconstruction, and they might win support from other elements in the party who agreed with particular parts of their program. This would affect both the platform and the candidate in 1868. The conservatives were worried. James G. Blaine wrote afterward, "I felt . . . that if we should carry everything with a whirl in '67 that such knaves as Ben Butler would control our National Convention and give us a nomination with which defeat would be inevitable if not desirable."[25]

The people of twenty states went to the polls from March to November 1867, and Republicans lost ground in nearly all of them. In March, Connecticut had replaced its Republican governor with a Democrat and elected three Democratic congressmen and only one Republican. Republicans lost 12,000 votes in Maine. The Democrats swept California, with Republicans running 20,000 votes short of their 1864 pace. The Republican vote in New Jersey fell 16,000 short of that polled in 1865, with seven of the twelve counties that voted Republican that year returning Democratic majorities in 1867. In Maryland, the Republican vote was reduced from 40 percent of the total to 25 percent. In Massachusetts, Republicans had won 77 percent of the vote in 1866; now they received only 58 percent.[26] Republican percentages were also reduced in Vermont, New Hampshire, Iowa, Minnesota, Rhode Island, and Wisconsin. Only in Michigan and Kentucky did the party improve upon its showings of a year earlier.[27]

Most ominous were the losses Republicans sustained in Ohio, Pennsylvania, and New York. All three were "swing" states, carrying great weight in the Electoral College; Republicans could not lose them in 1868 and expect to win the presidential election. The Ohio contest had been especially important. It was the only populous, northern, swing state where voters had the opportunity to vote directly on the issue of black suffrage. A combination black enfranchisement–deserter disfranchisement amendment to the Ohio constitution was on the ballot. Throughout the campaign it remained the central issue in the contest. Moreover, Ohio played a critical role in presidential politics. Both Wade and Chase were Ohioans; the legislature elected in 1867 would name a senator to fill the Senate seat held by Wade, whose term expired in 1869. Wade was a candidate for reelection, and his presidential ambitions could not very well survive the election of a Democratic state legislature. As the Ohio correspondent of the *New York Times* pointed out before the elections, Ohio "gives the keynote of the entire central West. If Ohio give [*sic*] a decided vote, you need not expect any of the ten States, west and north of it, including Missouri and Colorado to go otherwise. These states give about one hundred electoral votes in the Presidential election. . . . If Ohio carries the Constitutional Amendment [extending suffrage to African Americans] . . . and gives the Radical candidate . . . a decided majority, you may rely upon it, that these one hundred electoral votes will be given to an uncompromising Republican candidate for the Presidency. By that I mean a Republican, and one whose principles on important issues cannot be mistaken."[28] Contemporary readers would have known that the Ohio correspondent's reference to an "uncompromising candidate" meant someone other than Grant. (And as an Ohioan, the correspondent probably was intending to boost Chase or Wade.)

The Republicans had expected victory in Ohio. William Henry Smith, the Republican secretary of state and an important local politician, anticipated a two-to-one Republican majority in the state legislature, a 40,000 majority for the Republican candidate for governor, Rutherford B. Hayes, and a 5,000–10,000 majority for the black suffrage amendment. Instead the Democrats won the legislature, the black suffrage amendment lost by 38,000 votes, and the popular Hayes squeezed into the governorship by only 3,000 votes of 484,000 cast. The Republicans lost 13,000 votes from their 1866 total, while the Democrats gained 27,000. Twelve of the forty-five Republican counties returned majorities against Negro suffrage.[29] As the Democratic *Chicago Times* admitted, "Democrats as well as Republicans, are astounded at the result in Ohio."[30]

In Pennsylvania, the Republican state ticket lost by 1,000 votes, although the party retained control of the legislature by a slim margin. The previous year the Republican statewide majority had been 17,000 votes. In New York Republicans also lost, the narrow 13,000-vote Republican majority of 1866 converted to a 50,000-vote deficit. From the moment the first reverses were observable, the conservative Henry Adams grew confident. There was no reason to fear that "the American people are disposed to abrogate or alter the Constitution." "The duty of guarding the Constitution was put by the people in the hands of the Republican party," he wrote his brother. "That party has betrayed its trust, and the Democratic party has succeeded to it, since the people had no other choice."[31]

But in fact, the elections of 1867 were not disastrous for the Republican Party as a whole. Few major offices were lost; most states merely showed greatly reduced Republican majorities. Conservative Republicans were not despondent. If Adams had identified the danger that the people were beginning to perceive the Republican Reconstruction program as a threat to constitutional norms, the elections of 1867 had warned Republicans early enough to avoid it. As Blaine wrote, "[The losses] will be good discipline in many ways and will I am sure be 'blessed to use in the edification and building up of the true faith.' . . ."[32] But for the radicals the defeat was a disaster—"a crusher for the wild men," conservative congressman Nathaniel P. Banks, wrote happily.[33]

There had been many side issues distracting Republicans in various states, yet the cause of the setbacks was apparent. As John Sherman recognized, "The chief trouble is the [Negro] suffrage question. It is clearly right. . . . It is easy to convince people so, but harder to make them feel it—and vote it." Ben Wade, deprived of his Senate seat and his chances for the presidency, put it more simply: "We went in on principle, and got whipped."[34] The consequences were clear. The perceptive, conservative New York lawyer and political observer John Binney wrote hopefully, "The extreme Radicals must now open their eyes to the palpable fact, that they must moderate their impetuosity so as to carry the prudent conservative Republicans along with them." But the unhappy Wade put it another way: "I fear its effect will be to make the timorous more timorous and the next session [of Congress] more inefficient than the last."[35]

The elections' practical effects were felt immediately. The radical *Independent*'s correspondent found the change in Congress "startling." "Our friends have an overwhelming majority," he wrote, "but with the people apparently against the Radical members, it will he impossible to secure Radical legislation." As the session opened, he gloomily assessed the prospects:

> First, the impeachment movement is dead. . . .
> Second, all confiscation bills will fail. . . .
> Third, Congress will not pass a national Equal Suffrage bill till after the presidential election.[36]

All these predictions proved accurate. Neither confiscation nor suffrage bills passed, and fewer than one half of the Republicans in the House of Representatives supported the radical impeachment resolution in December 1867.[37]

Finally, the results of the elections of 1867 made Grant's nomination for president in 1868 inevitable. As the observant French journalist Georges Clemenceau informed his readers, "The real victims of the Democratic victory are Mr. Wade and Mr. Chase."[38] Even in Ohio, which both Wade and Chase had hoped to make the cornerstone of their campaigns for the nomination, opposition to Grant collapsed. In the presence of Governor-elect Hayes, who would dominate the Ohio delegation to the Republican national convention, Sardis Birchard, Hayes's uncle, announced to a Republican audience that General

Grant was as good as nominated, "though no convention had been held."[39] From other states came similar reports. The other candidates are "good men as we all know," a correspondent wrote the general's campaign manager, Elihu B. Washburne, "but we can only win with Grant." Most Republicans agreed.[40]

Disheartened, the dejected Wade lamented, "It is very strange that when men talk of availability, they always mean something squinting toward Copperheadism. They never think of consulting the Radicals. . . . Oh, no; we must take what we can get."[41]

The elections of 1867 marked a turning point in the history of the Republican Party. They set the limits on reform in Reconstruction. They confirmed leadership of the party in conservatives and centrists. They convinced Republicans that radicalism was not a viable political creed. They proved that no matter how deeply Republican leaders were committed to wide-ranging economic, social, and political reform, the northern electorate set limits that the party dared not transgress.

3　A New Look at the Impeachment of Andrew Johnson

When I wrote the book from which the original version of this essay was drawn, it had been just over one hundred years since the impeachment and trial of Andrew Johnson—the only president ever to have been charged by the House of Representatives with "high crimes and misdemeanors." No president had faced an impeachment inquiry since. The few impeachments seemed to be reserved for errant judges.[1] It seemed inconceivable that another president might be subjected to the process. Indeed, I ended the last chapter by concluding that the failure to convict Johnson had proved impeachment was a poor weapon with which to protect congressional prerogatives and that therefore "the only effective recourse against a president who ignores the will of Congress or exceeds his powers is democratic removal at the polls."[2]

It did not take long for the prediction to be proved wrong. The Watergate scandal suddenly reawakened interest in presidential impeachment, and many Americans naturally turned for insight to the Johnson precedent. But the version of the Johnson impeachment that Americans found in textbooks, studies of the presidency, and histories of the Reconstruction era was hardly likely to reassure them. The Johnson impeachment, one scholar concluded after reviewing the literature, had been "so immersed in political partisanship" and such a "sharp departure" from the "canons of moderation espoused by the Founding Fathers" that it had "almost succeeded in destroying the viability of the impeachment process as an important part of the system of checks and balances."[3] Looking to history to help understand the contours of impeachable offenses, Yale law professor Charles Black discounted the Johnson precedent. Understating the historical consensus, Black reported that it was "to say the least, by no means universally regarded today as a paradigm of propriety or unimpassioned law."[4] The Johnson impeachment had been portrayed as "the most insidious assault on constitutional government in the nation's history," "the culmination of a sustained effort to make [the president] . . . subservient to Congress, to alter the place of a coordinate branch in the constitutional

---

The original version of this essay was published in *Political Science Quarterly* 88 (September 1973): 349–67.

scheme."⁵ The leading book-length study of the Johnson impeachment was still David Miller DeWitt's 1903 study *Impeachment and Trial of Andrew Johnson*, which paralleled the anti–Radical Reconstruction historical orthodoxy of the times in which it had been written.⁶

Newer studies of Reconstruction, less sympathetic to Johnson's policies and more sympathetic to the congressional Republicans, still suggested that the impeachment "was a great act of ill-directed passion."⁷ John F. Kennedy had included one of the Republicans who had voted to acquit Johnson in his Pulitzer Prize–winning bestseller *Profiles of Courage*, crediting him with having "preserved for ourselves and posterity constitutional government in the United States."⁸ The most recent account, a chapter in Raoul Berger's influential *Impeachment: The Constitutional Problems*, blasted the Johnson episode as "a gross abuse of the impeachment process," "a frightening reminder that in the hands of a passion-driven Congress the process may bring down the very pillars of our constitutional system."⁹

Disdain for the Johnson precedent had encouraged the notion that the "high crimes and misdemeanors" for which a president might be impeached ought to consist of actual criminal conduct rather than the vague accusation of abuse of power. The Watergate scandal encouraged a reevaluation of this notion. The influential primer on impeachment that Black prepared during the crisis suggested that impeachable offenses should have "some flavor of criminality," but that they could not be limited to indictable crimes. They were "offenses which are rather obviously wrong . . . and which so seriously threaten the order of political society as to make pestilent and dangerous the continuance in power of their perpetrator."¹⁰ John R. Labovitz concluded that the Nixon impeachment articles "should . . . put an end" to the question of what constitutes an impeachable offense, concurring in Black's views that "high crimes and misdemeanors" means gross abuse of power.¹¹ In the wake of the scandal, this view became the new orthodoxy.¹²

The combination of new, sympathetic accounts of Republican Reconstruction and the experience of Watergate created the opening for new evaluations of the Johnson impeachment. Several works, including my own *The Impeachment and Trial of Andrew Johnson*, led to a revised, more balanced account that historians incorporated into Reconstruction history and legal scholars incorporated into studies of impeachment generally.¹³ A dissenting tradition persisted that treated Johnson as a heroic figure impeached for protecting the Constitution from radical Republican fanatics, but mainly in nonscholarly books, often published by southern presses, directed to a general public.¹⁴

However, the movement to impeach President Bill Clinton revived hostile accounts of the only prior presidential impeachment. In the view of many, the

Clinton impeachment constituted the sort of abuse of the process by a passion-driven Congress that Berger had warned against. The Johnson impeachment certainly had raised partisan passions, and now they once again seemed sinister. Critics of Clinton's accusers among historians and legal scholars suddenly decided that "history has not been kind to that impeachment effort," which had been founded "on unambiguously political grounds."[15] Journalists revived lurid accounts.[16] A Civil War and Reconstruction textbook, published since the Clinton impeachment, seems to imply that his impeachment was the unjustifiable product of emotion and anger.[17]

These interpretations do injustice to history and—more important—if they become a new orthodoxy they will lead Americans to fear the great constitutional remedy for official wrongdoing more than the wrongdoing itself. The Clinton impeachment *is* a sobering reminder of how political passions can cloud judgment, and it must sensitize a historian to the deep partisanship that swirled around the Johnson impeachment. But in a democracy it is inevitable that ideological and political beliefs will color how people evaluate charges of presidential wrongdoing. No impeachment can fail to stir powerful political emotions. But this fact does not mean that all impeachments must be basely political efforts to remove adversaries. If we are to comprehend the real nature of presidential impeachment, a correct understanding of the origins and causes of the Johnson impeachment is essential.

Most Americans are at least somewhat familiar with the background of the first impeachment of a president of the United States: Andrew Johnson became president after Lincoln's assassination in April 1865 and immediately faced the intimidating task of restoring the shattered Union. Like Lincoln, he assumed authority over the question himself, but denied Congress's power to participate in a way that his predecessor never did. Johnson embarked on a policy designed to restore the former Confederate states to civil government with maximum speed and a minimum disturbance of southern institutions beyond the abolition of slavery itself. But his policy placed former rebels in political control of nearly every southern state and left southern blacks to the mercies of the men who had fought so desperately to keep them in bondage.

Faced with returning southern congressmen-elect who so recently had tried to rend the nation, and with state "black codes" that reduced the freedmen to virtual peonage, Republicans in Congress felt the fruits of victory slipping from their grasp. They reacted by refusing to recognize the finality of Johnson's policy of Reconstruction and by legislating to protect the civil rights of the former slaves. Unsympathetic—if not antipathetic—to black aspirations, Johnson broke with his party and began a bitter conflict with its congressional majority, the so-called Radical Republicans.[18]

The Johnson impeachment was engendered by the partisan passions the conflict over Johnson's Reconstruction policies kindled among the Radical Republicans. Republicans approached impeachment reluctantly, unwillingly, and voted for impeachment only after they were convinced that the president had violated the law and intended to abort congressional authority over Reconstruction by any means necessary. Impeachment was, thus, the defensive response of a Congress faced by an aggressive executive using his presidential powers in a way that appeared to subvert the Constitution of the United States.

For almost a year after Johnson's final break with the party that elected him to vice-presidential office, many of the more conservative Republicans hoped for reconciliation. As late as February 1867, when Congress fashioned the Military Reconstruction Bill, these conservative Republican congressmen were still trying to negotiate a compromise with their powerful adversary.[19] When, at the same time, more radical Republicans announced their intentions to propose impeachment in the House, the Republican caucus, led by the influential John A. Bingham—author of the first section of the Fourteenth Amendment—and Elihu B. Washburne, forbade any Republican from bringing impeachment resolutions to the floor without first getting caucus approval. Moreover, the caucus required that any actual impeachment have the sanction of the House Judiciary Committee.[20] The radicals refused to obey the caucus dictate and proposed impeachment resolutions anyway, but the Republican majority, trying to stifle debate, hurriedly referred them to various committees.[21] To conform to one of these impeachment resolutions, the House Judiciary Committee began slowly to investigate the president's conduct. In March 1867, dismayed by the committee's slow progress and evident coolness to their project, radicals tried to bypass it and win caucus approval for impeachment. Again Bingham, now aided by Judiciary Committee Chairman James F. Wilson, thwarted his restive Republican colleagues.[22]

Defeated in their attempts to institute impeachment proceedings against Johnson, radicals, led by Representatives Thaddeus Stevens, Benjamin F. Butler, and George S. Boutwell, and Senators Charles Sumner and Charles Drake, hoped to keep Congress in session over the summer of 1867, both to guard against presidential intrigue and to maintain pressure for Johnson's removal. But here again more conservative Republicans, led by Bingham and James G. Blaine in the House, and Lyman Trumbull and William Pitt Fessenden in the Senate, checked the enthusiasm of their more radical colleagues.[23] When Johnson's provocative activities forced the 1867 summer meeting that conservative Republicans had sought to avoid, they limited business to amendments to the

Reconstruction Act and then squelched a radical effort to call an October session to deal with impeachment.[24] So the majority of Republican congressmen hardly displayed that eagerness for revenge upon the president that subsequent generations of Americans ascribed to them.

The reluctance to impeach President Johnson becomes even more apparent when one analyzes the dispute between radical and nonradical Republicans over the nature of impeachable offenses—a controversy still of importance. This controversy turned upon opposing interpretations of the terms "high crimes and misdemeanors," which provide, along with outright treason and bribery, the sole grounds for impeachment under the Constitution.[25] Conservatives, fearful of the institutional and political effects of impeachment on the stability of the country, turned to the theory propounded by the defense in several earlier nonpresidential impeachments, namely, that government officers could be impeached only for indictable violations of criminal statute or common law. Many historians studying impeachment have accepted this position, accusing the more radical Republicans, who insisted on a broader interpretation of "high crimes and misdemeanors," of perverting the impeachment process in a purely political vendetta. But those who espoused the narrow view had a very difficult task in sustaining it against the weight of precedent and authority that contravened it, and it has been rejected by modern scholars who have investigated the question, noting the innumerable English impeachments based on nonindictable offenses on the part of royal officials before the framing of the American Constitution. Every impeachment brought by the House before the Senate in 1868 had similarly alleged nonindictable but wrongful conduct, and in two cases the Senate convicted the defendants and removed them from office.[26]

Radical Republicans endorsed a much broader interpretation of impeachable offenses. Turning to the English precedents, examples of earlier American impeachments, and the almost unanimous agreement of the great American constitutional commentators of the early nineteenth century, the radicals argued that "our forefathers adopted a Constitution under which official malfeasance and nonfeasance, and, in some cases, misfeasance, may be the subject of impeachment."[27] They repeated the logic that preeminent legal scholars of the early Republic—Joseph Story, William Duer, James Kent, William Rawle, and the authors of the *Federalist*—felt compelled a broad construction of the impeachment power. The radicals recognized that the framers of the Constitution had defined the roles of the president, Congress, and the judiciary so loosely that maintaining the checks and balances that guaranteed liberty would in practice depend upon the good faith and mutual self-restraint of those entrusted with power. They felt that there was less danger that the president or other government officials might break explicit provisions of law or act outside their constitutional authority than that they might abuse the powers that the Constitution *had* delegated to them. Although earlier constitutional analysts had arrived at the same conclusion, the great nationalist legal scholar John Norton Pomeroy, writing at the very time the Johnson impeachment became a topic of popular discussion, stated this consideration most succinctly:

> The importance of the impeaching power consists . . . in the check which it places upon the President and the judges. They must be clothed with ample discretion; the danger to be apprehended is from an abuse of this discretion. But at this very point where the danger exists, and where the protection should be certain, the President and the judiciary are beyond the reach of Congressional legislation. Congress cannot . . . interfere with the exercise of a discretion conferred by the Constitution. . . . If the offence for which the proceeding may be instituted must be made indictable by statute, impeachment thus becomes absolutely nugatory . . . in those cases where it is most needed as a restraint upon violations of public duty.[28]

For that reason, this school of analysts agreed, impeachment should be "of a liberal and comprehensive character, confined as little as possible to strict forms."[29]

Radicals complained of precisely the type of offenses these legal authorities believed were impeachable. There can be little doubt that Johnson had provided ample grounds for impeachment under this doctrine, by exercising his discretionary power in a manner that undermined congressional legislation. For example, exercising his discretionary power under the Constitution, he pardoned nearly all those who had rebelled, specifically requiring the return to them of all of their previously abandoned land.

Under the Freedmen's Bureau Act of 1865, southern lands abandoned by owners, which were subject to confiscation, were put under the administration of the bureau to be used to aid black men in the transition from slavery to freedom. The commissioner of the bureau had been empowered, under the direction of the president, to set aside abandoned land and land the government had confiscated for the use of freed people and refugees. It was to be divided into forty-acre plots or less and rented to individual freedmen and refugees for three years. At the end of the three years, or any time earlier, the occupants could purchase the land they were working, receiving from the government "such title thereto as the United States can convey."[30] By pardoning ex-Confederates and ordering the return of their land, Johnson foreclosed the possibility of land reform in the South, in effect nullifying Congress's cautious steps toward confiscation and redistribution. His policy wreaked havoc upon the newly created Freedmen's Bureau, annulling its congressional mandate to rent land to freedmen at low rates or to rent to lessees who would deal fairly with black laborers. Within a year of the close of Civil War hostilities, the bureau had been forced by Johnson's policy to return to southern white owners over one-half of the land that it had held at war's end.[31] Convinced that the Freedmen's Bureau was a corrupt machine harassing whites and creating labor instability, he worked assiduously to undermine it.[32]

Moreover, when Johnson proceeded, without congressional authority, to begin the process of Reconstruction in the South, he ignored the Test Oath law in appointing certain provisional governors. The law required federal appointees to swear that they had never aided the rebellion. If strictly enforced, it would have effectively barred former Confederate military or civil officers from receiving appointments. Johnson also permitted the secretary of the treasury to ignore it in the appointment of southern treasury officials, thereby placing control of an immense patronage system in the hands of men Congress clearly had proscribed.[33] By his encouragement of former Confederates, his blatant antipathy toward racial equality before the law, his inflammatory speeches—none of which violated law—Johnson succeeded in creating a spirit of determined resistance in the South to concessions on great war issues of importance to northerners. The consequences for southern loyalists, especially African Americans, were disastrous.

Of course, Johnson had perpetrated these "offenses," as radicals viewed them, before Congress had clearly manifested its hostility to his lenient Reconstruction policy. Congress overrode his program with the Reconstruction Act of March 1867, which, while not dispersing outright the governments created under Johnson's authority, made these governments provisional only. That law placed them under the ultimate control of five military commanders until each state framed a constitution guaranteeing equal legal and political rights to its citizens. Throughout 1867, Johnson used his discretionary powers as chief executive and commander-in-chief of the armed forces in a systematic effort to defeat the Republican legislative program.

Within four months of the passage of the Reconstruction Act and the first supplement to it, Johnson's attorney general, Henry Stanbery, appeared with a formal opinion that virtually emasculated Congress's program, forcing Republicans to return to Washington to patch the torn netting of the law. Stanbery's interpretation minimized the power of the military authorities to which Congress had entrusted administration of the unreconstructed states. According to the attorney general, the military could not remove recalcitrant officials of the Johnsonian provisional governments, enforce national laws in military courts, take cognizance of crimes committed before Congress passed the Reconstruction act, or prohibit activities not in violation of state or national statute law. His interpretation also required registration boards authorized under the Reconstruction law to accept southerners' oaths that they were not disqualified from voting, denying the boards power to investigate whether the oath-taker had perjured himself.[34] General Daniel Sickles, whose acts as military commander in the Carolinas Stanbery had specifically denounced as illegal, angrily requested to be relieved from duty so he could defend his conduct before a court of inquiry. "The declaration of the Attorney General that Military authority has not superseded [the provisional governments] . . . prevents the execution of the Reconstruction acts, disarms me of means to protect life, property, or the rights of citizens and menaces all interests in these States with ruin," he wrote.[35] Congress was forced to return to Washington in July to pass amendments to the Reconstruction Act to repair the damage.[36]

When Congress again adjourned, Johnson acted to gain more direct control of the military authorities to which Congress had entrusted enforcement of the Reconstruction law. In August 1867, he suspended Secretary of War Edwin M. Stanton. He followed this act by ordering the removal of one of the five commanders in the South, General Philip Sheridan, who had come into conflict with the former rebels in Louisiana's provisional government. On August 27, the president removed the complaining Sickles, again because of differences between the military authorities and the Johnsonian officials.[37]

In none of these actions had Johnson violated a law and he had ample formal constitutional authority for each of them. But taken as a whole, it was plain by the winter of 1867–68 that the president of the United States was consciously and determinedly following a program designed to nullify congressional legislation through the exercise of his power as chief executive.

Moreover, Johnson was straining every power at his command to do it. As soon as he broke with Republicans over Reconstruction, he began to demand support from government employees who had been appointed under the patronage (or "spoils") system, making examples of those who resisted by removing them. In an era when successful political parties were responsible for filling government offices, furious Republicans charged him with trying to build a personal political machine. They responded with the Tenure of Office Act, establishing a fixed term for government appointees, who would be subject to removal before the expiration of their terms only with the consent of the Senate.[38] As political scientist Keith Whittington has observed, by trying to impose his will on the military and the federal bureaucracy, Johnson was unilaterally attempting to reconfigure the existing constitutional balance between the legislative and executive branches of government.[39]

Yet, in the last week of November 1867, when the House Judiciary Committee finally reported its conclusion that Johnson's conduct justified impeachment, only five of the seven Republican members signed its statement. Chairman Wilson and another Republican member joined the two Democratic members in opposition. With their colleagues on the committee divided and their chairman in opposition, the majority of Republicans on December 7, 1867, influenced by Bingham, Wilson, Blaine, and Washburne, voted with Democrats to table the impeachment resolution on the floor of the House.[40] Naturally, the radical minority was outraged. "If the great culprit had robbed a till; if he fired a barn; if he had forged a check; he would have been indicted, prosecuted, condemned, sentenced, and punished," the radical editor of the influential Congregationalist opinion journal *The Independent*, Theodore Tilton, fumed. "But the evidence shows that he only oppressed the Negro; that he only conspired with the rebel; that he only betrayed the Union party; that he only attempted to overthrow the Republic—of course, he goes unwhipped of justice."[41]

Radical anger was so great at this final failure that an outright party schism threatened. Voicing the feelings of the defeated Republicans, Tilton mourned, "[A] Republican majority of cowards gagged a Republican minority of statesmen." Two days after the vote, radicals met at Thaddeus Stevens's residence to discuss the prospects for creating a separate radical congressional party organization.[42]

But Johnson, believing himself freed from the threat of impeachment, embarked on an even more aggressive course. On December 28, 1867, he removed General John Pope from his command over Georgia and Alabama, and General Edward O. C. Ord from his command over Arkansas and Mississippi. He replaced them with the more conservative George Meade and the archconservative Alvan C. Gillem. At the same time President Johnson replaced Meade's subordinate, General Wager Swayne, who had been delegated immediate authority over Alabama. With the president's shifts of military personnel, control of the military in every reconstructed state passed to officers sympathetic to southerners who were resisting the Republican Reconstruction program.[43]

As Johnson continued his offensive, Freedmen's Bureau Commissioner Oliver Otis Howard expressed deep concern to one of his friends: "The President ... musters out all my officers.... Measures are on foot ... which are doubtless intended to utterly defeat reconstruction."[44] With the military "influence" in the hands of conservatives, southern loyalists despaired of winning their states' compliance with the Reconstruction acts. From throughout the South came warnings of the Johnson offensive's disastrous effects on congressional Reconstruction policies.[45] "Johnson defeats Congress at every point," the *Boston Com-*

monwealth lamented. "The work of reconstruction, at very short intervals, receives from him a staggering blow. . . . While Congress is passing acts to reconstruct the South, the President is driving a carriage and six through them."[46]

The success of the president's policy was made manifest when pro-Reconstruction forces were defeated in Alabama, the first state to vote on a new constitution framed under the terms of the Reconstruction Act. In fact, Republican forces would prove unable to bring about compliance with the Reconstruction law in four of the ten states that it covered.[47]

Johnson's course appeared to congressional Republicans to be fraught with danger. It seemed, at a minimum, that the president hoped to delay Reconstruction until an anti-Republican reaction developed in the North, born of frustration and weariness with constant crises. Of course, if voters in the states that had not left the Union elected a Democratic Congress before southern states were reconstructed along Republican lines, it would be a simple matter to repeal the Reconstruction Act, recognize the Johnsonian civil governments as legitimate, and admit their representatives to Congress. But this was extremely unlikely. The real danger was that a Democratic presidential candidate might win enough northern and border-state electoral votes in 1868 to win a majority of the whole if Democratic votes from unreconstructed southern states were counted. That might precipitate a real crisis, with Johnson, in control of the military, recognizing the Democratic body.[48]

A second anticipated peril was that Johnson might use the military to interfere with presidential balloting in those states that were yet to comply with the Reconstruction law and be restored by Congress. "Do you not suppose that next November a single soldier at each polling place in the southern country, aided by the whites, could prevent the entire negro [sic] population from voting?" the radical Boutwell asked. Again there was the danger that Democratic electoral votes from northern and border states combined with southern votes won through such illicit tactics might constitute a majority. If the Republican-controlled Congress refused to count southern votes in either case, as they undoubtedly would, President Johnson might view the refusal as a denial of the democratic process. As Boutwell grimly prophesied: "The next inauguration of a President . . . [would] be the occasion of renewal of fratricidal strife."[49]

Many Republicans believed the president capable of such audacity. During the summer and fall of 1866, Johnson supporters had hinted darkly that if enough Democrats were elected to Congress from the North, they might withdraw from the Capitol and join southern congressmen-elect in a counter-Congress, arguing that it represented more congressional districts than its Republican-dominated counterpart. Many Republicans believed the scheme had been abandoned only because northerners had returned an overwhelming Republican majority.[50] Again, in the fall of 1867, rumors of a Johnsonian coup d'état swept the country.[51] By 1868, Carl Schurz recalled, "The air . . . throughout the country was buzzing with rumors of iniquities which Johnson was meditating and would surely attempt if he were not disarmed. . . . There was a widespread feeling among well-meaning and sober people that the country was really in some sort of peril."[52]

Republicans knew that the success of such schemes would depend upon control of the army, and it was Johnson's apparent efforts to gain control of the military in February 1868 that convinced even the doubters that a real danger existed. On January 13 the Senate refused to acquiesce in Johnson's suspension of Secretary of War Stanton as appeared to be required by terms of the Tenure of Office Act, and the next day Stanton resumed his place at the War Office. When General William T. Sherman, who sympathized with the president's view on Reconstruction, suggested that Republican conservatives and moderates would be willing to dump Stanton in favor of the archconservative but independent-minded Jacob D. Cox, he found Johnson uninterested in reaching an accommodation. Johnson wanted his own man in the office. Sherman abandoned his efforts, realizing, as he wrote home, that "there must be something behind the scenes."[53]

Instead of compromising, Johnson determined to take the ominous step of creating a new army department, the Army of the Atlantic, with headquarters in Washington. The sympathetic Sherman would be placed in command. Sherman resisted the appointment, but Johnson ignored his protests. On February 6, 1868, he instructed Grant to promulgate an order creating the department and giving the command to Sherman. At the same time he acted to promote Sherman to General of the Army—the same rank that Grant held—sending the nomination to the Senate on February 13, 1868. Johnson knew the effect his action would have on his adversaries in Congress: "This would set some of them thinking," he told his secretary.[54]

Sherman refused the command and telegraphed his brother, Senator John Sherman of Ohio, to oppose confirmation of his new rank in the Senate. "The President would make use of me to beget violence," he wrote. "He has no right to use us for such purposes, [even] though he is Commander-in-Chief." On February 19, Johnson acceded to Sherman's pleas and rescinded his transfer to the new command.[55]

Two days later Johnson again removed Stanton, this time without complying with the provision of the Tenure of Office law. To Republicans it appeared to be another step in a course that threatened incalculable disaster to their program and to the country. But this time all Republicans agreed that Johnson had crossed the bounds of legality, that he had, as even Bingham conceded, "deliberately . . . violated . . . the laws of the country."[56] Conservative Republicans, feeling they were left no choice, bitterly joined the radicals in presenting articles of impeachment to the Senate.[57]

So the impeachment of President Andrew Johnson was no hasty, passionate decision by vindictive radicals. The longtime opponent of impeachment, Judiciary Committee Chairman Wilson, best expressed the spirit in which the majority of Republicans who had opposed impeachment finally decided to act: "Guided by a sincere desire to pass this cup from our lips, determined to drink it if escape were not cut off by the presence of a palpable duty, we at last find ourselves compelled to take its very dregs."[58] The Johnson impeachment was the reluctant decision of men who felt that they had been forced to take a stand to defend the constitutional prerogatives of Congress against presidential aggression. As even the most conservative of Republicans (in this case Representative Austin Blair of Michigan) finally saw it, President Johnson had "thrown the gauntlet to Congress, and says to us as plainly as words can speak it: 'Try this issue now betwixt me and you; either you go to the wall or I do.'"[59]

II

PARTIES AND FACTIONS IN
CIVIL WAR–ERA POLITICS

4

The Party, Going Strong: Congress and Elections in the Mid-Nineteenth Century

The constitutional politics of the Reconstruction era took place in an intensely partisan environment that was quite different from what most Americans have experienced in our lifetimes. Only recently have Americans become anywhere near as deeply polarized politically as they were in the mid-nineteenth century. Once more political rhetoric runs hot, and the presidential elections of 2000 and 2004 were bitterly contested. Political scientists, reawakened to the potentialities of partisanship, now stress the tenacity of party identification.[1]

Yet many more Americans continue to identify themselves as "independents" than did so before the decline of party identification of the second half of the twentieth century.[2] Voters continue to split their votes between candidates of the two parties.[3] Campaigns remain "candidate-centered."[4] The parties themselves still act more as candidate service providers than as the prime movers of political campaigns.[5] Political scientists Larry Sabato and Bruce Larson note that Americans who lean toward either of the two major parties are reluctant to admit to their real party identities, reflecting "a sea change in attitudes about political parties." Where adhering to a political party was once "a badge of good citizenship . . . signifying that one was a patriot," now political labels "are shunned as an offense to a thinking person's individualism, and a vast majority of Americans insist they vote for 'the man, not the party.'"[6] Americans no longer attempt to affect public policy collectively through party politics, but rather through a plethora of groups and institutional mechanisms that encourage more individualistic, "personal democracy."[7]

But something is happening.[8] If ordinary voters still betray the characteristics of the era of "dealignment," elites—party activists, congressional representatives and senators, pundits, journalists—are making the differences between the Democratic and Republican parties clear to a degree unknown in the decades from the 1950s through the 1980s, when the political columnist David Broder had summarized the situation for a popular audience by punning *The Party's Over*.[9] If political scientists are correct that the key to partisanship

---

The original version of this essay was published in *Congress and the Presidency* 9 (Winter 1981–82): 37–60.

among ordinary voters is the cues they receive from elites,[10] we may be entering a new, more partisan era, and a number of analysts are presenting evidence that this is so.[11]

What may be being replaced was an era that lasted from the 1950s into the 1990s during which party identification and loyalty had eroded and in which voters' comprehension of issues and the positions of candidates and parties on them were vague.[12] Suggested by studies of the electorate in presidential elections, the characterization seemed to be even truer for congressional elections.[13] Congressional behavior mirrored this political environment and, in light of recent studies of the impact of elite political behavior on ordinary voters, probably reinforced it. Studies of congressional roll calls found declining party cohesion.[14] In a political environment in which party labels had diminishing attraction for voters and in which party institutions had atrophied, the responsibility for getting elected and reelected fell primarily upon congresspersons' own individual efforts. Most congressional candidates ran their own independent election campaigns, with money they raised themselves and staffed by people they recruited. They strove to establish positive, personal images often irrelevant to that of their party; they took positions popular in their own districts, even if contrary to the general position of their party, and they eschewed those that were unpopular. They stressed the services they rendered their constituents; and they took care to conciliate powerful local interests. In short, congressional politics turned upon what David R. Mayhew called "the electoral connection" between congressperson and voter rather than party competition.[15] Political scientists still describe elections as candidate-centered rather than party-centered.[16]

Party leaders recognized this reality by tolerating mavericks, eschewing sanctions in favor of persuasion when trying to secure support for party positions, and even encouraging colleagues to "duck" or desert the party position on votes that would jeopardize their chance of reelection.[17] As candidates rather than parties had the main responsibility for communicating with voters, parties appeared increasingly irrelevant to decisions about how to vote in elections.[18] In a candidate-centered era, reorganized and strengthened party institutions emerged primarily to provide candidate services rather than partisan cues.[19] Naturally, this blurred the policy differences between the parties, while the relationship between individual congressmen and party policy was even fuzzier.

Thus, when the original version of this essay appeared in 1981, it described a lost world. But with the revival of partisanship, the political landscape of the 1860s and 1870s no longer looks so alien. Like the present, it was a time when many Americans, and certainly party activists, were convinced that the Democratic and Republican parties stood for radically different principles and that the future of American society was at stake in the nation's political contests. Still, a congressman's approach to politics was very different from the approach of congresspersons today. Looking at mid-nineteenth-century politicians and parties can give an idea of the potentialities of a truly partisan era.

The Party in the Nineteenth Century

The 1860s and the early 1870s were the early years of what political scientists and historians perceive to be the third-party system. In these years, the great struggle over slavery that had led to the birth of the Republican Party and to civil war was still fresh in the mind of the electorate; they worshiped at "the shrine of the party."[20] This was reflected by the pervasiveness of party in the Reconstruction-era Congresses. This is not to say that every issue was a party issue, especially when defined by the strictest measure. The median Rice indices of party likeness on final votes on substantive legislation were 36 and 56 in the Thirty-ninth and Fortieth Congresses, respectively; they were 56 and 39 in the Senate.[21] These were relatively low compared to scores later in the nineteenth century and in the first part of the twentieth. But, as tables 4.1 and 4.2 show, partisan differences were concentrated overwhelmingly in the area of Reconstruction legislation. By far the largest number of votes in a single area that the two houses recorded involved that subject. In fact as the proportion of Reconstruction to other legislation decreased in the immediately succeeding Congresses, so did the degree of partisan division in the House and, at first, in the Senate.[22]

Thus when Republicans won the presidential election of 1868 on a promise that their victory would mark the end of the great conflict over slavery, pledging in the words of one orator "peace . . . upon the basis of a restored Union, of results already accomplished and of a state of things already existing," they were consciously interring the issue that had led to the partisan realignment upon which their coalition was based.[23] Naturally, within a few months Republican congressmen were lamenting the collapse of party unity. "The Republicans are of one party only in name," complained one leader.[24] And Republican politicians and factions defeated in intraparty battles began to urge a fundamental restructuring of the party leadership.[25] This erosion of party unity continued until the spring of 1871, when Ku Klux Klan outrages in the South rekindled the slavery issue and Republicans responded with the Force Act. A small number of Republican dissidents refused to go along with this resurrection of a "dead issue" and organized the ill-fated Liberal Republican movement. But for most Republicans the Force Act restored party élan. As Attorney General Amos T. Akerman wrote a political ally, "All that is necessary to hold the majority of the

Table 4.1
Median Indices of Republican-Democratic Likeness or Various Issues, House of Representatives, 39th–40th, 43rd–44th Congresses

Issue	Number of Roll-Call Votes	Median Index of Likeness
Reconstruction		
39 Congress, 1 Season	(122)	10.5
39 Congress, 2 Session	(45)	6.1
40 Congress	(111)	6.0
43 Congress	(40)	22.6
44 Congress	(23)	21.8
Black Rights		
39 Congress, 1 Session	(Black Suffrage; votes = 11)	24.0
39 Congress, 2 Session	(Black Suffrage; votes = 5)	5.1
40 Congress	(Nonsouthern Black Rights; votes = 5)	0.1
43 Congress	(Civil Rights; votes = 17 not including filibuster)	9.9
44 Congress	(Civil Rights; votes = 1)	27.1
Southern Contested Elections		
43 Congress	(10)	13.5
44 Congress	(6)	7.1
1876 Electoral Vote Count		
44 Congress	(66)	11.4
Corruption in Government and Civil Service Reform		
44 Congress	(Civil Service Reform; votes = 8)	42.4
44 Congress	(Corruption Investigation; votes = 7)	5.3
Tariff		
39 Congress	(6)	41.0
43 Congress	(6)	21.8
44 Congress	(2)	23.8
Anti-Monopoly and Regulatory Legislation		
39 Congress	(5)	24.3
40 Congress	(9)	74.9
43 Congress	(6)	31.3

Corporate Subsidies

39 Congress	(16)	31.1
40 Congress	(14)	86.8
43 Congress	(11)	64.2
44 Congress	(6)	89.3

Presidential Term

43 Congress	(3)	37.0
44 Congress	(7)	56.5

Fiscal Policy

39 Congress	(20)	67.8
40 Congress	(16)	71.0
43 Congress	(23)	88.4
44 Congress	(26)	46.5

Public Works

43 Congress	(16)	76.5
44 Congress	(6)	92.5

Bankruptcy

39 Congress	(5)	93.7
43 Congress	(1)	93.9
44 Congress	(1)	84.2

NOTE: Near-identical votes on dilatory motions and amendments were generally excluded. These figures are the result of tedious search, and slight variations due to human error or differences in judgment might occur if another investigator embarked on the same project.

northern voters to the Republican cause, is to show them how active and cruel the Confederate temper still is in the South."[26] From that point until the realignment of the 1890s, Republicans regularly waved what battered opponents disgustedly called "the bloody shirt."[27]

During these years, the 1860s to mid-1870s, the institutions of party leadership in Congress were stronger than they have been until the recent revival of party discipline among Republican members of the House. The party caucus, in particular, played a much stronger role than it does now. It met regularly to devise legislation that all elements of the party could support.[28] Thaddeus Stevens's legendary "dictatorship" over Republicans in the House emanated from the forcefulness with which he enforced party, especially caucus, decisions.[29]

It was on the slavery and the related Reconstruction issues that congressional Republicans most differed from Democrats in the 1860s and 1870s,[30] and the electorate mirrored that division. From 1865 through 1876 the Republicans con-

Table 4.2
Median Indices of Republican-Democratic Party Likeness or Various Issues, Senate, 39th–40th, 43rd–44th Congresses

Issue	Number Votes	Median Index of Likeness
Reconstruction		
39 Congress, 1 Session	(293)	7.7
39 Congress, 2 Session	(67)	18.5
40 Congress, 1 Session	(60)	51.8
40 Congress, 2 Session	(57)	24.3
40 Congress, 3 Session	(59)	26.7
43 Congress	(25)	12.5
44 Congress	(General Reconstruction; votes = 52)	11.4
44 Congress	(Loyalty Oaths and Amnesty; votes = 4)	74.3
44 Congress	(Protection of Voting Rights; votes = 20)	0.0
Civil Rights		
43 Congress	(14)	10.4
Southern Contested Elections		
43 Congress	(8)	10.8
44 Congress	(15)	11.0
Army Appropriations		
43 Congress	(10)	33.4
44 Congress	(9)	21.1
Indian Policy		
43 Congress	(12)	29.8
44 Congress	(14)	44.9
Tariff		
39 Congress	(40)	56.5
43 Congress	(3)	19.5
Southern and Wartime Claims		
43 Congress	(7)	46.7
44 Congress	(2)	41.5

1876 Electoral Vote Count

44 Congress	(31)	42.1

Corporate Subsidies

39 Congress	(6)	54.4
40 Congress	(16)	60.1
43 Congress	(6)	61.5
44 Congress	(21)	73.7

Anti-monopoly and Regulatory Legislation

39 Congress	(3)	37.5
40 Congress	(5)	70.4
43 Congress	(10)	65.1

Civil Service Reform

43 Congress	(1)	61.0
44 Congress	(4)	91.3

Public Works

43 Congress	(24)	75.4
44 Congress	(23)	67.7

Fiscal Policy

40 Congress	(12)	77.8
43 Congress	(52)	88.8
44 Congress	(1)	74.9

Debt Funding

43 Congress	(4)	92.7
44 Congress	(3)	60.9

Bankruptcy

39 Congress	(1)	81.7
43 Congress	(6)	92.9

stantly stressed sectional issues—what Democrats, wishing they would go away, insisted were dead, "bloody shirt" issues, and what Progressive historians insisted were all-too-successful smokescreens to deflect the electorate's attention from the "real" economic issues of the time.[31] And these issues were profoundly constitutional. They went to the definition of citizenship, to the delineation of its rights, and to the power of the federal government to protect them and the states to maintain jurisdiction over local affairs.

Although many historians and political scientists have pointed out the strong link between party identifications and ethnocultural backgrounds,[32] Republican leaders suppressed nativist, anti-Catholic, prohibitionist, and Sabbatarian agitation throughout the era, and it did not begin to revive until the mid-1870s.[33] With large numbers of potentially antislavery Germans concentrated in key northern states, Indiana Republican and future vice president Schuyler Colfax merely stated the obvious when he warned that rhetoric linking Republicans and nativism "must be extinguished, or we shall lose Pa, N.J., Inda., Conn. & Lord knows how many more states."[34] A look at state party platforms from 1866 to 1872, gleaned from Edward McPherson's political manuals for those years, confirms this observation.[35] (Party platforms do not predict very accurately what a party will do when in power, of course, but they do constitute the issues that leaders think will win them votes.) As table 4.3 shows, planks on the national issues of Reconstruction, economics, and government operations far outnumbered the handful dealing with what may be called "social issues." Party differences were clearest in the areas of Reconstruction and black rights (especially before the Democratic "New Departure" of 1871–72, in which Democrats tried to put the catastrophic war issues behind them), state rights, the protective tariff, and the national banking system.

Proponents of equal political rights for African Americans, an issue closely related to antislavery, and of prohibition of alcoholic beverages consistently attempted to write their commitments into state constitutions. Although nativism, prohibitionism, and antislavery seem to have been rooted in the same soil of evangelical Protestant values, table 4.4 shows how strongly Republican voters identified with the party's antislavery mission by the 1860s. In the formative years of the third party system, until about 1856, voting patterns in prohibition referenda and in black-suffrage referenda had correlated at about the same level with Republican voting patterns. But by 1860 Republican voting patterns almost exactly paralleled the patterns of support for black rights, while the party eschewed the liquor issue.

Of course, the fact that the voting *patterns* were similar did not mean that every Republican voted to expand black rights in their states. It only meant that as the percentage of Republican voters went up in counties across a state, so did the percentage of votes to grant black citizens the right to vote. Indeed until the war's end a large proportion of Republicans opposed so radical a step as enfranchising black men living among them. However, after the Confederate surrender, support for black rights became virtually a party issue, dividing the electorate as completely as it did party leaders. Table 4.5 provides estimates of individual voting behavior derived from regression coefficients.[36] It indicates that only in Kansas was there major Republican opposition to the enfranchise-

Table 4.3
Common Northern State Political Platform Planks 1866–1872

	Number of Planks	
	Republicans	Democrats
	(N = 40)*	(N = 33)
Reconstruction and Race		
Endorsing State Rights, Opposing "Centralization"	0	19
Endorsing Congressional Reconstruction Policy	16	0
Condemning Congressional Reconstruction Policy	0	9
Pro-Test Oath, Anti-Amnesty	3	0
Anti-Test Oath, Pro-Amnesty	4	6
Pro-Black Suffrage	9	0
Anti-Black Suffrage	0	8
Protection of Voting Rights (after 1868)	4	0
General Endorsement of Equality in Unspecified Rights, 1871–72	7	4
Acquiescence in the Results of Reconstruction, 1871–72	—	8
Thanks to Union Soldiers	6	4
Bounty Equalization	0	3
Economic Issues		
Pro-Protective Tariff	17	0
Anti-Protective Tariff	1	12
Anti-National Banking System	0	5
Pro-Government Aid for Economic Development	4	1
Anti-Government Aid for Economic Development	11	4
Pro-Currency Inflation, Anti-Currency Contraction	2	1
Anti-Currency Inflation, Pro-Currency Contraction	3	1
Pro-Reserving Public Lands for Settlers Only	10	4
Anti-Monopoly	2	1
Government Operation		
Pro-Civil Service Reform	7	3
Pro-Reduction of Expenditures	3	4
Pro-Reduction of Taxation	9	11
Social Issues		
Pro-National Government Promotion of Education	2	1
Pro-State Promotion of Education	6	0
Pro-Prohibition	3	0

(continues)

Table 4.3
Continued

	Number of Planks	
	Republicans	Democrats
	(N = 40)*	(N = 33)
Anti-Prohibition	1	2
Pro-Religious Tolerance	0	2
Anti-Sectarian Influence in Schools (implicitly anti-Catholic)	2	0
Pro-immigration and Protection of Naturalized Citizens	3	3

*N = number of platforms. If more than one plank was devoted to one subject, the subject was nonetheless counted once.

ment of black state citizens after 1865. Where Republicans were unenthusiastic, they signified their dissatisfaction by abstaining; they could not bring themselves to vote for a position now completely identified with the Democratic Party.

Party and Personal Ambition

The powerful political partisanship of the mid-1860s and early 1870s alters many of the understandings of congressional behavior derived from the traditional view among political scientists that each congressperson's activities are best understood as a personal effort to win reelection. At minimum, in such a partisan environment, party must have played a larger role in each congressman's calculation of just what conduct would reelect him.

Moreover, even the premise may not have been true. With party and a single set of issues playing so crucial a role in politics, the ethic of the times seems to have been against such egocentric political calculations. In the 1860s and 1870s Americans believed that the man should not seek office; the office should seek the man, and he reluctantly agreed to a nomination for the sake of the principles that his party espoused. Thus George W. Julian recalled that he first stood for Congress "in compliance with the wishes of my anti-slavery friends, and by way of doing my part of the work" of organizing an antislavery party.[37] Democrat Henry Watterson began his short stay in Congress although "holding office, especially going to Congress, had never entered any wish or scheme of mine. Office seemed to me ever a badge of bondage." What happened? "The opportunity sought me out."[38] Pennsylvania Republican William D. Kelley

Table 4.4
Coefficients of Determination Between Party Voting Patterns and Referenda

	Republicans		Democrats	
	Black Rights	Prohibition	Black Rights	Prohibition
Illinois, black exclusion,				
1848–1856 presidential vote	.42		.28	
1858 congressional vote	.16		.28	
Michigan, black suffrage,				
1850/1856 presidential vote	.37		.22	
1858 congressional vote	.31		.41	
Indiana, black exclusion,				
1851/1856 presidential vote	.35		.27	
1858 congressional vote	.23		.08	
Ohio, license,				
1851/1856 presidential vote		.03		.31
1858 congressional vote		.10		.32
Michigan, prohibition,				
1853/1856 presidential vote		.26		.30
1858 congressional vote		.48		.42
Rhode Island, license,				
1853/1856 presidential vote		.77		.29
1858 congressional vote		.56		.53
Wisconsin, prohibition				
1853/1856 presidential vote		.18		.23
1858 congressional vote		.07		.23
Pennsylvania, prohibition,				
1854/1856 presidential vote		.12		.18
1860 presidential vote		.23		.14
Illinois, prohibition,				
1855/1856 presidential vote		.58		.66
1858 congressional vote		.49		.55
Iowa, prohibition,				
1855/1854 congressional vote		.90		.71
1856 presidential vote		.13		.31
1858 congressional vote		.02		.18
Wisconsin, black suffrage,				
1857/1857 gubernatorial vote	.64		.96	
1858 congressional vote	.19		.14	
Iowa, black suffrage,				
1857/1857 gubernatorial vote	.06		.25	
1858 congressional vote	.11		.25	
1860 congressional vote	.26		.34	

(continues)

Table 4.4
Continued

	Republicans		Democrats	
	Black Rights	Prohibition	Black Rights	Prohibition
Oregon, black exclusion,				
1857/1858 gubernatorial vote	.58		.56	
1860 presidential vote	.61		.07	
New York, black suffrage,				
1860/1860 presidential vote	.77		.81	
Connecticut, black suffrage,				
1865/1865 gubernatorial vote	.74		.96	
Minnesota, black suffrage,				
1865/1865 gubernatorial vote	.66		.79	
Wisconsin, black suffrage,				
1865/1865 gubernatorial vote	.85		.90	
Kansas, black suffrage,				
1867/1868 presidential vote	.58		.76	
Minnesota, black suffrage,				
1867/1867 gubernatorial vote	.61		.74	
Ohio, black suffrage,				
1867/1867 gubernatorial vote	.96		.98	
Iowa, black suffrage,				
1868/1868 presidential vote	.88		.94	
Michigan, prohibition,				
1868/1868 presidential vote		.62		.52
Minnesota, black suffrage,				
1868/1868 presidential vote	.96		.96	
New York, black suffrage,				
1869/1864–1868 mean party vote	.81		.67	
Michigan, black suffrage,				
1870/1864–1868 mean party vote	.71		.26	
Ohio, license,				
1874/1870–1873 mean party one		.31		.16
Michigan, license,				
1876/1872–1876 mean party vote		.37		.04
Kansas, prohibition,				
1880/1860 presidential vote		.22		.38

NOTE: Voting patterns are based on the proportion of the total eligible electorate voting for each party. The coefficient of determination is the square of the simple Pearsonian correlation coefficient (r). It expresses the proportion of the variation in the voting patterns or referenda explained by the Republican and Democratic voting patterns in years noted. In every case voting patterns in favor of black rights and prohibition correlated positively with Republican voting patterns and negatively with Democratic voting patterns.

Table 4.5
Republicans, Democrats, and Black Suffrage Referenda

	VOTES ON BLACK SUFFRAGE REFERENDA		
	% For	% Against	% Not Voting
Republicans			
Connecticut, 1865[1]	60.2	0 (−3.2)	43.1
Minnesota, 1865[1]	72.4	22.7	4.9
Wisconsin, 1865[1]	84.5	8.5	6.9
Kansas, 1867[2]	47.7	59.0	0 (−6.7)
Minnesota, 1867[1]	77.3	0	32.7
Ohio, 1867[1]	94.7	1.0	4.3
Iowa, 1868[2]	86.0	3.2	6.8
Minnesota, 1868[2]	92.2	5.1	2.7
New York, 1869[2]	61.7	4.0	34.5
Democrats			
Connecticut, 1865[1]	0 (−2.1)	100.5	1.6
Minnesota, 1865[1]	0 (−7.6)	91.6	16.0
Wisconsin, 1865[1]	5.5	83.9	2.2
Kansas, 1867[2]	0 (−8.4)	94.5	14.9
Minnesota, 1867[1]	0 (−11.9)	59.0	18.3
Ohio, 1867[1]	0 (−3.5)	102.7	.9
Iowa, 1868[2]	1.9	93.1	1.0
Minnesota, 1868[2]	0 (−2.8)	98.3	4.5
New York, 1869[2]	6.3	84.2	9.1

[1] With gubernatorial vote of the same year.
[2] With 1868 presidential vote.

would have retired in 1870, "if I could have . . . without ingratitude or indifference to the wishes of [his] constituency." Yet he did not want to seem ungrateful. "While . . . I cannot say that I gladly accept the honor you tender me," he explained, "I would be wanting in candor if I did not assure you that I do it with just pride and a renewed determination to prove myself worthy" of it.[39] Kelley reluctantly answered his constituents' call for another twenty years, leaving Congress only for a final trip to the cemetery.

Campaigning for a nomination, which suggested a desire for personal preferment, seems to have been regarded as unseemly. James A. Garfield wrote a friend shortly before his Republican district convention met to decide his renomination, "My policy . . . has been this: to secure the support of my constituents by doing my duty here (in Congress) in such a manner as to honor the District and myself . . . rather than by palaver and begging them to give me their votes. This is the only way for me to preserve my self-respect."[40]

In his reminiscences, the voluble Indiana Democratic politician David Turpie could not bring himself to say much about his political maneuvering. Naturally, he claimed to have been drafted for his first state legislative race. Years later, "in my absence, I was unanimously nominated by the Democratic convention of the ninth district as a candidate for Congress." Evidently without any action on his part, this occurred three consecutive times. A few years after that, "in the summer of 1874 . . . I was nominated by acclamation . . . as one of the candidates for the legislature. Having always been of the opinion that a member of our party should not decline a call thus made, I accepted the nomination."[41] According to his brother and admiring biographer, Roscoe Conkling, the New York Republican party boss, who was notorious for his vanity, likewise had to be coaxed into his first run for Congress: "At first Mr. Conkling refused to allow his name to be used, but his political friends would not take 'no' for a reply."[42]

The researcher becomes so used to this pattern that he is shocked by the candor of Schuyler Colfax's 1868 campaign biographer, who wrote, "It is certain that at a very early day when most boys are thinking of their games and play, he made up his mind to enter upon the stormy and uncertain career of politics at the first practicable moment, and to rise as high and as quickly as his ability would permit."[43] Rutherford B. Hayes's campaign biographer, William Dean Howells, was more traditional. Of Hayes's first congressional nomination, he wrote, "He had not, of course, sought the nomination, but at the urgence of friends, he had let the matter take its course."[44]

Beneath this decorous exterior, the politicians of the 1860s and 1870s must have been as ambitious as other men. Their behavior suggests it. Despite his protestations, Garfield fought like a lion to secure renomination the one time he was really threatened by local insurgents, after he was tainted by the Credit Mobilier scandal.[45] Charles Sumner resisted pressure from associates to seek the United States Senate nomination from the Democratic–Free Soil coalition that had won control of the Massachusetts legislature in 1850. "I have never been accustomed to think highly of political distinction," he wrote one of them. "I have not been able at any time in my inmost heart to bring myself to desire the post, or even to be willing to take it." But he refused to withdraw his name even when the reluctance of some of the Democrats to support him deadlocked the legislature for three months. He would not bargain for the office, but neither would he give it up.[46]

Such behavior does not mean that these diffident politicians were insincere. As he struggled for his 1874 renomination Garfield confided in his diary, "I can fight battles for others but to fight men for disliking me, for disapproving of my course, hurts my pride and self-love more than anything I have been called upon to meet."⁴⁷ The diary of Rutherford B. Hayes also indicates a deep ambivalence about his pursuit of political advancement. The researcher can look in vain for an avowal of ambition, for an apparently selfish thought. Every act is justified in terms of moral duty. And yet the acts themselves are not much different from those that a calculating self-seeker would undertake.⁴⁸

Perhaps the best example of the inability of mid-nineteenth-century politicians to admit their own ambition and their compulsion to justify it in terms of other commitments is a letter U.S. Supreme Court Chief Justice Salmon P. Chase sent an old friend in April 1868. "I really think that I am not half so ambitious of place as I am represented to be," he wrote. "Certainly I never used any of the ordinary means to get place. I worked for ideals and principles and measures embodying them; and was always quite willing to take place, or be left out of place, as the cause, in the judgment of its friends, required." Even as he sealed the envelope, the old antislavery radical was coquetting for the *Democratic* nomination to the presidency, since it had become clear he could not win that of the Republicans. His friend and sympathetic biographer had to concede, "Never was a heart more self-deceived than was the heart of our hero when he wrote that letter and others of like import."⁴⁹

The consequence of this aversion to public personal promotion, and of the public expectation that one should not engage in it, was the tendency to promote one's party rather than oneself when campaigning. A candidate to the House of Representatives was expected to stump his district thoroughly every two years. Slogging by carriage from one small town to another, at each of which he would be expected to speak for hours before a few hundred of the voters in what was for them both entertainment and a civic duty, the candidates developed a largely set piece that served with minor changes for the duration. One can find them in local weekly newspapers and in the daily press of the large cities. Almost invariably, these speeches were arraignments of the opposing party and encomiums for one's own.⁵⁰ The campaigns were most definitely not "candidate-centered." Rarely did a candidate ask for a vote for himself. Garfield recognized congressional elections as "the time . . . when the people . . . inspect the work of their servants to see if it has been done honestly and wisely." But he did not perceive it to be individual politicians who were judged. To Garfield, it was axiomatic that "the political party whose doctrines and aspirations accomplish most in this direction will enjoy the confidence of support of our people."⁵¹

To get their own views before the public, candidates even articulated party positions where none really existed. Julian, for example, drew a distinction between the Democratic and Republican positions on his pet scheme to reserve all government-owned western lands for actual settlers, ending the railroad land-grant system.[52] One would be hard pressed to sustain the distinction based on congressional action. Garfield, stumping for the Republican ticket in 1868, likewise insisted that only Democrats favored "repudiating" the national debt by paying off wartime bonds in greenbacks."[53] He must have known better, but if the position were popular among his constituents, he wanted his party to have credit for it. So complete was the identification in Garfield's mind between party and candidate that, he concluded, "The people of the Nineteenth District . . . will not now, I believe . . . become repudiators of the national obligations. But if they do, I should consider myself dishonored by accepting or continuing to hold office on any such terms."[54] One can hardly imagine a modern congressional candidate threatening to refuse his office if the rest of his party's ticket is defeated, even as a rhetorical device—an explicit rejection of ticket-splitting, even in one's favor.[55] On the contrary, one of the most important uses to which candidates put campaign funds nowadays is to distinguish themselves from unpopular aspects of their party image—to be seen as *in* party but not *of* it, as one analyst describes the effort.[56]

Perhaps nothing displayed better this nineteenth-century aversion to personal politics than the reaction in the North to Andrew Johnson's unusual campaign tour of 1866, designed to win support for his conservative Reconstruction policy. This policy had divided him from the Republican Party, and yet he refused to affirm himself a Democrat. Without a party with which to identify, he continually had to refer to "my policy" rather than to his party's policy. The number of references to "my policy" and uses of the first person in his speeches became a political joke. Satirist David Ross Locke dedicated a poem to the president, in honor of his campaign: "I, Me, I, Me, I, Me, 1, Me, I, Me, I, Me, I, Me," were its last two stanzas.[57] Needless to say, the tour was a political disaster.[58]

Given the degree of the mid-nineteenth-century partisanship, however, there was little danger in making such threats as Garfield's to refuse election if the rest of the ticket were defeated. In the case of those aspiring to the United States Senate, the mode of election itself required such a symbiosis. Since U.S. senators were elected by state legislatures, their fortunes depended on party success in their states. Any politician who hoped to get the party legislative caucus to select him was expected to campaign strenuously for his party throughout the state.

But even House candidates could not expect to succeed if the rest of their party's ticket failed. Party lines were too rigid for that. Whether in a presidential year or in an off-year, there was far less variation between the congressional vote and that for candidates for other offices than what we expect today. Looking at the difference between election percentages among candidates running for different offices in the same year, Paul T. David has found that the average difference for Republicans was 5.3 percent from 1872 to 1894, as compared to 8 percent from 1932 to 1970. For Democrats the figures are 6 percent and 8 percent, respectively.[59]

But closer analysis of returns for 1856 through 1880 indicates that the differences were even slighter. Table 4.6 shows the roll-off between the congressional vote and the presidential and gubernatorial vote from 1848 to 1880 in six typical states. From 1856 to 1880 the mean roll-off of the two-party vote for both presidential year and off-year elections in the average county was merely 1.7 percent. Moreover, tables 4.7 and 4.8 suggest how futile it was between 1856 and 1880

Table 4.6
Roll-off Between Congressional Vote Percentages and Presidential or Gubernatorial Vote Percentages for Six States

	Ill.	Iowa	Mass.	N.J.	Ohio	Penn.
1848	12	2	31	2	13	2
1850			20	0		
1852	4	1	16	0	1	1
1854			3*			7
1856	7	1	3	1**	1	1**
1858			0			
1860	1	1	7	1	0	4
1862			7	2		
1864	1	0	0	1	0	1
1866			0			0
1868	0	0	3	1	2	2
1870			0			
1872	1	4	0	1	3	8
1874			2	1		
1876	2	1	0	5	0	1
1878			3***			
1880	0	4	0	0	1	4

Mean roll-off in presidential years, 1856–1880 = 1.7
Mean roll-off in non-presidential years, 1858–1878 = 1.7
Mean roll-off, 1856–1880 = 1.7

NOTE 1: Unless otherwise noted, the parties are Whigs and Democrats through 1854 and Republicans and Democrats from 1856.
NOTE 2: Non-presidential year roll-off percentages are between congressional and gubernatorial votes.
  *Democratic and American parties.
  **Democratic and combined American and Republican parties.
  ***Combined Democratic and Greenback parties are Republican party

Table 4.7
Correlations Between Whig-Republican Congressional and Presidential or Gubernatorial Votes for Six States

	Ill.	Iowa	Mass.	N.J.	Ohio	Pa
1848	.50	.88	.49	.75	.66	.81
1850			.72	.96		
1852	.56	.83	.72	.99	.67	.79
1854			.97			.73
1856	.86	.90	.86	−.06*	.95	.54
1858			.98			
1860	.99	.99	.97	.98	.92	.91
1862			.84	.96		
1864	.86	.99	.98	.99	.92	.96
1866			1.00			.98
1868	.93	1.00	.97	.98	.99	.98
1870			.81			
1872	.97	.96	.99	.96	.97	.96
1874			.74	.98		
1876	.84	.85	.92	.53	.98	.97
1878			.86			.65
1880	.97	.99	.95	.99	.99	.90

*Republican congressional vote compared to Peoples Party presidential and gubernatorial votes.

Median Pearson r for presidential years, 1856–1880 = .96
Median Pearson r for non-presidential years, 1856–1880 = .91

NOTE: Non–presidential year correlations are between congressional and gubernatorial vote patterns.

for a congressional candidate to hope that the basic voting patterns would be any different for him than for the rest of his ticket. The median Pearson product-moment correlation between the congressional and presidential or gubernatorial vote over the counties in the six states was .96—fully 92 percent of the variation in the congressional vote could be explained by the presidential vote in presidential years or the gubernatorial vote in nonpresidential years. The notion that it might be better if opposing parties controlled different branches of government, widely expressed in the 1990s,[60] was completely foreign to mid-nineteenth-century voters. Therefore, even if a candidate were selfishly concerned with his own personal election, the best way to secure it was to promote the success of the whole party.

Yet another reason that congressional candidates may have stressed party rather than individual virtues while campaigning was the relative lack of commitment to a congressional career that characterized most of them. Scholars have long recognized that the nineteen-century Congress, especially the House,

Table 4.8
Correlations Between Democratic Congressional and Presidential or Gubernatorial Votes for Six States

	Ill.	Iowa	Mass.	N.J.	Ohio	Pa.
1848	.62	.90	.02	.99	.74	.79
1850			.30	.99		
1852	.69	.64	.79	.99	.76	.85
1854			.92			.70
1856	.99	.86	.55	.99	.96	.97
1858			.95			
1860	.93	.98	.59	.95	.85	.86
1862			.66	.98		
1864	.87	.98	.99	1.00	.97	.96
1866			1.00			.99
1868	.99	.98	.93	.96	.99	.98
1870			.94			
1872	.99	.93	.99	.97	.94	.84
1874			.74	.98		
1876	.93	.92	.95	.98	.96	.98
1878			.77			.24
1880	.93	.69	.99	.99	.99	.68

Median Pearson r for presidential years, 1856–1880 = .96
Median Pearson r for non-presidential years, 1856–1880 = .93

NOTE: Non-presidential year correlations are between congressional and gubernatorial vote patterns.

was marked by high turnover, few members with long terms of consecutive service, and slight regard for seniority.[61] Many of those congressmen who served only short stints in Congress looked forward to holding other elective or appointive office and their prospects, especially for patronage positions, depended on general party success.

The whole party organizational system demanded that candidates work for party rather than individual success. The party organization was sustained primarily through the custom of providing activists with positions in the national, state, and local civil service. These political appointees were expected to devote time and a portion of their incomes from government service to the party; reciprocally, party activists expected such rewards for their efforts. However, these rewards could be secured only if the party won control of the major appointing offices: the presidency, the state governorship, and local executive offices.[62] Party activists, who controlled party nominations, were hardly likely to feel kindly toward a congressional candidate who won political office for himself but ignored the rest of the ticket, to their own detriment.

Finally, the simple fact was that the congressman's success was intimately bound to that of his party. In this era of intense partisanship, one won or lost elections according to whether partisans turned out in the numbers required. Rarely did voters cross party lines. If disenchanted with recent party policies or dispirited because of the élan of opponents, they stayed home. If alienated by a candidate they scratched his name from the ballots their party gave them to deposit in the ballot box. The charisma of a particular candidate, an effort to distinguish one's positions from those of ones' party, "anything which detracted from the overt appeal of partisanship," as historian Robert Marcus has pointed out, "brought a decline in support."[63]

Conclusion

All of this may have reinforced partisan behavior in Congress. An elected congressman must have felt that he owed more to his party than present-day representatives do. As already noted, nowadays (or at least until quite recently), electioneering involves almost entirely the efforts of individual congresspersons in their own districts with little help from their party as a whole. That simply was not true of the elections of 130 years ago. The patronage system assured a supply of party workers and money, and because of the nature of the system, everyone owed his election to everyone else. They had all stressed the importance of a party vote on party issues, and the electorate had responded. Part of the congressional party's job was to keep those issues salient by proposing legislation involving them. Therefore, in the mid-nineteenth century, and perhaps during other periods following partisan realignments, Anthony Down's economic model of political action, which makes parties the units of analysis, may be more relevant than that of Mayhew and others who stress individual desire for reelection as the prime determinant of congressional legislative behavior.[64]

The original version of this article ended with the suggestion that it seemed unlikely that the process of decay in party loyalty among voters and officeholders could continue much longer. Experience suggested that when Americans feel that their parties no longer provide vehicles for dealing with salient questions, party lines are either reorganized or revitalized. The process was slower than I expected, but the evidence suggests that Americans are reentering a new partisan era. The militancy and cohesion of the Republican Party is tangible. Democrats finally seem to be responding with growing cohesion and militancy of their own. If so, the congressional elections of the future may begin to look more like the contests of the 1860s and 1870s.

5

Factionalism and Representation: Some Insight from the Nineteenth-Century United States

Historians of mid-nineteenth-century American politics know it to be an era when intraparty factional rivalry was almost as bitter as the struggle between parties. Studies such as Joel Silbey's *A Respectable Minority* and Michael Perman's *The Road to Redemption*, concentrate on disagreements between "legitimists" and "purists" in both parties.[1] My own *A Compromise of Principle* stressed factionalism among Republicans in the 1860s, while the first chapter of Robert D. Marcus's study of political structure in the Gilded Age, *Grand Old Party*, is entitled "Faction."[2] While Republican factionalism in the South has been a central concern of historians of Reconstruction,[3] however, few have attended closely to intraparty factionalism in northern states and localities.[4]

Moreover, although American historians are aware of the importance of factionalism in mid-nineteenth-century politics, none has drawn upon the general social-science literature on the subject, either to gain a broader perspective from that literature or to add new insights to it. They have generally concentrated upon issues and events rather than process. They have not studied the origins, structures, and functions of factions during Reconstruction. Most studies refer to differing positions that party subgroups took on issues and tactics, without relating these to factional organization and rivalries.

The Study of Factions

Factions have been analyzed primarily through case studies—especially of the political systems of Japan, India, and Italy. Somewhat different in orientation have been case studies of factional politics in American states, especially in the formerly one-party South, which have been informed by one of the few early efforts at theorizing about factions in general, V. O. Key's extremely influential *Southern Politics in State and Nation*.[5] Belle Zeller's seminal 1954 study of state legislatures for the American Political Science Association paid

---

The original version of this essay was published in *Social Science History* 9 (Fall 1985): 361–98.

close attention to factions, finding that in most states, "factions, blocs, pressure groups, personal followings, local interests, and logrolling combinations pay a much greater part in supplying legislative leadership than does partisanship."[6]

But interest in the study of factions at the state level has declined dramatically. In recent years, American political scientists have turned their attention to the study of coalition-building among ideologically oriented factions in the national parties.[7] Undertaken almost exclusively by political scientists, the historical content of these studies serves primarily to provide a background for current events. The state of knowledge about American political factionalism at the state level remains skimpy. In 1978 the authors of a text on American state politics wrote, "Theoretical literature and evidence are almost totally lacking on factionalism, though it is one of the more frequently used words in politics."[8] The 1982 edition of their work appears to have marked the highpoint of attention to state party factionalism.[9]

The decline of the faction-ridden one-party South is a large factor in the development. With the rise of the two-party South and the increasing ideological coherence within each party there, the perception of factionalism in the region declined, although it remained stronger among party activists.[10] By the 1990s, a summary of a collection of essays by the leading specialists on southern politics reported that "a southern politics more focused on issues has superseded the politics of personal factionalism described by Key."[11] Other political scientists proclaimed "the end of southern distinctiveness."[12] As the classic examples of the politics of personal faction faded from memory, analysts no longer studied factionalism as a characteristic of southern politics and shifted attention to ideological and interest-group divisions in the national parties.[13]

In 1992 an analyst still referred to factionalism as "one of the most understudied areas of American political science."[14] Little has changed. The rise of organized interest groups and their increasing influence seems to have diverted analysts' interest in the subject.[15] At the same time, cultural anthropologists' interest in clientelism and factionalism, which had been seen as a potential key for understanding the transformation of premodern societies into modern ones, shifted to other concerns.[16] Indeed, the entry for "Factionalism" in the *International Encyclopedia of the Social and Behavioral Sciences* says that a 1977 book of essays "is still considered the definitive work on the subject."[17]

Nonetheless, anthropologists, sociologists, and political scientists do address factionalism. Key's work and an early seminal essay by Raphael Zariski posing central questions have been augmented by theoretical articles and compilations of new or previously published essays.[18] In this effort scholars have developed four only moderately compatible approaches. Specialists in American politics began by following the lead of Key, whose *Southern Politics* framed the questions and articulated the approach. Although much of *Southern Politics* was narrative analysis of politics in particular states, throughout his career Key was first of all concerned with the relationship of the general public to politics, and he was also committed to statistical analysis of research problems.[19] Therefore Key chose to identify and analyze intraparty factionalism by looking at the records of party primaries, and this became the standard approach of specialists in American politics.[20]

Key did not analyze factions per se. Rather, he categorized *parties* according to their degree of factionalization and offered hypotheses about what determined whether parties were highly factionalized or not. One of the most influential of these hypotheses was that factionalism is related to the degree of party competition. The more competitive the political parties in a state, the less pervasive is factionalism within them.[21] Although he had clearly identified instances where factions were bound to interests and issues, Key concluded that factionalism obstructed truly representative government, reducing the ability of people to affect policy through electoral politics. In his discussion he stressed the personalist nature of factions—their dependence upon patron-client relationships and charismatic leaders. Factional politics, he wrote, are "issueless politics." They are "ill-designed to meet the necessities of self-government."[22] In fact, Key viewed factionalism virtually as pathological. Southerners had "condemned" themselves to factional politics, he wrote.[23] He titled his last chapter "Is There a Way Out?" Students of American politics tested and elaborated upon these conclusions, and where texts on American politics discussed intraparty factionalism at all, they did so in these terms.[24]

Another approach to factionalism descends from Moisei Ostrogorski's and Robert Michels's pioneering studies of party bureaucracy, by way of such analyses of political systems as Gaetano Mosca's *The Ruling Class*, Maurice Duverger's *Political Parties*, and Giovanni Sartori's *Parties and Party Systems*.[25] Unlike most American analysts, these scholars perceived factions to arise from competition for influence among established and aspiring party leaders, quite independent of any wider support in the general electorate. These analysts make explicit what Key and his successors have left implicit: politicians who want to advance their careers must wage intraparty battles to secure nominations or a high place on a party list before turning to the struggle against the nominees of rival parties. Factions are related to this effort to secure "the route to incumbency," as Sartori calls it.[26] Because they perceived the politician's central goal to be securing office, Key and Sartori each stressed the way in which the formal electoral system influenced the number and stability of factions.[27]

Third, American political scientists have turned to studying the issue-oriented and interest-oriented cleavages in the national Republican and Democratic parties.[28] Although they have not yet considered the degree to which these cleavages are entwined with the political ambitions of rival party leaders—an essential element of factionalism as others have defined it—in recent years there has been some effort to develop a theoretical understanding of coalition-building and competition among intraparty groups, suggesting insights that should be very useful for historians of Reconstruction.[29]

A fourth source of scholarly understanding of political factionalism has come from anthropological studies of premodern and transitional societies. Those studying the politics of transitional society in India, Southeast Asia, Latin America, premodern North and South America, and even southern Italy have found anthropologists' explications of "clientelism"—mutual personal obligations between individuals of unequal status—particularly informing. Such clientelism pervades the social environment of premodern societies, these analysts say, and is reflected in their political systems. Especially at times of social strain and stress, as during modernization, this translates into political factionalism, which they define as competition among different groups of patrons and clients. As societies modernize, leaders whose power derives from their governmental positions may replace traditional community leaders as patrons, because they control the local distribution of larger resources; or traditional patron-client relationships may pervade even a modernizing society, as social development lags behind economic development. Thus these scholars see factions as natural outgrowths of clientelist societies, related more to the distribution of power and control of resources than to the formal structure of politics and intraparty competition for nominations to office.[30]

Until recently, the dominant view was that in a completely modernized state, class and interest-group politics replace factional politics.[31] Like Key, those who approached factionalism from other perspectives concluded that personalist factionalism deprived the public of influence over government. "Most evaluations of intra-party factionalism are highly critical," Sartori wrote.[32] The reason is easy to see. As Harold Lasswell wrote in one of the earliest descriptions by an academic political scientist, "[A] faction seems to subordinate the public good to private gain."[33] By "distorting government policies to benefit their own particular ends," factions rendered political systems "unable to handle society-wide problems."[34] The more highly factionalized a state's politics, the more subject to the influenced of special, selfish interests.[35] Indeed, some analysts define clientelism as bordering on the criminal in its "favouring of exchanges based on private individual or group benefits instead of the exchanges demanded by law, universalist principles or institutional procedures."[36] The term connoted "illegitimacy, if not malevolence and pathology."[37]

Perceiving faction this way, most analysts naturally attended to the ways that factionalism obstructs representative government, hardly considering that it might in fact facilitate it. However, in the late 1970s, integrating the findings of scholars who approached factionalism from different perspectives, students of faction began to question this dismal orthodoxy.[38] As patron-client political relationships stubbornly continue around the world despite global modernization, analysts have become more aware of its ability to accommodate change and its persistence even in modern states.[39]

In sum, social scientists have studied factions far more intensively than have historians of American politics, and their work can help provide a more comprehensive context in which to place nineteenth-century American factions. At the same time, social scientists have not yet integrated differing approaches to the study of factionalism. These differing approaches have led to disparate definitions of faction itself, varying perceptions of their origins and their relationship to the public, and disagreement about their role in and effect upon representative government. An assessment of mid-nineteenth-century American factionalism in the context of the general social-science literature not only may help historians understand nineteenth-century American politics better, but it may also advance social scientists' understanding of factions in general.

The Nature of Nineteenth-Century American Political Factionalism

At the very outset, an effort to place nineteenth-century American factions within this broader context raises a difficult theoretical problem in the study of factionalism and representation—that of definition. Nineteenth-century American factionalism does not comport very well with factions as Key and his protégés defined them. Utilizing data from party primaries, they allowed their method to dictate their definition. To Key, a faction was "any combination, clique, or grouping of voters and political leaders who united at a particular time in support of a candidate." As he explained succinctly, a party primary "with eight candidates will involve eight factions."[40] Accepting this definition, investigators identified 438 separate state-level Democratic factions in the South from 1920 to 1980.[41]

A natural consequence of this approach has been that Key and his successors judged the degree of party factionalization by the number of candidates in primaries and the size of the vote they received: Where there were few meaningful contests, parties were "cohesive"; where primaries were regularly contested by two candidates, each of whom secured a significant proportion of the vote, parties were "bi-factional"; where a plethora of candidates divided the primary vote, parties were "multi-factional."[42]

The problem is that this equates individual candidacies in primaries with factionalism. However, mid-nineteenth-century American factions were informal alliances among party activists who sought to control party machinery in order to nominate for office men allied with their own groups. Obviously, such factions existed before primaries. In fact, the introduction of the primary system was one of the culminating events in a fifty-year struggle to break the power of intraparty factions. The primary was designed by reformers to permit individual party members to select candidates free of party bosses and political machines, in effect allowing capable men without factional connections to appeal over the heads of factional "bosses" to the party rank-and-file for support. Indeed, political scientist Austin Ranney titled his history and assessment of party reforms, including state promotion and regulation of political primaries, *Curing the Mischiefs of Faction*.[43] Nomination through party primaries was designed as an alternative to nomination through factional alliance.

Naturally, party factions adjusted to the primary system. Factions presented candidates in primaries and regularly succeeded in electing them. But not all candidates represented factions. Indeed, just as the rise of candidate-centered politics has weakened the significance of party in voters' decision making,[44] it may have made factional alliances less useful to aspiring politicians, although the question simply has not been studied. In any case, primaries are merely a mode of selecting candidates. They may affect how factions organize to secure those nominations, as Key and his successors demonstrated, but they are not themselves the cause of faction. Therefore, while there may be more candidates in a primary than there are factions, there also may be more factions than there are primary candidates. A "cohesive" party will likely still have factions, even though various factors lead them to avoid competition in primaries, and a "bifactional" party may well have more than two factions, even though various factors may encourage the factions to combine behind only two primary candidates. An awareness of the historical background of factionalism suggests that analyzing primary voting returns is not the best way to get at the roots, structure, and functions of factions themselves.

Another consequence of studying factions primarily through analysis of voting in party primaries was to define faction, in Key's words, as a "grouping of voters and leaders."[45] That is, Key made the voters a part of the faction. The aptness of such a definition has an important effect upon one's understanding of the relationship between factions and representation. It suggests that party factions *emerge from* and represent broader constituencies.

American political scientists studying competition and coalition among factions in the present-day Democratic and Republican parties take the same point of view. They stress one part of the most commonly accepted definition of faction, articulated by Nelson Polsby more than twenty-five years ago—that factions provide "a mass base, an ideological format, an organizational matrix, or all three for the expression of interests" within a party. But they miss the implication of his preceding sentence: "Factions *organize* interests, the felt needs of individuals which are seen to be in some sense capable of satisfaction by means of government policy" (italics added).[46] What Polsby implies, and what recent analysts of factions in American political parties do not attend to enough, is the role ambitious politicians play in organizing and marshaling potential sources of support on issues they believe may garner support.

Observation of nineteenth-century American factionalism suggests that factions did not arise spontaneously out of divisions among voters. Rather, ambitious politicians formed factional alliances that sought to garner support from voters with different interests and ideologies. For example, in the 1860s there existed among New York Republicans a factional alliance among former Democrats, a variety of upstate politicians, and the powerful editor of the *New York Tribune*, Horace Greeley. Originating in the 1850s, by the 1860s it was sustained by patronage of the Treasury Department under Secretary Salmon P. Chase from 1861 to 1864; by the patronage controlled by Reuben E. Fenton as governor from 1865 to 1868 and as senator after 1869; and by the influence of the *Tribune* itself, then the leading Republican newspaper in the country.

In the 1860s, this faction was generally perceived as "radical." It urged abolition of slavery before others did, demanded vigorous prosecution of the Civil War, advocated legal and political equality for black Americans before many whites accepted the idea, and favored a stricter Reconstruction program than did more conservative Republicans. In 1864 this faction opposed the renomination of Abraham Lincoln, promoting Chase instead; in 1868 it supported Chase against Ulysses S. Grant, who was backed by a rival, "conservative" state faction. Yet by the late 1860s and early 1870s, as it slowly lost control of the Republican Party to rivals, this faction swung toward what became known as "liberal Republicanism." It advocated reconciliation with the South and amnesty for Confederates; it criticized severely the black-influenced southern Republican governments and no longer treated the interests of black Americans sympathetically. It demanded that the Republican Party make its central political appeal upon a high protective tariff, hard money, and civil service reform rather than the war issues that had been its own chief concern from 1861 to 1869. In 1872 the *Tribune*, Greeley, Fenton, and most of their allies bolted from the Republican Party to join an alliance of other Republican factions and the Democratic Party. The alliance ran Greeley himself for president against the Republican Grant.[47]

Such shifts in factions' political positions were by no means rare. In Reconstruction Georgia, the Republican "carpetbagger" John E. Bryant and his associates swung from radical Republicanism to an alliance with the Conservative-Democratic Party and back to radicalism again in the 1860s and 1870s.[48] The Snopes-like McWhorter family went from Democrat to Republican and back to Democrat.[49] In Arkansas the "brindle-tail" faction of the Republican Party followed a similar course.[50] In Indiana the Republican faction identified with George W. Julian went from radical Republicanism to liberal Republicanism, much like the New York radical faction.[51]

Democrats, too, traveled such tortuous routes. In 1860, New York's Democratic Party was still divided into "Soft-shell" and "Hard-shell" factions. The former had welcomed back Democrats who had bolted to join the Free Soil Party in 1848. The latter had resisted the rapprochement. In the 1850s the Hards were perceived to be the more proslavery wing of the party, closely allied with the pro-southern Democratic president, James Buchanan. But when the Softs and their ex-Free Soiler allies gained control of the party machinery in the later 1850s, the hitherto proslavery Hards began to form alliances with the Republicans. Still, when the Democratic Party divided in the presidential election of 1860, the Hards backed the proslavery, southern candidate John C. Breckenridge, while the Softs backed the northern candidate Stephen A. Douglas. When the Civil War erupted in 1861, however, it was the Hards, out of power in their own party, who responded to the Republican invitation to join a nonpartisan, "Union" party, while the dominant Softs refused.[52]

In Ohio, the charismatic Clement L. Vallandigham appealed to his state's most extreme, pro-peace, anti-Negro Democrats during the Civil War. He parlayed his rigid adherence to principle into the Democratic gubernatorial nomination in 1863, over the objection of more moderate leaders. But by 1868 Vallandigham had lost control of the party to rivals. He responded by conniving to secure the Democratic presidential nomination for the former radical Republican Chase on a platform accepting the results of the war, including legal and political equality for southern blacks. In 1871 Vallandigham launched the "New Departure" movement, which called upon Democrats to cease agitation of Civil War issues and led to the 1872 coalition with the liberal Republicans.[53]

In sum, Civil War–era party factions behaved much like the description of pragmatic political behavior around the world and over broad swaths of time limned by social anthropologist F. G. Bailey.[54] Mid-nineteenth-century factions were primarily alliances among party leaders that did not arise out of different party constituencies but rather sought support from broader segments of the party by identifying with attractive positions, symbols, promises, and electoral strategies.

Political Patronage and Factionalism

Political appointments were a primary engine of mid-nineteenth-century party machinery. The key was the control over such appointments that the federal and state constitutions gave to the president and governors and the way customs developed to cement party organizations through the distribution of offices. Every official in the national, state, or local civil service was subject to removal by the executive power, with only the most tenuous restraints. No competence tests dictated appointments. Executives could name officers, often subject to legislative confirmation, on almost any criteria. Ultimately, the most important criterion became service to the executive's political party. But custom dictated that local party leaders provide the names and the references, and these leaders demanded personal as well as party loyalty. Thus the system created patron-client relationships, and one's influence in securing civil service positions was itself called "patronage."[55]

Patronage-structured, factional alliances ran up and down the different levels of government. For example, for over ten years during the 1860s and 1870s, Indiana Congressman George W. Julian's chief local Republican rival was Solomon Meredith. Each had a group of consistent supporters who worked to secure the Republican congressional nomination for him; each had the support of rival newspaper editors. Julian also had a statewide reputation and on several occasions challenged Republican governor, and later senator, Oliver P. Morton for control of the party and its nominations. Naturally, Meredith allied with Morton.

Over Julian's objections, in 1861 Morton appointed Meredith colonel of an Indiana army regiment, a prestigious position providing a base for future political support.[56] In 1865 and early 1866 Julian and Morton competed for the Republican nomination to the United States Senate. As they did so, Morton endorsed President Andrew Johnson's mild Reconstruction policy, while Julian blasted away at it and at Morton for supporting it. The recrimination between Julian and the Morton-supporting Meredith became so bitter that in November 1865 the two fought physically in the streets.[57] Even after Morton recanted his support for Johnson, Meredith served as presiding officer of the state convention of the pro-Johnson wing of the Union-Republican Party. At the same time Johnson named Meredith United States tax assessor in Julian's district.[58] As Morton succeeded in driving Julian out of the Republican Party and into the liberal Republican-Democratic alliance of 1872, Meredith was elected by the Morton-dominated Republican state convention as one of Indiana's six delegates-at-large to the national convention.[59]

In Illinois, returning General John A. Logan in 1865 began to maneuver to replace Senator Lyman Trumbull when his term ended in 1867. As Trumbull worked desperately to preserve harmony between President Johnson and the Republican Party, Logan gave the impression of being firmly committed to the president. Using the influence he acquired with Johnson's administration, Logan helped other returning soldiers to replace civilian politicians holding national civil service jobs in Illinois. Their argument that such positions should go to those who had made sacrifices to save the nation had obvious implications for the impending Logan-Trumbull contest. Afraid of alienating veterans among Republican activists, Trumbull watched helplessly as local ally after ally fell. He recovered only when Johnson was discredited among Republicans by his too lenient Reconstruction policy, forcing Logan to abandon him and the patronage he had provided, and allowing Trumbull to emerge as a symbol of opposition to him.[60]

Such vertical alliances were very common. If we had more studies of local politics in the nineteenth century, one might be able to say they were the rule. Thus rivals in the Chicago Republican Party lined up with rival state-level factions, mainly pitting former Whig politicians against former Democrats.[61] All over Ohio, local rivals were linked to the Chase faction of the state party, to that of Senator Benjamin F. Wade, or to the smaller faction associated with Columbus Delano.[62]

Naturally, with so much depending upon factional alliances and control of patronage, it was crucial for local and state factions to place allies in executive positions. On the state level, factions sometimes sabotaged their party's gubernatorial candidates rather than allow executive patronage and influence to come under the control of an intraparty rival. Thus Chase's allies in the Ohio Republican Party almost prevented the election of Rutherford B. Hayes in 1867, because he was perceived to be a Wade man, and they did succeed in turning the state legislature over to the Democrats, scuttling Wade's chances for reelection to the Senate.[63] Alabama Senator George E. Spencer and his allies permitted his rival, Republican Governor William H. Smith, to go down to defeat in 1870, and in the process they too prevented the reelection of a rival Senator.[64]

Even more bitter were struggles to control party presidential nominations. Greeley worked diligently to prevent his New York Republican rival, William H. Seward, from securing the nomination in 1860. Disgusted with his opponents' influence with Lincoln, he and his radical New York allies supported Chase's presidential ambitions in 1864. In 1867 the Greeley-Fenton faction again backed Chase for the coming year's nomination, while its rivals boomed the eventual winner, Grant. In 1872, Greeley himself ran for president as the candidate of the Liberal Republican–Democratic coalition, bolting Grant's renomination.[65]

Wade and other of Chase's Republican factional rivals in Ohio served him in the same fashion as Greeley served Seward and Grant.[66] Ohio Democrats

Vallandigham and Alexander Long successfully undermined the effort of their state's dominant Democratic faction to secure the 1868 presidential nomination for Ohioan George H. Pendleton. Their support for Chase as a Democratic candidate was part of that effort. Chase cooperated, but dissident New York factions, fearing the effect upon their party position, managed to prevent the plan from bearing fruit.[67]

Eight years later Samuel J. Tilden's factional enemies in New York's Democratic Party tried to keep him from securing the 1876 Democratic presidential nomination. Failing, they then diligently set to work to prevent him from getting a second chance in 1880. This time they succeeded.[68] Illinois' rival Republican factions had united behind Abraham Lincoln's candidacy for the presidential nomination in 1860—the friends of his rival, Lyman Trumbull, never imagining that he had a real chance to win it. So once he was elected they spent their time battling to control his choice of a Cabinet.[69]

By the 1870s control over national patronage had become rather clearly structured, with U.S. senators becoming the dominant figures in the process. During the bitter contest over Reconstruction between President Johnson and the Republican majority in Congress, Johnson began to remove Republicans holding patronage positions. Desperate officeholders persuaded Congress to pass the Tenure of Office Act, which protected civil servants from removal until replacements were confirmed by the Senate. Thus government employees became dependent upon the favor of senators to protect them from removal, no matter who else had been primarily responsible for securing their appointments. Despite efforts to repeal the law when Republicans regained the presidency, it remained on the books. This meant that the support of one's senators was crucial when an aspirant sought to oust an incumbent from a patronage position. (A critic observed that "as a pious disciple of Mohamet... must make a weary pilgrimage to the tomb of the prophet in Mecca," anyone seeking a patronage office in Michigan "must make a pilgrimage to Detroit" to see Michigan's Senator Chandler.)[70] Senators reinforced their positions by agreeing among themselves that they would refuse to confirm any appointee personally obnoxious to a senator representing his state—a practice that became known as "senatorial courtesy."

Informal understandings regularized the resulting system. Representatives were conceded the right to nominate postmasters—key patronage positions—in their own hometowns. They and their senators had to agree on post office appointments within their districts. Senators controlled all other appointments within a state and also the patronage in districts represented by members of the opposing party.[71]

The consequence was that senators became the dominant powers in the parties that controlled the presidency. It was in the aftermath of the passage of the Tenure of Office Act that Indiana's Senator Morton was finally able to overpower his rival, Julian, by gerrymandering him out of his safe congressional seat. Likewise, Minnesota Senator Alexander Ramsey was able to crush the aspirations of his nemesis, Representative Ignatius Donnelly, while Pennsylvania Senator Simon Cameron routed the faction led by ex-Governor Andrew G. Curtin.[72]

However, disparate sources of factional power continued to exist even under the new system. Naturally, senators achieved dominance most easily and completely where a party's two senators cooperated, or where the party controlling the presidency controlled only one of the two Senate seats. Thus Senator Zachariah Chandler rose to dominance in Michigan with the acquiescence of his less ambitious colleagues.[73] New York's Senator Roscoe Conkling consolidated his power with the aid of his ally, Senator Thomas C. Platt,[74] while Pennsylvania's Cameron could count on the support of his colleague John Scott.[75] Morton did not have to worry about his colleague, Thomas H. Hendricks, who as a Democrat had no access to patronage under a Republican administration.

On the other hand, if senators of the same party as the president were incompatible, the result was severe factional instability. Thus New York's Republican Party was wracked with division until Conkling destroyed the influence of his rival, Senator Reuben E. Fenton.[76] The faction led by Missouri Senator Carl Schurz bolted from the state's Republican Party rather than accept the dominance of rivals led by his colleague, Charles D. Drake.[77] Supporters of Alabama Senator Spencer's factional rival, Willard Warner, did the same after they lost their struggle with him.[78]

The state government was another source of patronage, and therefore another base for factional opposition to a state's senators. Rivalries between factions led by senators and those led by governors were extremely common. The Cameron-Curtin rivalry, already mentioned, was one instance. Alabama's Senator Willard Warner had the support of Governor Smith in his losing struggle with Spencer. Michigan's Chandler had fought off Governor Austin Blair in his rise to dominance. Mississippi's Governor James Lusk Alcorn and his allies struggled against rivals led by Senator Adelbert Ames,[79] while Louisiana's Governor Henry Clay Warmoth battled Senator William Pitt Kellogg and his allies in the New Orleans Customs House and the United States marshal's office.[80]

All this also draws into question Key's suggestion that factionalism is related to the degree of party competition. Unlike the mid-twentieth-century American South, the mid-nineteenth-century United States had a highly competitive two-party system, characterized by high voter turnout that reflected deep and interested partisanship. Yet factionalism was pervasive. Nonetheless, one ought not to discard Key's hypothesis, or consider it time-bound, without further research. Factionalism in the southern Republican Party, where it seemed most bitter, in many cases arose where the party's dominance seemed unchallengeable so long as it was united—around 1869–72 in such states as Louisiana, Florida, South Carolina, and Mississippi. But Felice A. Bonadio, analyzing Ohio politics in the 1860s, found that evenly balanced two-party competition promoted factionalism, because bolters could often exercise the balance of power.[81] New York, where both the Democrats and Republicans were riven by factions, was a highly competitive two-party state, as was Virginia, where Democrats joined dissident Republicans to gain control of the government in 1869.[82] Alabama too was a highly competitive two-party state, yet Republican factional rivalry there was among the bitterest in the nation.[83]

Clientelism and Nineteenth-Century American Political Factionalism

Many analysts suggest that political clientelism grows out of the clientelist nature of premodern societies or where social change lags behind political modernization.[84] As clientelism has persisted even in modernizing societies, they have stressed that "patron-client relations are based on very strong elements of inequality and power," indeed a virtual monopolization of the control of resources by individuals or patron organizations.[85] The political factionalism that led to the organization of the first political parties may have reflected a degree of clientelism in early American society,[86] but by the mid-nineteenth century, American society was extremely mobile geographically, individualistic, and egalitarian in outlook.[87] Except in a few of the largest American cities, the United States was not characterized by the sorts of disparities in power and control of resources that one identifies with clientelistic societies. The patron-client relationship common to American politics appears to have been fundamentally at odds with other aspects of American society.

Reformers certainly perceived structural factors rather than social ones to lie at the heart of factional "machine" politics. As already noted, they believed that the way to destroy the influence of factional leaders in politics was to change the political environment by substituting a professional civil service for the patronage system and later by instituting the party primary. Indeed, a study of how these reforms affected factions might add greatly to our understanding of the general phenomenon.

Sometimes American factions did seem to fit the pattern that social scientists have found in modernizing societies, where politicians and administrators use their control over government resources to build their own clienteles. Those who have observed this phenomenon usually associate it with modern government's distribution of important resources in the community, of which government jobs are merely one type, and not the most important. One certainly could find factions with access to these kinds of government-related resources. The Tammany Hall faction of the New York Democracy was a famous example; the "Gas Ring" and "Buildings Ring" that competed for influence in Philadelphia's Republican Party in the 1870s provide another.[88] Urban political machines in general seem to fit the pattern, and the anthropologically oriented social-science literature of factionalism cites studies of them rather than Key-influenced state studies when discussing faction in America.[89]

Certainly a degree of clientelism was apparent in most nineteenth-century American factions. For poverty-stricken black southerners and their socially and economically ostracized white allies, political jobs were a crucial means of support. Michael Fitzgerald calls this desperate necessity "the mainspring of it all" in describing the scramble for federal patronage in Mobile, Alabama.[90] With millions of former slaves emancipated with hardly any property, the post–Civil War South may have resembled impoverished premodern societies more than it did the rapidly developing North. Studies of black southern political leaders stress how they sought to promote the interests of their constituents. They rarely discuss how political influence may have enabled them to secure the influence as patrons in a clientelistic society. But one can easily imagine Georgia's Tunis G. Campbell, authorized to distribute confiscated land among the freed people, distributing favors to a grateful clientele.[91] Thomas Holt's description of black leadership in South Carolina implies the existence of similar patron-client relationships.[92] Frederick Douglass helped build a black middle class in Washington, D.C., with the low-level government jobs he was able to distribute, and Booker T. Washington's role as influential patron of a wide-ranging clientele is well known.[93] With access to white power brokers and the ability to navigate an alien commercial world, black leaders during Reconstruction may have filled the same roles that some *padrones* did in the Italian immigrant community at the turn of the twentieth century.[94]

Ostracized by the white southern community, even white Republicans could be put in a position where access to political influence became an economic necessity. For them, seeking office was not merely a matter of offering public service; they engaged in what an influential essay has called "The Politics of Livelihood."[95] Cultivating influential friends who could help them acquire government jobs became a necessity.

At least sometimes American politicians used control of resources to build up clientelist factions in ways that call to mind the connection between politicians and resources characteristic of Italy and Japan, for example. Most common were alliances between particular factions and railroads that needed special charters or government aid, or on whose boards sat directors appointed by state governors. Thus Virginia railroad promoter William Mahone backed sympathetic factions in his state's Republican and Conservative (Democratic) parties, while the competing Baltimore & Ohio backed rivals.[96] Republican Governor Powell Clayton of Arkansas used his power to disburse aid to deserving railroads while building his political machine during Reconstruction. Factional leaders in Georgia's and South Carolina's Republican parties tried to do the same.[97] Railroads also became involved in Republican factional disputes in such northern states as Massachusetts, Michigan, Wisconsin, Iowa, and California.[98] Likewise, Pennsylvania Railroad President Thomas A. Scott's quest for support from the national government to build his Texas & Pacific Railroad led him into the quicksand of factional disputes all over the country.[99]

One might also consider a politician's influence over law enforcement and bureaucratic decision making to be a source of power with which he might create a personally loyal clientele. The "Whiskey Ring" scandals may be viewed from this perspective. Avoiding taxes on their production, distillers could increase their profits by selling whiskey at the same or slightly lower prices than those who paid their fair share. But this required the cooperation of local Treasury Department employees, the district tax assessors and collectors who hired and supervised them, and, ultimately, the congressmen who recommended the appointment of the assessors and collectors. While the bribes themselves were no doubt most important to the low-level employees, it was the political benefits of the patron-client relationship established between themselves and the distillers that were most important to the higher-ups, and they fought bitterly against reform of the system.[100]

The ubiquitous development of "customs house" factions may provide another instance in which American politicians and bureaucrats used control of resources to develop clienteles. Control of the customs house meant control not only of the jobs but also of the distribution of government contracts. Perhaps more important, those who controlled the customs house could control the rigor of law enforcement and the valuation of goods. Once again this permitted the congressmen who controlled the major customs house appointments to establish clienteles dependent upon their continued favor.[101]

Similar potential for harnessing government control of resources to political ambition existed in the General Land Office, which distributed public lands under various land grant, preemption, and sales laws. Fraud in land claims was endemic, and no effective inspection system was established until the late 1880s. What is not known is whether frauds were merely local, turning on bribery, or whether they were part of a clientelistic system that exacted political loyalty as the price for governmental favors.[102] The same potential existed in the Pension Office, which processed pension and disability claims made by Mexican War and Civil War veterans and their survivors.[103]

Factions and the Structure of Nineteenth-Century Politics

When these examples are added to the practices of urban machine politicians, it becomes apparent that historians ought to look further into nineteenth-century American politics as a clientelist system for the distribution of resources. Nonetheless, on the whole the development of nineteenth-century American factions seems to have been influenced most by the way in which politics itself was organized. No matter why people sought office, whether to control the distribution of resources or for other purposes, it seems to have been necessary to establish the kinds of mutual ties that characterize factions.

One can see this in considering one of the most important "factions" in the Republican Party of the late 1860s through the 1880s—the "reformers" or (in the 1880s) "Mugwumps." Rigidly opposed to "class" legislation—such as the protective tariff, railroad and other subsidies, government manipulation of the money supply, or labor legislation—their primary goal was to prevent government favoritism in the distribution of resources.[104] Moreover, they were firmly committed to ending the patronage system, making "civil service reform" a central element of their program. Yet the structure of the American political system forced them to adopt many of the same techniques as their "machine-politician" enemies.

They may have wanted it for the best of reasons, but what the "reformers" wanted was power. Many of them were politicians who had lost factional struggles. Others were intellectuals who were losing influence in the Republican Party to professional politicians, whom they dismissed as mere "time-servers." "There has been for years in Mich. a 'Zach Chandler party' and a 'Republican party' and the two never have affiliated except in name," a disgruntled Michigan Republican wrote Chandler's rival, former Governor Austin Blair. "The first includes all the professional politicians, the last the great mass of the rank and file, headed by a few men who are Republicans from *principle*."[105] When reformers wrote each other privately that "I fear there is little hope for reform from regular politicians," they of course meant that the country ought to look to them.[106] Charles Nordhoff put it succinctly: "It belongs to us to be recognized as the true leaders of the Republican party. If we are not that we are nothing."[107] To carry out their program they had to secure nominations and office, and to do this they wound up creating a network of associates, bound to one another through ties of mutual obligation and interest, not that dissimilar from the "machines" they opposed. They, too, jockeyed for control of government departments and offices and sought to dominate party conventions. By the turn of the century they would succeed. As one historian has put it, their success "stemmed from their capturing and altering the party organization that the Mugwumps had so bitterly criticized. It was a case of fighting fire with fire.... To fight the machines one had essentially to join them."[108]

Thus, apparently, the bureaucratic model of factionalism with its stress on personal ambition offers the most insight into mid-nineteenth-century American factions. Indeed, much of the shape of factional politics in the 1860s and 1870s can best be understood in terms of Michels's "iron law of oligarchy" and related ideas. That rule posits that as a party becomes institutionalized, its leaders will begin to use their power over it for their own ends and will concentrate their energies on retaining that power. As aspiring leaders find the route to important positions closed, they begin to organize to oust the old guard, often under the banner of "reform," only to form an oligarchy themselves if successful.[109]

If one expands that understanding to recognize that those who have lost struggles for power to the "oligarchy" will join the effort, then it seems to apply precisely to the "reform" campaigns of the late 1860s through the 1880s. One need hardly read between the lines to perceive the relationship between ambition and reform implicit in the following enthusiastic statement of support for civil-service reform: "The consequences of the proposed severance of the patronage from the direct control of the members of Congress and the heads of departments can hardly be overestimated. It strikes a fatal blow at the whole existing process by which ... men have been kept in place and power.... It will bring a better class of men, not only into the executive offices, but into legislative places; ... it will displace or reform [local 'rings'] altogether."[110] As Morton Keller put it, "The real point of contention between reformers and regulars was political control. The advocates of civil service reform ... were in effect a distinct interest group, contesting with another bloc ... for government power."[111] In the effort, they were joined by fading Republican factions, such as Julian's in Indiana, Greeley's in New York, Donnelly's in Minnesota, Trumbull's in Illinois, Cameron's opponents in Pennsylvania, and a host of others, who echoed reformers' attacks on the "corruption" of the dominant party leadership.[112]

Factionalism and Representation

How did such pervasive factionalism affect representative government in the United States? According to contemporary "reform" leaders and, until fairly recently, most scholars, factionalism subverted it. The criticism read essentially the same as the traditional objections raised by social scientists. Concerned only with securing political power, factional leaders ignored real issues, they complained. "The machine is an oligarchy, a ring or clique of professional politicians . . . [with] no public purpose."[113] The government ought to be reforming the revenue system, establishing a stable currency, and professionalizing the civil service, reformers insisted. Instead, the government was controlled by "a network of rings . . . and members [of Congress] who are by their tastes disposed towards reform dare not move a finger."[114] But that complaint itself was part of a campaign to oust Republican regulars from their leading positions in the party, a campaign in which dissident political factions joined. And that suggests a more complex relationship between factionalism and representative government in the mid-nineteenth century.

In a state where the social environment does not sustain patron-client relationships, no faction can lay claim to influence purely because of its organizational strength. It must articulate a raison d'être related somehow to the public good. This is so much the rule that social scientists often include the articulation of an ideological position among the identifying characteristics of faction.[115]

In the mid-nineteenth century, rivals never described factional struggles solely in terms of personal loyalties. They always claimed that greater issues were at stake. In doing so, they might argue for firmer adherence to the party's central principles. Or they might, on the contrary, charge that "impractical" leaders were demanding such fidelity to principle that they guaranteed defeat by alienating the less committed and neutral. Austin Ranney referred to this as a conflict between models of political action—the "competitive" model in which the main goal of party politics is to win, and the "expressive" model in which the main goal is to articulate the beliefs of the party's adherents. Those who follow the "competitive" model try to shape the party appeal to win the floating voters by occupying the middle ground, downplaying principles if necessary. They urge compromise of disagreements over principle within the party and view it as an umbrella covering those with disparate views.[116]

According to Ranney, "expressives" prefer purity to such pragmatism. In fact, Ranney seemed to suggest that "expressives" prefer purity even to winning. But here his analysis does not fit nineteenth-century partisans, whether it fits more modern ones or not. When nineteenth-century factional leaders advocated an "expressive" rather than "competitive" approach, they argued that this was the surest way to win. "The strength of the Republican party consists in its adherence to principle," argued a Republican purist. "Yielding a principle . . . through fear it becomes occupied with sordid plans, disgusts the moralist, and dampens the ardor of the young and heroic," agreed another.[117] Greeley wrote, "The experience of all parties is that cowardice is the worst policy. Agitation, progress, constant advances are necessary to . . . strength. When a great principle is at stake we cannot gain a half victory. Such victories are surrenders, for we either concede that our enemy is right, or that we are weak."[118]

The Greeley-Fenton wing of the New York Republicans, the Julian wing of the Indiana party, the Chase faction of the Ohio party, Cameron's faction in Pennsylvania, and Republican factions throughout the South took this position, and as a consequence they were identified as "radicals"—the "fellows that 'believe in it,'" as one of them put it.[119] Their opponents were "croaking conservatives," "all that is fishy and mercenary in the Republican party."[120]

Rival factions often urged a more "competitive" approach. They did not necessarily challenge radicals' notions of the central mission of the Republican Party. "I have been a partisan long enough to know that extreme measures will not always promote the interests of a party," one of them worried. "What will our people at home think of these rank and radical measures? . . . Will not these matters react . . . ?"[121] "I have many agreements with them in principle," another cautious Republican said of radical leaders, "but [I] regard them as about the worst tacticians I ever heard of. Whenever there is anything in their cause or position involving possibility of defeat, they are sure to find and develop it."[122] In his study of the Democratic Party during the 1860s, Joel Silbey found this kind of disagreement, dividing what he called "purists" from "legitimists," to mark the main fault line among Democrats.[123] Michael Perman has discerned the same disagreement dividing southern Republicans and Democrats during the Reconstruction era.[124] However, both concentrated primarily on the arguments themselves and not on the connection between the arguments and the practical aspects of factional competition. There is no reason to doubt that most of the factional leaders who urged "competitive" or "expressive" oriented programs upon their parties sincerely believed in their proposals when they made them. But analysts must understand what contemporaries understood—that power in the party turned upon whose views were finally adopted.

If the Republican Party nationally or in any state decided to adopt the radical formula for success, they were almost certainly going to put radicals in positions of leadership. Thus Andrew Johnson's apostasy in 1866 permitted radical

Republicans to discredit the conservative factional leaders who had supported him.[125] When a nervous congressman worried about whether a vote for black suffrage in 1866 might cost his reelection, Illinois congressman "Long John" Wentworth growled, "You'd better get your nomination first. Haven't you learnt that it is the Radicals who do that job nowadays?"[126]

On the other hand, after Republicans followed the radical approach and went down to defeat in elections in 1867, their opponents noted with grim satisfaction that "these Republican defeats lay a good many men on the shelf who will be more useful *there* than they may have been elsewhere."[127] Throughout the country, conservative factions used the defeats to attack the radicals' influence in the party. At the national level, they insisted that the setbacks meant that Republicans must nominate the conservatives' candidate, Ulysses S. Grant, for president rather than the radical Chase or Benjamin F. Wade. On the state level, at least in those states where elections were closely contested, the 1867 defeats meant that moderate men and moderate views must prevail.[128] A typical conservative attack read: "Republicans throughout the country have to consider whether . . . they propose to follow Thad. Stevens and Wendell Phillips in the wildest and most desperate measures conceivable, to the end, or whether they will stop short. . . . If they listen to the babble of the intellectual lunatics . . . they will put the country next year into the hands of the Democratic party."[129] Coming from one of the principal newspapers supporting conservative Republican factions in Ohio, readers knew well enough that editor included local radicals Chase, Wade, and others among the "intellectual lunatics." New York Republicans understood just as well that the Seward-Weed organ, the *New York Times*, was aiming its shaft at Greeley and his Chase-supporting allies when it warned that if the Republican Party "[adopts] a Radical platform and nominates a Radical candidate—we venture the prediction that it will be beaten more disastrously than the Whigs were in 1852."[130] They knew that Morton's *Indianapolis Journal* was referring to Julian when it warned against Republicans who demanded "that the train shall move without looking to see if the track is clear."[131]

If the "competitive"–"expressive" dichotomy about tactics provided one set of issues that factions could use against rivals, disagreements over substantive issues provided another. In Massachusetts Benjamin F. Butler and his friends sought power not only by advocating the "expressive," radical position on tactics, but by urging inflationary financial policies and attacking the increasing influence of businessmen upon the established party leadership.[132] In the mid-1870s rival factions of state Democratic parties supported competing candidates for the party's 1876 presidential nomination. The struggle was fought not only in terms of "competitive" versus "expressive" campaign strategies but also in terms of inflationary versus restrictive financial policy.¹³³ Thus supporters of New York Governor Samuel J. Tilden rejoiced when Ohio and Philadelphia Democrats were defeated on pro-inflation platforms. "It will have the good effect to tumble out of the Presidential path several aspirants and possible candidates," one of them wrote the anti-inflation Tilden happily.¹³⁴

The demands made by "reform" Republicans that their party abandon the "dead" issues of the Civil War in favor of financial, tariff, and civil service reform offer a fine illustration of the link between issues and factional ambition. As already noted, "reform" ranks were made up largely of men who either had lost factional struggles or aspired to influence but were denied it. They understood full well that the dominant leaders of the Republican Party had achieved power through the related issues of slavery, emancipation, saving the Union, and Reconstruction. So long as these issues remained the central concern of the Republican Party, those identified with them were bound to retain their leadership positions.

Reformers may have honestly believed that the old slavery-related issues died with emancipation or with black enfranchisement, but they were not unaware of the implications of such a conviction for political leadership. Those who had risen to leadership positions on the slavery issue "are fit to fill them no longer," the reform-oriented *Nation* insisted.¹³⁵ The new issues were primarily ones of political economy. They required the attention of "the best men"—those with "the loftiest development of moral and intellectual education."¹³⁶ It is not hard to see who they meant. They could not come out and say so publicly, but among themselves the reformers might be less circumspect. "If you or I or any other honest economist ever seek office, we should get it," one of them wrote in a moment of brash candor.¹³⁷

Thus it is no wonder that the regular Republican leaders so resented reformers' self-righteousness. To them a faction was a faction, and one who sought office was a politician. "Reform" often was merely "a catchword and subterfuge for personal advancement or the success of a faction," they warned. "It will not do ever to trust the professions of superactive advocates of 'reform' without keeping an eye on their practices."¹³⁸ But everyone knew that if the Republican Party did abandon old issues in favor of financial and tariff reform, they would also turn for leadership to those who had advocated the change.

All this factional rhetoric was aimed at two audiences. One was made up of the party activists—often patronage appointees or aspirants—who determined nominations and decided who would fill party leadership posts. The other was the general public. In appealing to party activists, the idea was to bind one's supporters more closely to one's faction, to secure the neutrals, and to pry loose and win over those supporting one's rivals. An appeal to their principles might do it; an appeal to their interests might do it better. Factional rhetoric was designed to do both. This was aimed both at persuading activists that a faction's tactical approach or position on an issue was right on principle, and that its adoption was most likely to secure victory.

As for appeals to the general public—sometimes there really was widespread support for the position advocated by one faction or another, as when Republican radicals urged immediate emancipation during the Civil War. On other occasions, however, issues had to be promoted, as when reformers insisted that financial issues ought to take precedence over Civil War issues. In that case, factions had the difficult task of popularizing their views among the public at large at the same time that they warned Republican activists that the demand for change was so widespread that these activists risked defeat if they ignored it.

This assessment of mid-nineteenth-century intraparty factionalism in the United States suggests that rather than obstructing representative government, factional competition provided another opportunity for the public, and especially active partisans, to influence policy. A faction's strength depended not only on its ability to wield patronage and manipulate the levers of power, but upon its ability to harness issues with a broad public appeal.

Moreover, this suggestion may be true as well of present-day factions, both in America and elsewhere. While a stress on factionalism provides a useful corrective to studies that treat issues and ideology as if they were the sole motivating force in politics, analyses that describe factional structure and strength without describing the positions they take on issues are just as incomplete. A political system does or does not permit the public to influence public policy. That the leaders of personalist factions themselves may not have firm convictions on public issues may well be irrelevant to that question, judging by the post–Civil War factional system. Social scientists and historians should investigate the personalist factional bases of apparently ideological intraparty splits, such as the Populist-Bourbon Democratic divisions in the American South during the 1890s, the Progressive-Conservative split in both parties in the early twentieth century, divisions between "new Democrats" and "the Democratic wing of the Democratic Party," as presidential nomination candidate Howard Dean put it in 2004,[139] and similar divisions within non-American parties. Such studies might elucidate the relationship between factional ambition and the articulation of issues.

On the other hand, the nature of factions may make them less effective conduits for public opinion than are cohesive parties. Are factional positions clear enough for a long enough period of time? Do those legislators affiliated with a faction display similar voting patterns?

Nineteenth-Century American Politics
and the Literature of Political Factionalism (Reprise)

It is clear that historians of nineteenth-century American politics must become more familiar with the social-science literature on factionalism if they wish to present a faithful portrait of the past. To speak of issues, ideology, and the development of public policy without connecting them to the personal ambitions of political actors is to remove them from the real world to an abstract one. It not only misrepresents reality but also leaves out an important explanatory variable in the analysis of causation. Moreover, attention to the social-science literature expands the context in which the historian must place nineteenth-century American factionalism. Generally, American political historians have viewed it simply as the reflection of intraparty divisions on issues or political strategies.[140] At most, they have perceived factionalism as a manifestation of political ambition.[141] But historians should inquire whether the roots of factionalism lay deeper in American social and political structure.

III Politics, the Constitution, and the Retreat from Reconstruction

6

The Politics of Reconstruction

Despite the immense literature on politics in the Reconstruction era, few historians have discussed the practical way politics *worked* during that era and then related the system to changes in Reconstruction policy. Joel Silbey linked grassroots politics and Democratic policy toward Reconstruction in his study of Democrats from 1860 to 1868, *A Respectable Minority*.[1] But no one has yet done the same for the Republicans. In fact, few historians have written much at all on the politics of the period that followed the establishment of Republican Reconstruction policy. Until recently, most general studies of Reconstruction slighted national policy in the 1870s, shifting attention to developments in the southern states. William Gillette's *Retreat from Reconstruction*, published in 1979, was the first book-length study of post-1868 national Reconstruction politics since volumes 6 and 7 of James Ford Rhodes's *History of the United States from the Compromise of 1850*, which appeared in 1906.[2] It remains the only such study today. However, Eric Foner's magisterial *Reconstruction: America's Unfinished Revolution* broke the usual pattern among general histories by attending as much to later as earlier national Reconstruction developments, and several historians have since addressed the attitudes toward race and political economy that influenced post-1868 policy.[3]

The paucity of histories linking public policy to the political system and grassroots voting behavior reflects a general problem in political history: Political historians have had a difficult time making the connection. Foner's study of how and why Reconstruction policy changed in the 1870s is told at a very high level of abstraction—tensions between employers and labor in the North led powerful northern interests to sympathize with southern conservatives instead of black southern workers and their Republican allies. He has described the macropolitics of Reconstruction, but he has not described the actual politics—the way public opinion was translated into public policy.

Eschewing discussion of the political system, Foner neither cites nor incorporates what was once called the "new political history," whose practitioners

---

The original version of this essay was published in *American Political History: The State of the Discipline*, ed. John F. Marszalek and Wilson D. Miscamble (Notre Dame, Ind.: University of Notre Dame Press, 1997), 54–107.

utilized statistical methods to analyze mass voting behavior during the Civil War era. Their conclusions do not fit very well into his story. Where Foner sees a clash between a free-labor and slave-labor society, a battle about moral issues that grew out of rival economic systems, they perceived a clash of ethnic and religious cultures. Republicanism permitted evangelical Protestants and voters of New England heritage to vent their hostility toward southerners, immigrants, Catholics, and "liturgical" Protestants.[4]

Although most of the ethnocultural political studies concentrated on the origins of the Republican Party, at least one—Paul Kleppner's *The Third Electoral System*—assessed the whole Civil War and Reconstruction era, continuing on to 1892, while Melvyn Hammarberg published a statistical study of Indiana voting in the 1870s.[5] Archetypically of ethnocultural studies, Kleppner's work sharply challenged the notion that the issues debated by the political elites motivated the voting of the masses. "That assumption ignores the enormous differences in kind between mass and elite cognitions," he wrote.[6] So while elite intellectuals, newspaper editors, and politicians debated about the nature of the Union, slavery, and the place of the freedmen in American society, Kleppner argued that ordinary voters voted their cultural antipathies, with local elections that raised such issues more important than national ones. The Republican Party originated in nativism and anti-Catholicism, expressed anti-southernism during the Civil War era, and turned back to nativism and anti-Catholicism in the 1870s.[7]

This darker view of the motivations of rank-and-file Republican voters coincides with doubts other historians have expressed about the degree of Republican commitment to racial justice. Concentrated especially among scholars studying the antebellum race relations and the origins of the Republican Party,[8] the conviction that Republicans shared the racism endemic in American society led the great southern historian C. Vann Woodward to describe racism as the deepest rooted of the "Seeds of Failure in Radical Race Policy" during Reconstruction.[9] Sensitivity to northern racism informs Gillette's work as well. Having in an earlier work attributed the passage of the Fifteenth Amendment to Republicans' need for black votes rather than commitment to racial justice, in his study of Reconstruction in the 1870s Gillette concluded that a racist reaction in the North led Republicans to abandon their southern program.[10] Civil War and Reconstruction textbooks repeat the dismal explanation.[11]

The purpose of this essay is to link the shifts in Reconstruction policy more closely to the political system of North and South than these excellent works have done. Mid-nineteenth-century public policy was driven more directly by public opinion and election concerns than we may realize from our modern perspective. Despite reformers' complaints, there were few well-organized interest groups; lobbying was primitive.[12] A campaign like Tom Scott's effort to get government funding for the Texas & Pacific Railroad—a forerunner of modern lobbying—was a thing of wonder, and like most nineteenth-century lobbying it was an effort to get a benefit—a charter, a land grant, a subsidy—from an essentially distributive system of public policy. It was not an effort to determine the direction of general public policy; in fact, Scott failed to secure his subsidy at least in part because public opinion had come to oppose such subsidies as a whole.[13]

Money was growing more important in politics, but levies on officeholders and cash siphoned from public projects accounted for more of it than the donations of organized interest groups—which hardly existed.[14] There were influential individual donors who had important economic interests, but when one looks at the correspondence of congressmen, one finds such men trying to cajole or persuade their legislators much like any other correspondent. And the common currency of such lobbying was the claim that the correspondent reflected a public opinion that would affect the political fortunes of the party and the individual politician. As Joel Silbey put it in his study of the nineteenth-century political system, "Independent party leaders were rarely the puppets of the new economic elites. They had other masters."[15]

When it came to Reconstruction, the most important factor affecting immediate policy decisions was their perceived impact on public opinion and politics. Elections seemed never-ending in mid-nineteenth-century America. Congressional elections were held at various times of the year, rarely at the same time as the presidential election in November. States reelected governors every year, or every second or third year. The elections rarely coincided with presidential or local elections, although often with congressional elections. Observers regarded these rolling elections as an ongoing public opinion poll. Historians may think that local issues were more important than national ones in these canvasses. But in an era of intense partisanship, contemporary politicians and other analysts regularly found in them portents of great meaning for national politics. The state and local elections of 1867, in which Republican setbacks were accounted a repudiation of radicalism on Reconstruction issues, were a classic example.[16]

Like all polls, those implicit in local and state elections could be self-fulfilling. Thus, politicians watched the results of the elections of fall 1875 in Ohio, Pennsylvania, and other northern states with intense interest. Another loss after the shellacking of 1874 was held to doom Republican chances for the presidency in 1876. Republican victories would mean that the Democrats had frittered their great chance away.[17]

It was in this environment that President Grant in 1875 refused to accede to Governor Adelbert Ames's plea to intervene to stop violence in Mississippi's election. Grant's decision on that occasion probably did more than any other single judgment to seal the fate of Republican Reconstruction. As is well known, Grant made it in direct response to warnings from Republican leaders that it would cost the party 1875's crucial elections in the North and consequently the presidency in 1876.[18] The Republicans did win in 1875, and the predicted consequences—a victory in 1876—followed.

It is usual to think that such a decision reflected a broad change in public opinion in the North—that out of some combination of racism, economic and class interest, and the revival of ethnocultural issues, in the 1870s northerners turned their backs on the commitments that had sustained Reconstruction. A closer look makes the political process by which that happened—if it happened at all—more understandable.

But before we take that look, one must pay particular attention to the politics of Reconstruction in the South. After all, had southern Republicans succeeded in creating a viable party there, there would have been no need for national intervention, no occasion for northerner Republicans to retreat from their commitments. Indeed, throughout the Reconstruction era, the chief goal of Republicans North and South was to create a competitive Republican Party in the South. At all times, national Republicans relied on southern Republicans for information and advice about how to do it. Southern Republicans presented alternative strategies for achieving that goal. These alternative strategies provided the context for the determination of national policy throughout Reconstruction.

From the vantage of more than a hundred years, the failure of Republicans to create a multiracial party in the South and the subsequent collapse of the party there seem to have been preordained. As Eric Foner has pointed out, no emancipation effort had ever attempted to empower newly freed people to the degree that Republicans had empowered them in the South.[19] The social and economic implications of racial equality in basic rights were so radical and the Republicans' black constituency so poverty-stricken and inexperienced, that success now seems to have been impossible. North Carolina carpetbagger Albion Tourgee conceded years later that he had been on *A Fool's Errand*.[20] The final end to federal intervention to protect southern Republicans seems to have been, as one historian of Reconstruction titled his last chapter, "The Only Possible Ending."[21]

But that had not been the perception when Tourgee and others enlisted in the southern Republican Party. Black politicians may have had no choice, some white Republicans may have been idealists and others short-term opportunists, but none of them expected to be political martyrs. Such savvy and experienced southern politicians as Joseph E. Brown and William Woods Holden knew what they were doing. Both had been powers in Democratic politics since the 1850s (Holden, in fact, since the 1840s). Many other Republicans were experienced, if not so eminent, Whig and Democratic politicians.[22] The fact was that these men had weighed the chance of success and found it attainable. Indeed, at the time Grant ascended to the presidency, southern Republicans were confident that their party would attract widespread support from *white* southerners, assuring its legitimacy, its competitiveness, and even, they believed, its dominance.

Although they expected massive support from the freedmen, these Republicans knew that they needed white support as well to create viable parties in the southern states. Brown saw this clearly. "The negro vote will not do to rely on," he wrote Georgia's Republican Governor Rufus Bullock. "It is impossible to maintain the [Republican Party] . . . in the South, without a division of the white vote."[23] In the early years of Reconstruction, they were sure that they would be able to attract such white support, and this confidence led many of them to eschew the proscriptive, disfranchising policies radical unionists had advocated ever since the war broke out.

Southern Republicans' confidence was based on assumptions that most American held about the relationship between politics and social and economic institutions, and their understanding of the southern political heritage. They shared the Republican ideology of free labor, according to which the equal opportunity of all men to bargain freely for goods and services, in an environment where education and enterprise were encouraged, promised general liberty and prosperity.[24] To Republicans, North and South, their party was as surely a manifestation of a modern, progressive society as were enlightened Protestant churches, schools, temperance, and industry. "Wherever railroads, telegraphs, and common schools are plenty, democrats are very soon to be in a minority," a California Republican wrote a colleague in a typical statement of his party's faith. "When you get away from these civilizing and enlightening influences democratic majorities are often enough to swamp the whole."[25] Republicans were convinced that the slavery system was responsible for the general economic and social stagnation that they thought characterized the South. Frederick Law Olmsted, the most influential prewar critic of the economics of slavery, had put it simply: "The average progress in happiness and wealth, which has been made by the people of each State, is in almost exact ratio to the degree in which the democratic principle has been radically carried out in their constitution, laws, and customs."[26] "Freedom has given to the North unexampled prosperity and constantly increasing wealth and power," Republicans believed. "Freedom and free institutions will secure for the South the same results."[27]

Since economic and social progress and Republicanism were inextricably linked, emancipation inevitably would lead southerners to revise their political perceptions. Already many white southerners conceded the abolition of slavery to have been a blessing. Republicans were confident that "the day is not far distant when the [same] men . . . will be equally free to confess that Reconstruction, with its common schools, Republican newspapers, Northern capital, and universal suffrage, was even more salutary and effective in the great work of southern redemption."[28] In the wake of Ulysses S. Grant's inauguration, many Republicans thought they saw clear signs of the expected change. As early as 1869 both the *New York Tribune* and *New York Times* were referring to "the New South."[29] The political consequence was clear. Southern Republicans were confident that "the progressive element is destined, sooner or later, to shape the policy of every Southern State."[30]

Republicans thought they had a fertile field from which to harvest white recruits. They believed that there had been an undercurrent of hostility to slavery among nonslaveholding whites before the war and that their party inevitably would be its beneficiary. They were well aware of the intrastate sectionalism that in nearly every southern state had pitted slaveholding regions against regions where nonslave agriculture predominated. They knew that slave agriculture had priced fertile land beyond the reach of ordinary farmers, that underrepresented yeomen farmers had protested tax policies, that entrepreneurs wanted state support to develop railroads, that reformers had urged expenditures on education, and that slaveholder-dominated legislatures had resisted.[31] They were convinced that large numbers of white southerners would have opposed secession in 1860–61, had not slaveholders so completely controlled the media and pulpit, and had they not utilized violence to suppress opposition.[32] Moreover, southern Republican leaders were acutely aware of the unionist resistance to the Confederacy during the war itself, especially since many of the them had been active in it.[33] Republicans believed that these antislavery materials were still at hand—what Wendell Phillips called "the labor, the toil, the muscle, the virtue, the strength, the democracy, of the Southern States . . . the poor white, a non-slaveholder, deluded into rebellion for a system which crushes him."[34]

To build their party with these materials, southern Republicans regularly tried to fan resentment against the old slaveholding elite while stressing the issues they believed had divided slaveholder from nonslaveholder. Some of the rhetoric was aimed directly at poorer whites and suggested class-based appeals.[35] However, most Republicans stressed the benefits to all sure to follow good-faith adoption of the free-labor system. "Roast Beef and good times ahead, boys. That's the talk," the aptly named *Atlanta New Era* advised Republican campaigners. That was the way to overcome antipathy to the party's northern origins. "I tell you Yankees and Yankee notions are just what we want in this country," a North Carolina Republican declaimed. "We want some of those same Yankee tricks played down here that have covered the North with rail roads and canals."[36]

As they organized from 1867 to 1869, southern Republicans worked to enact the policies that would secure their political future. They promised to reform "the iniquitous and unequal taxation and assessments which, discriminating against labor and laborers, have born[e] so unjustly and unequally upon the people."[37] In Louisiana and South Carolina, they explicitly promised to frame policies that would break up large estates and make small landholdings available to ordinary citizens.[38] And in South Carolina, at least, they tried to carry through, trying to force redistribution through high taxation of uncultivated farmland. The tax laws established by the state constitutional convention called under the Reconstruction Acts "are the death blow to the large plantation system," a leading black delegate exulted.[39]

Republicans wrote ad valorem and equal taxation provisions into nearly every southern state constitution they framed in 1867 and 1868. Some Republican state constitutions allowed for slightly progressive taxation, establishing exemptions for certain amounts of property or income. Some banned poll taxes as well.[40] In most, Republicans liberalized homestead exemptions.[41] Republican state legislatures gave workers prior liens upon employers' property to guarantee fulfillment of employment contracts. They gave merchants priority over employers in liens on the property of employees, enabling workers to secure credit from merchants rather than having to borrow from their employers.[42] All these provisions were designed to demonstrate a common interest between white and black workers. "The real issue is not over a 'white man's party,' but the *poor-man's party*, and of equal rights to all," the *Vicksburg Republican* urged.[43]

Throughout the South Republicans placed special emphasis on promoting free public education. Education was the handmaiden of progress. It promoted intelligence, moderation, discipline, thrift, energy, and morality, all of which bred Republicanism, unlike the Democratic party, which drew its support from "the ignorance and vice of mankind," from "the old slave-owner and slave-driver, the saloon-keeper . . . the criminal class of the great cities, [and] the men who cannot read and write."[44] Education would solve the central problem for Republicans—to break the influence of the old elite "over the poor, illiterate class, who never had a political opinion of their own, but have always voted as their *masters* dictated," as one Mississippi activist put it.

Moreover, the establishment of free public schools would provide tangible evidence of Republican concern for ordinary white men and women. State-supported education was an area of public policy where their interests coincided with those of the freedmen and ran contrary to those of the old planter elite. Once public schools for their children were established, surely white southerners would rally against a party that threatened to dismantle them. Republicans were sure that "[a] schoolhouse . . . is an argument for the new order of things . . . that cannot be resisted."[45]

Republicans placed even greater reliance on their ability to use government to promote prosperity and spread it to a larger proportion of the population than ever before. Economic development was crucial to the success of their party. Southern Republicans were well aware that nascent hostility to slavery among small farmers and laborers had included a large component of hostility to the black slaves themselves. Confident that emancipation would lead to increased prosperity for all southerners, Republicans would demonstrate that emancipation was not what economists now would call a zero-sum game, in which the economic gains of freedmen had to come at the expense of whites. The exhortation of the Republican provisional governor of Texas was typical: "To have a successful Republican party in Texas," he wrote a party worker, "it . . . must . . . advance the material interests of the whole people."[46]

An ambitious effort to extend railroad facilities was central to the Republican program in nearly every state. Railroads would bring every part of a state into the national and international economy. They would permit farmers to exchange subsistence farming for cash crops; they would increase land values; they would end intellectual and cultural isolation; they would bring in capital investment and immigration. Moreover, railroad legislation would appeal to those elements of the southern electorate—many Whigs and some dissident Democrats—that had worked futilely for similar legislation before the war. It was impossible to overstate the importance to the Republicans of a successful transportation policy. "The *success* & the *prudence* with which our policy of internal improvement is carried out will realize or defeat our hopes," a North Carolina state legislator exhorted Holden.[47]

Southern Republicans argued that only an activist national government could augment state internal improvement programs. They were quick to point out that theirs was the party of broad construction of the Constitution, the party that had already expended millions of federal dollars to develop transportation throughout the North and West. "When a large appropriation is asked for the North, let us ask a million of dollars to improve the harbor of Savannah, and another for Charleston," Brown urged on the Georgia campaign trail. "When a Pacific railroad is to be built for the West, let us ask a few millions to rebuild the levees on the Mississippi river."[48]

Even more important to the southern economy than federal aid for internal improvements was the distribution of the currency. The South was desperately cash- and capital-short because the distribution of the currency was closely linked to the distribution of national banks established during the war, which had the sole right to issue United States bank notes. The South, out of the Union and then destitute, had been able to secure hardly any national banks. There were none at all in Mississippi, two each in Alabama, Arkansas, and Louisiana. Of nearly $318,000,000 in national bank notes circulating in 1869, only $7,160,000 had been issued by southern banks—less than the amount issued in Maine alone.[49] Since a national capital market had not yet developed, money did not flow easily from North to South to fill the void. To secure capital, southerners had to pay a premium in high interest rates.

Desperately, southerners sought direct northern investment. "There has never been a time when so much general good could be done with so little capital at so small a risk," they pleaded.[50] The same conviction impelled the influx of the "carpetbaggers" whom southerners would later condemn so bitterly. Carpetbaggers originally came not to fatten off politics but in hopes of making a killing with the investment of modest amounts of capital. But these minimal amounts were not enough to revitalize the southern economy. Only action in Washington could secure national banks and national bank notes for the South, Republicans pointed out. Conservative/Democratic[51] representatives could not hope for sympathetic consideration from the Republican government in Washington. "We want . . . government aid and sympathy in a hundred things—not one of which a Democrat could control if he were elected and sent to Congress," southern Republicans insisted.[52]

Convinced that securing white support was critical to the survival of their party, many southern Republicans believed it essential to make overtures to white southerners, to signal that they were welcome in the party and that they need not worry about proscriptive public policies. Thus, they advocated the repeal of laws disfranchising Confederates that border-state Republicans had passed during the war. They successfully blocked such provisions in most of the new constitutions ratified under the Reconstruction Acts and were appalled at their inability to do so in Texas, Virginia, and Mississippi. They urged Congress to remove the office-holding disqualification the Fourteenth Amendment imposed on many who had held office under the Confederacy. Such proscriptions could only alienate the very population Republicans so desperately needed to recruit. Those who advocated it were proposing government by a small white population of diehard unionists and a large former-slave population over what would be a large and certainly alienated and restive population of whites—in many cases a majority of the population as a whole. No economic policies could overcome the hostility thus engendered. No success could legitimize the resulting governments.

Not only was proscription inconsistent with a Republican appeal for southern white support, many southern Republicans warned, but so also was too much attention to the interests of black southerners. Conservative southern Republicans recognized the ineluctable fact of southern white racism. Appeals to white resentment of the planter elite and to hopes for economic development would work only if the race issue were muted, they worried. As the Republicans' issue was the promise of prosperity, the Democrats' issue was race.

Therefore, from the beginning both southern and northern Republicans urged restraint on the southern party's black rank and file.[53] "The black man . . . must win over to his side, if not through sympathy or humanity, then through interest, enough of the whites to give him . . . the opportunity of influencing the government," the *Nation* cautioned. "The way to do this is to refrain as far as possible from stimulating white prejudices and arousing white passions, to avoid every step or measure that is likely to unite the whites *as whites* against the blacks."[54] The Louisiana Republican leader, Henry Clay Warmoth, told a black audience that he hoped significant numbers of freedmen would vote Democratic. "Race conflicts are sure to ensue if party lines are based on race," he warned. "More negroes becoming Democrats will bring whites into the Republican party and in that is the safety of the Republic and the prosperity of the people." Years later, Warmoth recalled how he had campaigned for white votes.[55]

Such advice was easy for white Republicans to give, but hard for black Republicans to take. While the freedmen and their leaders were as anxious for economic prosperity as the next man, and equally hostile to the planter "aristocracy," they had essential interests as black people and as laborers. If aspiring Republican politicians took radical positions to appeal to those interests, was it realistic to think that the freedmen would withhold their support in order to expand the appeal of the Republican Party? In essence, many white Republicans were counting on the freedmen to sacrifice short-term to long-term interests. It would have required a discipline that few groups of white American voters have ever displayed.[56]

There is little evidence that black workers expected to secure land through confiscation. What was crucial for them was to have local courts and law-enforcement officials that would enforce contracts fairly and protect the right of workers to move freely from job to job.[57] With those rights protected, the freed people could hope for significant economic gains. As planters universally complained, the freed women and children quickly withdrew from the full-time agricultural work force. Many freedmen moved to towns to seek work unassociated with slavery. In a free-labor system, the remaining agricultural workers could not be forced to work the long hours extorted from them under slavery.

The result was a severe labor shortage that promised higher wages or, as southerners moved toward sharecropping, greater independence and a larger share of the profits for the croppers. In a society with a shortage of labor, it was not labor organization that was crucial to workers, it was freedom from laws limiting mobility and freedom of contract and enforcement of the common-law rules that secured them. A real free labor regime would lead to a radical redistribution of the product of labor away from the planter and to the laborer.[58] Clearly, such an evenhanded legal regime would alienate both large and small planters, who relied on black workers. Republicans would have to choose. No Republican who endorsed legislators who might be soft on this issue, or who advocated the appointment of "intelligent" judges who might favor planters in employment disputes, could expect black support.

Much of the leadership of the black community came from those who had been free before the war or who immigrated from the North. The interests of these people, a professional class influential far out of proportion to their numbers, went beyond those of the mass of black workers. They wanted equal access to transportation and entertainment facilities, to higher education, and to the professions.[59] For some black men politics was the only way they could earn enough money to sustain a middle-class living, or to raise capital for other investments.[60] When Republicans asked such men to surrender their interests and ambitions for the sake of their party and their race, they were asking for sacrifices few people would have been willing to make. Nonetheless, the desire to attract white southern support was so strong that the argument could be made, and men who advocated such conservatism could hope to win support from party activists.

Disfranchisement, the role of African Americans in the party, and civil rights legislation immediately became the focal points for factional conflict within the southern Republican Party—an illustration of how a key part of the political system, intraparty factionalism, affected public policy. The winner-take-all American political system channels aspiring public servants into two parties—in some states and localities into one party—where they must compete for nominations and appointive positions. As I have discussed elsewhere, in the nineteenth century it was usual for politicians to form intraparty alliances of varying durations.[61] In the South, rival factions of ambitious Republican politicians identified with one position or the other, trying to win support from party activists and the rank and file. The factionalism was the more bitter for the fact that Republican leaders often were ostracized by white southerners and unable to earn a living equal to their education and social positions outside the public arena.⁶² More radical Republicans, in many cases northern immigrants to the South, agreed that economic development was crucial to winning white support, but they argued that conciliation would not work. Instead, both the state and federal governments had to demonstrate that there was no alternative for southern whites but to accept the new situation. Southern whites would become reconciled, and even enthusiastic, as freedom brought economic prosperity. Until then southern Republicans had to rely on black voters.

Naturally, black southerners responded to the courtship of politicians who were prepared to recognize their interests. We "were up to be knocked down to the highest bidder," a local black leader made clear. The freedmen might not yet have enough educated leaders to govern, but they knew enough to choose representatives "from among our white friends who were to be depended upon . . . to look after their interests." White Republicans had better get the message. As a black politician in Memphis told them, "We want candidates to stand by principles and their friends. . . . If you leave the principles of the Republican party, we shall leave you."⁶³

Futilely, conservative southern Republicans urged caution. The potential of securing white votes in the South was clear. White unanimity had broken down after the passage of the Reconstruction Act in 1867. Important white leaders had openly urged their people to accept the situation, or privately began to negotiate with conservative Republicans. The adhesion of such politicians as Brown and Holden, who had made their careers through anti-aristocratic politics, suggested the potential of the Republicans' own anti-aristocratic appeal. Large numbers of whites, concentrated in the old nonslaveholding regions, had voted to hold constitutional conventions under the Reconstruction Acts—about 30 percent of the registered white voters in North Carolina, Alabama, and Georgia, and about 10 percent in Virginia, Florida, and Texas.⁶⁴ If they wanted to turn these floating voters into Republicans, conservatives argued, the party must avoid alienating them with disfranchisement, racially progressive legislation, or African American nominations to office.⁶⁵

Frustrated southern conservatives complained to northern Republicans that a tiny minority of no more than three thousand white radicals were alienating tens of thousands of potentially Republican white voters. Efforts to secure this white support were being defeated by "a small set of men who fancied that by appealing to the ignorance & prejudice of the freedmen they could monopolize the offices of the state."⁶⁶ Of course, the reality was quite different. African Americans had interests and they backed politicians who served them. As a South Carolina Conservative perceived, "The negroes have been accused of being easily led by demagogues; but they really rule the demagogues, not the demagogues them. Let the politicians do anything which is distasteful, and opponents spring up in every quarter."[67]

Conservative and radical Republicans cooperated uneasily. In most, but not all, southern states, Republicans at first nominated more moderate leaders for the top state offices, while more radical Republicans were elected to the Senate and the House of Representatives. Since congressional delegations, and especially senators, had the strongest influence over federal appointments, federal officeholders often formed the backbone of more radical southern Republican factions, while state appointees backed more moderate policies. The complaint of a North Carolina native Republican was typical: "Our Federal office holders, composed almost entirely of the carpet bag class, are utterly inefficient, politically worthless and intensely selfish.... Deserving men ... and first rate politicians of our own people are thrust aside to keep these men in power."[68] Moderates were continually weakened in the party by the desertion of allies, who bolted party nominations to nominate rival tickets backed by the Democrat/Conservatives. Where such bolting tickets were successful, as in Virginia and Tennessee in 1869 and West Virginia and Missouri in 1870, they led not to stronger, conservative Republican parties but to Democratic/Conservative supremacy.

Northern Republicans and the administration of Ulysses S. Grant, inaugurated in 1869, wavered over whom to support. They continued to vacillate even in the face of growing violence in the South, manifest in the rise of the Ku Klux Klan. By spring of 1870 this violence was already growing serious, and it exacerbated southern Republican divisions. Those who were committed to conciliating white southerners tended to deny that it was as pervasive as more radical Republicans alleged, and they especially denied that it had the support of the conservative, business-minded southerners whose support they were courting. To concede otherwise would have serious political ramifications; it would mean a diminution of their own influence and the rise of that of their harder-line rivals.

Although there were exceptions, as a whole Republican governors of the southern states, responsible for maintaining the peace, tended toward conciliation, while Republican senators, responding to appeals from frightened local activists and black Republicans, criticized their caution. Of crucial importance to southern Republican factional politics, the violence and the failure of conciliationist Republicans to deal with it, led black Republicans, who made up the overwhelming majority of the party's rank and file in the Deep South, to swing decisively toward the southern hardliners. By 1871 the more radical factions— often led by northern immigrants to the South—were ascendant there, with their leaders taking over the top state offices. As Mississippi Senator Adelbert

Ames explained to a colleague, "The Carpetbagger . . . has a hold on the hearts of the colored people that nothing can destroy. He is the positive element of the party and if the South is to be redeemed from the ways of Slavery it must be done by him."[69] African American leaders secured larger numbers of official positions, and they demanded that Republicans support new state and federal civil rights acts to secure equal access to public educational institutions, hotels and transportation facilities, theaters and places of amusement.[70]

More conservative southern Republicans fumed at the support black Republicans gave the hardliners. "The trouble is, that they will vote for any man who makes a noisy demonstration of devotion to their rights, without the slightest regard to his past public career, or his private character," a disillusioned southern unionist lamented. "Life-long devotion to the Union . . . went for nothing."[71] Black voters "were not disposed . . . to take counsel from *leading high-minded Union men*," another southern Republican echoed, "but only from irresponsible white adventurers who pandered to their wishes."[72]

The politics of Reconstruction in the South had led to hard-line Republican ascendancy in the region, and it was this ascendancy that made federal intervention in the South necessary. Eschewing conciliation, promoting the interests of their mostly black constituency, nominating African American aspirants to important political offices, southern Republicans had slight hope for southern white support in the short term. When the depression of 1873 dashed prospects for the economic prosperity all Republicans had counted on to win southern whites over to the party of progress, the Republican position in the South was dire indeed.[73] White electoral support eroded. Table 6.1 indicates how completely the racial distribution of the electorate predicted opposition to Republicanism in the South.

Denying the legitimacy of the governments imposed by federal action, the overwhelming majority of whites perceived the Republican Party as an engine of class legislation. As Republicans provided public services to African American constituents, southern Conservatives charged that corrupt politicians were enriching themselves with government offices, bribery, and theft, retaining power by supporting legislation that transferred resources from white taxpayers to venal African American voters. Judges who attempted to provide impartial justice were denounced as showing favoritism to black workers.[74]

Where whites made up a significant majority of the population, Democrats returned to power, often aided by dissident conservative Republicans and utilizing some degree of intimidation and violence. In states where African Americans were a majority or so close to it that Republicans needed few white votes to win, more and more Democrat/Conservatives turned to leaders who advocated violence. Only the willingness of the federal government to intervene—that is,

Table 6.1
Correlations between Republican Voting Patterns and the Distribution of White Voters, 1868–1876

	1868	1869–1871	1872	1873–1875	1876
Alabama	−.74	−.71	−.69	−.81	−.57
Arkansas	−.46		−.79		−.86
Florida			−.82		−.90
Georgia	−.55		−.44		−.39
Louisiana	−.56		−.76		−.67*
Mississippi		−.81	−.89	−.80	−.43
North Carolina	−.61		−.83		−.75
South Carolina	−.73	−.79	−.81	−.60	−.91
Tennessee	.32	.02	−.17	−.25	−.04
Texas		.23	.26	.26/.19**	.13
Virginia		−.89	−.81	−.82	−.83

NOTE: Correlations for 1868, 1872, and 1876 based on presidential election returns; correlations for off-year elections based on gubernatorial returns. As yet unreconstructed, Mississippi, Texas, and Virginia cast no votes for president in 1868. Florida's electoral vote was determined by the state legislature in 1868, without a popular vote.
*The correlation between Democratic voting patterns and the distribution of white voters was .84.
**Gubernatorial elections in 1873 and 1875.

the resolve of northern Republicans—inhibited them. As long as forceful federal action demonstrated that violence was counterproductive, more moderate Democrats could argue that appeals to conservative southern Republicans were more likely to succeed, especially if national Republican leaders could be persuaded to use their influence to bolster them rather than the dominant radicals.[75] When the Grant administration failed to counteract the Democrats' open use of intimidation in the state elections of 1874 in Alabama and 1875 in Mississippi, it cut the ground from under Democratic moderates, opening the way for the violent campaigns of 1876 in South Carolina and Louisiana. As we all know, the Republican regimes of the South collapsed before the onslaught.

How and why did northern Republican resolve dissipate? That question takes us back to the politics of Reconstruction in the North. When one looks at the voting behavior of the northern electorate, some key facts stand out. First, there almost certainly was an ethnocultural aspect to the voting alignments of the Civil War era. Tables 6.2a and 6.2b show the correlation between Democratic and Republican voting patterns from 1864 to 1868 and different ethnocultural variables in a number of northern states.[76] They indicate that anywhere from about 25 to 85 percent of the variance in Republican voting patterns can be explained by the distribution of ethnic and religious groups within the states.

Table 6.2A
Republican Voting Patterns and Ethnocultural Variables

	N.Y.	Pa.	Ohio	Ind.	Mich.	Ill.	Wis.	Iowa	Minn.
Austria	−.62	x	x	x	x	x	x	x	x
Baptist	.61	.32	.41				−.43**		
Canada								−.38	
Congregationalist	.41	x	.38**	x		.33	.46(.60)**	x	x
Dutch Reformed	−.38	−.32**						x	
England & Wales						.34		−.51	
Episcopalian	−.61		x	x		x		x	
France		−.36***		−.41					
German Reformed	−.39**						x		x
Germany	−.64	−.44	−.61		−.39		−.48		
Indiana	x	x	x	x	.39		x		x
Ireland	−.71	−.30			−.63				
Lutheran			−.43	−.36					−.47(−.62)
Maryland	−.55***			x	x	x	x	x	x
Methodist	.38								

	1	2	3	4	5	6	7	8	9
New Jersey	−.45***	−.32							
New York	x	x	.33(.50)	x	.70	.51	.66	x	.60
Ohio	x		x		.56		.37(−.53)		
Pennsylvania	x	x	x		.43				
Presbyterian		.36						.37	
Quaker	x	x	x	.36	x	x	x	x	x
Roman Catholic	−.60	−.30	−.50	−.33	−.60		−.37	−.47	−.50
Scandinavia		x			−.41				
Scotland						.33		−.34	
Switzerland	−.35						x		
Universalist	.35**								
Vermont/Mass.	.46*	x	x	x	.60	x	.71	x	x
Wisconsin	x	x	x	x	x	x	x	x	.54
Total explained variance (R^2)	87%	35%	62%	26%	66%	27%	82%	44%	59%

NOTE: The figures are simple Pearsonian correlations (r). The figures in parentheses are partial correlations, with the relationships among all other ethnocultural variables controlled; they are given when they indicate a relationship clearly stronger than that indicated by simple r. An x means that the census records did not provide data on the variable for the given state; a blank means that the variable did not correlate with the partisan division at more than .30 or was not significant at the .01 level.

*Massachusetts
**1850
***1880

Table 6.2B
Democratic Voting Patterns 1864–1868 and Ethnocultural Variables

	N.Y.	Pa.	Ohio	Ind.	Mich.	Ill.	Wis.	Iowa	Minn.
Austria								x	.38
Baptist	−.36	x	x	x	x	x	x	−.33	
Canada	−.39	−.38	−.47	−.33(.44)	−.53	−.51	−.58(−.70)	−.63	
Congregationalist	.48	x	−.42*	x	−.33	−.62			
Dutch Reformed		x	x	x	x	x	.44	x	x
England & Wales				−.53		−.58	.66	−.32	
Germany	x	x	x	x	x	x	−.34	−.45	.54
Illinois	x	x		.32	x	.49	x	.57**	x
Kentucky	.40	.30	.42				.46(.75)*		
Lutheran	−.36	−.54**	x	x			x	x	
Massachusetts									

The Politics of Reconstruction

New York	x	-.42	-.58	-.51			-.75	-.36	-.65
Ohio	x	-.33	x	-.33					
Pennsylvania	x	x		-.41				-.37	
Quaker	x	x		-.32(.47)		x	x	x	
Roman Catholic						.32		.36(.52)	.51
Scandinavia		x			-.58	-.41	-.51(-.70)	-.34	
Scotland		-.35	-.43		-.43	-.57		-.43	
Switzerland								.31(.46)	
Vermont	-.49	x	x	x	x	x		x	x
Total explained variance (R²)	45%	42%	61%	40%	49%	65%	81%	62%	37%

NOTE: The figures are simple Pearsonian correlations (r). The figures in parentheses are partial correlations, with the relationships among all other ethnocultural variables controlled; they are given when they indicate a relationship clearly stronger than that indicated by simple r. An x means that the census records did not provide data on the variable for the given state; a blank means that the variable did not correlate with the partisan division at more than .30 or was not significant at the .01 level.

*1850
**1880

Figures 6.1, 6.2, and 6.3 tell a similar story. They indicate the dramatic shift in election behavior that took place in counties of Ohio, Indiana, and Illinois with high concentrations of voters of New England–upstate New York, or "Yankee," heritage. The emergence of the Republican Party clearly energized these voters.

German-dominated counties, in contrast, remained Democratic. But one does not see the dramatic shift in voting that characterized the Yankee counties. In Ohio and Indiana, the German counties remained safely Democratic, but only slightly more so than during the 1840s and 1850s. In Illinois, where the Republicans aimed a powerful appeal at Germans, they were far more competitive in predominantly German counties than the Whigs had been. (Note, too, that table 6.1 shows that while the pattern of German settlement correlated negatively with Republican voting in several northern states, it did not in Illinois or Indiana.)

These charts certainly say something about the Republican appeal to Yankee voters and the continued appeal of Democrats to German and Irish immigrants. But despite significant ethnic polarization, it is not so certain that the basis of the Republican appeal was hostility to immigrants and Catholics. Democratic voting by Germans in Illinois, Indiana, and Ohio persisted, but it did not increase. This suggests a continuation of a prior allegiance established during the second, Whig-Democratic party system or perhaps during the Know-Nothing agitation that preceded the Republican Party's emergence as the second party in a new two-party system.

There are clear indications that the Republican appeal was based more on antislavery than nativism. Table 6.3 shows the correlations between Republican voting and a variety of statewide referenda that related to either issues of race or to one of the leading issues separating ethnocultural groups—prohibition and liquor license. They indicate that race-related issues almost completely displaced the prohibition issue during the 1860s and that the prohibition issue revived after the ratification of the Fifteenth Amendment appeared to take African American voting rights out of northern state politics. There was an extraordinarily high correlation between Republican voting patterns and voting patterns on African American suffrage referenda as early as 1860, significantly higher than correlations between party and ethnocultural issues.

Of course, by the mid-1860s African American suffrage had become a party issue, inclining Republicans to support it out of party loyalty. But if so, Republican politicians had succeeded in making it so. One wonders why they would do that, if northern white racism was as overwhelming a force as some historians have said. The answer lies in the fact that politicians do not merely respond to public opinion, they attempt to shape it—with luck, to promote the public

THE POLITICS OF RECONSTRUCTION 113

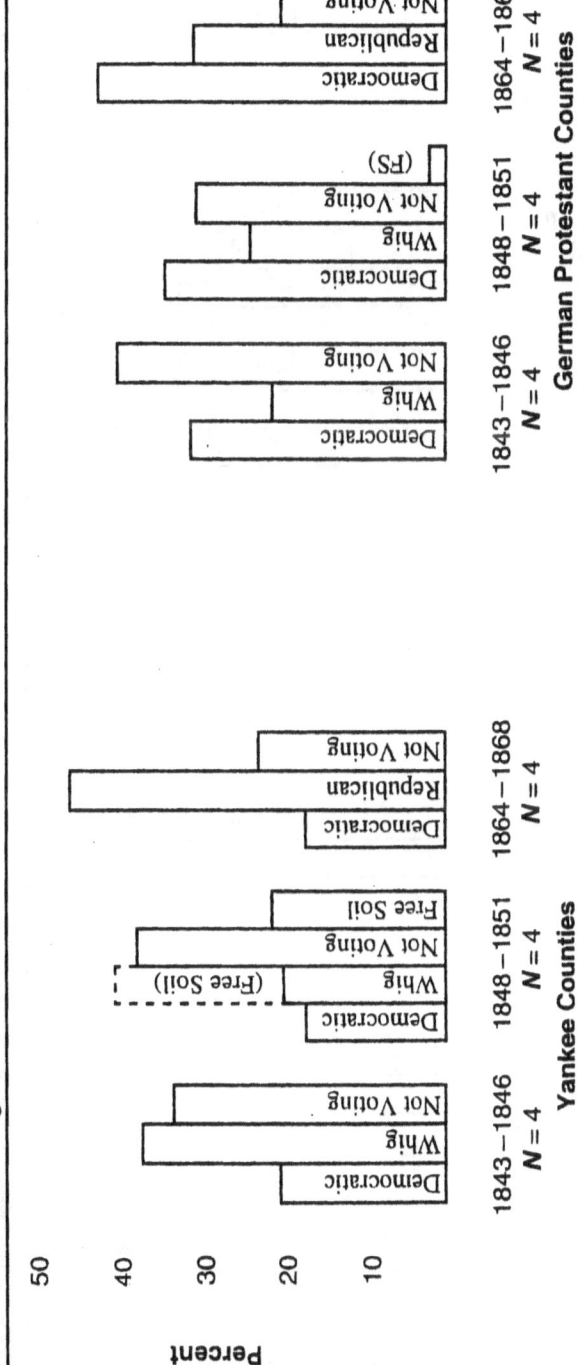

Figure 6.1
Ohio Counties and Voting Shifts, 1840s to 1860s

NOTE: For 1843–1846, elections include 1843 congressional, 1844 presidential, 1846 gubernatorial; for 1848–1851, elections include 1848 presidential, 1850 and 1851 gubernatorial; for 1864–1868, elections include 1864 presidential, 1865 gubernatorial, 1866 congressional, 1867 gubernatorial, 1868 presidential. N refers to the number of counties included in the analysis.

Figure 6.2
Indiana Counties and Voting Shifts, 1840s to 1860s

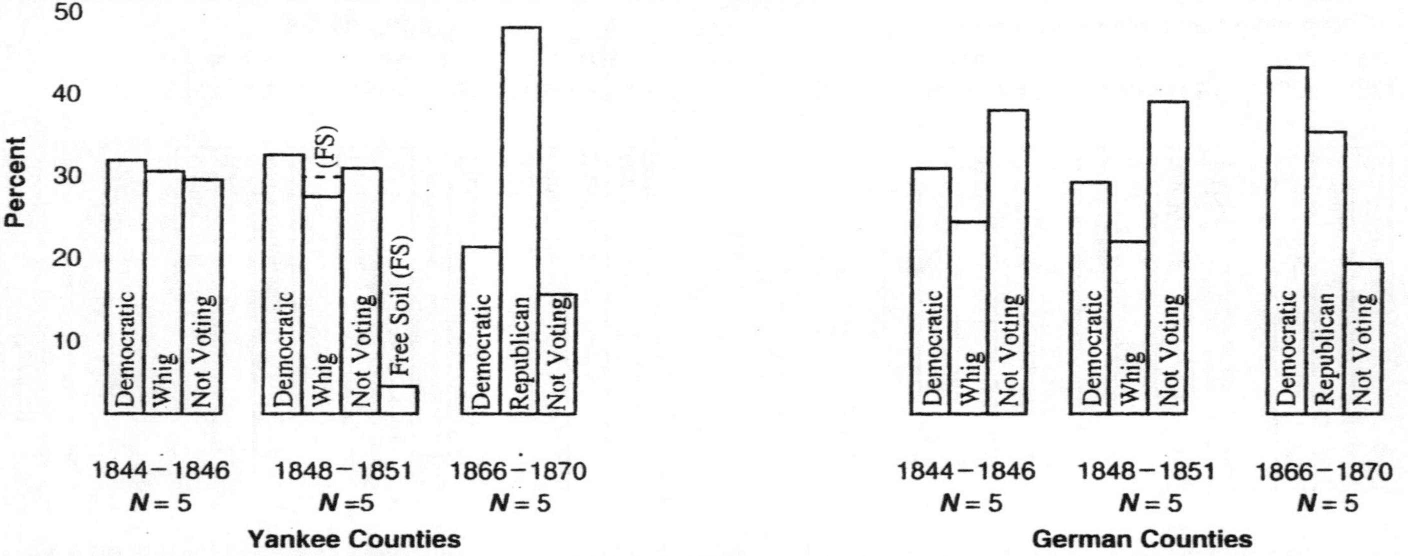

NOTE: For 1844–1846, elections include 1844 presidential, 1845 congressional, 1846 gubernatorial; for 1848–1851, elections include 1848 presidential, 1849 gubernatorial, 1851 congressional; for 1866–1870, elections include 1866 congressional, 1868 presidential, 1870 congressional. N refers to the number of counties included in the analysis.

The Politics of Reconstruction 115

Figure 6.3
Illinois Counties and Voting Shifts, 1840s to 1860s

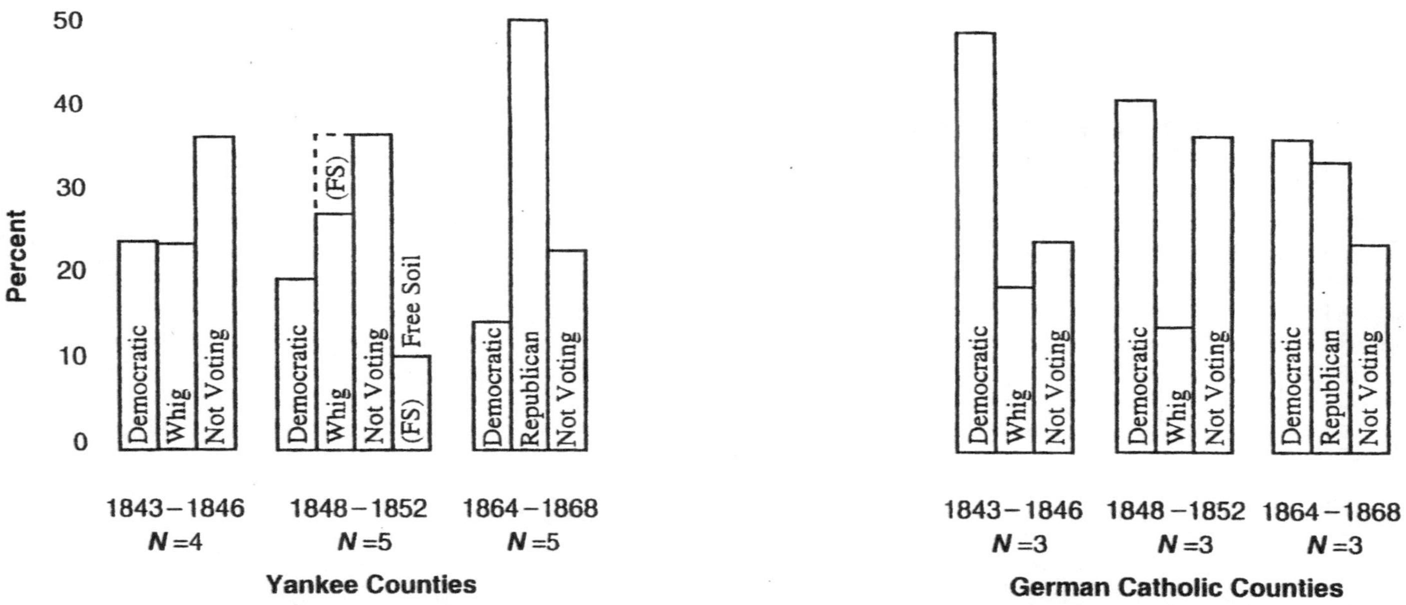

NOTE: For 1843–1846, elections include 1843 congressional, 1844 presidential, 1846 gubernatorial; for 1848–1852, elections include 1848 presidential, 1850 congressional, 1852 presidential; for 1864–1868, elections include 1864 presidential, 1866 congressional, 1868 presidential. N refers to the number of counties included in the analysis.

Table 6.3
Correlations for Referenda and Elections

	Republican	Democratic
Pre-War		
Illinois, black exclusion, 1848		
1856 presidential vote	.65	.53
1858 congressional vote	.40	.53
Michigan, black suffrage, 1850		
1856 presidential vote	.61	.47
1858 congressional vote	.56	.64
Indiana, black exclusion, 1851		
1856 presidential vote	.59	.52
1858 congressional vote	.48	.29
Ohio, license, 1851		
1856 presidential vote	.16	.56
1858 congressional vote	.32	.57
Michigan, prohibition, 1853		
1856 presidential vote	.51	.55
1858 congressional vote	.69	.65
Rhode Island, license, 1853		
1856 presidential vote	.88	.54
1858 congressional vote	.75	.73*
Wisconsin, prohibition, 1853		
1856 presidential vote	.43	.48
1858 congressional vote	.26	.48
Pennsylvania, prohibition, 1854		
1856 presidential vote	.34	.43
1860 presidential vote	.48	.38
Illinois, prohibition, 1855		
1856 presidential vote	.76	.81
1858 congressional vote	.70	.74
Iowa, prohibition, 1855		
1854 congressional vote	.95	.84
1856 presidential vote	.36	.56
1858 congressional vote	.15	.42
Wisconsin, black suffrage, 1857		
1857 gubernatorial vote	.80	.98
1858 congressional vote	.44	.37
Iowa, black suffrage, 1857		
1857 gubernatorial vote	.25	.50
1858 congressional vote	.33	.50
1860 congressional vote	.51	.58
Oregon, black exclusion, 1857		
1858 gubernatorial vote	.76**	.75
1860 presidential vote	.78**	.27
New York, black suffrage, 1860		
1860 presidential vote	.88	.90

Post-War
Connecticut, black suffrage, 1865
    1865 gubernatorial vote   .86   .98
    1864–68 mean party vote   .86   .93
Minnesota, black suffrage, 1865
    1865 gubernatorial vote   .81   .89
Wisconsin, black suffrage, 1865
    1865 gubernatorial vote   .92   .95
    1864–68 mean party vote   .83   .92
Minnesota, black suffrage, 1867
    1867 gubernatorial vote   .78   .86
Kansas, black suffrage, 1867
    1868 presidential vote   .76***   .87
    1864–68 mean party vote   .69***   .76
Ohio, black suffrage, 1867
    1867 gubernatorial vote   .98   .99
    1864–68 mean party vote   .92   .97
Iowa, black suffrage, 1868
    1868 presidential vote   .94   .97
    1864–68 mean party vote   .92   .96
Michigan, prohibition, 1868
    1868 presidential vote   .79   .73
    1864–68 mean party vote   .84   .57
Minnesota, black suffrage, 1868
    1868 presidential vote   .98   .98
Minnesota, black suffrage, 1865–68 mean vote
    1865–68 mean party vote   .90   .95
New York, black suffrage, 1869
    1864–68 mean party vote   .90   .82
Michigan, black suffrage, 1870
    1864–68 mean party vote   .84   .51
Ohio, license, 1874
    1870–73 mean party vote   .56   .40
Michigan, license, 1876
    1872–76 mean party vote   .61   .21
Kansas, prohibition, 1880
    1880 presidential vote   .47   .62

NOTE: Voting patterns were based on proportion of the total eligible electorate. This gave individual correlations for Republican and Democratic patterns with both support and opposition for black rights and prohibition. The highest correlation is reported on the table, without signs. The highest Republican correlation was always with support for the pro-black rights or prohibition position—either a positive correlation with support for those positions or a negative correlation with opposition. The opposite held true for Democrats.

   *Also correlated with anti-license position at .48.
  **Also correlated with anti-black rights position at .41 in 1858 and .64 in 1860.
 ***Also correlated with the anti-black rights position at .47 in 1868 and at .60 for the mean 1864–68 vote.

good, and certainly to promote their political careers. Like modern politicians, Reconstruction-era politicians tested issues, molded them, abandoned them, and revived them in a delicate dance with public opinion. Naturally, they chose issues and tried to present them in a form that they thought promised political success for themselves and (more than today) their party.

Despite the racism endemic North as well as South, Republicans chose to stress the slavery and civil-rights issues rather than prohibition, Sabbatarianism, immigration restriction, and similar ethnoculturally charged issues that might have appealed to much of their constituency. That is certainly apparent in the issues they chose to make in Congress. Table 6.4 indicates the types of legislation both parties proposed in the House of Representatives between 1869 and 1880.

Moral regulation made up less than one-half percent of the total. Of course, the nineteenth-century federal system lodged authority to regulate morals in the state rather than federal government. But Republicans generally avoided such issues in state campaigns as well. And for good reason. Such issues divided Republicans more than they united them. They might energize part of the party's rank and file, but in most states the losses exceeded the benefit. When Republicans raised such issues, they always seemed to lose votes.[77] Therefore,

Table 6.4
Proposed Legislation in the House of Representatives, 1869–1880

	Congress						
	41	42	43	44	45	46	Total
Economic Promotion	674 (19%)	533 (13%)	512 (10%)	421 (9%)	508 (8%)	383 (5%)	3031 (9%)
Reconstruction and Civil Rights	583 (16%)	425 (10%)	290 (6%)	268 (6%)	322 (5%)	305 (5%)	2193 (7%)
Economic Regulation	169 (5%)	213 (5%)	257 (5%)	146 (3%)	244 (4%)	331 (4%)	1360 (4%)
Financial Legislation	122 (3%)	133 (3%)	215 (4%)	165 (3%)	299 (5%)	219 (3%)	1153 (4%)
Moral Regulation	15 (.4%)	11 (.3%)	16 (.3%)	13 (.2%)	20 (.3%)	41 (.5%)	116 (.4%)
Other (primarily pension appropriations)	2060 (57%)	2961 (69%)	3761 (75%)	3889 (79%)	5301 (79%)	6342 (83%)	24,314 (76%)
Total	3623	4276	5051	4902	6694	7621	32,167

as table 6.5 shows, only about 7 percent of the planks of Republican state platforms from 1869 to 1880 were directed to what we may call "social issues," such as prohibition, church-state relations, and immigration restriction.

Because local issues could be dangerous, Republicans tried to keep voters focused on national issues. Even during years where no national officer was up for election, more Republican platform planks referred to Civil War issues than any other single issue. Moreover, planks dealing with economic development

Table 6.5
Issues in Northern Republican Platforms, 1869–1880

	Presidential Election Years	Congress-Only Election Years	Odd Election Years	Total
War Issues	78 (22%)	63 (22%)	83 (29%)	224 (24%)
(Reconstruction & Civil Rights)	(56)	(53)	(59)	
(National Sovereignty)	(13)	(5)	(13)	
(Veterans' Legislation)	(9)	(5)	(11)	
National Finances	27 (8%)	38 (13%)	30 (10%)	105 (11%)
Economic Development and Regulation	19 (5%)	27 (10%)	52 (18%)	98 (11%)
Taxation and Economy in Government	17 (5%)	13 (5%)	27 (9%)	57 (6%)
Civil Service Reform and Honesty in Government	21 (6%)	11 (4%)	25 (9%)	57 (6%)
Social Issues	18 (5%)	23 (8%)	27 (9%)	68 (7%)
(Prohibition)	(1)	(5)	(4)	
(Church-State Relations)	(2)	(1)	(6)	
(Immigration Restriction)*	(2)	(3)	(4)	
Other (principally endorsements of candidates and administration)	181 (50%)	110 (39%)	47 (16%)	328 (35%)
Total	361	285	291	937

*Includes 3 anti-Chinese immigration planks

and regulation, taxation and retrenchment, and civil-service reform rarely pertained to state government alone. Even some social issues, such foreign immigration, inherently implicated national action. Although it will take further research to demonstrate it conclusively, if one excludes the pro forma endorsement of state and national candidates and administrations, table 6.4 suggests that at all times well over half of the planks were devoted to national issues.

Analysis of electoral behavior seems to confirm that voters found national issues more salient than local ones. Figure 6.4 graphs the median estimated voter turnout in presidential and gubernatorial elections at the state level from 1855 to 1880.

Not only was the median turnout in presidential elections higher than the median gubernatorial election turnout in any year but 1868, but gubernatorial turnout also consistently peaked in presidential-election years. Table 6.6 demonstrates that—to different degrees—voting patterns were more consistent in presidential elections than in elections for state officers, even though most states elected governors every year or every other year. (The correlations in

Figure 6.4
Presidential and Gubernatorial Turnout, 1855–1880

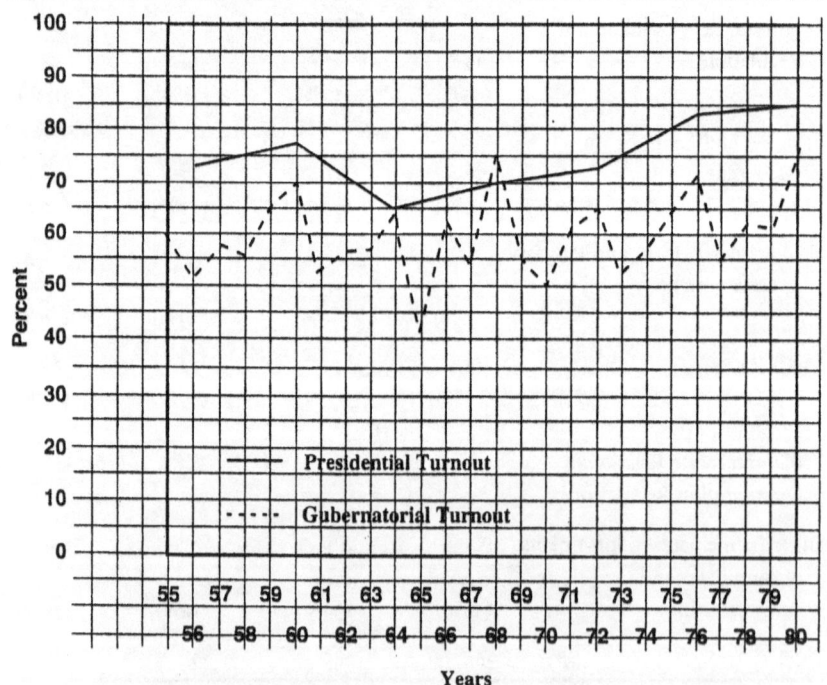

Table 6.6
Median Correlations between Republican Voting Patterns in Succeeding Elections in Various Northern States, 1855–1880

	Presidential Election Years	Non-Presidential Election Years
Illinois	.83	*
Indiana	.89	*
Iowa	.74	.72 (.65)
Kansas	.63	.47 (.58)
Maine	.91	.83 (.65)
Massachusetts	.69	.58 (.61)
Michigan	.83	.77 (.58)
Minnesota	.63	.35
New Jersey	.89	.88
New York	.95	.95 (.91)
Ohio	.95	.90
Pennsylvania	.92	.90
Vermont	.90	.44 (.39)
Wisconsin	.83	.74

*Gubernatorial elections in Illinois and Indiana took place only in presidential years.

parentheses are those for non-presidential years four years apart.) These stable voting patterns and higher turnouts in presidential elections led to Republican victories, while more volatile elections for state officers led to losses of voters if not outright defeats.

The voting pattern in the congressional elections of 1866, familiar to all students of Reconstruction, is most illustrative. Despite the fact that congressmen were national officers, voting patterns in off-year congressional elections varied much more than those in presidential-year elections, which closely resembled the pattern of the vote for president. Democrats seemed always to do better in off-year than on-year elections. The exception was the election of 1866, which Andrew Johnson turned into a referendum on Reconstruction when he broke with the Republican Party, orchestrated the formation of an anti-Republican alliance, and launched an ambitious speaking tour through the North—the "Swing Around the Circle."[78] That off-year election galvanized voters almost as effectively as a presidential canvass, and the high correlation between its voting pattern and those of presidential elections between 1860 and 1880 showed it, as did the highest turnout in an off-year congressional election between 1858 and 1874.[79] Table 6.7 gives the correlation between presidential elections and succeeding, off-year congressional elections.

Table 6.7
Median Correlations between Republican Voting Patterns in Succeeding Presidential and Congressional Elections in Northern States, 1855–1880

1856–1858	.72
1858–1860	.71
1860–1862	.70
1862–1864	.77
1864–1866	.83
1866–1868	.84
1868–1870	.67
1870–1872	.70
1872–1874	.58
1874–1876	.63
1876–1878	.66
1878–1880	.70

NOTE: Northern states included are Illinois, Indiana, Iowa, Kansas, Maine, Massachusetts, Michigan, Minnesota, New Jersey, New York, Ohio, Pennsylvania, Vermont, and Wisconsin. Not included: California, Connecticut, Nevada, New Hampshire, Oregon, and Rhode Island.

Compare the correlations among the elections of 1864, 1866, and 1868 to the others. If only all off-year elections could look like that one, Republicans lamented. In 1866 they hardly lost a congressman, following a huge gain in 1864. In most other off-year elections they lost twice as many or more, often from smaller pools.[80]

Throughout the 1870s, Republicans would do best when they could convince voters that the South was resurgent and again brutalizing its African American people. That consideration was one of the main reasons that the Grant administration and northern Republicans finally endorsed the hardliners rather than the conciliationists in the South. In 1871 they ended a dangerous period of drift by uniting on the Ku Klux Klan Act; they carried the elections of 1872 on the southern issue. In 1876 they did it again. As Georgia Republican and former Attorney General Amos T. Ackerman wrote that year, Rutherford B. Hayes "will be elected, if the people can see that the old issues are not settled, particularly in the South." Southerners intended that the extension of rights to African Americans "shall be only nominal." "Let the North know this, and the battle is won."[81] Democrats knew it too. Furiously, they denounced Republicans for waving the "bloody shirt"—cynically keeping the old war issues alive. "What they want now is the very thing they constantly shed tears over—a first-class 'southern outrage,'" the *Richmond Dispatch* editorialized scornfully.[82] But when southern whites provided it—in the form of the bloody Hamburg Massacre in South Carolina—the *Dispatch* recognized the consequences. "We know as well as any one else that it would take only a few such affairs to . . . make Hayes's election sure," it wrote.[83] As anyone familiar with the election of 1876 knows, southern outrages did not quite make Hayes's election sure. But they made it possible.

On becoming president, Hayes ostentatiously repudiated Republican intervention in the South, dividing and demoralizing his party.[84] How then did the Republicans manage to recover and win the presidential election of 1880? In 1879, having gained control of the both the House and Senate in off-year elections, the Democrats tried to force the repeal of the Reconstruction-era election laws. The Democrats attached the repeal to the military appropriations bill, guessing that Hayes would not veto so essential a piece of legislation. They guessed wrong, and they paid for it. The independent but Democratic-leaning *New York Herald* knew it from the beginning. "The republican leaders have not until within a few weeks entertained any confident expectation of carrying the Presidential elections next year. . . . Then came the Democratic idiocy . . . . The democrats could hardly do better if they received their orders directly from the other side."[85]

Given the potency of the Civil War issues, it should not surprise us that many Democrats urged that the party end its diehard opposition to the extension of equal civil and political rights to African Americans and turn to other issues instead.[86] Republicans had succeeded in linking equal civil and political rights for African Americans with the triumph of loyalty and Unionism in the war. Despite northern racism, presented the right way, the civil-rights issue was a winner, not a loser.

By 1871 Democrats advocating a "New Departure" were gaining strength. Their problem was that the war issues united the Democratic minority as thoroughly as they united the Republican majority. On most other issues—finances, banking, even the protective tariff—they were as divided as their opponents. They could unite on the "corruption" of the Grant administration and the well-oiled state Republican Party machines. But that hardly seemed a winner, because the outs always charged the ins with corruption. If they could convince northerners that they really meant to concede civil and political rights to the freedmen, they could appeal to a widespread desire in the North for peace and reconciliation—a sentiment that persisted despite distrust of southern intentions. In those circumstances, moreover, Democrats could give their own spin to the race issue. Echoing the charges of their southern white allies, northern Democrats insisted that black southerners, now protected in their civil and political rights, were being duped into supporting the political ambitions of white adventurers and thieves. Sustained blindly by a constituency with no property to lose, carpetbaggers and scalawags were plundering the South. In this form, one that did not explicitly challenge the freedmen's civil and political rights, Democratic appeals to Republican racial prejudice could be effective.

What made these appeals credible was that they were echoed by important elements within the Republican Party itself—another illustration of how intraparty factionalism affected public policy. In the fluid circumstances surrounding the organization of the new Republican Party, there had been an immense amount of jockeying among these factions, with none securing too much control for too long a time. But by the late 1860s and early 1870s, most party organizations had stabilized. The Tenure of Office Act of 1867 had the unintended effect of strengthening the influence of Republican United States senators within their state parties.[87] Senators such as Roscoe Conkling of New York, Zachariah Chandler of Michigan, and Oliver P. Morton of Indiana slowly emerged as the heads of formidable "machines" that controlled local political patronage and nominations, just as southern Republican senators had gained predominant influence in their states.[88]

The process is an example of what the great political scientist Robert Michels called the "iron law of oligarchy"—the inevitable institutionalization of political movements into bureaucratized political parties, with a concomitant loss of internal democracy and openness.[89] There were a large number of losers, among them not only the members of declining factions but also Republican newspaper editors, who had exercised a great deal of independent influence on the party in its formative years, and intellectuals, whose role as articulators of antislavery ideals had been crucial in broadening the party's appeal but whose skills were less important than hacks who got out the vote now that partisan identifications had solidified.

Members of these groups howled in protest as mere machine politicians took over the party. But how could they oust the dominant leaders from power and regain their old influence? One thing was certain. They could not do it as long as the main issue dividing Republican from Democrat continued to be the antislavery, Civil War, civil-rights issue that riveted rank-and-file Republicans to their party and made the key political skill the simple ability to turn them out at election time. The simple fact was that the dominant leaders—even reluctant warriors, who like Morton had sought to stem the tide of radical Republicanism—were now firmly associated with that issue. No one was going to wave the bloody shirt better than they. E. L. Godkin, the disgruntled editor of the *Nation*, articulated the situation clearly. "People came to look upon fidelity to the antislavery cause . . . as the one test of statesmanship, and under cover of this feeling a large number of gentlemen have won their way to places in public life." But now, "the circumstances have . . . so changed, and the problems presented for solution are so different, that they are fit to fill them no longer."[90]

But this argument could carry weight only if Republicans agreed that the great moral issue was settled. So it was that after the southern states were restored to normal relations in the Union, after Grant was elected president in 1868, and after Congress sent the Fifteenth Amendment to the states for what was expected to be certain ratification, dissident Republicans launched a great campaign to convince Republican voters that it was time to close the Civil War with amnesty and to turn to new issues of finances and reform.

When the regular Republican leadership proved surprisingly resilient, dissidents perceived the machinations by which they retained power—the control of the patronage, the distribution of governmental largesse to sympathizers, the appeal to dead issues—to be essentially corrupt. Claiming the mantle of "reform," they linked this corruption to what they feared was a growing tendency to exercise governmental power to redistribute resources by giving tariff protection to manufacturers and their workers in industrializing states at the expense of consumers in the less developed regions of the country, passing Granger legislation to serve the interests of farmers and shippers at the expense of railroad investors, making huge public works expenditures in the cities at the expense of property-owning taxpayers, and manipulating the money supply to benefit farmers and entrepreneurs at the expense of creditors. They were easily persuaded by southern Democrats that Republican programs to benefit the freedmen in the South at the expense of white taxpayers constituted another example.

The combination of their desire to move away from Civil War issues and their opposition to redistributive government economic policies—what they called "class legislation"—led Republican "reformers" into a de facto alliance with Democrats. Occasionally this alliance took on a concrete form, as in the Liberal Republican and Democratic nomination of Horace Greeley for the presidency in 1872. But generally it was limited to parallel attacks on the leadership of the Republican Party—accusations of corruption and of ignoring the real issues facing Americans while making demagogic appeals to the settled ones surrounding slavery, race, and the war.[91] At the same time both reform Republicans and Democrats had an interest in portraying white southerners as reconciled to the results of the war, including the extension of basic civil and political rights of the freedmen, and in fact now the victims of cynical carpetbaggers and scalawags. Finally, both dissident Republicans and Democrats pointed to the stress intervention in the South to protect civil and political rights placed on government institutions, especially the federal system.

The constant reiteration of these themes in the dissident-controlled journals of the northern press, whose influence was enhanced by the claim that the reformers' independence of party organizations made them reliable and neutral observers, did undermine the appeal of the Civil War issues to the rank and file.[92] The effect was especially apparent after 1870 and in non-presidential year elections, when it was more difficult for Republicans to keep their voters focused on national issues. Table 6.6 shows the correlations between Republican voting patterns in succeeding national elections. The trend down from the Republican heyday of 1864 through 1868 is clear.

Foner links this trend to growing class tensions in the North. Faced with growing labor unrest, "consciousness of being members of a separate capitalist class . . . spread within the business community. . . . In the face of agrarian unrest and working-class militancy, metropolitan capitalists united as never before," he writes, and several recent studies echo him. Now identifying more with white southern property-owners than the black southern working class, fearful of an activist state, capitalists and businessmen turned against Reconstruction.[93]

There is a good deal of truth to this portrayal of the reaction of many businessmen (and financiers—a group to which Foner and other recent historians give too little attention) to Reconstruction in the South. But there is no evidence that their distaste for Republican Reconstruction policy was determinative of the result. Although the sharp sectional divisions among business interests were slowly giving way to greater harmony in the 1870s, the business community was by no means united. And its influence was clearly limited; the passage of Granger legislation either demonstrated that business interests could not control policy in states like Wisconsin, Illinois, and Iowa, or that their class consciousness was not so well developed after all. As Joel Silbey has observed, when businessmen came to perceive their common interests, they turned against the nineteenth-century political system because they could *not* exercise enough influence within it to secure them.[94]

Moreover, the business community as a whole had *never* sympathized with radical Reconstruction. Many of businessmen and financiers were Democrats. Others clearly favored conservative Republicans rather than radicals. The few who had been ostentatious radicals, such as Boston textile manufacturer Edward Atkinson, turned toward conservatism as early as 1867.[95] The real damage was done by the reform Republicans, who articulated a philosophy of laissez-faire moralism that appealed not only to businessmen and capitalists, but which resonated with the tenets of free-labor ideology to which nearly all northerners adhered.[96] It was they who lent credibility to the charge that the Republican regimes of the South were violating basic American norms in an orgy of plunder and class legislation.

Still, we must be careful about what we mean by the "abandonment" of Reconstruction by northern voters. The problem for Republicans was not that their rank and file had turned against the freedmen or against Reconstruction. The reaction to southern outrages demonstrated that. The problem was that in between southern outrages the reformers convinced a large enough minority of Republican voters that the fruits of the antislavery victory were secure to make elections doubtful. Republicans had always been divided on issues unrelated to slavery. If that glue weakened, the party's base was bound to erode.

The party leaders' difficulty was exacerbated by the fact that an even smaller minority of Republicans did actually turn against further intervention in the South as a matter of political and constitutional principle. Republicans not only faced the problem that their best issue was losing its salience; in some important states, such as New York and Ohio, reformers hostile to Reconstruction might hold the balance of power between the parties. In those states an appeal to Civil War issues, while energizing the rank and file, might alienate enough dissidents to lose the election. Recognizing these facts, Republican leaders searched desperately for an issue that would augment or replace the Reconstruction issue without putting their own party positions in jeopardy. They tried combinations of anti-Catholicism and hard money between 1873 and 1875 and an early version of anticommunism in 1877 and 1878. Later they would try the protective tariff.

But nothing could replace the Civil War issues when it came to marshaling ordinary Republican voters. So Republicans turned to an expedient that had tragic results for the freedmen of the South. They did raise the Civil War issues, but in a way that avoided driving dissidents to the Democrats. The potential of this approach first became clear in the great amnesty debate of 1876. Having recently persuaded President Grant not to send troops to Mississippi for fear of losing the elections of 1875 in the North, the Republican leader in the House, former Speaker James G. Blaine, moved to exclude Jefferson Davis from a bill designed to give him amnesty. Southern Democrats rose in a bitter defense of Davis and the Confederate South and an equally bitter attack on postwar Republican policy in the South; Blaine's response and that of James A. Garfield electrified the party's rank and file. "Hundreds of thousands of ardent, oppressed hearts responded with a battle-cry of joy," Garfield's friend Albert Gallatin Riddle recalled a few years later.[97]

Republicans considered the amnesty debate, which followed closely upon the Republican victories in the 1875 state elections, to have been the turning point in the remarkable recovery from the disastrous congressional elections of 1874. The lesson was not lost upon Republican leaders. The best political course was to raise the war issues that excited the majority of Republicans without proposing to do anything that might alienate the minority. One way to do that was to shift the issue from the rights of freedmen in the South to the behavior of the Democrats during the war. Blaine had done that successfully in the amnesty debate, and it became more and more the pattern afterward—although southern racial outrages did continue to reinforce the partisan allegiance of many northern Republicans as well.

The consequences of the Republican strategy were tragic for African Americans. It broke the crucial link Republicans had so carefully crafted among African American civil and political rights, loyalty, moral progress, unionism, and patriotism. It eliminated the counterweight that held northern racism in check among Republicans, allowing southern Democrats to shape the race issue as they wished. Thus, it was not increased racism that led to the erosion of northern support for Reconstruction, but the erosion of support for Reconstruction that led to increased racism.[98]

The new Republican strategy converted the living issue of equal rights into the dead one of Democratic perfidy in the Civil War. Although such a constricted waving of the bloody shirt triggered a host of associations binding Republicans to their party, it could not last forever. In the late 1880s, as fading memories of the war undermined the effectiveness of merely rhetorical attacks on Democrats' wartime sins, Republicans tried to revitalize bloody-shirt rhetoric by again linking it to the civil and political-rights issue, bringing forward the Force Act of 1890. But by then the Republican strategy had done its damage. As their leaders allowed the issue of equal rights to atrophy, too many northern Republicans had become indifferent to the fate of African Americans.[99] In light of that indifference it is no surprise that Republican politicians did little to protest the open violation of African American rights in the 1890s and after. That was no longer the way to energize their voters; it was certainly not the way to attract new ones. The politics of Reconstruction was over.

7

Salmon P. Chase and Constitutional Politics

In 1868, Salmon P. Chase, chief justice of the Supreme Court of the United States and one of the preeminent leaders of the radical wing of the Republican party since its founding in 1854–55, became a serious contender for the presidential nomination of the racist, anti-Reconstruction Democratic party. It was the most incredible and puzzling event in his long political career. It amazed contemporaries and stuns historians. But a look at Chase's career makes the remarkable development intelligible while at the same time fostering an understanding of nineteenth-century constitutional politics.

I

Salmon P. Chase was a towering figure in mid-nineteenth-century American public life. Abraham Lincoln, who emerged as a significant national figure only after his great debates with Stephen A. Douglas in 1858, was a newcomer in comparison. By that time Chase had been a leader of the antislavery political movement since the 1840s. He had represented Ohio in the United States Senate, had served two successful terms as the state's governor, and was about to be sent back to the Senate. A lawyer like Lincoln, Chase was the leading expositor of the Republican constitutional argument about the relationship between the federal government and slavery. Upon his death, the *New York Tribune*, the most influential Republican newspaper in the country, credited him "more than any other one man," for converting antislavery sentiment into an organized political movement.[1]

Chase and New York Senator William H. Seward were the giants of the early Republican Party, the leading contenders for its presidential nomination in 1856 and 1860. To consolidate his administration, Lincoln named Seward secretary of state and Chase secretary of the treasury, the two most important positions in his cabinet. Each expected the other to try to dominate; each intended to do so himself. Neither succeeded.

This essay is adapted primarily from "Salmon P. Chase and Constitutional Politics," *Law and Social Inquiry* 22 (Spring 1997): 459–500, and secondarily from "Salmon P. Chase as Jurist and Politician: Comment on G. Edward White, Reconstructing Chase's Jurisprudence," *Northern Kentucky Law Review* 21 (Fall 1993): 133–50.

Chase proved a great secretary of the treasury, managing the nation's finances during its most critical trial and establishing the national banking system we still have, fostering the transition of the United States into a modern, capitalist economy.[2] The accomplishment lent further luster to his reputation. Such was Chase's stature that leading Republicans considered him an alternative to Lincoln even as he served in the Cabinet. That notion dissipated as Lincoln demonstrated his abilities; Chase damaged his standing by allowing dissident elements to boost him for the nomination in 1864. Bedeviled by the rivalry between Chase and Seward and knowing of Chase's ambition to replace him, Lincoln finally accepted Chase's resignation in June of that year. A few months later, Lincoln nominated him to be chief justice and the Senate immediately confirmed him. He took the oath December 15, 1864.

Despite the wound Chase had inflicted upon himself by challenging Lincoln's renomination in 1864, he still was considered a leading, probably *the* leading, candidate for the 1868 Republican nomination, until his opponents brought forward Ulysses S. Grant. Chase cut so great a figure that as his chances for the Republican nomination faded that year, he became a serious candidate for the Democratic nomination as well. Senator, governor, secretary of the treasury, chief justice—it was a record few have equaled. No wonder that, despite their tense relationship, Lincoln conceded that "Chase is about one and a half times bigger than any other man that I ever knew."[3] Two long biographies appeared within a year of his death. Yet Chase is not much remembered now, except among specialist historians of the Civil War.[4]

At the turn of the twentieth century a new generation of southern and southern-influenced historians came to blame antislavery radicals for precipitating the Civil War and imposing harsh terms of reconstruction at war's end. They were strongly antipathetic toward radical Republicans like Chase, who had demanded a tougher antislavery policy and a radical reconstruction of the South based on equal civil and political rights for the freedmen. Because he had connived with radical Republicans to replace Lincoln in 1864, Chase became a special target, the representative "Jacobin," as one leading historian denominated the radicals.[5] Donnal V. Smith's brief and evenhanded study of *Chase and Civil War Politics* did little to stem the tide.[6]

The reputation of the radical Republicans improved in the 1960s, as the civil rights movement committed Americans to racial equality. No longer vindictive fanatics, Chase and his allies were now portrayed as "Lincoln's Vanguard for Racial Justice."[7] As part of this wave of historical revisionism, historians reevaluated the lives of many leading Republicans. Chase was one of the last. Frederick Blue's *Salmon P. Chase: A Life in Politics* and John Niven's *Salmon P. Chase: A Biography* did not appear until 1987. It was followed by John Niven's *Salmon*

P. Chase: A Biography eight years later.[8] Thoroughly familiar with antebellum antislavery politics, Blue and Niven were able to utilize sources unavailable to Chase's earlier biographers. (Niven edited a microfilm edition of the Chase papers and published selections from it.[9]) Both biographies reflect the now orthodox sympathy toward antislavery politicians.

II

Chase's ambition was legendary. In an age when public figures were supposed to affect disinterested modesty, when the office was supposed to seek the man rather than vice versa,[10] Chase could not hide his political aspirations. His all-too-apparent ambition diminished him in the opinion of his contemporaries. He was "a great man," his Supreme Court colleague Samuel F. Miller wrote, but his greatness was "perverted, shriveled by the selfishness generated by ambition."[11] Chase was well aware of the criticism. "I really think that I am not half so ambitious of place as I am represented to be," he wrote a friend. "I worked for ideals and principles and measures embodying them, and was always quite willing to take place, or be left out of place, as the cause, in the judgment of its friends, required."[12] It was no use. Commenting on a similar letter to another correspondent, even his sympathetic biographer Robert Warden recognized, "Never was a heart more self-deceived than was the heart of our hero when he wrote that letter and some others of like import."[13]

Although Chase was born into a branch of a leading New England family, his father's death left his mother in straitened circumstances. Nonetheless, Chase's family connections enabled him to secure a good education. His uncle was the Episcopal bishop of Ohio and ran an Episcopal academy near Columbus. Chase lived in the austere clergyman's household from the age of twelve to fifteen, moving to Cincinnati during the last year of his stay. He may have learned from the bishop the habits of severe rectitude and reserve that controlled what was clearly a passionate nature. Chase did not establish many warm personal relationships; worse for a politician, he could not establish the rapport with audiences or readers that made a politician popular in the nineteenth century. Much respected, Chase was never much loved, and his inability to connect emotionally with the public was one of the main obstacles to achieving his goal of the presidency.

After leaving Cincinnati, Chase entered Dartmouth College, again with the help of relatives.[14] Through family connections with politicians in Washington, Chase was able to open a school in the nation's capital. He hated teaching, but impressed his students' parents, including William Wirt, attorney general under John Quincy Adams. Seizing the main chance, Chase persuaded Wirt to allow him to study law in his office. He was admitted to the District of Columbia bar on December 14, 1829. But Andrew Jackson had defeated Adams's re-election, rendering Chase's anti-Jacksonian political connections useless. The disappointed young lawyer returned to Cincinnati, now a booming river town full of promise for an ambitious and capable attorney. There he developed his social life among the town's elite. He secured a reputation by publishing a highly regarded compilation of the Ohio statutes. His financial situation improved rapidly as he served as legal counsel to the Cincinnati branch of the Bank of the United States, the city's largest financial institution. Chase would never again lack material resources, cementing his social and economic standing with a good marriage into an influential Cincinnati family.

It is not clear why this rising young lawyer, apparently conservative in every way, decided in 1837 to take the case of a young woman named Matilda, alleged to be a runaway slave, who was living in the household of the controversial antislavery editor James G. Birney. Did the mobs that had rampaged through Cincinnati's defenseless black community and now threatened Birney offend his conservative love of order? Did an antislavery stand reaffirm his patrician New England origins, reflecting the genteel antislavery of its elite? Was his rigid Victorian morality shocked by the possibility that the slave-owner seeking Matilda's return may have been her father? Was he more sensitive to the evil of slavery because Matilda was white, her grandmother being her only black forebear?

If the antislavery that characterized New England Federalism and Whiggery was genteel, it was tempered into stronger stuff in the furnace of the West. Only the Ohio River appeared to separate Cincinnati from slavery. In reality it was more a highway than a barrier; Cincinnati's commercial relations were entirely with the South. It is a tribute to Chase's ability to project a conservative image that he escaped the ostracism so many antislavery westerners endured in the 1830s and early 1840s. But from the time he took on Matilda's case, Chase was committed. He was a good lawyer and a better polemicist. His legal briefs and arguments against slavery were the most widely circulated in the country. He threw himself into antislavery politics.

One of the great paradoxes of Chase's political career is that despite his contempt for Andrew Jackson, his connection to the Bank of the United States, his Federalist heritage and orthodox New England background, despite the strength of antislavery sentiment in the Whig party and its weakness in the Democratic Party, Chase consistently and adamantly identified himself as an antislavery Democrat. It is remarkable how firmly Chase maintained this identification, only reluctantly accepting the appellation Republican rather than

Free Democrat as the new antislavery party was born. Throughout his career as a Republican, Chase would vigorously portray himself as the representative of the Democratic element of the party, even when his radicalism seemed to place him at the polar opposite of the racist, pro-southern Democracy Party.

As he became identified with antislavery, Chase led a small cadre of self-described independent, antislavery Democrats who worked in tense cooperation with a larger cadre of antislavery Whigs and the small, antislavery Liberty Party. In 1848 these elements combined to run former president Martin Van Buren as a "Free-Soil Democrat," dedicated to barring slavery from United States territories acquired from Mexico. Although the Free-Soilers could not elect Van Buren, they did elect eleven candidates to the Ohio state legislature. This gave them the balance of power in the closely contested body, which was due to elect a United States senator in 1849. After a long deadlock, Chase secured the place as part of a deal between two of his antislavery supporters in the legislature and the Democratic Party—a deal that outraged the other nine antislavery legislators, who wanted to cooperate with the Whigs. But the arrangement also led to the repeal of highly symbolic laws designed to discourage black immigration into the state and to African American access to the public school system—although generally on a segregated basis. Chase hoped it was the beginning of the process that would turn the northern Democracy Party into an antislavery party.

In his effort to increase political support for the antislavery cause, Chase tried to make antislavery nominations and platforms more pragmatic. Chase was among the organizers of the new Republican Party in 1854 and 1855, at first referring to the movement as one of "Independent Democrats." As the new party organized, Chase left the Senate to serve as a successful Republican governor of Ohio from 1855 to 1859, encouraging political allies who launched strong but unsuccessful campaigns to secure him the Republican presidential nominations of 1856 and 1860.

III

As historians have recognized, in the course of his pre–Civil War career, Chase became the most important exponent of the mainstream antislavery constitutional argument.[15] But even those who have attended more closely to Chase's antislavery constitutionalism have missed its implications for protecting black rights after emancipation. A closer look helps to explain how and why traditional American constitutional commitments limited efforts to empower the national government to protect the rights of American citizens.

It is natural for analysts to identify antislavery agitation with a strong federal government, determined to overthrow slavery through national action, and to think of state rights as the slave-owners' defensive bulwark against federal legislation. This conception is reinforced by the fact that the most important specific issue involving slavery was its extension in United States territories. After 1846, antislavery northerners demanded that Congress fully exercise its constitutional power to "make all needful Rules and Regulations respecting the Territory . . . belonging to the United States" (U.S. Constitution, Art. IV, sec. 3) to ban slavery there.

But the situation was far more complex. Proslavery southerners ultimately responded to the pressure for "free soil" in the territories by demanding that the federal government pass a slave code applicable in all of them, repudiating the deal, embodied in the Missouri Compromise of 1820, whereby northerly territories would be free while southerly ones would countenance slavery. This demand was part of a general pattern by which southerners construed federal power to interfere with slavery narrowly but construed federal power to promote and defend it broadly.[16] The most egregious examples were the Fugitive Slave Acts of 1793 and 1850.[17] These were essentially federal extensions of southern slave codes into the North. The earlier law was designed to facilitate the reclamation of runaways. The second was passed to circumvent northern laws that provided procedural protections for those alleged to be fugitives and to overcome the reluctance of northern state authorities to aid in their capture.

Chase devised his antislavery constitutional argument in response to the first of these fugitive slave laws. Chase insisted that the nation's founders had recognized the natural right of human beings to liberty in the Declaration of Independence and myriad other enactments.[18] Citing English and American cases that declared freedom the natural state of persons under the common law,[19] Chase insisted that only positive laws could establish slavery. Wherever they failed to do so, liberty was the rule. Nowhere did the Constitution refer to slavery, he pointed out. Indeed, the framers had used convoluted euphemisms to avoid countenancing it. Even the so-called Fugitive Slave Clause of the Constitution referred only to persons "held to Service or Labour in one State . . . escaping into another" (Art. IV, sec. 2). Thus the Constitution completely divorced the federal government from the barbaric institution. Insofar as the government of the United States was concerned, all persons were entitled to liberty. The Fifth Amendment enjoined it from depriving any person of that liberty except by due process of law. Thus the Bill of Rights should have precluded Congress from countenancing a slave code in Washington, D.C. There could be no slave code for the territories. Nor could Congress pass a law authorizing the recovery of fugitive slaves. Chase's rule, adopted by the antislavery movement as a whole, was "Freedom National, Slavery Local."[20]

Chase acknowledged that the "Fugitive from Labour" Clause of Article IV referred to slaves, but he denied that the framers had intended it to empower Congress to legislate to protect slavery. The clause appeared in Article IV of the Constitution, which dealt with matters of interstate relations and comity. The Constitution had been framed both to create a national government and to "adjust and settle certain matters of right and duty, between the states," Chase argued. "These different ends of the constitution . . . are entirely distinct in their nature. . . . The clauses of compact confer no powers on the government; and the powers of government cannot be exerted, except in virtue of express provisions, to enforce the matters of compact."[21] Like the Full Faith and Credit and the Privileges and Immunities clauses, which also appeared in Article IV, the Fugitive Slave Clause was a compact among the states, to be enforced solely by their own voluntary action. "The parties to the agreement are the states. The general government is not a party to it, nor affected by it."[22]

In 1842, the Supreme Court repudiated Chase's argument in *Prigg v. Pennsylvania*,[23] sustaining the constitutionality of the Fugitive Slave Act of 1793 and striking down state laws and actions inconsistent with it. But it also handed antislavery forces a practical victory by declaring that the federal government could not require state officers and judges to aid in its enforcement. Federal courts and officers were few and far between in the antebellum United States; slavecatchers had depended almost entirely on ubiquitous local courts and constables. Relying on *Prigg*, many northern states barred state and local officers from enforcing the federal act. Where still permitted to aid in enforcement, more and more state judges refused to certify the removal of alleged runaways.[24]

The Fugitive Slave Act of 1850 was designed to circumvent this resistance. It authorized the appointment of as many fugitive-slave commissioners as necessary to enforce the Act efficiently and denied alleged fugitives the right to present any evidence in the proceedings. It made federal officials liable to slaveowners if they failed to enforce the law, and it subjected anyone who obstructed the seizure and transport of alleged runaways to criminal penalties and civil damages. Chase and other antislavery people blasted the law as an exercise of undelegated power and for violating due process rights protected by the Bill of Rights. Opponents of slavery harassed slavecatchers with writs of habeas corpus, kidnapping charges, civil suits for damages, and rescues.[25] In response, Democratic leaders in the Senate proposed a law authorizing anyone claiming rights under a federal law to transfer his or her case to the federal courts.[26] It was precisely the sort of removal act that Republicans would utilize to protect the rights of African Americans and other American citizens after the Civil

War.²⁷ Chase, serving in the Senate, bitterly opposed it. It was "a bill for the overthrow of State rights," he thundered. "It is a step, let me say a stride rather, towards despotism." It was "the complete humiliation of the States."²⁸

Chase's great contribution to the antislavery constitutional argument, then, was not a brief for the exercise of federal power on behalf of liberty but a defense of the right of the states to protect the liberty of their citizens against other citizens claiming rights under federal authority. He was arguing against the constitutionality of federal enactments designed to enable American citizens to exercise their rights in a hostile environment. The American citizens were slave-owners and the right was to recover runaway slaves, but the argument cut both ways. If Chase's argument denied the constitutionality of federal laws protecting the rights of slave-owners to recover runaway slaves, it also denied the constitutionality of any law the federal government might have passed to secure "the citizens of each State" the "Privileges and Immunities of Citizens in the several States." As Chase construed federal power, there was nothing Congress could do to counteract southern and western state laws barring African American settlers from other states, laws forbidding black seamen from going ashore in southern ports, or mob action preventing northern lawyers from coming South to lodge cases in federal court challenging the discriminations. If Congress could enforce the Fugitive Slave Clause, it could enforce the Privileges and Immunities Clause, he had warned southerners. Were they "prepared to adopt the broad proposition . . . that wherever the Constitution confers a right or enjoins a duty, a power arises to the Federal Government to enforce [it]?" he asked. "Is it not obvious that it will open a new and very copious source of powers to the General Government; and that it must tend towards the subversion of the rights of the States, and the establishment of a consolidated central power, dangerous to their independence and sovereignty?"²⁹

The implications—and the differences among Republicans on the issue—are clear from an exchange between Lincoln and Chase in 1859. Feeling out Lincoln's views, Chase hoped that Illinois Republicans would second the Ohio Republican Party's call to repeal the Fugitive Slave Act of 1850. (Chase was hoping to ride the issue to the 1860 Republican nomination.) Opposition to the Fugitive Slave Act "illustrated strikingly the leading ideas" of the two parties, he urged. It contrasted "the centralizing tendency towards consolidated despotism of the selfstyled democracy" with the Republicans' "liberal bias toward constitutional Liberty for States & Persons."³⁰ Lincoln's response showed the difference between his Whiggish constitutional nationalism and Chase's orientation toward state rights. "My view . . . is, simply this," Lincoln explained. "Whatever the constitution says *'shall be done'* and has omitted saying who shall do it, the government established by that constitution, ex *vi termini*, is vested with the power of doing." The execution of such constitutional mandates could not be left to the states. After all, "the constitution was adopted, in great part, in order to get a government which could execute it's own behests, in contradistinction to that under the Articles of confederation, which depended, in many respects, upon the States, for its' execution."[31]

Unlike Chase, Lincoln believed that having a constitutional right imposed a duty on the government to see that one could exercise it. In contrast to Chase, Lincoln consistently acknowledged the obligation of Congress to provide a fugitive-slave law. "There is a Constitutional right which needs legislation to enforce it. And although it is distasteful to me, I have sworn to support the Constitution, and having so sworn I cannot conceive that I do support it if I withheld from that right any necessary legislation to make it practical."[32] Thus Lincoln the conservative was more likely than Chase the radical to find constitutional power to protect rights. Chase denied that Congress had any power to enforce the Privileges and Immunities Clause; in his first inaugural address, Lincoln called for legislation to do so.[33]

Even where Chase advocated federal action, his argument was strict constructionist. By "Freedom National, Slavery Local," he meant "the disconnection of the National Government from all support of Slavery, and the exercise of its legitimate influence on the side of freedom."[34] Therefore he urged Congress to abolish slavery in the territories and Washington, D.C. He wanted to ban the interstate slave trade. He wanted to forbid slavery on forts, ships, and other federal property. But the argument was negative. As a violation of natural rights, slavery could only be instituted by positive law, he insisted, and the Constitution did not delegate power to Congress to establish it. "Our government is one of enumerated and specific powers," he averred. "Among them, we find none to legislate upon slavery. . . . On the contrary, the whole matter of slavery seems to have been carefully excluded from national legislation, and left to the disposal of the state sovereignties."[35] In Chase's view, the abolition of slavery in Washington, D.C. and the territories would not be the discretionary exercise of a constitutional power, but the repeal of an unconstitutional exercise of power.

Chase's commitment to state rights was consistent with his self-identification as an antislavery Democrat. So, he thought, was his advocacy of equal rights for all Americans, black and white. He was, he affirmed, "a Democrat, recognizing and well known to recognize the duty of carrying out Democratic principles in their practical application to every subject of legislation." "Equal rights" was a watchword of the Democratic party, and he was a Democrat who refused "to except slavery from the universal and impartial application of those principles."[36]

Many of the Republicans who went into the Civil War with Chase's constricted view of the federal government's responsibility to secure constitutional rights came out of it with Lincoln's capacious view. The Civil War demonstrated that federal power could be utilized on behalf of liberty as effectively as on behalf of slavery. Having been subjected for four years to Chase's pressure to take radical antislavery action, Lincoln must have expected him to have undergone the same conversion. Chase was still well known to be more radical on war and slavery issues than Lincoln himself.

IV

Contemporaries regarded Chase as a great antislavery lawyer, constitutionalist, and chief justice of the Supreme Court. Upon his death, lawyers viewed the decisions rendered in his term as equal in importance to those of the Marshall court. As one of them wrote, "None of his predecessors were ever called upon to consider questions so grave, so pervading and far-reaching in their consequences . . . questions which go to the foundation and structure of the government, and touch its very right to exist."[37] But his career is little known among legal scholars now. His name does not appear when historians and legal scholars list the great justices.[38] He was not included among the justices portrayed in the American Bar Association's *The Supreme Court and Its Justices*,[39] drawn to mark the bicentennial of the Constitution from portraits that had appeared over the years in the *ABA Journal*. Felix Frankfurter titled his influential history *The Commerce Clause Under Marshall, Taney, and Waite*,[40] as if Chase had never served as chief justice. He is one of the few chief justices to have no book written about his judicial career—Fred M. Vinson and Warren Burger are the others—although specialists are familiar with David F. Hughes's quite good doctoral dissertation,[41] and constitutional historian Harold M. Hyman recently published a brief account of aspects of his judicial role in Reconstruction.[42]

Despite the apparent radicalism of his political career, Chase proved relatively conservative on the bench, as did the Republican justices who served with him. This was a relief to lawyers. There was real potential for destabilizing the ordinary commercial relationships essential to maintaining the southern economy. Southern courts were instruments of governments whose illegitimacy lay at the foundation of the Civil War. A radical might have held their decisions and the ordinary legal rights based upon them void. Contracts for which slaves or Confederate currency had been the consideration were vulnerable to attack.

The potential for revolutionizing federalism was just as troubling. Republicans trying to protect civil and political rights in the postwar South faced the same resistance, carried to even greater extremes, than proslavery legislators had faced in trying to secure the rights of slave-owners to recover fugitive slaves. Among the tools Republicans utilized were the same procedures for removing cases to federal courts that Chase had condemned when proposed by Democrats in the 1850s. Moreover, the rights Republicans sought to protect went much further than the right to recover runaway slaves. Federal laws to protect the rights secured by the Fourteenth Amendment made federal crimes of offenses traditionally at the heart of state jurisdiction. The limits that the Amendment itself placed on the states threatened to subject nearly every state law to challenge on federal constitutional grounds.

The first generation of lawyers and historians to assess Chase and his court praised its restraint. Chase was "by no means" a radical, his protégé, Ohio Governor George Hoadly, eulogized. Despite his reputation for political radicalism, "by disposition and education he was a conservative. His function was not that of a destroyer, but a restorer."[43] Neither Warden nor fellow biographer James W. Schuckers paid much attention to Chase's career as chief justice. Albert Bushnell Hart provided a good overview in his 1899 biography, observing with approval that the Chase court "inherited the conservative spirit of its predecessors" and that "Chase's influence bore for caution and restraint, and not for radical changes."[44] Charles Warren quoted Hart in his *Supreme Court in United States History*, the most influential constitutional history of the early twentieth century, noting that Chase's course proved once again "that even in times of stress, the men who ascended the Supreme Bench, dropped 'their politics when they assumed the black robes.'" Chase was "not only a great lawyer, but a great statesman."[45]

Warren echoed turn-of-the-century historians in portraying a bitter conflict between the Court and the Congress that forced radical Reconstruction on the South.[46] The radicals attacked the justices, according to Warren, using "revolutionary methods"[47] to deprive the Court of jurisdiction over threatening cases and ultimately proposing "to destroy the constitutional function of the Court."[48] The struggle petered out as the last of the southern states returned to normal relations in the Union. By the 1930s historians reinterpreted this tension between Court and Congress into an institutional assault upon the Court by radical Republicans intent on achieving congressional supremacy in the government, a view that remained dominant among historians into the 1960s; only the Court's retreat and acquiescence saved it.[49]

According to historians writing in the first half of the twentieth century, it was this drive for legislative supremacy that led to the impeachment of President Andrew Johnson. They denounced that episode as the gravest excess of post–Civil War Republican radicalism.[50] The chief justice played a leading and crucial role. The great historian James Ford Rhodes described the impression he made: "Chase, distinguished in appearance, of great natural dignity, easily conscious of the awe and veneration inspired by the Chief Justice of the Supreme Court, made an imposing presiding officer."[51] Nowhere did Chase demonstrate his judicial statesmanship as clearly as in the impeachment trial, according to his early biographers. "At no time in his life did he show more calmness, good judgment, and foresight," Hart wrote, "and for his effort to raise the proceedings above a partisan investigation . . . he deserves the credit of averting a great public danger."[52]

As historians' attitudes toward the radical Republicans changed, so did their understanding of the Republicans' relationship with the Supreme Court. Rather than a defensive institution, avoiding conflict with the congressional juggernaut, they have described a confident and activist Court, wisely avoiding conflict with Congress over essentially political questions. This is the tenor of Charles Fairman's volume on the Chase Court in the Oliver Wendell Holmes Devise History of the Supreme Court, which is the most thorough and detailed study.[53] Moreover, far from assaulting the federal courts, Congress dramatically expanded their jurisdiction. It created new, specialized courts. It passed laws permitting federal officers to remove cases brought against them from state to federal courts, when the cases grew out of official actions. It authorized similar removals when defendants claimed rights under the Constitution or federal laws. "The Court was not bashful about accepting its enhanced role and powers," observes a leading recent chronicler.[54] By the end of Reconstruction, concludes another, "the Court stood stronger than ever, and at the threshold of its own heyday of power and glory."[55]

While turn-of-the-century commentators praised the Supreme Court's conservatism on Civil War and Reconstruction issues, modern analysts see the Chase court's seminal decision in *The Slaughterhouse Cases* as the first step by which the justices betrayed the egalitarian promise of the postwar amendments. According to the view dominant since the 1960s, the Court, in "one of the most blatant examples of judicial legislation in the Court's history . . . nullified a revolution in American constitutionalism."[56] Chase wins praise not for encouraging this conservative reaction but for joining the dissent.[57]

Chase was a powerful personality who consistently tried to influence those around him. Even his bitter enemy Rutherford B. Hayes recognized his "commanding presence."[58] His correspondence is filled with missives to superiors, colleagues, and protégés exhorting them to various actions. His effort to persuade Lincoln and Illinois Republicans to endorse the repeal of the Fugitive Slave Act, noted above, is just one example.[59] There is no doubt that as chief justice he tried to lead his colleagues on the Supreme Court. "One of the elements of his strength was that he was always 'thoroughly persuaded' before he acted," his colleague Justice William Strong remembered, and that explained his "imperious manner."[60] But leadership is most potent when directed at how best to achieve shared goals. Chase was not much interested in questions of ordinary law, except for issues related to the international law relating to wartime blockades. Prize cases were the only area of nonconstitutional law in which he assigned many opinions to himself, at first taking an expansive view of a belligerent's power to interdict shipping[61] but later rejecting many seizures and libels, a development that paralleled his growing public commitment to restoring good feelings North and South.[62]

Chase was far more interested in areas of constitutional law. But in those dearest to Chase's heart, constitutional issues relating to Reconstruction and to currency, the Court was badly divided. Justice Samuel F. Miller recollected that Chase's colleagues "quietly and courteously . . . resisted his imperious will," and Chase had to settle for the role of "Moderator and presiding officer . . . not possessed of any more authority than the rest of the Bench chose to give him."[63] His position of leadership was weakened further when he suffered a stroke in August 1870. Chase did not return to the bench until the spring of 1871, and he never fully regained his faculties.

V

Perceived as a radical because of his commitment to racial justice, Chase in fact had not kept pace with other Republicans, who concluded that it was necessary to empower the federal government to protect constitutional rights. Faced with an apparent fait accompli on the part of Lincoln's successor, Andrew Johnson, who had facilitated the reorganization of state governments in the South on a white-voter-only basis, Republicans shied away from black suffrage in 1866. Instead they passed the Civil Rights Act,[64] which defined citizenship to include African Americans and secured equality in basic civil rights to all. This effort to protect the basic civil rights of the freed people led to a break with Johnson, who was committed both to white supremacy and to the states' exclusive power to define the rights of their inhabitants. To settle the war issues, Republicans then proposed the Fourteenth Amendment, which among other things wrote the Civil Rights Act's definition of citizenship into the Constitution, forbade states from infringing upon fundamental rights or denying the equal protection of the laws, and authorized Congress to enforce its provisions. But Chase thought this "rather too big a contract." Although he claimed to think the broader proposition "all very well, if it can be carried out," he may have revealed his deeper reservations when he wondered, "Will not these propositions be received with some alarm by those who, though opponents of secession or nullification, yet regard the real rights of the States as essential to the proper working of our complex system?"[65] He had urged nothing more than a ban on the payment of the Confederate debt and a reduction of southern-state representation in Congress as long they denied African Americans the right to vote.[66]

In sum, at war's end Chase wanted to instill changes in the southern states *before* their restoration to normal relations in the Union, before they were once more entitled to state rights. As Chase later explained his position, "Becoming freemen, the emancipated people became necessarily citizens . . . as citizens they were entitled to be consulted in respect to reorganization, and to the means of self-protection by suffrage."[67] Restore the southern states to their rightful place in the Union with all their (male) citizens enfranchised, Chase insisted, and all would be well. There would be no need for intrusive federal supervision. If only President Johnson had reorganized the southern state governments upon this basis, he lamented in 1866, "can it now be doubted that the practical relations of every State in the Union would have been already reestablished, and with the happiest consequences?"[68]

Chase's commitment to equal political rights was enough to maintain his reputation for radicalism in the early years of Reconstruction. As Johnson and Seward, who continued to sustain the president after he broke with the party, were discredited as potential Republican candidates for the presidency in 1868, Chase emerged as the frontrunner. Despite his earlier hesitation, he came around to the idea that the federal government must have the power to protect the civil and political rights of its citizens. On circuit he upheld the Civil Rights Act as a constitutional exercise of Congress's power under the Thirteenth Amendment.[69] He still pressed for black suffrage. Privately, he opined that the Thirteenth Amendment authorized Congress to enfranchise African Americans by simple legislation. "Is not *suffrage* the best security against *slavery* and *involuntary servitude*?" he asked. "Is not the legislation which provides the best security the most *appropriate*?"[70]

When southerners, encouraged by the truculent Johnson, rejected the Fourteenth Amendment, Republicans finally concluded that they had to impose black suffrage if they were to restore the southern States to the Union without undue delay. To supervise the Reconstruction process, the Republican Congress turned to the army. The Reconstruction Act of 1867 declared the governments created under President Johnson's authority provisional, and the South was put under the control of military commanders instructed to superintend the organization of new governments by constitutional conventions elected by both black and white voters.⁷¹ Chase helped write the supplementary legislation specifying the process in greater detail.⁷²

The Republican endorsement of equal suffrage, the measure with which Chase was most conspicuously identified, solidified his position as the likely Republican presidential nominee in 1868. Determined to prevent it, his enemies brought General Ulysses S. Grant forward as a conservative alternative, known for his moderation on Reconstruction issues. Faced with this challenge from the army's highest-ranking officer, Chase began to hint that he disapproved of the Reconstruction Act's reliance on the military for its administration.⁷³ At the same time, he began to stress his desire for reconciliation with former Confederates.

His delay in holding circuit court for the trial of Jefferson Davis on charges of treason began to look like an expression of his desire for amnesty, especially after his close ally, Horace Greeley, the owner and editor of the *New York Tribune*, put up Davis's bail.⁷⁴ The following month Chase offered an exegesis on amnesty from the bench. In *Shortridge & Co. v. Macon*⁷⁵ he confirmed that waging war against the United States was treason; the fact that the Confederacy had acquired the status of a de facto belligerent did not exculpate offenders. But

> wise governments never forget that the criminality of individuals [does] not always or often equal that of the acts committed by the organization with which they are connected. Many are carried into rebellion by sincere thought and mistaken convictions. . . . When the strife of arms is over, and such governments . . . address themselves mainly to the work of conciliation and restoration, and exert the prerogative of mercy . . . complete remission is usually extended to large classes by amnesty.⁷⁶

But Chase's efforts to counteract Grant's candidacy proved fruitless. When Republicans lost ground in the state elections of 1867, frightened party leaders interpreted the result as a repudiation of radicalism. Chase's support collapsed in the rush to Grant.⁷⁷ Disappointed, Chase began his drift toward the Democrats.

It was in this frame of mind that Chase entered his duties as presiding officer of the impeachment trial of Andrew Johnson, where he did everything he could to undermine the Republican position. Chase played his cards masterfully to enhance his role at the trial. His success was an important ingredient in stressing the judicial rather than political aspect of impeachment, badly damaging the Republican efforts to place Johnson's offenses in a political context where, in my opinion, it belonged. Chase created a trial-like environment in which such efforts looked more and more partisan and out of place, eroding public support for Johnson's removal. When the Senate failed to convict Johnson, Chase received a good deal of the credit and the blame.[78]

Chase's course as presiding officer in the impeachment trial and rumors that he opposed much of the Republican Reconstruction program led influential Democrats to contact him about their party's nomination. Remarkably oblivious to the ethical problem involved in negotiating with the Democrats as he presided over the impeachment, Chase became deeply enmeshed in an ultimately unsuccessful effort to secure the nomination. Conservative eastern Democrats, attracted to Chase's hard-money views, put him forward to stop the likely nomination of the inflationist, radically anti-Reconstruction Ohioan George H. Pendleton. There seems little question that Chase's desire for their presidential nomination blinded him to the danger that Democrats would use his great reputation for their own ends, betraying his ideals upon achieving power.[79]

As he maneuvered to secure the prize, Chase became ever more critical of the Republican Reconstruction program. He insisted that he had always favored "universal amnesty" as well as "universal suffrage." But this was at best an exaggeration. The Reconstruction legislation he helped to write in 1867 temporarily banned many ex-Confederates from voting. At that time he was urging white southerners to cooperate in Reconstruction "upon the basis of universal suffrage and equal rights for all,"[80] not upon "universal suffrage and universal amnesty." He had wanted amnesty "just as soon as magnanimity can be indulged with reasonable certainty that equal rights for all will not be endangered thereby."[81] Nonetheless, in letters to Democrats and to his shocked friends, Chase now insisted that he had been concerned all along about the centralization and militarization of American government.[82]

As Chase dallied with leading Democrats in the spring of 1868, observers wondered whether he had shaped his course on the bench to serve his political ambitions. But Chase did not have to tailor his judicial opinions to his political aspirations. The plain fact was that his judicial positions inevitably had political implications. Because of his political stature, his appointment to the Supreme Court did not remove him from the political calculations of the day, and Chase never rejected the possibility that he might leave the bench for yet higher office. Quite the contrary, the activity of his Republican friends from 1865 to 1867 and his political discussions with a wide group of Democratic correspondents in 1868 made his willingness to serve quite apparent. As he perceived the situation, he was taking positions on issues of political consequence, and if those who shared his positions wanted him to run for the presidency, he would be happy to do so. As he wrote in the letter that so many observers and historians discounted, "I worked for ideals and principles and measures embodying them;

and was always quite willing to take place, or be left out of place, as the cause, in the judgment of its friends, required."[83]

Still, all those letters explaining his position to Democrats simply were not discreet. As indicated above, his friend and biographer Warden thought Chase deceived himself about his feelings. Others, like his colleague Miller, were more offended and their judgment was harsher. But Chase's willingness to be considered for the presidency while on the Court does not mean that he tailored his opinions to his political possibilities. Rather, his judicial opinions and positions made him a leading representative of public policies with widespread appeal.

Democrats had been uniformly and rigidly opposed to Republican Reconstruction policies, appealing to Americans' commitment to states' rights and to their racism.[84] At the same time, Civil War financial and banking policies created a deflationary shortage of currency in the states west of Pennsylvania and in the South. Many Democrats in those states abandoned their party's traditional commitment to specie currency and advocated an inflated paper currency and uncontrolled, so-called free banking rather than the new system of national banks created under Chase's administration of the Treasury Department.[85]

By 1868, some of the leaders of the Democratic Party, especially in New York, recoiled from the growing radicalism of their party. With the inflationists strongly identified with root-and-branch opposition to the Republican reconstruction program, the hard-money Democrats urged acceptance of the results of the war, including equal rights, coupled with opposition to further federal intervention in the South and support for traditional Democratic hard-money currency policies. They tried to convince other Democratic party activists that the only way to return to national power was to make this "new departure," as it would later be called. This would attract the support of Republicans who were dissatisfied with some of the consequences of Radical Reconstruction, win over undecided voters who believed some changes in the South essential, and retain the support of eastern Democrats alienated by inflationary proposals. Because of the positions Chase had taken on and off the court, his nomination would be the best way to symbolize the change.[86]

It was this record that made Chase a logical representative of the policy advocated by the hard-money, eastern Democratic moderates. They were also encouraged by the fact that after entering third-party antislavery politics, Chase had always advocated coalitions with Democrats in preference to Whigs. He had often referred to himself and his allies as the "Independent Democracy" and the "Free Democrats."[87] Within the Republican Party his firmest allies had been ex-Democrats, especially in Ohio and New York.[88] As rumors of discussions between Chase and leading Democrats percolated, some Republican radicals were convinced that there was a conspiracy among Johnson, Democrats, and the seven Republican senators who had broken with their colleagues over impeachment to nominate Chase as the presidential candidate of a coalition of dissident Republicans and Democrats.[89]

Democratic leaders carefully sounded out Chase's opinions on future Reconstruction policy. Satisfied with his answers, they artfully planned a strategy to secure him the 1868 Democratic nomination. Hard-line inflationist Democrats frustrated these machinations at the Democratic national convention, and the Democrats went down to defeat in the ensuing congressional and presidential elections.[90] By 1869 Chase represented the road not taken and was a formidable candidate for the 1872 nomination. After a spontaneous Chase demonstration in the Tammany Society Wigwam, the *New York Herald* pronounced him "far ahead of all other competitors" among the Democratic rank and file.[91] At the same time Chase came to represent Republicans who had been thoroughly antislavery but who now favored a liberal amnesty for ex-Confederates and worried about centralization, militarism, and southern Republican radicalism. When these dissidents launched the Liberal Republican movement in 1872, one of its leaders would call Chase "the father of the party."[92]

Chase's activities on the bench continued to make him the leading representative of moderation on Reconstruction and a potential candidate who could appeal both to Democrats and to Republicans who favored liberality toward the South—people who by 1869 were beginning to be called "liberal Republicans." In November 1868, after the presidential election and several months after the ratification of the Fourteenth Amendment, Jefferson Davis's lawyers moved to have his treason indictment quashed, arguing that the office-holding disqualification of its third section repealed the treason statute under which the indictment was brought. Chase and the district court judge sitting with him certified their disagreement over this farfetched argument, sending the question to the Supreme Court. Chase let it be known that he had favored the defense motion.[93] At the same time he suspended the Test Oath for grand jurors in his circuit, saying that too many good grand jurors scrupled to take it. Greeley's *Tribune* gave his action front-page attention.[94]

In May 1869, as Virginia's radical Republicans struggled to prevent a coalition of liberal Republicans and Democrats from gaining control of the state as it emerged from military occupation, Chase quashed a campaign by Virginia radicals to force the resignation of all ex-Confederate state officials continuing to hold office in violation of the disqualification section of the Fourteenth Amendment. Failing to persuade President Grant to order the military commander to remove the offending officials, the radicals sought a writ of habeas corpus to release a felon convicted in a trial presided over by a judge disqualified from holding office. Radical District Court Judge John C. Underwood granted it. Chase immediately intervened. In what a scholar calls a "frankly bullying" letter,[95] he forced Underwood to reverse himself and join Chase's decision that the disqualification section of the Amendment was not self-executing and could be enforced only by congressional legislation.[96] Construing the Amendment to dislodge all officials for their past actions smacked of a bill of attainder and ex post facto law.[97] The following month Chase charged a grand jury that the sanction of the Confederate government excused acts of a strictly military character, rendering their perpetrators immune from prosecution.[98]

Grateful southern Democrats recollected that "a short time sufficed to dispel all doubts" they had entertained about how Chase's legal rulings would affect them:

> Rising at once to the greatness of the occasion, he deliminated and declared ... principles of public law ... which operated as amnesty, peace, and security for life and property.... [H]is decisions ... did more to restore confidence, to reconstruct our shattered institutions, and rehabilitate peace than all other acts of all other functionaries.[99]

The *New York Herald* observed that "Chief Justice Chase, in his tour of the Southern States, is gaining golden opinions from all the anti-radical Southern elements, and, plank by plank, is building up a strong democratic platform for 1872."[100]

Democrats also found Chase's view of federalism attractive. Reconciling federal power to restore the South with his old commitment to state rights, in 1869 Chase wrote his conception of the Union into American constitutional law. In his great opinion in *Texas v. White*,[101] he denied that states could secede. Like Lincoln,[102] he insisted that the Union was older than the Constitution. "The Union of the States was never a purely artificial and arbitrary relation," he wrote. "It began among the Colonies, and grew out of common origin, mutual sympathies, kindred principles, similar interests, and geographic relations. It was confirmed and strengthened by the necessities of war and received definite form, and character, and sanction from the Articles of Confederation." The Articles "solemnly declared" the Union to be "perpetual," and the Constitution was expressly ordained to form "a more perfect Union." "It is difficult to convey the idea of indissolubility more clearly than by these words," Chase concluded. "What can be indissoluble if a perpetual Union, made more perfect, is not?"[103]

But if Chase repudiated secession, he also rejected the view of the most extreme radical Republicans that the attempt had destroyed the states, leaving them open to government as United States territories. There "can . . . be no loss of separate and independent autonomy of the States," he insisted. "The Constitution, in all its provisions, looks to an indestructible Union, composed of indestructible States."[104] Yet Chase also confirmed the power of Congress to provide for the reorganization of the state governments after the war. "When the war closed there was no government in the States except that which had been organized for the purpose of waging war against the United States." That government disappeared with the defeat of the Confederacy. "There being then no government in Texas in constitutional relations with the Union, it became the duty of the United States to provide for the restoration of such a government."[105]

Chase's opinion in *Texas v. White* both sustained congressional power over Reconstruction and reconfirmed the importance of state rights once the process was completed. He made the two sides of his opinion clear in a carefully and beautifully crafted statement: "[T]he preservation of the States, and the maintenance of their governments, are as much within the design and care of the Constitution as the preservation of the Union and the maintenance of the National government."[106] That language supported the government's right to subdue the rebellion; it recognized the government's responsibility to restore state government to the South; it also suggested that the Constitution mandated the protection of state sovereignty against federal encroachment.

The state-rights potential of Chase's formula was apparent in *Lane County v. Oregon*,[107] in which Chase ruled that Congress could not have intended the Legal Tender Act to have nullified state laws requiring taxes to be paid in specie. "Both the States and the United States existed before the Constitution," Chase wrote in a preview of *Texas v. White*, which would be decided two months later. "In many articles of the Constitution the necessary existence of the States, and, within their proper spheres, the independent authority of the States, is distinctly recognized," and "to the existence of the States, themselves necessary to the existence of the United States, the power of taxation is indispensable. It is an essential function of government."[108] Congress could not have subjected the states' taxing power to the Legal Tender Act if it had wanted to, he hinted. "There is nothing in the Constitution which contemplates or authorizes any direct abridgment of this power by national legislation."[109] Two years later, in *Collector v. Day*,[110] the Court would use similar reasoning to rule that state judges need not pay federal income tax. Relying on *Lane County*, the Court averred that American federalism posits "separate and distinct sovereignties, acting separately and independently of each other, within their respective spheres."[111] In this system, the federal government was not supreme. Rather, "the two governments are upon an equality."[112]

Chase was too ill to sit as the Court heard and decided *Blyew v. U.S.*[113] There the Court denied that the Civil Rights Act meant that a criminal case could be brought in federal court because black witnesses were not permitted to testify in Kentucky or because the victims of the crime were black. To hold otherwise could bring every case in the state to the federal courts, simply by alleging there were black witnesses. Likewise, in the seminal *Slaughterhouse Cases*,[114] the majority of the Court narrowly defined the privileges and immunities of citizens of the United States protected against state infringement by the Fourteenth Amendment. Using Chase's terms of analysis, it distinguished the rights associated with state citizenship from those associated with national citizenship. To do otherwise would revolutionize the federal system, the majority warned, encouraging people to challenge the constitutionality of almost any state legislation they opposed and "constitute this court a perpetual censor upon all legislation of the States."[115] Even worse, the enforcement clause of the Amendment would authorize Congress to intervene as well.[116] Despite the majority's appropriation of his terms of analysis, Chase, too weak to write his own opinion, joined the dissent. Still, it is not clear how firmly Chase would have sustained broad federal power to protect equal rights had he lived longer. Like many on the Court, he was torn between his desire to preserve the fruits of victory and to preserve the basics of the federal system as he had known it.[117]

Chase's calls for sectional reconciliation reinforced his standing with Democrats and dissident Republicans. Although Chase overembellished his early record on the issue, after 1868 he consistently and vigorously advocated amnesty. From that time on he took a broad view of the president's pardoning power. He wrote the opinion in the case of *Armstrong's Foundry*,[118] which held that amnesty purged former rebels of all guilt and entitled them to the return of their property unless the rights of third parties had intervened. In 1870 he held for a unanimous Court that pardoned ex-Confederates were purged of all taint of wrongdoing. Thus they could make claims for property seized by Union forces on the same basis as loyalists; Congress could not require claimants to take an oath that they had not aided the rebellion.[119] Congress responded by passing a law instructing the Court of Claims to regard pardons as conclusive proof of disloyalty and to dismiss claims by those who had accepted them. The law expressly withdrew the jurisdiction of the Supreme Court to hear appeals of such decisions. With Chase again writing the opinion, the unintimidated Court ruled the law an unconstitutional invasion of judicial authority.[120] At the end of his life, as he helped organize the reports of his circuit court cases, Chase punctuated his desire to overcome wartime bitterness, striking out the loaded words "rebellion" and "rebels" wherever the sense of the text would permit, and substituting "civil war" and "belligerents."[121]

Even more important to the South, Chase took the lead in repudiating the notion that the illegality of the Confederate governments rendered their court decisions void, or that contracts made in Confederate currency were unenforceable. His circuit court opinion in *Keppel's Administrators v. Petersburg Rail Road Company* recognized acts done by the Confederate state governments and the decisions of their courts as binding, as long as they were not directly in aid of the rebellion.[122] Chase reiterated his views for the whole Court in *Texas v. White*.[123] Likewise he spoke for the Court in sustaining the enforceability of contracts made in Confederate currency.[124] As already noted, he forcefully intervened when a radical Republican district judge prepared to release defendants convicted of crimes in state courts presided over by judges disqualified from holding office by the Fourteenth Amendment.[125] These decisions, a grateful southern lawyer said, reflected Chase's "clear perception of great principles" that "so greatly contributed to the peaceful reorganization of society in the South."[126]

Chase's decisions with regard to the currency likewise set out a political platform. He had always been a hard-money man. He had only with the greatest reluctance concluded that the federal government must issue a paper currency in excess of specie reserves and make it legal tender. He signaled his continued commitment to a specie-based currency in 1868, in his opinion for the court in *Bronson v. Rodes*.[127] Implicitly criticizing the Legal Tender Act for its "introduction of varying and uncertain measures of value"[128] to the heart of the financial system, he insisted that "gold and silver . . . are the only proper measures of value."[129]

To the amazement of contemporaries, Chase the chief justice overturned the work of Chase the secretary of the treasury. Chase had no doubt about the government's power to establish a paper currency—the so-called greenbacks; what he had always doubted, even as he exercised it, was its power to make that currency a "legal tender"—that is, to require creditors to accept it in payment of all debts. Forcing creditors to accept payment in a depreciated currency effectively redistributed wealth from creditor to debtor. Moreover, Democrats had always complained that the rich would hoard specie, while the poor would have to accept paper. Chase had resisted the measure as long as he could but had been forced to it.

At first Chase was successful in his effort to undo on the Court what he had done at the Treasury Department. In what seemed a great triumph, he delivered the Court's opinion ruling the Legal Tender Act itself unconstitutional.[130] Chase became the hero of eastern hard-money men. But his campaign ended in humiliation. Ulysses S. Grant, who had deprived him of the Republican nomination in 1868, deprived him of this victory as well. Two new Court appointees joined the dissenters to overturn the decision, over Chase's furious objections.[131]

While he denied that the national government could require creditors to accept greenbacks as legal tender, Chase remained a staunch proponent of the national banking system. When he sustained the federal tax on state-chartered bank currency in *Veazie Bank v. Fenno*,[132] he manifested his commitment to both positions, overcoming any state-rights scruples he might have considered. Again, his position linked him both to the conservative, hard-money wing of the Democratic party and to the liberal Republicans, who also shared his anti-inflationary views. Had he not been incapacitated by a stroke, Chase would have been a leading candidate for the Liberal Republican and Democratic presidential nomination in 1872, which instead went to his old ally, *New York Tribune* editor Horace Greeley.

Chase was a great man—a man of powerful convictions and strong passions. Convinced that he was right in his principles, Chase was determined to make them public policy. He was a master of constitutional politics, utilizing politics and law to achieve change. In this, Chase represents something profoundly, perhaps uniquely, American. Nowhere can popular commitment to fundamental constitutional principles be harnessed to secure political ends as they can in the United States. Nowhere else do the courts provide so powerful an alternative forum to executives and legislatures in which to advocate and secure social and economic rights and interests.

At the same time, Chase's career helps to explain why the effort to secure equal rights fell short after the Civil War. Chase embodied the ambivalence of the people of the North. Both out of humanitarian concern and in order to make the Union more secure, they wanted to guarantee the equal rights of the former slaves. But they wanted to do it within the framework of the old federal system. They wanted to empower the national government to protect rights without depriving the states of the primary responsibility for enforcing law and regulating society. If the Chase Court, under a vacillating chief justice, annulled a constitutional revolution, it was because Americans, like Chase himself, had wanted to reform the federal system, not revolutionize it.

8

The Problem of Constitutionalism and Constitutional Liberty in the Reconstruction South

As much as we venerate the Constitution, Americans must remember that it has no meaningful life of its own. Many nations have written constitutions, some of them guaranteeing more liberty than ours. Article 35 of the constitution of the People's Republic of China declares, "Citizens of the People's Republic of China enjoy freedom of speech, of the press, of assembly, of association, of procession and of demonstration." It did not prevent government troops from firing upon the tens of thousands who demonstrated for reform in Tiananmen Square in 1989, nor would it be wise for any public critic of the Communist government to rely on it today. It is not the text of a constitution but a community's commitment to the rule of law and principles of constitutional liberty that gives meaning to a written constitution. In the absence of such commitments, a constitution is no more than what its name indicates, a document that sets up an institutional framework of government—that "constitutes" it. South Carolina's able Republican governor Daniel Chamberlain, driven from office in the violent "Red Shirt" election of 1876, learned the lesson well. Evaluating his experience twenty-five years later, he wrote, "Rights, to be secure, must, in the last resort, rest on stronger supports than constitutions, statutes, or enrolled parchments."[1]

During Reconstruction, ten of the eleven Confederate states were required to frame new constitutions. Most had to do so twice—once under the prodding of President Abraham Lincoln or Andrew Johnson and again under the semi-compulsion of the congressional Reconstruction Acts. The resulting constitutions established governments similar in structure to those of other states and not terribly different from those established by preceding state constitutions or those that followed. As Kenneth M. Stampp realized years ago, "They were neither original nor unique."[2] Although several did concentrate a larger appointment power in the governor than was usual,[3] as a whole they established democratic procedures for electing government officials common to the states of the Union before Reconstruction and after. Yet, with the exception of Vir-

---

The original version of this essay was published in *An Uncertain Tradition: Constitutionalism and the History of the South*, ed. Kermit L. Hall and James W. Ely (Athens: University of Georgia Press, 1989), 225–49.

ginia, every one of these states witnessed transfers of government power accompanied by the kind of fraud and violence we now associate with third-world nations. In three of them—Arkansas, Louisiana, and South Carolina—there were what can only be described as insurrections (more than one in Louisiana) and civil war.[4] Conditions in Texas were similar in character but not degree.[5] In Mississippi and Alabama, and perhaps also Florida, the transfer of power from Republicans to Conservatives involved brutal violence and intimidation that approached civil war but probably fell short of a proper definition of it.[6]

Not only did violence accompany transfers of power in these states, but continued violence and fraud also eliminated viable political opposition. In Georgia, violence played a role in undermining the dominant party but probably was not determinative, and in North Carolina a similar campaign of violence led only to a partial transfer of power and did not destroy the opposition entirely.[7] In Tennessee, the transfer of power was accomplished through an open violation of the law, sponsored by the governor of the state.[8] Only in Virginia were political contests relatively fairly and freely conducted, and bitter complaints about intimidation emanated even from there.[9]

Conflict beyond the bounds of constitutional democracy occurred within state legislatures as well. The most extreme abuse was the attempted coup by Conservatives (that is, Democrats and former Whig opponents of Republicans allied with the national Democratic Party) in the Louisiana legislature in January 1875. The bitter election of 1874 resulted in an evenly balanced House of Representatives. Control would turn on which of the claimants were given five contested seats. Before a regular vote could be taken on organizing the House, the Conservative candidate for speaker seized the chair and gavel, claiming election on the basis of the votes of the Conservative contestants. He then announced the election of a Conservative clerk and sergeant at arms. Suddenly men who had forced their way into the chamber turned down their lapels, displaying badges marked "assistant sergeant at arms," and threw the Republican House officers out of the room. Forcibly detaining enough Republicans to make a quorum, the Conservatives then decided the disputed contests in favor of their claimants, securing a majority of the house. Republicans persuaded the commander of the federal garrison, which had been billeted in New Orleans to keep peace between the parties, to intervene. In what came to be known as "DeTobriand's Purge" (a reference to "Pride's Purge" of Parliament, which made Oliver Cromwell dictator), the commander ousted the Conservative claimants to the contested seats, restoring the status quo ante.[10]

Nearly as bad was the Conservative purge in 1869 of black Republicans elected to the Georgia state legislature and the seating of their defeated white Conservative rivals, on the grounds that the Georgia state constitution did not expressly authorize blacks to hold office. That purge precipitated a crisis in Georgia politics and Congress that led directly to the collapse of the Republican party in the state.[11] In North Carolina Conservatives converted the simple majority of legislative seats they had won in the Ku Klux Klan–influenced election of 1870 to a two-thirds majority by refusing to seat Republicans elected from districts where the Republican governor had sent militia to protect voters. They then proceeded to convict and remove him on flimsy articles of impeachment.[12] Conservatives forced Mississippi Republican governor Adelbert Ames from office on similarly flimsy charges after they secured control of the state legislature in the violent election of 1875.[13] After winning overwhelming majorities in the Georgia state legislature in 1871, Conservatives forced the Republican governor to resign under threat of impeachment and then called a special election to fill the vacancy, rather than permitting the Republican lieutenant governor to finish out the term.[14]

Conservative violence and chicanery engendered Republican responses that also transgressed the limits of constitutional government. The most obvious abuses occurred in the various boards authorized to count and confirm election returns. Convinced that black southerners uniformly voted Republican, Republican returning boards were quick to accept evidence that deviant returns were the result of violence or fraud. They were probably right, but the returning boards did not demand the kind of evidence that would compel that conclusion, and they were constituted in such a way as to invite charges of partisanship.[15] In Georgia, Republicans reacted to Conservative machinations by trying to persuade Congress arbitrarily to extend the term of the state legislature in new Reconstruction legislation.[16]

All of this occurred despite the trappings of constitutional government established by state constitutions. Plainly, southern white Conservatives did not concede those governments the legitimacy that a constitution is designed to impart, and Republicans were forced to take measures that subverted commitment to constitutional values in response.

Of course, one explanation is that most white southerners simply did not have a commitment to democratic and libertarian constitutional values. And that is how nearly all historians have portrayed them since the transformation of Reconstruction historiography of the mid-twentieth century.[17] But that certainly is not how southern Conservatives characterized themselves and their struggle. Reconstruction itself was "the betrayal of constitutional liberty," they insisted, "a crime against the principles of free government."[18] It was the Republican governments that were tyrannical and undemocratic. That is why white Louisianans in 1891 gave the name Liberty Monument to a memorial, located at Liberty Place, commemorating their unsuccessful effort to overthrow the Republican state government in 1874.[19] (And nothing could signal new attitudes better than the refusal of New Orleans authorities to restore the monument to its prominent location on Canal Street after it was removed "temporarily" for street repairs in 1989.[20]) It is time historians took seriously southerners' rhetoric and comprehended their resistance to Radical Reconstruction as a manifestation not merely of blind racism and class exploitation but also of the failure of the Republican constitutions and governments to secure constitutional legitimacy in the eyes of a large part of the population from which Republicans expected obedience.

Perhaps it is fatuous to suppose that Republicans could have established a constitutional system of government in the South that would have secured both the allegiance of white and black southerners. Had Republicans been willing to sacrifice the interests of the freedmen or to rely primarily on national power to protect their rights, it probably would have been possible to establish a constitutional basis for government acceptable to southern whites. But northern Republicans were willing neither to leave freedmen's interests in the hands of southern whites nor to transfer primary responsibility for protecting their rights to the national government. Nor would they simply exclude ex-Confederates from constitutional government by imposing massive disfranchisement. "We do not want oligarchies of professed Union men," they insisted.[21] "Our policy towards the mass of our enemies must be liberal. . . . Otherwise you nourish alienation and encourage the elements of treason and war."[22] The federal system gave the states the responsibility for protecting people against private wrongs, and Republicans did not want to change that fundamental principle—nor, they believed, could they retain political support if they tried. Ultimately, they determined that the best way to assure that states fulfilled the responsibility to protect their citizens was to establish systems of government in which blacks and whites shared power and to which they would recognize a common allegiance.[23]

It was skepticism about the possibility of establishing such a constitutional consensus that led more radical Republicans to urge long-term national supervision of the southern states as territories. "There are no symptoms that the people of these provinces will be prepared to participate in constitutional government for some years," Thaddeus Stevens said bluntly. Participating in territorial government under the watchful eye of Congress, southerners could "learn the principles of freedom."[24] Radicals urged radical land reform and the establishment of nationally supervised school systems. The idea was to establish a new social and economic system—"small farms, thrifty tillage, free schools, social independence, flourishing manufactures and the arts, respect for honest labor, and equality of political rights."[25] In such a society the consensus necessary for constitutional government might be established. Radicals understood, George W. Julian wrote later, "that no theories of democracy could avail unless adequately supported by a healthy public opinion. They saw that States must grow, and could not be suddenly constricted where materials were wanting."[26]

Republicans did not simply impose new governmental systems on the South. Many of the more conservative Republican congressmen urged their colleagues to make no specific provision for constitutional conventions at all. Simply refuse to recognize the southern states' restoration to normal relations in the Union until they voluntarily modified their constitutions to guarantee equal civil and political rights, they urged. "The formation of a State government must be the voluntary act of the people themselves."[27] In practical terms, conservative Republicans expected, this step would divide southern whites, with more moderate southerners urging the framing or amending of constitutions in a way that would satisfy Congress. Sooner or later they would be successful, and southern states would be restored with acceptable constitutions that had gained the support of a large proportion of the white population, as well as that of the black.

Ultimately, however, congressional Republicans rejected this advice. Radicals complained that it would give ex-rebels control over the pace of Reconstruction. All worried that if southern whites remained recalcitrant, impatient northerners might repudiate the Republican Party and turn to Andrew Johnson and the Democrats to end the stalemate. As a consequence, Republicans imposed a process for establishing new state governments. Yet they still left a good deal to voluntary southern action. Their Reconstruction legislation required southerners to vote on whether to hold constitutional conventions in the first place, to elect convention delegates, and then to ratify the constitutions proposed. These requirements were consistent with the Republicans' constitutional justification for their program: that the national government could hold the South in "the grasp of war" until its citizens voluntarily agreed to conditions of peace.[28] But they also corresponded to the procedure that had become customary throughout the country for establishing fundamental law, an embodiment—theoretically problematical, it is true—of the American conviction that government is based on a compact among the governed.[29] In fact, as originally conceived, ratification would have required the participation of an absolute majority of the registered voters in the ratification elections, as well as in the elections to call the constitutional conventions in the first place. The effect of this requirement was to increase the proportion of the population that would have to approve the new constitutions and to obligate an absolute majority to acquiesce in the new systems, on the principle that those given a fair opportunity to participate in a canvass are bound by the result.

However, Republicans also barred from registering and voting all men who had sworn to uphold the U.S. Constitution before the war and then joined the rebellion.[30] They mistakenly believed that this rule would disfranchise a relatively few men who prior to the rebellion had held higher-level federal offices, but in fact the restriction disfranchised large numbers of minor state and local officials as well.[31] Of course, people barred from participating in the process by which constitutions are established will hardly feel bound to support them. There is also no way to know how the participation of the disfranchised might have affected the results.[32] Moreover, the purpose of the disfranchisement was to deprive potential opponents of the new constitutions of their most experienced and senior political leaders. It was natural that even those who were not disfranchised might believe that ratification under such circumstances failed to reflect the considered will of the people.

Faced with the alternative of continued military supervision of government and the prospect of possibly more radical congressional action in the future, a significant number of southern white leaders did come out for ratification of new state constitutions. A larger number, however, urged whites to register and then abstain from voting, in order to deny backers the participation of the absolute majority of the registered electorate required for ratification. Had Republicans been willing to risk adhering to this element of their program, southern whites might have successfully defeated the new constitutions when initially proposed, as they did in Alabama, the first state to hold a ratification election. This result would have given Republicans a second opportunity to follow the course advocated by their more conservative wing: allow white southerners to defeat proposed constitutions until the moderates among them gained the upper hand, providing a firm, white base for new constitutional systems.

However, with Andrew Johnson working successfully to maintain Conservative control of the provisional governments, southern Republicans pleaded with their national allies to drop the absolute-majority requirement. The other course left them at the mercy of ex-rebels. In fact, as long as Johnson kept them in control of day-to-day administration, southern Conservatives preferred staying under military supervision to adopting constitutions that would give black-supported Republicans a real chance at power. There was a good chance that southern Conservatives might outwait northerners, many Republicans feared, precipitating Democratic victories in the North.

Rather than risk it, Republicans dropped the requirement. A simple majority in a ratification election, no matter what the total vote, would suffice to establish a new state constitution. They even applied the new requirement retroactively to Alabama, restoring the state to normal relations in the Union even though its people had rejected its constitution according to the rules in place when they voted.³³ Such a proceeding proved that "the constitution they impose is not the constitution of the people of Alabama, but a constitution of the minority of the whole people, and that, a negro minority," Alabama Conservatives averred.³⁴ In Arkansas news that Republicans had repealed the absolute-majority requirement arrived on the second day of the two-week ratification election. There too opponents had worked, apparently successfully, to persuade voters to abstain. Over twenty years later, William M. Fishback remembered the outrage with which he and other Conservative leaders had received the news. "Such an election could not be in any sense regarded as fairly expressing the wishes of the people of the state," he insisted.³⁵ Throughout the South, whites refused to vote either in the elections to call conventions or in the ratification elections.³⁶

The results were stark. Only in Virginia and North Carolina, among states for which the votes were published by race, did over 40 percent of the registered white voters even cast a ballot in the elections to hold conventions.³⁷ Evidence indicates the situation was much worse in the ratification elections. It suggests that in every state the vast majority of the votes sustaining the constitutions were cast by black southerners, although significant proportions of the white voters may have joined them in North Carolina and Georgia. The votes were not reported to Congress by race, but figures have been discovered for Louisiana parishes except New Orleans. In those parishes 40,409 of the 41,861 votes favoring ratification were cast by black voters.³⁸ A historian of Alabama Republicanism during Reconstruction has estimated that 62,000 of the approximately 68,000 votes in favor of that state's Reconstruction constitution were cast by freedmen.³⁹ Conservatives in Mobile, Alabama, published the names of those voting for ratification, listing 76 "White Renegades" among the 4,585 voters sustaining the constitution.⁴⁰

A racial division of such proportions over the fundamental law was bad enough. But because a constitution must ultimately win the acquiescence of its opponents in order to serve its legitimizing function, the failure of whites to vote at all was most ominous. The result was that Conservatives considered the ratification process a sham. Years later the Conservative North Carolina leader Zeb Vance lumped the disfranchised and those who had abstained together and repeated the conclusion that had undermined hopes for constitutional government in the South: "At least 40,000 citizens," he recalled, "by a pure fraud . . . [were] deprived of the right to vote for the Constitution of their choice."⁴¹

Yet when one considers the constitutions themselves, what is striking is how similar they were to previous southern state constitutions. It was a time of constitutional ferment in the northern states. Constitutional conventions there would soon establish new forms of regulatory agencies, at the same time severely limiting the general authority of state legislatures, restricting local autonomy, and also transferring a variety of municipal powers to the states. Almost none of these changes were reflected in the southern constitutions, which in many ways were the last of the Jacksonian documents, expanding suffrage and treating state legislatures as direct representatives of the people, rather than threats to them.[42] Only in Arkansas, Florida, and North Carolina did the Republicans who dominated the state conventions eschew reliance on earlier state charters. Mississippi's constitutional convention followed previous constitutional language establishing the executive branch and about half of the preexisting provisions on the judiciary, substantially altering the rest. In the other states, the framers followed earlier declarations of rights and articles establishing the legislative, executive, and judicial branches, largely repeating previous language word for word. In Tennessee, the 1834 constitution, amended by sections disfranchising rebels, abolishing slavery, and enfranchising freedmen, continued to serve as the state's fundamental law during Reconstruction. Although disfranchisement was agitated in nearly every convention, only four constitutions—those of Alabama, Arkansas, Louisiana, and Tennessee—incorporated any such provisions.[43] Most also expanded significantly on earlier articles dealing with education and corporations and attended in more detail to state finance and taxation. Some—especially Virginia's—made detailed modifications in local government or established special bureaus to promote immigration or land distribution.

The difference that enraged white southerners, of course, was the extension of civil and especially political rights to black southerners. Much of the new Alabama constitution merely restated the state's previous constitutional provisions, Conservatives conceded. "But these are rendered delusive and useless by the diabolical ingenuity of other provisions, contrived . . . to insure . . . the ascendancy of the negro race."[44] To white southerners the black suffrage provisions themselves promised unconstitutional, tyrannical government.

Without question, white southerners were bitterly, violently, and unreasoningly racist, and it is certainly possible to find those who with grim pleasure engaged in race war, pure and simple, who needed no justification to vent their racial hatred. But judging by what white southerners said to each other in public print and private communication, for most southerners racism interacted with deeply held principles of constitutional liberty in a manner that convinced them that they were the oppressed, not the oppressors; the victims, not the tyrants. As the resolutions of a Mississippi Conservative party convention indicated, they saw themselves engaged in a struggle to "vindicate alike the superiority of their race over the negro, and their political power to maintain constitutional liberty."[45]

This conviction grew out of basic understandings about government shared by most Americans—notions at the heart of what legal scholars have denominated "laissez-faire constitutionalism."[46] One of the most central of these is that the purpose of government is to promote the general welfare rather than the special interests of particular individuals or groups. Acts that violated this principle were denounced as "special" or "class legislation." Not only did opponents fight such legislation in the political arena, but courts also sometimes ruled that it violated various constitutional limitations on legislative power. Most twentieth-century Americans believe that the general community can derive benefits from legislation that helps particular groups. Therefore modern American government engages in a wide range of redistributive activities. But nineteenth-century Americans' notions of what might be in the general interest were far narrower. Whig and Republican promoters of active government might convince people that a protective tariff or railroad subsidies helped the community at large, but they fought a deep current of Jeffersonian and Jacksonian suspicion that such measures reflected the ability of the powerful to pervert government to their own ends.

Of course, in prevailing nineteenth-century opinion, autocratic or aristocratic governments always degenerated into machines for the enrichment of the few who controlled them. As Vernon L. Parrington summarized the common view (represented by Jefferson), "A class will serve class interests. Government by aristocracy is government in the interest of aristocracy."[47] But democratic governments were subject to similar risks. There were two ways in which democratic government might be perverted into an engine of special privilege. First, the rich and powerful might exercise authority over a horde of dependents, gaining an influence far out of proportion to their numbers. "Place power in the hands of those who have none, or a very trivial stake in the community, and you expose the poor and dependent to the influence and seductions of wealth," and the poor "will become subservient to the ambitions of the rich."[48] This was a fear that had long led advocates of republican government to favor property requirements for voting and to regard independent, yeoman landowners as the guarantors of republican liberty.[49] But democracy also raised an opposite danger: Demagogues, seeking power and plunder, might gain control of government by promising to pass legislation to improve the condition of the poor at the expense of the rest of society, in effect confiscating a part of the property of the prosperous for the benefit of the poor, the ignorant, and the venal.[50]

White Americans' racism, both North and South, interacted with these understandings. Even as they concluded in the 1820s and 1830s that all white men, in whatever economic circumstances, were independent enough to be entrusted with the ballot, they disfranchised black men on the grounds of their supine dependence on wealthy employers or, alternatively, their dangerous susceptibility to demagoguery because of their innate ignorance and cupidity.[51] Thus Pennsylvania's Democratic senator Charles Buckalew, a respected expert on legislative representation, warned Republicans against black suffrage: "By pouring into the ballot-boxes . . . a large mass of ignorant votes, and votes subjected to pecuniary or social influence, you will corrupt and degrade your elections."[52] And Ohio Democrat Durbin Ward warned of black voters, "It is preposterous to suppose they will be, during this generation, at least, anything more than pawns on the chess-board of politics—puppets in the hands of political wire-pullers."[53] Even the sympathetic commander of the Freedmen's Bureau, General Oliver Otis Howard, worried that unless the state or national governments undertook a massive education program, the freedmen "will become the tools of demagogues and a power for evil rather than for good."[54]

Thaddeus Stevens and other radical Republicans were more concerned about their dependence on ex-rebels. Enfranchisement alone could not secure the fruits of Union victory in the South, they warned. Unless Republicans secured the freedmen economic independence through confiscation and land reform, the southern aristocracy would simply control their votes.[55] In this matter their worries coincided with those of poorer southern whites. "Give them [freedmen] a vote now and what would inevitably result?" a southern columnist editorialized. "The rich landed proprietors, employing large numbers of ignorant laborers whom they could control . . . would hold the elections in their own hands. The poor white man, with his single vote, would be voiceless as the grave in the counsels and legislation of the state."[56]

Southern whites were quickly relieved of the prospect, or perhaps the hope, that the wealthy among them might control the black vote. As they watched native and immigrant whites—that is, whites who were native or immigrant to the South—begin to organize black voters (they never could conceive that black leaders played their own, independent role in this process), they realized with horror that the danger all ran in the opposite direction. "Political adventurers had taken the colored people in hand [and] . . . united them in an oath-bound political party."[57] A southern moderate reported to the influential Republican senator Henry Wilson how whites saw things: "Vast power is placed under the control of ignorance and passion, and . . . bad men are preparing to use it recklessly for selfish and sinister purposes."[58] In family letters, the same correspondent exchanged concerns about "the small, low and mischievous white men who are endeavoring to ride into power on the negroes' back."[59] It was an article of faith among the vast majority of southern whites that Republicans "make tools of the poor deluded creatures to advance their own purposes."[60]

Of course, in the opinion of most white southerners, such political managers were bad by definition. It was plain that the only way they could ride black votes to power was to appeal either to the freedmen's passions or to their interests, and to nineteenth-century Americans, with their firm conviction that government must act for the benefit of the whole community, neither was legitimate. President Andrew Johnson's denunciation of black suffrage indicates how southerners understood matters: Black people were "enemies of free institutions," he insisted. "If the inferior race obtains the ascendancy over the other, it will govern with reference only to its own interests—for it will recognize no common interest."[61] One need hardly point out the hypocrisy of men who had supported slavery—the most extreme form of class legislation ever enacted in the United States—complaining that Republicans' success in winning black votes must "mean the ... virtual enslavement of the white race."[62] But that does not mean they were insincere about the fears they expressed. On the contrary, who knew better the potential of state power to oppress?

As Michael Perman has shown, Republicans desperately sought to achieve legitimacy in the eyes of southern whites.[63] But political reality made that an impossible goal, given southern commitment to laissez-faire constitutionalism. The fact was that, like any politicians, Republicans had to respond to the demands of their constituents. Black southerners wanted access to public services that had been denied them as slaves—orphanages, asylums, hospitals, and especially educational institutions. The Republicans were in the position of having to serve a free population doubled in size by emancipation at the same time that emancipation had eliminated one of the largest prewar subjects of taxation, the slaves themselves. Worse, emancipation and the dislocation of war had lowered the value of the other major subject of tax revenue, plantation lands. Increased taxation of other property was inevitable, and even with higher taxes it is difficult to see how southern state governments could have maintained balanced budgets and paid for even basic social and educational services.

But what made this difficulty a matter of constitutional liberty to southern whites was the fact that parties promised to be divided largely along color lines, and therefore along class lines as well. As they considered the prospects under their new constitutions, southerners protested, "Taxation and representation are no longer to be united. They who own no property are to levy taxes and make all appropriations. The property-holders have to pay these taxes, without having any voice in levying them!"[64] Even the moderate James L. Orr, who would join the South Carolina Republican party, cautioned, "There will be presented the anomaly of a class of people wielding the political power of the State and levying taxes on the property of another class who will have in reality no political power."

As an example, Orr pointed to black demands for state-supported public education. "Property holders will be compelled to build schools for this class who will not contribute a dollar for the education of their own children," he worried.[65] Conservatives were more strident. Thomas S. Gathright, who would later serve as Mississippi's superintendent of education under a Democratic administration, in 1870 lambasted public schools as "an unmitigated outrage upon the rights and liberties of the white people of the state."[66] "The appropriations to support free schools for the education of negro children, for the support of old negroes in the poor-houses, and the vicious in jails and penitentiaries ... will be crushing and utterly ruinous," South Carolina Conservatives exclaimed. "The consequences will be, in effect, confiscation."[67] Mississippians echoed South Carolinians: Constitutional "provisions, on the subject of 'Public Works,' 'Houses of Refuge,' etc. . . . are all designed to establish means to rob the people." Mississippi's new constitution amounted to "the licensing of ... CONFISCATION by means of taxation."[68] Louisianans likewise insisted, "Negro suffrage would be tantamount to confiscation."[69]

As these southern protests indicate, the enfranchisement of southern blacks raised pressures in the Reconstruction South for the kinds of redistributive governmental policies that would not be acceptable to most Americans until after the turn of the twentieth century—in fact, perhaps not until the New Deal. The transfer of wealth inherent in Republican programs to provide public services to the freedmen violated the basic tenets of laissez-faire constitutionalism. The lament of a southern newspaper indicates how closely linked to this objection calls for white supremacy were: "Shall the white man be subordinated to the negro? Shall the property classes be robbed by the no-property herd?"[70]

This resentment may have been exacerbated by an apparent willingness of southern Republicans to use local government as a sort of government works program, another example of redistributive public policy. We need further research to learn whether Conservative complaints to this effect were based on fact, but at least one researcher sympathetic to the Republicans, looking closely at Charleston, South Carolina, has concluded that Republicans "created the impression among many voters, especially blacks, that the first priority of city government was to provide employment for the many destitute and unemployed."[71] At the same time, white Republican leaders were often ostracized and black activists blacklisted. As a consequence, many Republicans became dependent on government jobs as their sole means of support. It may well be that this dependence on government jobs led Republicans to pass the salary increases that Conservatives attacked so bitterly—salary increases necessary merely to compensate for the depreciating value of the state scrip in which they were paid.[72] But no matter how reasonable the explanation, most southern whites regarded Republicanism as a conspiracy among political adventurers, a "villainous scheme for transferring the earnings of the people to the pockets of the spoilsmen." "Taxation is robbery," they insisted, "when imposed for private gain."[73]

The situation would have been grim enough if Republican spending had been limited to expanding public services and meeting an increased payroll. But southern Republicans knew they had to devise programs whose benefits extended to white southerners, in order to establish the legitimacy of the governmental system they had enacted. They could not proceed in the one way sure to win white support—by imposing restraints on black freedom—so they tried to meet the goal by promoting economic prosperity, especially through the expansion of transportation facilities. But this attempt, too, cost money, stretching the already strained resources of the states. Republicans tried to escape from their dilemma by creating "contingent" debts, guarantees of loans to private enterprises for which they would become responsible only if the businesses failed. But the businesses did fail in the economic downturn of the 1870s, leaving the states with even greater obligations. Like third-world nations in recent years, the Republican governments found themselves in a cycle of raising taxes and refloating loans at ever steeper discounts and higher interest rates to pay off currently due interest and principal.

Worse, just like other states and the national government at the same time, the Reconstruction governments entered into their promotional efforts and their financing arrangements without having established systems that would enable them to differentiate worthy from unworthy projects or having instituted the controls over expenditure necessary to avoid fraud. The result was disastrous. Projects were funded, contracts let, and financial agents chosen on political rather than economic grounds, in a cycle that opened the way for widespread influence peddling and bribery. When the business ventures collapsed, southern taxpayers were left holding the bag. And the vast majority of those taxpayers were white, whereas the constituency of the party that had incurred the states' obligations was overwhelmingly black.[74] Horace Greeley saw the problem with unusual clarity:

> The old Slave governments of the South were . . . very rarely corrupt or prodigal. The planters paid most of the taxes; they decided who should be legislators; and they did not abide jobbers. . . . They had no public support of the poor; each subsisted, after a fashion, his own used-up slaves. The Poor Whites lived or died as they might; and, except for the Whites of two or three great cities, there were no public schools: and this made government cheap and taxes light. With Emancipation came a great change. There was

an urgent demand for schools . . . for the public support of paupers, White and Black . . . ; and so with many public institutions. Just when the people were poorest, they were required to bear the heaviest public expense, though only accustomed to the lightest. Dissatisfaction and complaint were inevitable.[75]

The Republican finance and internal improvement fiascoes of course confirmed southern whites' worst expectations. Reconstruction had, they were convinced, established exactly the sorts of governments they had feared. Taxes and state debt had risen dramatically, but there was little to show for it. In fact, because of the increase in the free population, spending per citizen had actually dropped since the war. Moreover, taxes had been shifted from slaves to land, so that the taxes levied on small farmers increased disproportionately to what they had paid before emancipation.[76] By 1874 the state auditor of Mississippi reported that one-fifth of all the land in the state was technically forfeit for taxes.[77] By 1873, 20 percent of Alabama's tax receipts went to pay off the interest on its bonded debt. These payments accounted for all of the state's deficit.[78] The interest on Louisiana's debt accounted for 11.5 mills of the state's 21.5-mill property tax in 1874.[79] In Texas, auditors increased the assessed value of property to gain tax revenues.[80]

Until new research into southern finances during Reconstruction is completed, one cannot judge just how heavy southern tax and debt burdens really were, although a historian undertaking that job has said that the debts did exceed the capacity of the weakened state economies to repay.[81] But it was not only the amount of the taxes that was at issue. "It is not taxation, nor even an increase of taxation, that the people of South Carolina object to," a sympathetic journalist reported, but rather "it is taxation without representation, an unjust, tyrannical, arbitrary, overwhelming taxation, producing revenues which never get any further than the already bursting pockets of knaves and dupes!"[82] Taxpayer protests did lead to retrenchment in southern Republican policies, but as a South Carolina Conservative insisted to reform Republican leader Carl Schurz, "The evils . . . are not of a transient character. They arise out of the very nature of things." The true problem was that "property is held almost entirely by the white race, political power is almost entirely with the African race."[83] That is, black southerners did not directly feel the tax consequences of the state policies they sustained. The militantly racist Louisiana paper *Alexandria Caucasian* thundered that for eight years "the negroes of the South [have] organized . . . [to obtain] class legislation over and over again for their exclusive benefit."[84] "This is the rule of the proletariat," Mississippi white-liners exclaimed; "it is naked communism—and negro communism at that."[85] As it prepared for the violent Mississippi election of 1875, the Democratic Party organ headlined, "The Robbery and Oppression of the South, and Not Negro Rights, [Is] the Issue."[86]

Some revisionist historians of Reconstruction have perceived growing northern sympathy for white southerners to have been a manifestation of renascent northern racism.[87] But as Heather Cox Richardson has recently demonstrated, southern complaints of black "class legislation" naturally resonated with northerners committed to laissez-faire constitutionalism, especially as they grew more concerned about potential "class legislation" in the North.[88] What southern Conservatives described seemed uncomfortably similar to the corrupt machine politics developing in northern cities, where taxpayers were at the mercy "of greedy and irresponsible crowds controlled by adventurers as reckless as themselves, whose object is nothing but plunder"; where "the educated and wealthy [man] . . . felt himself as much disfranchised as if he had been excluded from the polls by law"; and where taxes took on the character of confiscation—"organized communism and destruction of property under the guise of taxation."[89] "Ten years ago the North was nearly united in . . . sympathy for the freedmen," the *New York Times* wrote. "Now . . . not a few believe that the rights of the whites have been infringed on."[90] E. L. Godkin, the editor of *The Nation*, was surely one of them. "Instead of establishing equal rights for all, we set up the government of a class," he lamented in 1871. By 1874 he was editorializing on "Socialism in South Carolina."[91]

In effect, the governmental system established in the South during Reconstruction pitted democracy against a concept of equal rights many Americans believed inherent in liberty. Benjamin F. Butler perceived the issue clearly and understood its implications for the North as well as the South. According to southern Conservatives, he told his largely working-class constituents, "republican government means, that the majority shall not rule unless the majority are the owners of the property of the State, that the majority shall not rule unless that majority is composed of the educated classes."[92] But southern Conservatives did not perceive themselves to be rejecting democracy. To them, a system in which ambitious men acquired power by making impossible or illicit promises to voters Conservatives considered too ignorant or venal to regard the common good was not really democratic. On the contrary, it violated democracy by in effect giving bad men—"a few thousand white vampires" who controlled an "unbroken black line" of "political chattel"[93]—more votes than good men.

Therefore, white southerners could claim with all sincerity that the South would vote Democratic "if left to a fair ballot"—that is, a ballot that discounted black votes.[94] They insisted that "the carpet-bagger . . . has become, with the scalawag, through their influence with the negro, a sort of aristocrat or autocrat."[95] White southerners could calmly contemplate frauds from which they would have recoiled if elections had been "between intelligent voters" rather than being occasions "where whole hordes [are] hustled to the poles & voted."[96] Robert Toombs could promise to fashion a new Redeemer constitution "by which the people will rule and the nigger will never be heard of!"[97] Indeed, they could believe that "to rescue the government from Republican control involves the very salvation of Republican institutions."[98]

The Redeemer constitutions accurately reflected this southern white constitutionalism. More significant, they showed how congruent southern white concerns were with growing northern concerns, for these constitutions were very similar to those being framed in the North at the same time. The constitutions of the 1870s through the 1890s, North and South, reversed the trend toward broader suffrage, imposed strict limits on state legislative power, withheld state authority from a variety of areas, and withdrew power, by constitutional restrictions and gerrymander, from polities where the "dangerous classes" were large and politically potent.[99]

Thus we have the irony and the tragedy of Radical Reconstruction in the South. The irony was that Republicans sought to establish democratic constitutional government but in the process threatened constitutional liberty, as white southerners understood it. The written constitutions that created southern Reconstruction governments could not establish their legitimacy in the eyes of most southern whites, unless they corresponded to deeper, unwritten understandings of the essentials of constitutional government. To southern Conservatives, the war against those constitutions was a struggle not against liberty and democracy but for them. The tragedy was not only that southern whites were successful but that by the 1870s and 1880s their ideas were no longer just southern.

9 Reform Republicans and the Retreat from Reconstruction

The general verdict of historians is that Republicans failed to achieve their goals in Reconstruction. They had hoped to eliminate the vestiges of slavery, to secure the civil and political rights of the freed people, to establish a body of rights of all Americans that would be protected both by the federal government and by reconstituted state governments responsive to the interests of all their citizens, and to reap the political benefits of a successful program in the form of votes for Republican candidates North and South. The subtitle of Eric Foner's standard synthetic history of the effort reflects historians' judgment—Reconstruction was "America's Unfinished Revolution."[1]

Most studies of national Reconstruction policy have concentrated on the origins of Reconstruction policy from 1863 to 1869 rather than its decline. William Gillette's *Retreat from Reconstruction* and Heather Cox Richardson's *The Death of Reconstruction* are the only studies of later national Reconstruction policy published after the first decade of the twentieth century.[2] Historians have instead concentrated on politics in the South, pointing out the weaknesses of the Republican party there and white southerners' dogged and violent resistance.[3] But while white southern opposition played the greatest role in the Republicans' failure to achieve their goals, nearly as important was the decline of northern support—a change that reflected more than just battle fatigue.

Historians have recognized the importance of this fading support for Reconstruction in the North—especially among Republicans themselves, as manifested most dramatically in the liberal Republican movement.[4] Yet at the time the original version of this essay appeared, historians had only glancingly analyzed the decline of Republican radicalism, attributing it variously and vaguely to the death of radical leaders, northern racism, and commitment to federalism or laissez faire. But the essay was part of a trend. In his work on Reconstruction, Eric Foner had already paid more than usual attention to developments in the North. Influenced by the earlier work of W. E. B. Dubois and David Montgomery, he explained the change as a result of class conflict in the North, especially

---

The original version of this essay was published in *The Facts of Reconstruction: Essays in Honor of John Hope Franklin*, ed. Alfred Moss and Eric Anderson (Baton Rouge: Louisiana State University Press, 1991), 53–78.

a reaction against northern labor militancy, which led northern intellectual and business elites to abandon free-soil radicalism for a conservative version of free-market capitalism.[5] In recent studies, Richardson and Nancy Cohen have built upon Foner's foundation.[6] Like Foner, both have stressed elites' reaction to labor issues, and both have linked the reaction to growing northern racism. As Cohen has put it, "At the very moment that Radicals were heralding the irresistible advance of liberal-democratic civilization and a new era of national harmony and prosperity, workers and their allies ensured that the dawning era would be roiled by a new axial conflict, the status and condition of propertyless wage workers in a democracy."[7]

The most crucial element in weakening Republican resolve on the Reconstruction issue was the defection of self-consciously reform-oriented Republicans. These reformers included academicians such as Charles W. Eliot, David A. Wells, Francis Lieber, and Amasa Walker; litterateurs and editors such as Horace White of the *Chicago Tribune*, Edwin L. Godkin of the *Nation*, James Russell Lowell and Charles Eliot Norton of the *North American Review*, George William Curtis of *Harper's Weekly*, and Parke Godwin and Charles Nordhoff of the *New York Evening Post*; and intellectually inclined businessmen and lawyers such as Edward Atkinson, John Murray Forbes, Dorman B. Eaton, and Richard Henry Dana. They identified themselves as an intellectual elite—"the best men"—who bore a special responsibility to the nation but who also were entitled to special deference.[8] During the war and the early years of Reconstruction, most of these reformers had been firm supporters of radical antislavery action, providing an intellectual foundation and political support for radical Republican demands for emancipation and equal rights.[9] By 1870, most of them were clearly hostile to much of the leadership of the Republican party and were helping to create the movement, already known as "liberal Republicanism," that would sap the party of much of its intellectual vigor and its crusading spirit.

Liberal Reformers and Laissez-Faire Morality

Until recently, the most common historical understanding attributed the reformers' desertion of Reconstruction to racism, and new studies continue to stress that factor among others.[10] It is difficult, however, to see how the reformers' racism differentiated them from other Republicans. Few Republicans during the war or Reconstruction believed blacks to be the equals of whites. Even as he campaigned for black suffrage in the summer of 1865, James A. Garfield confided to a friend, "It goes against the grain of my feelings . . . for I never could get in love with the creatures." As the Senate seated its first black member, the old Republican warhorse Simon Cameron admitted, "It somewhat shocks my old prejudices . . . that one of the despised race should come here to be my equal."[11] Republicans had insisted only that the freed people be secured equality in basic civil and (after some hesitation) political rights, not that they be conceded what was called at the time "social equality." Even Thaddeus Stevens affirmed that associating with African Americans as equals was "a question of our own choice"—"a matter of taste."[12] The radical Republican Ignatius Donnelly expressed the outlook that most Republicans shared: "If it be true . . . that the negro belongs to an inferior race . . . the more reason is there why he should be protected by equal laws." Or as a California Republican legislator put it when he voted to eliminate the state's ban on black testimony, "It is not elevating the negro to give him justice."[13]

To understand what did alienate liberal reformers from Republican reconstruction policy after 1869, one must assess their ideas in the context of the almost idolatrous faith in science that swept European and American intellectuals in the nineteenth century. Science made sense of a physical world that for millennia had been rationalized through superstition or religion. By the mid-nineteenth century, educated men clamored for the application of the same tool to human relationships. They were convinced that these relationships were subject to laws just as certain as those that governed the physical universe. The new "social science," as it was called, would ferret out these laws. Charles Francis Adams Jr.'s recollection of his scientific awakening indicates science's almost mystical attraction. The revelation occurred while he lay abed in Europe in 1865, recovering from the rigors of his Civil War service and reading an essay by John Stuart Mill on Auguste Comte. "That essay of Mill's revolutionized in a single morning my whole mental attitude," Adams remembered. "I emerged from the theological stage . . . and passed into the scientific."[14]

In no area were reformers more certain that scientific truth had been discovered than in economics—the "science of wealth," as one of its most influential students called it. Not only did economics (or "political economy," as it also was called) belong "to the same class of sciences with mechanics, astronomy, optics, chemistry, [and] electricity," but its laws also were already known and needed only to be applied to specific circumstances. They were laws "like those of other sciences," laws "universal and invariable in their operation."[15]

Most nineteenth-century economists concluded that because natural laws of economics existed, they were beyond human interference. The clergyman-economist Lyman Atwater put it most trenchantly: "Legislation cannot alter the laws of nature, of man, of political economics."[16] Moreover, contemporary economists confused the notion of *interfering* with economic laws with that *of harnessing* them. It was no part of economics, as the reformers understood it, to study how human economic activities might be modified to achieve some social goal. Rather, political economy was, as Godkin put it, the science of "what man, as an exchanging, producing animal, would do, if let alone." That was "a real science," in Godkin's estimation. Years later, as young economists urged social reform, he lamented that political economy "has assumed the role of an advisor, who teaches man to make himself more comfortable through the help of his government"; it had "no more claim to be a science than philanthropy."[17] Thus economists, and the reformers who so ardently had popularized their conclusions, laid upon government the famous injunction *laissez-nous faire*, which the influential American astronomer and financial writer Simon Newcomb translated as the "let-alone principle."[18]

As the historian Sidney Fine observed, "Free trade and liberty were synonymous to the foes of protection." He might have said the same of almost every position the laissez-faire liberal reformers took, whether on the tariff, finances, taxation, or labor legislation. Despite its scientific trappings, the laissez-faire economic theory was in essence a commitment to liberty as the theorists perceived it—that is, to the "right of every man to employ his own efforts for the gratification of his own wants."[19] Therefore, the social science that the reformers worshiped was shot through with value judgments that would be considered inappropriate by modern scientific standards. It was not unusual for a "scientific" reformer to insist, for example, that "any honest man" could understand financial questions "because they are also, and equally, moral questions."[20]

The great threat to liberty lay in the temptation to use the power of the state to promote the interests of one group at the expense of others—that is, to enact "special" or "class" legislation. The struggle against kings and aristocrats had been waged to free the people from the inordinate power that enabled such persons to use the state to levy special, monopolistic exactions from the rest of society.[21] Such power also had been the essence of the slave system in the South, where the entire weight of the state was thrown behind the expropriation of the labor of black workers by white masters. "The highest right of property is the right to freely exchange it for other property," reformers insisted. "Any system of laws which denies or restricts this right for the purpose of subserving private or class interests, reaffirms . . . the principle of slavery."[22]

To the liberal reformers, all efforts specifically to benefit one group, even a group hardly able to protect itself without such intervention, shared this dangerous, antilibertarian tendency. "Wealth gained . . . by means of a protective tariff or a . . . law enforcing the use of paper money . . . [or] the leisure secured by eight and ten-hours laws . . . are all gained at the cost of the mass of consumers," Edward Atkinson insisted, even though demands for these various things came from disparate sources. Indeed, Atkinson identified protectionism with communism. "The two ideas are identical in principle," he insisted, explaining that "protection . . . attempts to enforce an inequitable distribution of our annual product," whereas communism "invokes the force of law under the mistaken idea that a more equitable division may be had."[23] William Graham Sumner, one of the few reformers to have remained a steadfast Democrat, in the 1880s would summarize the laissez-faire, liberal-reform position: "[Whenever] the question is raised, What ought the State to do for labor, for trade, for manufacturers, for the poor, for the learned professions . . . that is[,] for a class or an interest, it really is the question. . . . What ought Some-of-us to do for Others-of-us?" In the democratic United States, such government action would establish a tyranny in which "a man's neighbors are his masters."[24] Thus at the heart of the reformers' laissez-faire ideology lay a continued adherence to the notion of "equal rights" that had fueled Jacksonian resistance to "special privilege" in economic areas and Republican opposition to privilege based on race. With the establishment of majoritarian democracy by Jacksonian Democrats and radical Republicans, however, the great threat to equal rights no longer seemed to emanate from above, but from below. Weak-minded sentimentalists or corrupt demagogues would promise ignorant or venal voters benefits that could be acquired only by invading the rights of those whose abilities had lifted them above the crowd. "The problem," one reformer wrote, "is, to make men who are equal . . . in political rights and . . . entitled to the ownership of property . . . content with that inequality in its distribution which must inevitably result from the application of the law of justice."[25]

Of course, socialism posed one such threat to liberty, and after the uprising of the Paris Commune in 1871, liberal reformers would be deeply fearful of that threat. Another danger lay in the perceived willingness of corruptionists to harness the ignorance of voters and gain power through out-and-out demagoguery. This problem was especially acute in big cities—populated, the reformers believed, with ignorant immigrants who had no heritage of liberty or training in American democracy. Such people were "the dangerous classes," and the Tammany Hall–like corruption built upon their votes was no more than "organized communism and destruction of property under the guise of taxation."[26]

To the liberal reformers, nothing was more symbolic of the dangers of demagoguery than the political success of the radical Republican Benjamin F. Butler. Butler was the only important Massachusetts Republican ostentatiously to repudiate the doctrines to which the reformers were so firmly committed. Combining adroit use of political patronage with "demagogic" calls for government intervention in the economy, he defied the efforts of "better" men to mold public opinion and exert political influence. "Butlerism," the reformers fumed, was simply a plan for "the use of Government to carry out the poor and ignorant man's view of the nature of society." For the next thirty years, they would fight its author tooth and nail.[27]

Not surprisingly, the reformers' convictions had serious implications for their attitudes toward democracy. The reformers believed that "the highest allegiance of every man is due to liberty and civilization.... The possession of the suffrage by anybody ... is but a means to these ends," not an end in itself. If this belief alone were not enough to undermine their commitment to democracy, to it was added their conviction that there was a science of society—and the more one perceives measures to govern society to be matters of science, the less they can be matters of public opinion. As Frances Lieber put it while agitating for free trade, "Truth is not settled by majorities."[28] So the reformers did not conceive politics to be the mechanism by which the will of the majority was translated into action. Instead, it was "the art by which the teachings of social science are put into practice." Legislators at all times had to keep in mind the "laws of social order and well-being," laws as "immutable as that of gravitation."[29]

It followed that, as Henry Adams put it, "the great problem of every system of Government has been to place administration and legislation in the hands of the best men"—those with "the loftiest developments of moral and intellectual education."[30] As Adams perceived, this conviction "clash[ed] with our fundamental principle that one man is as good as another." Although Adams admitted, at least at first, that he did not know how to escape this dilemma, most reformers were unabashedly elitist. "It is curious, that, in a country which boasts of its intelligence, the theory should be so generally held that the most complicated form of human contrivance ... can be worked at sight by any man able to talk for an hour or two without stopping to think," James Russell Lowell wrote. "Experience would have bred in us a rooted distrust of improvised statesmanship, even if we did not believe politics to be a science, which ... demands the long and steady application of the best powers of men as ... [can] master even its first principles."[31] To a reformer like Lowell, democracy was "after all, nothing more than an experiment," to be judged by whether it fulfilled its function of elevating "the best men" to leadership.[32]

Convictions like these naturally led the liberal reformers to endorse proposals to reform the civil service so as to make ability the criterion for appointment and to make tenure independent of politics. Of course, there was a good deal of self-interest in this. Well-educated and certain of their own talents, the liberal reformers could not help but expect that under such standards the jobs would go to men like themselves—a conviction reflected in Atkinson's brash affirmation to David Wells: "If you or I or any other honest economist ever seeks office, we should get it." Several historians of the civil service reform movement have noted that liberal reformers' interest in such reform blossomed when they failed to receive appointive offices for which they believed themselves particularly suited.[33]

Other specific policies followed logically from the reformers' scientific understandings and moral convictions. The first of these involved the money question. The reformers were convinced that political economists had demonstrated that the value of goods and services was determined by their supply and the demand for them. That intrinsic value could not be affected by changes in how it was measured. To insure a stable economy, people needed a stable standard, free of fluctuation, by which to measure value so that they could compare the value of one kind of goods with that of another. In the opinion of nearly all American economists—and of the liberal reformers—experience had proved "scientifically" that only gold could serve that function, although a few believed silver also might do. "Money," the medium of exchange, therefore had to be based on gold, or perhaps gold and silver, in order to reflect the real value of goods.[34]

To repeat, one could not alter the intrinsic value of goods, that is, the value determined by supply and demand, by changing the standard by which it was measured—for example, by inflating the amount of money in circulation irrespective of the availability of gold to back it. Such artificial inflation was no different from trying to change the weight of goods by altering the scales, "as if more hay scales would mean more hay," the liberal reformer-businessman John Murray Forbes scoffed. Such an effort would not increase the value of the goods, but would rather make people uncertain of the value of the money, and thus it would introduce serious instability into the economy.[35]

As always with the reformers, however, beyond the question of the expediency of tampering with the standard of value was that of its morality. Speculative fever associated with inflation would lead to "the diffusion of a taste for luxury, dissipation, and excess," not to mention "gambling . . . scoundrelism and effrontery."[36] Moreover, as the supply of money grew, its purchasing power would depreciate. Creditors, who in good faith had lent money to those seeking it, would be repaid in currency of less value. Thus, a policy of inflation was a dangerous example of state action that threatened liberty. When debtors pressed for such a policy, they were seeking to use state power to benefit themselves at the expense of creditors, since inflation amounted to an appropriation of the property of one group for the use of another. Following this reasoning, the liberal reformers perceived currency based on gold to be "honest money" or even "moral money." During the Civil War, the government had been forced to issue "legal tender notes"—the so-called greenbacks—backed by no more than a promise to repay them in gold or silver someday. After the war, the reformers favored steady "contraction" of the currency—that is, a steady reduction in the amount of greenbacks circulating—and they believed deeply that those who agreed with them were "the friends of sound money and sound morals." [37] Those who pressed for "easy money" presented "the bald issue whether the nation shall be a liar and a thief or not."[38]

Closely linked to the currency question was the issue of how to repay the national debt incurred in suppressing the rebellion. Those who pressed for inflation generally also urged that the debt be repaid in the paper currency in which it had been incurred. Of course, this policy would keep paper money in circulation, as the inflationists wanted, and therefore would violate the same fundamental economic laws that inflation did, in the opinion of the liberal reformers. Moreover, the reformers thought that this issue raised the moral question even more starkly than did inflation. They insisted that refusal to repay the debt in gold amounted to its repudiation.[39]

Another violation of scientific principles and republican liberty was the protective tariff. Laissez-faire economists and their liberal reformer allies were certain that, if left alone, people would exchange those goods they could produce at least cost for other goods produced more cheaply elsewhere. The "great laws of human nature which are the natural forces of the science" of economics would accomplish this as surely as "universal gravitation will construct the solar system as it is." Such free trade would benefit both parties and permit the widest distribution of goods, since goods always would be produced where this could be done most cheaply, thereby keeping prices low.[40]

Besides flatly scorning arguments that protective duties were necessary to promote American industrial development, laissez-faire economists and liberal reformers once again raised an even more compelling moral objection: Protection imposed higher prices on American consumers so that the capitalists and laborers in a particular industry might survive foreign competition. Like inflationary schemes, the protective tariff was but an effort to use the power of government to enrich one group at the expense of another. A petition for tariff protection, wrote Atkinson, ought to read as follows: "Whereas we, the undersigned, are desirous of establishing certain branches of industry . . . for which we have not either the capital nor the skill, we ask that our countrymen shall be compelled to purchase our products at such prices as it may be found necessary for us to impose, while we are learning our trade and accumulating wealth at the cost of our said neighbors."[41]

Reformers and Radicals

Historians generally have perceived the defection of the reformers to have begun after the restoration of most of the southern states to normal relations in the Union and the election of Ulysses S. Grant to the presidency in 1868, culminating in the Liberal Republican bolt of 1872. Yet on all counts, from general principles to specific policies, future liberals began to drift away from their radical allies and toward the more conservative elements of the Republican Party as early as 1867. In doing so, the reformers robbed radical politicians of one of the strongest elements of their appeal, for the alliance with the reformers had given radicals something of a cachet, of somehow being more than "mere" politicians. By the 1870s, the more radical Republicans seemed no more virtuous than any other politicos—less so, in fact, than those who had replaced them in the reformers' affections.

The reformers' conviction that one can arrive at a science of society was, as Godkin recognized, "based on the theory that society is not an artificial arrangement regulated by contract like a business partnership, but an organism that grows in accordance with certain laws."[42] This evolutionary sociology approximated the central principle of Burkean conservatism, and the statement itself embodied a none-too-subtle slap at the traditional American notion, rooted in the nation's Lockean heritage, that men enter into society by free acts of will, which in turn implies equality of rights within society. Thus, the radical Republican argument that all men, including black men, had certain rights by virtue of their entering society was nonsense. A community's understanding of what rights individuals and groups possessed grew naturally out of its earlier development, and no one had an abstract right to anything more. Within the framework of American development, individual liberty had become a paramount value, and the extension of legal and political equality to the former slaves had been an appropriate method of securing liberty to them. But this was a matter of expedience and egalitarian tradition, not of right, and if the consequences were evil, no theory of abstract rights could stand in the way of a different solution to the problem of the freedmen's status.[43]

The reformers' commitment to new "scientific" ideas about social relations made enthusiasm for any major social or economic reform suspect. For if society was governed by natural laws, there were distinct limits to the possibilities of social improvement through "artificial" changes imposed by human will. Reformers scoffed at the "inordinate belief, common among the half-educated, in the potency of legislation." Thus the new social science was profoundly conservative. "Social science," Godkin wrote, "seeks to convince people that in sociology, as in medicine, all vendors of panaceas are quacks, that anybody who goes about saying that either equality, or freedom, or female suffrage, or prohibition, or common schools, or the ballot will make the world what it ought to be, should no more be listened to than the patent pill-man."[44]

Their disagreements with radical politicians over specific issues disturbed reformers even more than the growing divergence between the two groups' general understanding of society and reform. By 1867, Republicans were engaged in a bitter struggle over financial and tariff policy, barely hidden by the facade of unity imposed by their battle against President Johnson and the Democrats over reconstruction. Manufacturing interests in developing industries, bankers who had not joined the newly established national banking system, western bankers, capitalists who were inclined to aggressive investment programs, railroad promoters, agrarians, and labor reformers pressed for easy money and high tariffs. Merchants involved in international trade (and their local agents and independent wholesalers), manufacturing interests in established industries, and leading bankers urged contraction of the currency and reduction of tariff rates.

Blind to the economic self-interest that motivated the hard-money, low-tariff forces, the liberal reformers allied with them as a matter of "scientific" and moral principle. The reformers were dismayed, however, to find the most important Republican radicals among the leading proponents of soft money and high tariffs. Thaddeus Stevens, Benjamin F. Butler, William D. Kelley, Benjamin F. Wade, and Zachariah Chandler all were tainted. Many of the reformers shared the feelings of the Ohio Republican congressman Rufus P. Spalding, who complained: "It would seem that no man can come fully up in these days to the standard of radicalism unless he be prepared to put a tariff upon foreign goods that shall amount to a prohibition, and to open and extend the paper circulation of the country without limitation."[45]

In fact, the reformers' fear was misplaced; radical Republicans were not united on these issues. But the identification of key radical leaders with soft money and high tariffs was so strong that the differences among less prominent radicals were overlooked. Even Charles Sumner came under suspicion until he proved his financial orthodoxy in 1868, and several historians have suggested that there was an implicit radical Republican "ideology" in which soft money, high tariffs, and racial liberalism were manifestations of an underlying egalitarianism.[46]

The liberal reformers were shocked by the early successes of the soft-money, high-tariff forces. In 1867 the soft-money, pro-tariff lobby persuaded Congress to repeal the authority under which Treasury Secretary Hugh McCulloch had been restricting the circulation of greenbacks since 1866. Congress also had come close to passing a general upward revision of tariff rates and had succeeded in increasing the tariff on wool and wool products. Support seemed to be growing for a proposition to pay the national debt in greenbacks. Early in 1867 the worried special commissioner on revenue, David A. Wells, wrote an intimate, "I am afraid the extremists and inflationists will have it pretty much their own way." [47]

Aware of the reformers' concern, conservative Republicans worked assiduously to widen the break. "There is not a man who fought against us in the rebellion in whom I have not more confidence and for whom I have not more respect than I have for Mr. B. F. Butler . . . [and] Thad. Stevens is no better than Butler," Iowa's conservative Republican senator, James W. Grimes, wrote Atkinson. "The great question in American politics today is the financial question," he insisted, and he believed that this question "ought to override . . . reconstruction." As radicals attacked Republican conservatives such as William Pitt Fessenden, senator from Maine, as "clogs and obstructions" to a thoroughly just reconstruction program, Grimes warned, "Let . . . 'clogs and obstructions' be removed from Congress and Thad. Stevens and Butler be in controul [sic] as they then would be with their revolutionary and repudiating idea in the ascendancy and our government would not last 12 mos."[48]

The implications of a radical victory within the Republican Party for its position on financial and tariff issues drove the reformers into a de facto alliance with Republican conservatives. On the money question, the reformers joined the conservatives in praising the contractionist policies of Secretary McCulloch, in a campaign that culminated in highly publicized plans for a testimonial dinner in McCulloch's honor in Boston. The movement was a public rebuke to the radicals, who bitterly opposed extending honors to anyone openly supporting Johnson's reconstruction policy. As arranged, McCulloch declined the invitation but used the opportunity to defend his hard-money policies in a letter that was then broadcast by the Boston group.[49]

The reformers' cooperation with McCulloch cooled their ardor for one of the most important radical proposals, the impeachment of Andrew Johnson. If Johnson *were* removed from office, the high-tariff, inflationist Ben Wade, president pro tem of the Senate, would succeed him. McCulloch certainly would lose his position as secretary of the treasury, and an inflationist just as surely would replace him. Moreover, the circumstance would give Wade a crucial boost in his quest for the 1868 Republican presidential nomination.[50]

The radicals' flirtation with a policy of land confiscation and redistribution in the South, along with southern radicals' endorsement of former Confederate disfranchisement and courtship of black voters through promises of further change, also alienated the reformers. Land confiscation and redistribution was, of course, the quintessential case of using state power for the benefit of one group at the expense of another. When radical Ben Butler justified such a policy on the grounds that "a landed aristocracy is fatal to the advance of the cause of liberty and equal rights," the hitherto sympathetic, reformer-linked *Boston*

Advertiser asked, "Why a *landed* aristocracy? This mode of argument is two-edged. For there are socialists who hold that *any* aristocracy is 'fatal to the advance of the cause of liberty and equal rights'—socialists who would not hesitate to say that General Butler's large income places him . . . in the ranks of an aristocracy." Driving the same point home, the conservative *Cincinnati Commercial* began to refer to Butler and Stevens as the "Red Rads."[51]

The liberal reformers also felt threatened by southern radicals' appeals to the former slaves for their main support and by their desire to disfranchise large numbers of formerly Confederate southern whites. The reformers shared the certainty of nearly all white Americans that blacks were incapable of the intellectual achievements of whites, or at least of Anglo-Saxon and Germanic whites. Therefore, black enfranchisement, although just and necessary, was dangerous. As James Russell Lowell put it, "What is bad among ignorant foreigners in New York will not be good among ignorant natives in South Carolina." Like lower-class white northerners, especially Irish immigrants, southern blacks might be easily manipulated. Charles Francis Adams Jr. was expressing a common concern among reformers when he wrote that Americans were lifting voting restrictions despite the development of a "Celtic proletariat on the Atlantic coast, an African proletariat on the shores of the Gulf, and a Chinese proletariat on the Pacific."[52] Disfranchisement of the white southern "intelligent class" would only make things worse.

As they pondered these prospects, reformers found southern radicals themselves something less than attractive. The radicals' campaigns for black support on such issues as confiscation, civil rights laws, expanded public services, and hostility to the white upper class seemed the obvious counterpart to those of such freebooters as Ben Butler and the Tammany Hall Democrats in the North. Godkin thought it was "plain" that the freedmen were "in danger of falling into the hands of demagogues who will use them without scruples for purposes which will finally prove disastrous to the race," and he demanded that "the national leaders of the party . . . find some means of liberalizing the party managers at the South."[53]

To counter the danger, Massachusetts reformers organized the Massachusetts Reconstruction Association at about the same time they endorsed Johnson's treasury secretary McCulloch. The association's purpose was to "prevent the creation of an exclusive black men's party and to kill the scheme of confiscation," Atkinson informed McCulloch. Not coincidentally, its organizers also hoped "to secure the election of a southern congressional delegation who shall not be under Thad [Stevens's] lead on tariff and currency questions." The *Nation* quickly endorsed the effort. "We need not urge such men to see to it that nothing is done to excite the freedmen to feelings of revenge or with delusive hopes of direct benefits from Government," Godkin noted with satisfaction. What the freedmen needed, and what the Reconstruction Association would provide, was a crash course on the laws of political economy. "The more demagogues rave and rant, the more carloads of teachers and books we ought to send off," Godkin urged.[54]

Thus, by the summer of 1867, Republican conservatives and liberal reformers were allied in a bitter war upon the radicals. As the conservative organs blasted radical "one idea men, fanatics," Godkin's *Nation* echoed them, in its genteel way, with a new definition of "True Radicalism": "Many well-meaning persons . . . are so anxious to be considered 'radical' in their views that they fear to stop even when they have attained all that is really desirable or practicable." Efforts to transform southern society overnight by further radical legislation were doomed to failure because social science taught that social institutions evolve naturally. "The wise radical is content to wait . . . and slowly to build up when the work of pulling down is properly over."[55] Henry Adams began to refer to himself, Richard Henry Dana, and their allies as representing the "conservative liberalism of New England." By late August, *Chicago Tribune* editor Horace White also found himself in an anomalous position. "I call myself a Radical," he mused, "and yet find myself more in harmony with those . . . Conservatives than with any other branch of the party."[56]

At the same time, the *Nation*, recognized as the reformers' organ, leveled its guns at Stevens, Butler, and especially Wade, the radical, high-tariff, easy-money candidate for the 1868 Republican presidential nomination. The reformer-linked *Boston Advertiser* chimed in, charging that Wade's protectionism and inflationism and his criticism of labor-capital relations were "simply and wholly . . . an avowal of agrarian sympathies." The *Nation* sarcastically asserted that Wade exemplified the undertrained "self made man in politics" who "takes any bull by the horns, mounts the stump, and disposes of the most troubling problems . . . in a few sentences."[57]

This attack on Wade's lack of professional training raises the question of just what the reformers' goals were, as they opened fire upon their former allies. They always insisted that they wanted only to purify the American political system and upgrade its leaders, and they recoiled with horror from the manipulation and boss rule that they perceived to be implicit in backroom politics. Yet they themselves continually engaged in similar conduct, attempting to control policy and fix appointments from behind the scenes.[58] Sincerely believing that they were more honest and more capable than those in power, the reformers were ambitious men. "A man can have no truer satisfaction than in knowing that he has made himself a power," Lowell wrote Godkin in 1868, congratulating the editor on his influence; Lowell knew this would be taken as a compliment. In seeming contrast, Henry Adams wrote his brother Charles in 1869: "You like strife in the world. I detest and despise it. You work for power. I work for my own satisfaction." Yet Henry's insight into his brother's character may have been better than his insight into his own, considering the obvious pleasure with which he informed a friend a few months later that "I am . . . winding myself up in a coil of political intrigue and getting the reputation of a regular conspirator. . . . I am on the side which has the strongest men, and Reform is always a sure card."[59]

What ailed Henry Adams, his fellow reformer Oliver Wendell Holmes Jr. wrote later, was his failure to get public office "handed to him on a silver platter." The reformer-economist Amasa Walker was disturbed by similar traits in two other reform leaders: he found David A. Wells "distracted by vanity and [wanting] to be at something sensational"; the *Chicago Tribune*'s liberal editor, Horace White, was "not free from the same complaint."[60]

To achieve their goals, the reformers had to pursue power. "I fear there is little hope for reform from regular politicians," Godkin wrote Charles Eliot Norton privately in 1867. "If the country is to be saved and purified it must be by some force outside their ranks." Godkin thought the reformers needed to organize for "the hunting down of corrupt politicians, the stoppage of unscrupulous nominations." By "corrupt politicians," however, he did not mean actual crooks; he meant those who got their nominations through political manipulation—that is, by the common methods of the day. And "unscrupulous nominations" were, of course, in the eye of the beholder.[61]

Repelled by political ambition in others, Godkin perhaps was psychologically incapable of admitting that such a political revolution as he advocated inevitably would mean the elevation of men like himself. A similar combination of self-righteousness and ambition is detectable in Richard Henry Dana's lament, "There will be no more politics for me in Massachusetts until this set, who now rule us . . . of low toned, ill taught men pass aside." Charles Nordhoff made the connection plainer still. "It belongs to us to be recognized as the true leaders of the Republican party," he wrote Carl Schurz in 1870. "If we are not that we are nothing."[62]

Newly allied with the conservative elements of the Republican organization, the reformers aimed for nothing less than the elimination of radicals from the party's leadership. The argument that future leaders must be capable of applying the teachings of social science to government was the lever with which they hoped to dislodge them. The moral issue of slavery had required radical leadership, the reformers admitted. "People came to look upon fidelity to the antislavery cause, and a generally philanthropic tendency as the one test of statesmanship, and under cover of this feeling a large number of gentlemen have won their way to places in public life"; however, "circumstances have . . . so changed, and the problems presented for solution are so different, that they are fit to fill them no longer." Meanwhile, "the state and nation are constantly injured by their chosen servants, who lack the simplest rudiments of knowledge . . . of the principles essential to the public welfare."[63] As Nancy Cohen has pointed out, the reformers moved to make "administration" a political issue distinct from underlying principles,[64] which they claimed had been settled by the Civil War.

This argument could carry weight only if Republicans agreed that the great moral issue *was* settled. The radicals' firmness on that issue had secured them their power, the reformers recognized, and so long as Republicans perceived the war issues to be paramount, the radicals could not be dislodged. On the other hand, as Atkinson wrote McCulloch, "Let the reconstruction matters be once settled, and the fight between Protection and Free Trade will be upon us, and Free-Trade views will win."[65] Therefore, the scope of the great Civil War issues had to be narrowed. As the radicals proposed land redistribution, nationally supervised education, and long-term congressional control as means by which to secure real equality in the South, the reformers urged Republicans to be content with the elimination of unequal laws. "Let us be content with securing equal justice in the South, and then combine to attack corruptions nearer home," they urged.[66]

The reformers understood that the radical Republicans had secured their positions by appealing to the antislavery sentiment of the Republican rank and file. The reconstruction issue was the natural outgrowth of the antislavery movement, and it tapped the same underlying sentiment. The reformers understood very well that if they could eliminate the "Negro question" from politics, they would deprive the radicals of the vehicle by which they had driven to power. With the restoration of all but three of the southern states to normal status in the Union in 1868, the election of Ulysses S. Grant to the presidency in the same year on a platform of "Let Us Have Peace," and the passage in 1869 of the Fifteenth Amendment, securing black suffrage, the reformers insisted that the old issues were dead and would be superseded by questions of finance, taxation, and reform in the administration of government. The implications for the future leadership of the Republican Party were plain, as James Russell Lowell made clear in a January 1869 article designed to serve as the keynote of the reformers' campaign for power. In the fight over slavery and equal rights, Lowell observed, "ethics have been called on to perform the function of jurisprudence and political economy"; consequently, "an easy profession of faith is getting to be the highest qualification of a legislator." But the times dictated a change: "The Republican party, so long accustomed to deal largely with problems into which morals entered largely and directly, is now to be tried solely by its competency for other duties."⁶⁷ The point was clear. The new problems required the expertise of the reformers rather than the sentimental moralism of the radicals.

All this implied a new attitude toward southern whites. As early as 1866, Horace White had looked forward to a post-Reconstruction, free-trade alliance between West and South, a prospect apparently endangered by what conservatives thought was the pro-tariff bias of southern Republican radicals.⁶⁸ Moreover, hostility toward the former rebels played into the hands of the radical southern "demagogues" who were courting black support by stressing the differences between the interests of southern blacks and whites. As a result, by 1867 reformers and conservative Republicans already were urging Republican leaders to conciliate white southerners by stressing the moderation of Republican Reconstruction policy and by disavowing radical demands for further change. Reconciliation with white southerners remained a staple of the liberal-reform program throughout the 1870s.⁶⁹

The liberal reformers' sympathy for southern whites was based on more than political calculation, however. It was reinforced by their perceptions of politics in the South under Republican governments—and in this connection the reformers' racism came into play. It was not that the reformers' growing sympathy with conservative white southerners was founded on race hatred, nor did racism ever lead them, as it did most white southerners and northern Democrats, to justify legal discrimination against black people. Rather, the reformers' belief in black intellectual and moral inferiority led them to perceive the freedmen as posing the same threat to liberty in the South that the so-called dangerous classes of whites posed in the North—the threat of oppressive "class legislation." Having slight faith in blacks' political intelligence or political integrity, the reformers were quick to respond to the pleas of southern whites, who as early as 1868 were charging that the reformers' fears already had come true.

By the 1870s, most southern Conservatives—particularly those moderate Conservatives with whom the liberal reformers most closely identified—no longer framed their criticism of Republican Reconstruction in terms of white supremacy. That was the coin of the White League and color-liners, whose extremism more moderate whites claimed to resist. Promising acquiescence in the political and legal equality guaranteed by the Reconstruction amendments, moderate Conservatives lambasted scalawags and carpetbaggers, who "control the politics of the State through the control which they have obtained over the colored man."⁷⁰ The result of this control, they charged, was a massive system of class legislation. Penniless blacks elected governments that taxed whites to support bloated payrolls, expensive and corrupt building and internal-improvement programs, inefficient and largely black schools, and unnecessary public services. Whereas "all persons in the community who receive the benefits of government ought to contribute equally according to their means," southern Republicans "boast that one class of the population is required to bear only a small share of the burdens of taxation," the Conservatives claimed. "Taxation is robbery, when imposed for private gain, or to build up monopolies for the benefit of the few at the expense of the many."[71] No complaint could have been better framed to win the reformers' sympathy.[72]

Controlling the nation's leading intellectual organs, the liberal reformers ultimately had an immense influence upon the intellectual currents of the United States, and their distaste for the redistributive policies of the southern Republican regimes spread through the North. By the mid-1870s, it would be a common sentiment that, in the words of the conservative Republican *New York Times*, "these freedmen must he convinced that public affairs must not be managed solely for pillage and oppression."[73] Many Republicans came to believe that black suffrage and Republican control of the South were at best necessary evils, justified only by the threat southern Conservatives posed to freedmen's civil rights and to the Union. To stress that threat, Republican leaders desperately employed the rhetoric that came to be known as "waving the bloody shirt." But as southern Conservatives pledged to protect black rights under Conservative regimes and as charges that white southerners continued to nurture treasonous designs against the nation became ever more fatuous, national Republican support for southern Republicanism became less and less tenable.

The change seriously affected power relationships within the Republican party. During the Civil War and Reconstruction years, ambitious Republicans had sought to harness the radicalism of most party activists and the rank and file in order to advance their party careers. Pressure from such radicals often had forced intraparty rivals toward radicalism in self-defense. But under the reformers' attack, radicalism lost much of its appeal to activists and rank and file. By the 1870s, liberalism was a more attractive position from which to attack factional rivals than radicalism. Allying with the reformers, ambitious challengers insisted that Republicans had to replace the reconstruction issue with others that would mobilize the rank and file and reconcile "the best men" to the party.[74]

Just as established leaders had been pushed toward radicalism by such challenges in the 1860s, many were pushed toward conservatism in the 1870s. While some hard-liners urged firmness, the more flexible of the Republican leaders searched for new issues. After the terrible Republican defeats in the elections of 1874, that search became desperate. In the state elections of 1875, some Republican candidates experimented with a mix of support for hard money, anti-

Catholicism, and attacks on agrarian and labor radicalism—all of which resonated with the laissez-faire morality of the liberal reformers. The experiment proved especially successful in the key state of Ohio. There Republicans demonstrated how to win victories on new issues, electing a governor who by virtue of his triumph came to be perceived as the embodiment of the possibilities—the supremely flexible Rutherford B. Hayes.

10

Southern Democrats in the Crisis of 1876–77: A Reconsideration of *Reunion and Reaction*

In 1951, C. Vann Woodward published two books that established him as one of the premier historians of the American South. In one of these, *Origins of the New South*, Woodward exploded the myth of southern Bourbonism after Reconstruction. The so-called Redeemers, he demonstrated, were not the diehard planter reactionaries depicted by Populist and Progressive enemies at the turn of the century and by historians since that time. Rather, they were entrepreneurs who shared the values and interests of their northern counterparts and who opposed the anticapitalist reforms championed by such radical dissidents as Thomas Edward ("Tom") Watson, the Georgia agrarian whose life Woodward had chronicled earlier.[1] Looking backward from the 1880s and 1890s, when these conservative capitalists were ascendant, Woodward discerned a new meaning in the end of Reconstruction, one that confirmed the predominant historical understanding of the 1940s that Reconstruction embodied an effort by northern capitalists to secure their interests against renascent western and southern agrarianism.

Progressive historians had suggested that Republicans had abandoned their pretense of concern for ex-slaves' well-being when it became apparent that southerners no longer threatened the economic supremacy of the industrial interests they represented.[2] In *Origins of the New South* and more fully in his second 1951 volume, *Reunion and Reaction: The Compromise of 1877 and the End of Reconstruction*, Woodward bolstered the thesis by presenting evidence that Rutherford Birchard Hayes's emergence as president in the crisis following the disputed election of 1876 resulted from a definite bargain between northern Republicans and Whiggish southern Democrats over primarily economic issues. In return for southern Democratic support for his inauguration, Hayes agreed to end the interference in southern states that was now irrelevant to northern Republican industrial interests. More important, he promised to support economic legislation beneficial to the South—especially national help in building the Texas and Pacific Railroad, which would link the South to the Pacific Coast, and in repairing the war-wrecked Mississippi River levees. With

---

The original version of this essay was published in the *Journal of Southern History* 46 (November 1980): 489–524.

such an economic alliance cemented, the southerners would desert the Democratic Party and join the Republican, the vehicle of triumphant American capitalism.[3] Thus, *Reunion and Reaction* was one of the last, most important, and most sophisticated works of the Progressive school of history. Informed by the assumptions of economic determinism, Woodward took for granted "a class, or at least an economic, basis for our major parties," as David Herbert Donald observed in 1970. Appropriately, Woodward specially acknowledged his debt to Charles A. Beard in the preface to his book.[4] But Woodward went beyond the simple assertion, so common to the genre, that key historical events were determined by economic factors; he offered compelling evidence from the papers of the actors themselves.

Although some reviewers were dubious, the force of Woodward's prose, his ability to marshal evidence from eclectic sources, and perhaps the existence of the de facto southern Democratic–northern Republican congressional alliance that scuttled so much progressive legislation in the 1940s and 1950s convinced most historians.[5] A greater tribute to Woodward's ability than the acceptance of his account, however, was its endurance. Even though historians in the 1960s and 1970s abandoned the postulates of economic determinism, exploded the notion that Reconstruction-era Republicans fronted for northern capitalists, and came to agree that racial rather than economic issues determined the course of Reconstruction, Woodward's thesis weathered the storm.

Woodward's interpretation was trenchantly challenged by Allan Peskin, who pointed out that the economic terms were never carried out, and much more circumspectly questioned by Keith Ian Polakoff in what is still the standard history of the election of 1876. But Woodward responded to Peskin forcefully and effectively. He conceded that the bargain over home rule was more important to both sides than "the lesser parts," but he insisted upon the relevance of economic bargains and the crucial role played by "Whiggish" southern Democrats. The fulfillment of terms is not the test of whether there has been a bargain, Woodward urged, effectively pointing out that the terms of the Compromise of 1850 were not fulfilled either. Conceding that the Electoral Commission secured Hayes's victory, Woodward still maintained that it was the southern Democrats, in pursuance of their bargain with Hayes's supporters, who guaranteed that Hayes would be peacefully inaugurated and thereby exorcized the specter of civil war. Woodward's thesis, especially as modified by his response to Peskin, persisted in textbooks and was repeated in new scholarship at the time I published the original version of this essay in 1980.[6]

Undertaking a direct assessment of Woodward's evidence, the actual voting patterns of southern Democrats in the electoral-count controversy, and southern opinion during the crisis, I found that Woodward had accurately described a Republican effort to break down Democratic unity in the South, but that this effort had not been the determining factor in Democratic acquiescence in Hayes's inauguration. Moreover, he greatly overestimated both the role southerners played in moderating Democratic opposition to Hayes and the part the railroad played in influencing the southerners.

At the time I sent him a copy of an initial draft, Woodward was still recovering from a bitter dispute over his role in rescinding an invitation Yale students had issued to the Communist historian Herbert Aptheker to lead a seminar on W. E. B. DuBois. Regarding the draft of my article, he wrote me, "I don't know when I have been so thoroughly clobbered. That is saying a good deal, considering my experience in some quarters of late." Ever gracious, he sent a cordial three-page, single-spaced typed reaction that helped me modify and reshape the argument, but it was clear he was pained.[7] In his memoir *Thinking Back*, Woodward effusively praised the research, thought, and presentation of my essay. "It is the sort of criticism a historian dreams of—only to wake up in a cold sweat," he wrote.[8]

Explaining that *Reunion and Reaction* had been an "unanticipated book," the by-product of more general work on the post-Reconstruction South, he conceded that this fact had led to some distortions. He had indeed stressed too much the importance of the economic aspects of the Compromise of 1877 and had paid too much attention to southern Democrats and not enough to their northern allies. The facts he had uncovered were still a significant part of the story but by no means the central explanation for events as he had once thought.[9] This reassessment has generally found its way into the Reconstruction and American history textbooks, although it did not go as far as I did.[10] (My essay indicated that the effort to use economic blandishments to split southern Democrats had failed.) Thus, there is no longer any point in republishing "Southern Democrats in the Crisis of 1876–77" as a refutation of Woodward's thesis. But it does provide important information about the events surrounding the resolution of the disputed election, factionalism among southern Conservatives and among Republicans, Hayes's southern policy, and his relation to the Republican Party.

In *Reunion and Reaction*, Woodward delineated the large influence pre–Civil War Whigs had in the Reconstruction-era southern Democratic Party. In two beautifully crafted chapters, he pointed out that the economic notions of these old Whigs resembled those of probusiness Republicans more than they did those held by Jacksonian, antigovernment northern Democrats. The practical expression of the attitudes of these southern conservatives, he wrote, was their support for government aid in building a new transcontinental railroad to connect the South with the Pacific coast. Most of them favored Pennsylvania Railroad president Thomas A. Scott's Texas and Pacific Railroad scheme, which was lobbied throughout the South and in Congress in the 1870s. This support was only representative, Woodward wrote, of demands for aid in rebuilding the Mississippi levees and other improvements.[11]

However, in stressing southern Democratic support for the Texas and Pacific Railroad, one should not ignore economic issues of far greater moment to most Americans. As Carl V. Harris has demonstrated, on financial issues, the tariff, taxation, and business regulation southern Democrats in Congress voted more like western radicals than northeastern conservatives.[12] Also, although Woodward correctly observed that Republicans hoped to capture the old Whig vote, the evidence of the effort that Woodward found of an attempt to strike a distinct bargain between Republicans and Whiggish southern Democrats, based on support for such internal improvements as Scott's railroad, lay almost entirely in the correspondence among three men. The first of these was Hayes's close adviser William Henry Smith. The two others were journalist Henry Van Ness Boynton and newspaper publisher and editor Andrew J. Kellar.[13]

Woodward saw Kellar as the prototypical southern conservative with whom Republicans reached their understanding—a prewar Unionist, though a Democrat, now "aligned with the Whig-industrialist wing of the Democratic party led by Colonel Arthur S. Colyar of Nashville and opposed to the state rights-planter wing led by Isham G. Harris, unreconstructed Confederate."[14] However, Woodward seriously misconstrued Kellar's position in Tennessee politics, imposing the alignments of the 1880s upon the 1870s.[15]

Kellar was hardly a "Whiggish" conservative Democrat. In fact, he was barely a Democrat at all and certainly did not symbolize a new southern Democratic identity of interests with Republicans. As the *Memphis Ledger* noted, he had "been consistent in the efforts to disintegrate and break up the Democratic party ever since Grant was elected in 1868."[16] Editor of the *Memphis Avalanche*, Kellar wrangled incessantly with his chief local competitor, the orthodox Democratic *Memphis Appeal*, which received government patronage when regular Democrats were in power. Challenging regular Democrats first for being too quick to sacrifice war-related Democratic principles and then for being too slow to do so, Kellar's political zigzags were aimed primarily at dislodging the "Memphis ring of office-seekers," which persistently favored his competition. When Democratic leaders themselves endorsed the "New Departure" in 1872, as Kellar had been urging, he abandoned that line of attack and began to demand that the Democratic state administration repudiate a large part of the state debt. From this distinctly un-Whiggish position, Kellar's *Avalanche* joined former President Andrew Johnson's assault upon the regular party leadership, supporting Johnson's insurgent candidacies and sponsoring local bolts in the

Memphis area, which sometimes succeeded with tacit Republican support. When Johnson's death in 1875 left dissidents leaderless his organization began to crumble, and by 1876 Kellar and the *Avalanche* had openly left the Democratic ranks. In that year Kellar backed the low-tax, anti-debt payment gubernatorial candidacy of Dorsey B. Thomas, who ran as an independent with some Republican support. In the presidential election, he and the *Avalanche* supported the Greenback candidate Peter Cooper, hardly the favorite of Republican conservatives, and outspokenly promoted inflation and denounced eastern bondholders.

Far from representing the industrial Redeemer elite, Kellar worked assiduously in the 1870s to undermine its political power. Within the framework of Tennessee politics, he belonged to the agrarian wing of the Democratic Party led by Johnson in the early 1870s and Robert Love ("Bob") Taylor in the 1880s. In his relation to the Republicans Kellar was a precursor of the Virginia Readjusters and North Carolina and Tennessee Populists. Like them, he had his own interests to promote, and his goal was not to extend Republicanism in the South but to precipitate "a grand political smashup."[17] To accomplish this, he wanted control of the federal patronage in Tennessee, impossible if Democrat Samuel J. Tilden became president, and toward that end he pressed for the appointment of his new ally, former Senator David M. Key, to a Hayes cabinet.[18]

Boynton was the pugnacious Washington correspondent of the *Cincinnati Gazette*. Combining a preacher's son's hostility to corruption with a passion for political intrigue, Boynton—like most newspapermen of his era—was not above slanting his reports to reflect his views. "Boynton is universally regarded here as a liar and a libeller," John Sherman wrote his brother in December 1875, after one of Boynton's journalistic escapades—a book minimizing General William Tecumseh Sherman's role in the Civil War.[19] Bitterly hostile to the Republican leaders sustained by the Grant administration, Boynton had hammered away at its corruption and promoted the reputation of Benjamin Helm Bristow, his paper's candidate for the Republican presidential nomination. Boynton recognized that the events of the winter of 1876–77 were to determine both which party's candidate occupied the White House and which elements would control the Republican Party if Hayes were successfully inaugurated.

Boynton was not certain that his wing of the party would emerge victorious in this infighting. Hayes had been nominated as a compromise among diverse Republican factions battling one another largely over the issues of reform within the party and in the national civil service. Such a reform would deprive the dominant factions of the patronage that welded their "machines" and made them so hard to dislodge. Bristow had been the candidate of the "reformers," and their shift to Hayes had made his nomination possible. But some of the established "machine" forces—especially Oliver Perry Morton's Indiana delegation—had played critical roles, and all the "machines" had worked hard for Hayes in the canvass. Now it was the regulars—Zachariah Chandler, William Eaton Chandler, Morton, and others—who were most active in saving the disputed states for Hayes, and Hayes was depending upon Grant himself to guarantee his inauguration against forcible resistance.

Boynton also knew that if there was an issue besides civil service reform that separated "reformers" from "regulars" in the party, it was what to do in the South. Republican dissidents stressed the necessity for purifying the political system; regulars emphasized the issues on which the party had been founded and that still mobilized its rank and file. Although reform elements had gained ground since 1874, the Republican campaign of 1876 had been run largely on war issues. And Republican leaders and newspapers continued to describe southern antiblack and anti-Republican violence in lurid detail as they justified the rejection of Democratic votes in the disputed states.[20] The more Hayes was beholden to the orthodox party regulars and the more Republicans stressed southern violence and rebelliousness in defending his claims, the more likely it seemed to dissidents like Boynton that the same elements that controlled Grant's administration would control Hayes's.[21] Likewise, Kellar's dream of a general party realignment would evaporate if Hayes sustained leaders who stressed sectional issues.

So Kellar's and Boynton's activities were aimed both at dividing southerners and at convincing Hayes and his advisers that they had succeeded in the accomplishment—that Hayes owed his inauguration not to the old Republican hardliners but to the party's reform element, and that continued reliance upon their advice on civil service reform and the southern question promised similar success in the future. As he kept William Henry Smith informed of his lobbying activities, Kellar pressed Hayes's advisers to be wary of "Blaine & his class," urging that "the old secession element and the ultra Radicals under Blaine & Butler ought to be together in the same party."[22] Boynton's letters manifest the same concern. At the same time that he worked to divide Democrats in Congress, Boynton pressed Bristow's claims for patronage and influence in the new Republican administration. Copies of his correspondence with Smith went to Bristow, and Boynton noted, "You will see how I united the two things, and they *belong* together."[23]

Close attention to the chronology of Boynton and Kellar's activities during the electoral crisis makes clear the degree to which they—and through reliance upon them, Woodward—exaggerated the impact of their efforts to win southern acceptance of Hayes's inauguration. For the fact is that Hayes owed his peaceful inauguration far more to the course taken by northern Democrats, particularly northeastern Democrats, than to that of the southerners.

Democrats were in a weak position from the beginning as they watched in frustration while the returning boards of Florida, Louisiana, and South Carolina overturned apparent Democratic majorities there. Republicans controlled the presidency, the army, and the Senate, whose presiding officer was directed by the Constitution to open and count the vote of the Electoral College. The legal argument that the presiding officer of the Senate, Senator Thomas W. Ferry of Michigan, had to determine which electoral votes were certified by the appropriate state authorities was plausible enough to satisfy the Republican rank and file. Perhaps the Democratic counterargument that the framers of the Constitution could not have intended to permit one man to make that decision was just as plausible; but in the days before the Supreme Court was recognized as the ultimate arbiter of practically all such constitutional disputes, the Democrats had no tribunal to which to present it.[24]

Democrats had few alternatives. The Democratic House of Representatives could send committees south to gather evidence that the elections there were fair and that the returning boards had thrown out Democratic majorities for partisan reasons. If that evidence was compelling enough, Americans might recoil so violently from the fraud that Republicans would be forced by political pressure to abandon their program. In that event, Democrats would object to counting the votes from the disputed states, the two houses of Congress would not agree on what to do with them, and they would be thrown out. Neither candidate would have a majority of the electoral vote, and the Democratic House would elect the President, as the Constitution provides in such a case.

But it soon became apparent that the situation in the South was not as clear as Democrats had believed. Tales of violence and terror firmed the Republicans' determination, and they seemed committed to going forward. To put Tilden in the White House, Democrats would have to refuse to accept the validity of Ferry's count and have the House elect the president despite it; but there would be no way to enforce the decision except through a popular revolt against Grant's army. Democrats did not have the stomach for this. Yet if they buckled Republicans would surely succeed in electing Hayes. So Democrats had to stand firm and hope that public fear of violence would become so great that Republicans would be forced to abandon their scheme and concede the House's authority.[25]

In all this, it was the course of northern rather than southern Democrats that would be critical. With the electoral crisis following a bitter campaign turning largely on sectional issues, southerners knew that they could not take the lead in resisting Hayes's inauguration. "Our opponents are eagerly hoping for some outbreak upon the part of southern Democrats in Congress," the

Memphis Appeal warned in December. "Let them be disappointed."[26] That advice was echoed throughout the South. "It is for the northern people to consider the situation and do what they think is right. The South will not by impulsiveness increase her own sufferings nor in any way embarrass the northern people who are endeavoring to rescue the public places from the corrupt, dishonest, and cruel men who have so long profaned them."[27] It was all up to the North. "Will Tilden, our president elect—will the hundreds of thousands of northern men who voted for him—stand it? The south waits for an answer."[28] Over and over again southern Democrats urged boldness upon their northern allies. "Men of the North, rise up and rescue the once fair name of this land from disgrace," the *Charleston News and Courier* declaimed. "To you belongs the task, and to you it should be a pleasing duty. . . . Military Despotism on one hand—Constitutional Liberty on the other. Choose this day between the two."[29] While the South could not take the lead in preparations for resistance, there could be no doubt where it would stand when the crisis came. If northerners "prefer a dangerous contest to submission, we think that we can promise that the South . . . will be found . . . ready to peril life for liberty," the *New Orleans Picayune* assured its allies.[30]

But southerners were stunned to find little ferment among Democrats in the North. Many western Democrats echoed their calls for firmness and agitation, but serious problems made most national Democratic leaders hesitate.[31] Despite Democratic charges that Republicans had promoted radical changes in American government and society, Republicans had at critical moments been able to label the Democrats as the real threat to American stability.[32] With their large ex-Confederate constituency and their Copperhead heritage, Democrats were terribly vulnerable to attacks on their loyalty. The slightest indiscreet act "would do the Democratic party great damage," one of Tilden's advisers wrote. "It is so largely made up of the Southern States that nothing would please the Republican party better than to see it assume an attitude of war, or something that could be perverted into a threat against the Government. They would at once cry a new rebellion and endeavor to consolidate the North against the Democratic party, as being the rebel party, and with much show for success."[33] Moreover, conservative capitalists and businessmen, influential in the northern Democracy, could be relied on to repudiate measures that threatened economic stability. Throughout the crisis the northeastern Democratic leaders, who controlled much of the party apparatus, refused to take any step that might precipitate the feared reaction.[34] This caution was justified by the glee with which Republicans labeled *every* hint of resistance as "revolutionary."[35] The Republicans' reception in late November of Representative Clarkson N. Potter's statement of the Democratic position on counting the vote was particularly instructive. Republicans universally denounced it as "Tilden's Revolution."[36]

Democrats seemed to be in an impossible situation. "When Democrats... talk about resorting to legal and peaceful remedies to prevent the actual consummation of a glaring infamy," they complained, "the Republicans and the hypocritical Independents rush into print and twaddle about 'war,' 'bloodshed.'"[37] But it worked. Boynton reported that the flurry seriously demoralized Democrats in Washington, a conclusion corroborated by the Washington correspondent of the Democratic *Chicago Times*, who quoted party leaders there as warning, "If the democrats do not act with great prudence we will be again found on the defensive."[38]

As Democrats drifted southerners grew more and more restive, worrying that "if we announce by our silence beforehand that we intend to acquiesce in any outrage... [Republicans] perpetrate, we only invite aggression from them and prepare our own friends for a degrading submission." "The bad men, who are conspiring against liberty, feel only contempt for those who whine about the obligation of law and the necessity of peace," they warned.[39]

Although they enjoyed a brief moment of enthusiasm as the Democratic caucus selected hardliner Samuel J. Randall as Speaker when Congress convened early in December, it soon became clear that the firm leadership southerners wanted from the North was not forthcoming.[40] By mid-December those who urged an aggressive policy were thoroughly demoralized at the timid course of Tilden's advisers and northeastern Democrats generally. "Only the most prompt and determined resistance can avert the utter destruction of Constitutional government," incoming North Carolina governor Zebulon B. Vance wrote a friend. "The South *cant* make this resistance, for obvious reasons, and the North will not. They are too busy making money." Complaints flooded Tilden from throughout the South, whose Democrats, he was told, "feel more than ever that they are leaning on a bag of wind when they look for aid and comfort from the North."[41]

As the Democratic paralysis continued, southern Democrats began to worry that the fruits of their apparent victory would be lost; in particular, they feared that if Democratic inaction led to Hayes's inauguration it would mean continued national government patronage and protection for the southern Republican party that they loathed and still feared.[42] "What the South has expected from Gov. Tilden's election, no man who does not live in the South can be made to know," wrote a despondent Alabama Democrat. "It was resurrection after burial. And what our disappointment will be at his failure is beyond the possibilities of language to express. It is to have been resurrected only to be reinterred."[43] Furious at their confused northern allies, some southerners likened their course to that of their "cowardice" of 1861 and began to warn, "If the Northern Democracy is too timid to uphold the right, or unequal to the maintenance of victory achieved by our help, there is no tie to bind the South forever to defeat."[44] In *Reunion and Reaction*, Woodward cited such criticism of the course of northern Democrats in 1861 as evidence of southern restraint in the face of northern Democratic warmongering in 1876.[45] In fact, they were precisely the opposite—warnings to northern Democrats to adopt more aggressive measures. The Washington correspondent of the *Cincinnati Enquirer* explained the situation cogently: "The Northern Democrats are not taking the firm course necessary to secure a unity of action with the South." From Washington, an informant with close links to southern congressmen wrote Tilden urgently, "I am convinced if we fail to secure them the victory they have assisted us in obtaining they will make conditions with Hayes . . . . [They will] abandon the democracy if there . . . [is] a failure to maintain every right in the present contest!"[46]

As southerners' fears grew, more and more of them began to sound out Hayes's intimates. By mid-December, *Cincinnati Commercial* editor Murat Halstead, former governor William Dennison of Ohio, James A. Garfield, and William Henry Smith all reported such overtures.[47] But, as Tilden's correspondent suggested, southern Democrats approached Hayes not because they sought economic benefits for their section, and least of all because they feared northern Democrats would drag them into war. They began to talk to Hayes's friends because they were afraid northern Democrats were going to fritter away Tilden's victory. As one of them explained, "We have got to see that, whatever horse loses, our horse wins."[48] So when William Henry Smith, Kellar, and other Hayes advisers met in Cincinnati on December 14 and "arranged a programme" to split enough southern Democrats from Tilden to guarantee Hayes's inauguration, they were taking advantage of a situation precipitated not by southern but by northern—especially northeastern—Democratic moderation.[49]

To judge how much this "programme" contributed to Hayes's ultimate success, one must remember just what its purpose was. The goal of the operation Woodward described so beautifully was to convert southern overtures into commitments to oppose efforts in the House to recognize Tilden after Hayes was counted in by the presiding officer of the Senate. This would guarantee Hayes's inauguration. "Without the passage of resolutions which are essentially revolutionary the hands of the House are tied," Boynton noted. Thus "the practical question was to secure thirty-six democrats, who . . . will vote 'no' upon every proposition in the least revolutionary in its tendency."[50] Further, they hoped to make the breach irreparable. A new Republican southern policy following such an open division would break Democratic hegemony in the Solid South—and explode the influence of bloody-shirt bosses in the North. Kellar, Boynton, Garfield, Dennison, Stanley Matthews, Representative Charles Foster, and other Hayes representatives assiduously wooed southerners with assurances of his sympathy. Suddenly Republican newspapers announced that the threat to peace emanated from northern Democrats, expressed certainty that the South would oppose violence at all hazards, praised its restraint extravagantly, and openly announced that such a course would impose on Hayes and the Republican party "an obligation of the most binding kind to protect its interests to the utmost."[51]

Such Republican propaganda was rendered plausible by the course of a few southern Democratic leaders, like Lucius Q. C. Lamar of Mississippi, Benjamin H. Hill of Georgia, and former Confederate Vice President Alexander H. Stephens of Georgia, who consistently reassured northerners that the South intended no new rebellion. In an anonymous interview of December 24, Kellar insisted that while Hill and Lamar were resisting Republican overtures, Memphis Representative Hiram C. Young, and about twenty-five other former Whig congressmen intended to support Hayes on crucial votes. At almost the same time, an interviewer reported Hill's hints that Hayes would not make so bad a president.[52]

But despite Kellar's enthusiastic, and self-serving, report that "The situation in Washington has changed immensely, from the warlike to the most peaceful" due to his efforts, southerners' real response ranged from suspicion to denunciation.[53] "It is true that overtures have been made to Mr. Hayes by persons who gave him to understand they represented the South," the *Nashville Weekly American*'s Washington correspondent reported, "but it is not a fact that any man or set of men of any prominence in the South have given ear or support to any such scheme." Probably referring to Kellar, whose past efforts to disrupt the Tennessee Democracy were familiar to his readers, he noted, "There is a set of plotters in the South who seek personal ends alone, and they are the class who made the representation to Mr. Hayes."[54] Democratic correspondents unanimously concurred. The Republican effort was designed to inspire northern Democratic distrust of their southern allies and thus make them even more reluctant to make a stand. From throughout the South came renewed assurances: "The Democrats of the South have not been demonstrative . . . because any exhibition of the sort would injure our northern friends by cementing the northern Republicans. . . . But if war should be precipitated, it is useless [that is, unnecessary] to say that the northern Democrats would have the sympathy of a 'solid south,' and that a hundred thousand southerners would be found ready to join the northern Democrats battling . . . to preserve the rights bequeathed to us by our fathers."⁵⁵

As Democratic observers complained that Lamar, Hill, and other outspoken southern moderates had shaken Democratic confidence, these men hastened to recant. His only purpose was to promote a peaceful adjudication, Hill insisted. If Republicans spurned such overtures, he would sustain Tilden to the end. "I am brave enough to want peace, but not cowardly enough to accept dishonor," he wrote. Lamar, Stephens, and Young made similar denials.⁵⁶ Southern interest in Republican overtures waxed and waned in direct proportion to their confidence in Democratic resolution, Democrats reported, "but let the North show a bold front and assert its rights, and the South will not be found wanting."⁵⁷

But on December 30, newspapers published a letter to Hayes from Wade Hampton, assuring him that South Carolina would participate only in peaceful attempts to resolve the crisis; and Hill's explanation of his position—while denying any sympathy with Hayes—still seemed ambiguous about how to resist his inauguration.⁵⁸ Both appeared to corroborate Republican reports of southern irresolution, even if they scotched rumors of an actual bargain. Those who were convinced that only fear of resistance would dissuade Republicans from their course reported from Washington that "the letters . . . have fallen like a wet blanket on the Democrats here."⁵⁹

Convinced that only bold action would prevent further demoralization Democrats made one final effort to convince Republicans they would not submit sheepishly to usurpation—and, added the Washington correspondent of the *New York Times*, "to arrest the conciliatory feeling of the Southern Democrats, and . . . counteract the charge of pusillanimity made by the southern against the northern wing of the party."⁶⁰ Western and border-state Democrats called for nationwide protest meetings to be held on Jackson Day (January 8). Once again southern journals promised to follow any Northern lead, relieved that "the long silence of the Democrats . . . will be broken in a few days."⁶¹ With Tilden's secret approval, Representative Henry Watterson of Kentucky prepared an ominous call for 100,000 Democratic "petitioners" to converge on Washington on February 14 and timed its publication to coincide with the Jackson Day meetings. But on the crucial day the Democratic meetings were smaller than anticipated. Resolutions were watered down. In several states the party refused to endorse the protests officially. The Washington rally failed to attract any nationally known Democrat except Watterson.⁶² In the aftermath of the fizzle, New York Representative Abram S. Hewitt, Tilden's confidant and hand-picked chairman of the Democratic National Committee, refused pleas to convene the committee to endorse formally Watterson's mass protest. "He thinks the very first step to force by arms the inauguration of Tilden would deprive the Democratic party of its most valuable support in New York, Connecticut, and New Jersey," the *Richmond Dispatch*'s Washington correspondent reported. "The moneyed men of the Democratic party of those States of course desire the inauguration of Tilden, but they are a unit for peace at any price."[63]

Throughout the sputtering Democratic offensive, Boynton reported to his *Cincinnati Gazette* readers that it was southern Democratic moderation that stood in the way of Tilden's nefarious designs, and when resistance finally broke down, he characteristically took credit for it.[64] But it is plain that he exaggerated his role. The leading southern moderates—Lamar and Hill—had issued their cautious advice well before Boynton and Kellar went to work. Kellar had admitted in his anonymous interview that neither Hill nor Lamar was involved in his negotiations for southern Democratic support. When both Hill and Lamar came under attack from southerners and some westerners for their "demoralizing" position, Hewitt and other northern Democratic leaders informed the critics that their prudence reflected the strategy of northern leaders.[65] Southerners were receptive to the blandishments of Hayes's agents primarily because of the "timidity" of northeastern Democrats. And as of mid-January there was no real evidence, outside of Kellar's and Boynton's assurances, that southerners would not have stood solidly behind a firm northern Democratic front if there had been one.

Naturally, if there is little to indicate that Boynton and Kellar's efforts were successful up to this time, the Texas and Pacific lobby could not yet have had much effect. In fact, as of mid-January it had not even come into play. Boynton first broached the idea of enlisting Scott's forces on December 20, proposing that if Hayes favored the project some "recognized friend" should tell Scott so. While Hayes assured Smith that he would be "liberal" with regard to southern internal improvements, it is not clear whether Boynton and Smith could consider this a strong enough endorsement to assure Scott of Hayes's specific support of the Texas and Pacific. While the Republican press immediately began hinting that southerners were more likely to win Republican than Democratic support for such projects, it was not until January 14—after the collapse of the last Democratic offensive—that Boynton finally met with Scott and his lobbyist Grenville M. Dodge to propose their cooperation.[66]

Furthermore, Boynton grossly overestimated—or exaggerated—the strength of the Scott lobby. "It is as if an army had made a juncture with us," he wrote Smith.[67] As Allan Peskin has pointed out, Scott was never even able to get his scheme to the floor of the House for a vote; his efforts were a catalogue of frustrations. The day before Boynton enlisted Scott in Hayes's interest, General Richard ("Dick") Taylor, the most influential southern lobbyist in Washington, wrote wirepuller Samuel L. M. Barlow that Scott's bill was dead. "Out of seventy-three southern members," he wrote, "forty will oppose it."[68] Nonetheless, the Republican efforts might have borne fruit if Boynton, Kellar, Scott, Garfield, and others had had time to test them. But they did not. Only four days after Boynton finally met Scott, and in the immediate aftermath of the Democrats' abortive Jackson Day offensive, the Electoral Commission bill was reported by a joint committee set up a month earlier to find a compromise. Just when it had become clear that Democrats could mount no effective opposition, Republican unity had collapsed. Unwilling to risk the odium of inaugurating their candidate by force, pressured by important business interests from throughout the Northeast, and in a few cases none too friendly to the "reform" factions gathering around Hayes, leading Republicans had abandoned their party's hard line and agreed to submit disputed electoral votes to a fifteen-man commission during the count.[69]

Most Democrats welcomed the Electoral Commission bill, perceiving that it provided Tilden's only chance to be president. Given their desperate position, the compromise seemed "too good to be true," an astonished southern newspaper editorialized, "one of those things hard to believe. The Democrats have everything to gain and nothing to lose."[70] As the *Nation* reported, "The Democrats are much more disposed to ... agree on some middle course ... because they are at a disadvantage and know it. Their opponents ... are in possession ... they have the administrative machinery and the army in their hands, and are therefore able to do ... lawless things, which if done by the other side would ruin it." Many Democrats saw it differently: The compromise provided Tilden's only chance because of "the backdown of Chairman Hewitt and other weak-kneed bondholding Eastern Democratic capitalists."[71] But despite the pressure for the bill, a higher proportion of Democrats from the South than any other region held out for total victory. Of the eighteen Democratic representatives who opposed the compromise, thirteen were from the South.[72]

As Democrats united behind the bill Hayes and his closest advisers bitterly opposed it. "It is a clumsily constructed machine to allow timid or treacherous men to defeat your election," John Sherman wrote Hayes. "The bill of surrender—the astute terms of capitulation to the rebel yell," the disgusted national party organ characterized it. The reason for the opposition was simple: The measure was "a surrender of a certainty for an uncertainty."[73]

The Republican retreat was particularly galling for Boynton. His goal had been to win Hayes's gratitude by preventing House Democrats from recognizing Tilden; he thought his finally consummated alliance with Scott would guarantee success. The compromise frustrated those plans, bringing his efforts to a halt.[74] While Scott's ally Dodge worked to get the compromise through Congress and Kellar's *Avalanche* endorsed it, pretending to find it a victory for moderation against Tildenite extremism and Kellar's southern opponents, Boynton fumed that "In the pending compromise the Democrats have finally secured the only chance of success which remained to them after the results . . . became known" and bitterly detailed what his paper called the "Steps in the Surrender."[75] William Henry Smith also commented disgustedly that "the crafty policy of Tilden is about to receive the aid of Republicans in Congress" and lamented that Hayes's only alternatives now were to try to persuade Republican Supreme Court justices not to serve on the commission or to challenge the constitutionality of the law itself.[76]

However, by January 25, when it became known that Justice David Davis would not serve on the Electoral Commission and that Republicans would have an eight-to-seven majority on it, Boynton recovered his élan. He informed Hayes's friends of his conviction that their candidate had a good chance of winning before the commission and announced that the Electoral Commission bill had, after all, been passed because he and Kellar had broken Democratic morale by wooing the South.[77]

Boynton, Smith, and Kellar were really rescued when outraged Democrats threatened to renege on the compromise after the commission voted along party lines to deliver the Florida and Louisiana electoral votes to Hayes. An angry minority of Democrats determined to delay the electoral vote count beyond the March 4 expiration of Grant's presidential term, intending to recognize Tilden at that time. When these filibusterers failed to gain the votes necessary to carry out their plan, Boynton immediately claimed credit. "The good seed we planted brings pleasant fruit," he wrote Smith. "Enough southern men stand in the way of filibustering to make it certain . . . the Democrats cannot beat Gov. Hayes by delay." Scott and Kellar did the work, he announced happily. "It is difficult to distinguish between the comparative effects produced by the two elements—the purely political, and the Scott forces."[78]

Indeed, both Kellar and Scott were hard at work.[79] But once again Boynton overstated the influence of his efforts. There were far more compelling reasons for Democrats to accept the decision of the Electoral Commission than promises of railroad subsidies, or even of "home rule" for the South. A large majority of Democrats, northern as well as southern, recognized both the futility and danger of further resistance. Democrats had helped frame the Electoral Commission bill; they had given it overwhelming support when the Republicans had been badly divided. They could not repudiate it now that it had resulted in the victory of their opponents. This would simply allow Republicans once more to charge Democrats with incendiarism.[80] In fact Sherman was already counseling Hayes, "There is no cause now of doubt [as to the commission's decision] and every movement made by the Democrats to delay the count will be regarded as proof of a revolutionary intent, and need not be carried much farther to justify us in finishing the count without their assistance."[81]

Moreover, Democrats were in no better position to fight after the Electoral Commission decision than they were before the compromise had been framed. They had neither plan nor organization. Nearly all the state forces they controlled were in the South, leaving them vulnerable to charges of treason. "The Democratic members of the South who are members of the next Congress would be hustled out of their places, and their opponents sworn into office," one Democratic representative predicted. "We would lose the House, destroy our vantage ground in the Senate, and our party would be paralyzed and broken up throughout the length and breadth of the land, and the conspirators would . . . pass their force bills, and suspension of the *habeas corpus*, and reconstruct the States to suit themselves."[82]

This general Democratic understanding led to the most crucial single action taken against the filibuster: Speaker Samuel J. Randall's decision on February 24 to enforce the electoral count resolution's ban on dilatory motions. Had this decision gone the other way, the filibusterers would not have needed a majority to prevent completion of the count. But in quashing the Democratic extremists, Randall did not enforce his own will but that of the Democratic caucus. Randall himself favored the most extreme resistance in the caucuses that followed the commission decisions on Florida and Louisiana, but he and the filibusterers had been voted down. Had he sustained the minority in the face of formal caucus resolutions that the count be continued, his ruling could (and probably would) have been overturned upon appeal to the House. Randall had only a tenuous hold on the speakership, having been elected to fill the term of Michael C. Kerr, who had defeated him for the place in 1875,[83] and he would have sacrificed his chance for the speakership of the following Congress had he disobeyed the caucus.

Southerners who opposed further resistance could not resist acid responses to the minority of northerners who now urged it. "The Eastern Democrats . . . should have had more backbone at the right time. A want of nerve made arbitration a necessity. It was proposed. It was properly accepted and the Democrats of the West and South are properly absolved from all blame," the more moderate observed. Others, like Henry W. Grady, the *Atlanta Constitution*'s Washington correspondent, were less kind: "The Tilden campaign received its fatal stab six weeks ago," he wrote, "from the hands of Mr. Abram S. Hewitt. And he stabbed it with the same pair of shears that he uses for clipping coupons from his bonds."[84]

Randall's decision meant that the filibusterers could prevent the consummation of the electoral count only by overturning his ruling or by forcing continuous adjournments of the House. Either course required a majority of the votes. Boynton claimed credit for preventing the filibusterers from securing the majority, but despite his claims, southern Democrats opposed the filibuster in no higher proportions than northern Democrats. As figure 10.1 demonstrates, northern and southern Democratic voting patterns on the electoral count were almost identical, with southerners, if anything, a little more inclined to stopping the count. Moreover, if the filibuster votes are broken down by smaller regions, as in figure 10.2, it is clear that northeastern Democrats consistently opposed further resistance in greater proportions than southern or border-state Democrats. In fact, a majority of southern Democrats opposed the filibuster on only twelve of forty-three roll calls, and on each of those occasions a majority of all other Democrats did the same. In contrast, a majority of northeastern Democrats voted with Republicans twenty-four times. Although southern Democrats made up 17 to 20 percent of voting representatives, on the median vote they constituted only 9.1 percent of the anti-filibuster coalition. Boynton and Kellar had spoken of obtaining twenty-five to thirty anti-Tilden southern votes. But on the critical roll calls, only between eighteen and twenty-three of

Figure 10.1
Percentage of Democrats Voting With Republicans on Electoral Count Roll Calls

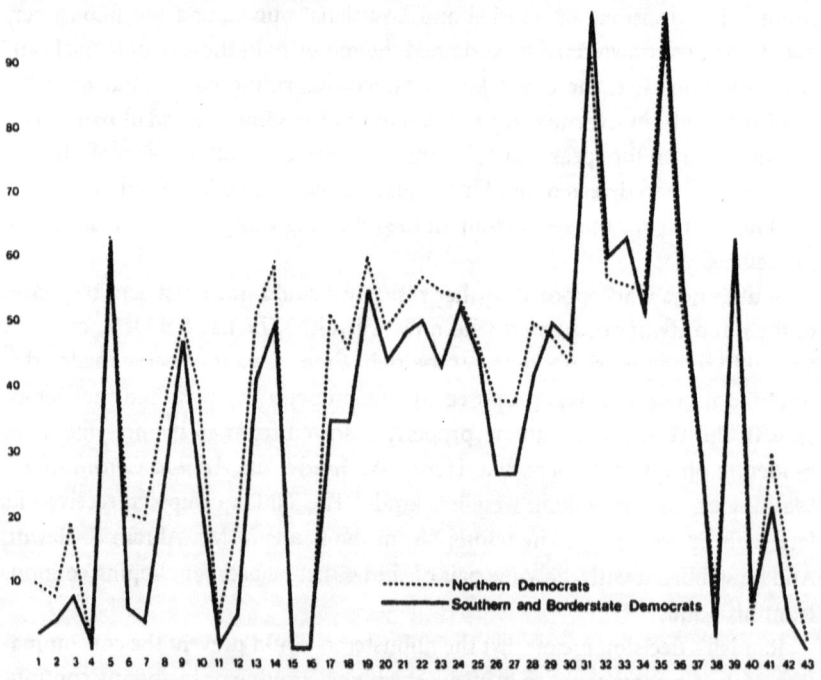

Figure 10.2
Percentage of Democrats Voting With Republicans on Electoral Count Roll Calls

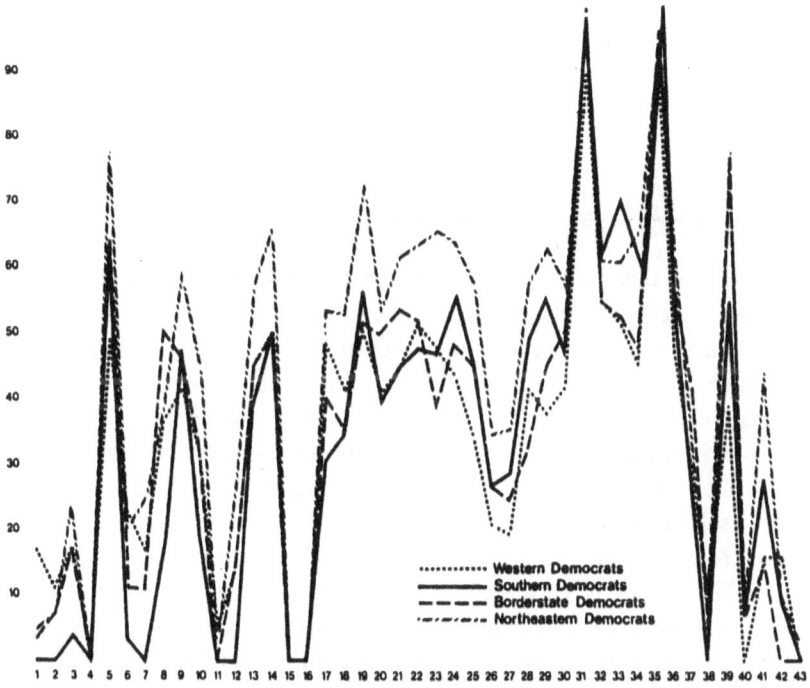

the forty to forty-eight southern Democrats voting sustained the Republicans. Over the whole series of delaying roll calls, the median number of southern anti-filibuster votes was thirteen, while the median number of northeastern Democratic anti-filibuster votes was seventeen, out of a smaller pool.

The anti-filibuster coalition lost the majority only fourteen times on the forty-three votes dealing with the electoral count and only twice in the critical period between February 24 and March 1. If every southern Democrat voting against the filibuster had changed his vote, not once would they have changed the result. If every anti-filibuster border-state Democrat had changed his votes as well, the combined defection would have affected the outcome only twice. Table 10.1 provides the result of Guttman scale analysis of the roll calls dealing with the electoral count.[85] Again, it is apparent that southerners made no disproportionate contribution to ending the filibuster. Moreover, the low value of the statistic *eta* indicates how little region had to do with Democrats' positions.

As the foregoing suggests, there is no evidence that southern Democrats who supported subsidies for pet southern projects were more likely to oppose the

Table 10.1
Democrats and the Electoral Vote Count Filibuster

Section	Antifilibuster	Profilibuster
Northeast	25	19
West	20	22
South	22	28
Border	14	13
Eta = .01		

filibuster than those who did not. Although congressmen never got the chance to vote on the Texas and Pacific Railroad subsidy directly, they did have the opportunity to vote for or against Representative William S. Holman's well-known resolution opposing further subsidies of any kind.[86] Moreover, statistical analysis indicates that the pattern of the vote on that resolution parallels closely the vote on the bill to subsidize the repair of the Mississippi levees. The two roll calls enable a researcher to rank representatives according to their attitudes toward subsidizing internal improvements in the South.

The resulting table 10.2 demonstrates the ineffectiveness of Republican economic blandishments. Of the fifteen southern Democrats who voted both for the Mississippi levee subsidy and against the Holman resolution, only seven opposed the filibuster. Of the forty southern Democrats who favored subsidies to some degree, only 42.5 percent opposed the filibuster, a smaller proportion than one finds among those opposing subsidies. The value of *gamma* indicates that attitude toward southern internal improvements had little impact on whether southern representatives supported or opposed the filibuster.

Table 10.2
Prosubsidy and Antisubsidy Southern and Border-State Democrats and Filibuster Roll Calls

Votes on Subsidies	Antifilibuster	Profilibuster
Opposed to all subsidies	6	6
Voted for Holman Resolution; did not vote on levee subsidy	11	8
Voted for Holman Resolution and for levee subsidy	7	12
Did not vote on Holman Resolution; voted for levee subsidy	4	2
Voted against Holman Resolution; did not vote or voted for levee subsidy	7	8
Gamma = −.06		

The voting patterns illustrated in these charts and tables suggest that whatever motivated Democrats to support or oppose the filibuster movement, it affected all of them—northern or southern—pretty much the same way. The simple fact was that most of them realized that the battle was lost and were determined not to make matters worse.

It is significant that there is no evidence of continued Republican–southern Democratic discussions while Tilden still had a chance to win through the decision of the Electoral Commission. Gone from Republican newspapers were references to southern moderation; Garfield recorded no visits from southern congressmen in his diary; Hayes received no letters from his Washington agents detailing negotiations. Not until the commission awarded Florida's electoral votes to Hayes on February 8 did southerners express renewed interest and not until its decision upon Louisiana on February 16 did negotiations begin in earnest. "My people . . . expected me to do all that I could to secure Mr. Tilden in his rightful possession, and I felt unwilling to hold any consultation [with Republicans] . . . so long as there was a hope or prospect of seating Tilden," explained Edward A. Burke, the principal Washington representative of Louisiana's Democratic gubernatorial claimant. "When that hope passed away (on the 16th of February) we were then ready to discuss the subject with Mr. Hayes's friends."[87] Democrats knew that they could not secure a majority for the filibuster. Any tactical maneuvers designed to convince Republicans otherwise were, in Burke's words, "a bluff game."[88]

If the victory was already won, why did Hayes and his allies deal with the southerners in the waning days of February? Polakoff suggests that they were taken in by the Democrats' bluff, and there is certainly evidence to sustain his view.[89] But, as Polakoff also emphasizes, Hayes and his friends had their own reasons for reaching an understanding with the southerners. By February 1877 Hayes had decided to commit himself to the reform wing of his party.[90] A new southern policy was inextricably entwined with that decision. If southerners reinforced the filibuster, even in a hopeless cause, Republican newspapers could be counted upon to renew their "bloody-shirt" attacks upon the Democracy, rekindling the sectional hostility upon which the Republican regulars thrived. Moreover, reports from Louisiana indicated that Democrats were determined not to submit to a Republican state administration in any case and intended to precipitate a crisis by moving against it with force.[91] This would have brought matters to a head during Hayes's first days in office, presenting him with equally untenable alternatives: to allow the Republican state governments to be overthrown by palpable violence, giving Republican regulars the opportunity to solidify a shocked party against "reformers" who condoned such an outrage, or to sustain the Republican claimants, alienate both southern whites and reformers, and be forced to turn to the regulars for support, just as Grant had done in 1871.[92] "We must go cautiously—slowly," Hayes had written Carl Schurz a few weeks earlier, and his Washington agents emphasized to southern Democrats the necessity of letting the southern Republican claimants down easily.[93]

Thus, the anticlimactic negotiations which culminated in the "Wormley House Bargain" served the purposes both of Hayes's friends, who wanted time to carry out "by gradual process such methods as result in your full possession of the government," as they promised Louisiana Democrats, and the southerners, who wanted definite, written assurance that Hayes would not double-cross them when he came under pressure from Republican party regulars.[94] But it was not this bargain—and still less any deals involving patronage, the Texas and Pacific Railroad, or the Mississippi levees—that broke the filibuster and guaranteed Hayes's inauguration. "Hayes was already as good as seated," one of the Wormley House conferees wrote years later. "If the States of Louisiana and South Carolina could save their local autonomy out of the general wreck there seemed no good reason to forbid."[95] As the leading southern newspaper correspondent wrote, rebutting "the silly charge of the bargain": "Southern Congressmen did not give away Mr. Tilden, nor could they do so. . . . The prize [was] . . . lost by the inaction and submission, or prudence—call it what you will—of our northern allies. They—not the South or her Congressmen—went back on Mr. Tilden."[96]

One should not infer that economic factors played no role in the events in 1877. Fear of violence, or at least of instability, played a large role in moderating the belligerence of the Democratic businessmen whose influence predominated in the northeastern wing of the party as southern Democrats disgustedly recognized. Republican businessmen exerted similar pressure on their party.[97] But the outright bargain Woodward described did not take place, and this eliminates the only evidence yet presented that there was a "settlement" in 1877 designed to secure the economic fruits of the Civil War at the sacrifice of its human achievements.

Appendix 1: Electoral Count Roll Calls

Note: Data for these roll calls provided by the Institute for Social Research, University of Michigan, Ann Arbor, Michigan. A fuller description of each vote can be found in the original version of this article, including the yeas and nays and the proportion of Democrats from different regions who voted with Republicans on the filibuster and other issues dealing with counting the electoral vote.

1. Resolution to notify Senate of the House's intent to meet for the counting of the electoral vote. *Congressional Record*, 44 Congress, 2 Session, 1665 (Feb. 17, 1877) (Hereafter only page and date will be recorded.)
2. To recess. 1665 (Feb. 17).
3. To recess. 1684 (Feb. 19).
4. That the Republican electoral vote from Louisiana not be counted. 1703 (Feb. 20).
5. To recess. 1705 (Feb. 20).
6. To recess. 1723 (Feb. 20).
7. To recess. 1884 (Feb. 23).
8. To amend a House electoral count resolution to notify the Senate that the House will meet the Senate today. 1886 (Feb. 23).
9. To table a motion to reconsider passage of the electoral count resolution as amended. 1886 (Feb. 23).
10. To recess. 1906 (Feb. 24).
11. To amend a resolution to count the Oregon electoral vote in conformity with the decision of the Joint Electoral Commission so as to reject a Republican elector. 1916 (Feb. 24).
12. To recess. 1919 (Feb. 24).
13. To recess. 1939 (Feb. 26).
14. To table a motion to reconsider the vote to recess. 1939 (Feb. 26).
15. To suspend the rules and pass a resolution recognizing Wade Hampton governor of South Carolina. 1984 (Feb. 27).
16. To suspend the rules and pass a resolution recognizing Hampton governor of South Carolina and Francis Nicholls governor of Louisiana. 1985 (Feb. 27).
17. To call the roll of the House to ascertain absentees before proceeding to count the electoral vote. 1989 (Feb. 27).
18. To recess. 2006 (Feb. 28).
19. To table an appeal from the ruling of the chair that motions to recess are out of order. 2007 (Feb. 28).
20. To read the testimony taken by the Electoral Commission in the investigation of the South Carolina election. 2008 (Feb. 28).
21. To table reconsideration of the vote on reading the South Carolina testimony. 2009 (Feb. 28).
22. To order the main question on rejecting the Electoral Commission decision on South Carolina's electoral vote. 2019 (Feb. 28).
23. To call the roll to ascertain absentees. 2025 (Feb. 28)
24. To table reconsideration of the vote on calling the roll. 2026 (Feb. 28).

25. To suspend the rule requiring the reading of the journal at the beginning of House business. 2030 (Mar. 1).
26. To amend a resolution declaring the Senate presiding officer's refusal to open the South Carolina electoral vote package illegal, by requiring that it be opened and submitted to the Electoral Commission for decision. 2048 (Mar. 1).
27. Second motion to amend a resolution declaring the Senate presiding officer's refusal to open the South Carolina electoral vote package illegal, by requiring that it be opened and submitted to the Electoral Commission for decision. 2049 (Mar. 1).
28. To table reconsideration of the vote on opening the South Carolina electoral vote package. 2050 (Mar. 1).
29. To table a resolution against counting the electoral vote of a Vermont elector. 2051 (Mar. 1).
30. To reconsider the vote on the resolution that the electoral vote of a Vermont elector not be counted. 2051 (Mar. 1).
31. To amend the Vermont electoral count resolution by providing the vote of an elector not be counted. 2052 (Mar. 1).
32. To table reconsideration of the amendment to the Vermont electoral count resolution. 2052 (Mar. 1).
33. To table the Vermont electoral count resolution. 2053 (Mar. 1).
34. To table reconsideration of the vote to table the Vermont electoral count resolution. 2053 (Mar. 1).
35. Vermont electoral count resolution. 2053 (Mar. 1).
36. To table reconsideration of the Vermont electoral vote count resolution. 2054 (Mar. 1).
37. To recess. 2056 (Mar. 1).
38. To amend the resolution that a Wisconsin elector not be counted, so that his vote be counted. 2067 (Mar. 1).
39. To suspend the rules and release witnesses in the Louisiana electoral count investigation. 2109 (Mar. 2).
40. Second motion to suspend the rules and release witnesses in the Louisiana electoral count investigation. 2121 (Mar. 2).
41. To pass a bill to provide a remedy for wrongful entry into the position of president of the United States. 2130 (Mar. 2).
42. To suspend the rules and release Louisiana investigation witnesses from custody. 2131 (Mar. 2).
43. To amend a resolution recognizing Samuel J. Tilden as president of the United States so as not to challenge the certificates of men recognized as electors of the president. 2228 (Mar. 3).

Appendix II: Electoral Roll Calls Utilized for Scale Analysis

Note: Those voting against the pro-filibuster position on the roll call in Group 1 opposed the filibuster throughout. Those opposing the filibuster on the roll calls in Groups 2 and 3 can also be described as anti-filibuster Democrats. Those supporting the pro-filibuster position on the roll calls in Groups 1 through 3 were pro-filibuster Democrats, and those taking the pro-filibuster position on the roll call in Group 4 were the most strongly committed to it.

Group 1: *Congressional Record*, 44 Cong., 2 Sess., 1884 (Feb. 23, 1877; pro-filibuster position = yea; vote = 131–108).

Group 2: *Congressional Record*, 44 Cong., 2 Sess., 2056 (Mar. 1, 1877; yea; 99–148).

Group 3: *Congressional Record*, 44 Cong., 2 Sess., 1886 (Feb. 23, 1877; nay; 156–89); 2006 (Feb. 28, 1877; yea; 92–170); 2008 (Feb. 28, 1877; yea; 87–176); 1989 (Feb. 27, 1877; yea; 76–156); 2030 (Mar. 1, 1877; nay; 175–85); 1939 (Feb. 26, 1877; yea; 84–178); 2050 (Mar. 1, 1877; nay; 171–80); 1886 (Feb. 23, 1877; nay; 175–74); 2009 (Feb. 28, 1877; nay; 177–73); 2025 (Feb. 28, 1877; yea; 68–169); 2051 (Mar. 1, 1877; yea; 64–162); 2019 (Feb. 28, 1877; nay; 190–73); 2026 (Feb. 28, 1877; nay; 66–173); 2051 (Mar. 1, 1877; yea; 61–167); 1939 (Feb. 26, 1877; nay; 182–67); 2053 (Mar. 1, 1877; nay; 170–58); 2054 (Mar. 1, 1877; nay; 176–59); 2007 (Feb. 28, 1877; nay; 184–61); 2052 (Mar. 1, 1877; nay; 172–55); 2053 (Mar. 1, 1877; yea; 53–180).

Group 4: *Congressional Record*, 44 Cong., 2 Sess., 2109 (Mar. 2, 1877; yea; 20–115)

Notes

Introduction: Constitutional Politics and Reconstruction

1. *National Anti-Slavery Standard*, May 18, 1867. At the same time, Phillips warned against complacency, cautioning delegates that if relieved of radical pressure, politicians would backslide.

2. Henry Ward Beecher, address at the second annual meeting of the American Equal Rights Association, May 10, 1867, in Elizabeth Cady Stanton, Susan B. Anthony, and Matilda Joslyn Gage, *History of Woman Suffrage*, 6 vols. (Salem, N.H.: Ayer, 1985; orig. 1881–1922), 2:218.

3. The perceived apposition of law and politics is reflected in the titles of such works as Robert Bork's *The Tempting of America: The Political Seduction of the Law* (New York: Free Press, 1990), complaining that political commitments have corrupted judicial decisions, and Michael J. Perry's *The Constitution in the Courts: Law or Politics?* (New York: Oxford University Press, 1994), which denies the charge. For the crucial role the separation of law and politics played in the development of judicial review, see Stephen M. Griffin, *American Constitutionalism: From Theory to Politics* (Princeton, N.J.: Princeton University Press, 1996), 11–19. Morton J. Horwitz has reflected on how the apposition between law and politics has discouraged historicism in legal analysis. Morton J. Horwitz, "Why Is Anglo-American Jurisprudence Unhistorical?" *Oxford Journal of Legal Studies* 17 (Winter 1997): 551–86.

4. See, for example, Louis Fisher, *American Constitutional Law*, 6th ed. (Durham, N.C.: Carolina Academic Press, 2005), the first chapter of which is entitled "Constitutional Politics" but limits that concept to seeking to secure interests through strategic litigation.

5. See Raoul Berger, *Government by Judiciary: The Transformation of the Fourteenth Amendment* (Cambridge, Mass.: Harvard University Press, 1977); James E. Bond, *No Easy Walk to Freedom: Reconstruction and the Ratification of the Fourteenth Amendment* (Westport, Conn.: Praeger, 1997); Michael Kent Curtis, *No State Shall Abridge: The Fourteenth Amendment and the Bill of Rights* (Durham, N.C.: Duke University Press, 1986); Earl M. Maltz, *Civil Rights, the Constitution, and Congress, 1863–1869* (Lawrence: University Press of Kansas, 1990); and William E. Nelson, *The Fourteenth Amendment: From Political Principle to Judicial Doctrine* (Cambridge, Mass.: Harvard University Press, 1988). Some scholars, such as Berger, have sought to divine the *intentions* behind the Civil War amendments. Searches for "original understandings" have generally replaced searches for "original intent" in constitutional scholarship, however. Compare Nelson's work, noted above, to Berger's.

6. At least most of us do. There is a significant literature on how and why historians do what they do. Some classics are Marc Bloch, *The Historian's Craft: Reflections on the Nature and Uses of History and the Techniques and Methods of the Men Who Write It*, trans. Peter Putnam (New York: Vintage Books, 1953); Edward Hallett Carr, *What Is History?* (New York: Vintage Books, 1961); and Henry Steele Commager, *The Nature and Study of History* (Columbus, Ohio: Charles E. Merrill Books, 1965). Two excellent contributions that take into account postmodern critiques of historical quests for

knowledge are Joyce Appleby et al., *Telling the Truth About History* (New York: Norton, 1994) and John L. Gaddis, *The Landscape of History: How Historians Map the Past* (New York: Oxford University Press, 2002). For the differences in how academic historians and law-faculty historians (and lawyers, for that matter) approach history, see Michael Les Benedict, "Constitutional History and Constitutional Theory: Reflections on Ackerman, Reconstruction, and the Transformation of the American Constitution," *Yale Law Journal* 108 (June 1999): 2011–38, esp. 2017–23; Laura Kalman, "Border Patrol: Reflections on the Turn to History in Legal Scholarship," *Fordham Law Review* 66 (October 1997): 87–124; Jack N. Rakove, "Fidelity Through History (Or to It)," *Fordham Law Review* 65 (March 1997): 1587–1609; Rakove, "Two Foxes in the Forest of History," *Yale Journal of Law and the Humanities* 11 (Winter 1999): 191–213; John Phillip Reid, "Law and History," *Loyola of Los Angeles Law Review* 27 (November 1993): 193–224. For a clear example of how using historical and legal criteria for weighing evidence leads to differing interpretations, compare Benedict, "Preserving the Constitution: The Conservative Basis of Radical Reconstruction," *Journal of American History* 61 (June 1974): 65–90, revised and republished in this volume, to Robert J. Kaczorowski, "Revolutionary Constitutionalism in the Era of the Civil War and Reconstruction," *New York University Law Review* 61 (November 1986): 863–940.

7. See Michael Les Benedict, *A Compromise of Principle: Congressional Republicans and Reconstruction, 1863–1869* (New York: Norton, 1974); William R. Brock, *An American Crisis: Congress and Reconstruction, 1865–1867* (New York: Harper & Row, 1966); William A. Dunning, *Essays on the Civil War and Reconstruction, and Related Topics* (New York: Macmillan, 1898); Eric L. McKitrick, *Andrew Johnson and Reconstruction* (Chicago: University of Chicago Press, 1960); Harold M. Hyman, *A More Perfect Union: The Impact of the Civil War and Reconstruction on the Constitution* (New York: Knopf, 1973); James E. Sefton, *Andrew Johnson and the Uses of Constitutional Power* (Boston: Little, Brown, 1980); Xi Wang, *The Trial of Democracy: Black Suffrage and Northern Republicans, 1860–1910* (Athens: University of Georgia Press, 1997).

8. Bruce Ackerman's study of the popular role in transforming the Constitution outside the formal amendment process is part of this transition, although his purpose is still to establish principles to guide judges. Ackerman, "Constitutional Politics/Constitutional Law," *Yale Law Journal* 99 (December 1989): 453–547; Ackerman, *We the People*, 1: *Foundations* (Cambridge, Mass.: Harvard University Press, 1990), 2: *Transformations* (Cambridge, Mass.: Harvard University Press, 1998). Michael J. Klarman has placed Supreme Court decisions regarding racial discrimination within a panoramic social and intellectual context, making clear that they are only a part of a much larger social and political process. Klarman, *From Jim Crow to Civil Rights: The Supreme Court and the Struggle for Racial Equality* (New York: Oxford University Press, 2004). In *Religious Liberty in America: Political Safeguards* (Lawrence: University Press of Kansas, 2002), Louis Fisher points out that over history the political branches of state and federal government have done more to protect the rights of religious minorities than have the courts.

9. For example, Griffin, *American Constitutionalism*; Griffin, "Constitutionalism in the United States: From Theory to Politics," in *Responding to Imperfection: The Theory and Practice of Constitutional Amendment*, ed. Sanford Levinson (Princeton: Princeton University Press, 1995), 37–61, esp. 54–61; Keith M. Whittington, "The Political Constitution," *Constitutional Construction: Divided Powers and Constitutional Meaning* (Cambridge, Mass.: Harvard University Press, 1999); Wayne D. Moore, *Constitutional Rights and Powers of the People* (Princeton, N.J.: Princeton University Press, 1996).

10. Griffin, *American Constitutionalism*, 3.

11. This is the thrust of Larry Kramer's *The People Themselves: Popular Constitutionalism and Judicial Review* (New York: Oxford University Press, 2004). Recent studies of Jacksonian constitutionalism likewise stress Democrats' appeals to the people to correct

the errors of the Marshall court. See Gerald Leonard, "Party as a 'Political Safeguard of Federalism': Martin Van Buren and the Constitutional Theory of Party Politics," *Rutgers Law Review* 54 (Fall 2001): 221–81. Kramer calls for legislation to the curb the court. Mark Tushnet calls for a constitutional amendment to eliminate judicial review entirely so as to rely entirely upon popular constitutionalism. Mark V. Tushnet, *Taking the Constitution Away from the Courts* (Princeton, N.J.: Princeton University Press, 1999).

12. As William J. Novak has made clear, the courts recognized broad legislative power to enact measures for the general welfare. Novak, *The People's Welfare: Law and Regulation in Nineteenth-Century America* (Chapel Hill: University of North Carolina Press, 1996). By modern standards, some early- and mid-nineteenth-century regulations infringed civil liberties. But as John J. Dinan indicates, perhaps a bit too tendentiously, what stands out is the degree to which legislators acted to promote liberty and restrained themselves from infringing it. Dinan, *Keeping the People's Liberties: Legislators, Citizens, and Judges as Guardians of Rights* (Lawrence: University of Kansas Press, 1998). For the "Restricted Field for [Courts'] Legal Decision Making" in one state, see Keith R. Schlesinger, *The Power That Governs: The Evolution of Judicial Activism in a Midwestern State, 1840–1890* (New York: Garland, 1990), 9–40.

13. James Roger Sharp, *American Politics in the Early Republic: The New Nation in Crisis* (New Haven, Conn.: Yale University Press, 1993), 276. See also Andrew Lenner, "A Tale of Two Constitutions: Nationalism in the Federalist Era," *American Journal of Legal History* 40 (January 1996): 72–105, and Michael Les Benedict, "The Jeffersonian Republicans and Civil Liberties," in *Essays in the History of Liberty: Seaver Institute Lectures at the Huntington Library* (San Marino, Calif.: Huntington Library, 1988), 23–42.

14. In general, see Kramer, *The People Themselves*. For the Democratic Party's self-identification as protecting the Constitution through the democratic process, see Leonard, "Party as a 'Political Safeguard of Federalism': Martin Van Buren and the Constitutional Theory of Party Politics," and Joel Silbey, *The American Political Nation, 1838–1893* (Stanford, Calif.: Stanford University Press, 1991), 94–98. For Republicans and the courts, see Don E. Fehrenbacher, *The Dred Scott Case: Its Significance in American Law and Politics* (New York: Oxford University Press, 1978), 417–48, and Harold M. Hyman and William Wiecek, *Equal Justice Under Law: Constitutional Development, 1835–1875* (New York: Harper & Row, 1982), 86–202. Donald Grier Stephenson's account of the Supreme Court as an issue in political campaigns clearly indicates the conviction that the judiciary did not have the final say in constitutional interpretation. Stephenson, *Campaigns and the Court: The U.S. Supreme Court in Presidential Elections* (New York: Columbia University Press, 1999), 53–106.

15. For the courts' sorry record, see Robert M. Cover, *Justice Accused: Antislavery and the Judicial Process* (New Haven, Conn.: Yale University Press, 1975). By the 1850s, northern state courts were doing more to protect the rights of their black citizens, but all knew that this was the consequence of political change—the result of what we would call "constitutional politics." See Paul Finkelman, *An Imperfect Union: Slavery, Federalism, and Comity* (Chapel Hill: University of North Carolina Press, 1981), and Finkelman, "Race, Slavery, and Law in Antebellum Ohio," in *The History of Ohio Law*, ed. Michael Les Benedict and John F. Winkler, 2 vols. (Athens: Ohio University Press, 2004), 2:748–81.

16. *Congressional Globe*, 39 Cong., 1 Sess., 1033–34 (February 26, 1866).

17. Ibid., 42 Cong., 1 Sess., appendix, 83–84 (March 31, 1871).

18. Hurlbut to Stevens, December 25, 1865, q. *Selected Papers of Thaddeus Stevens*, ed. Beverly Wilson Palmer, 2 vols. (Pittsburgh, Pa.: University of Pittsburgh Press, 1999), 2:58.

19. James M. McPherson, *For Cause and Comrades: Why Men Fought in the Civil War* (New York: Oxford University Press, 1997), 93, 121.

20. *Scott v. Sandford*, 60 U.S. (19 Howard) 393 (1857).

21. Frederick L. Blue, *Charles Sumner and the Conscience of the North* (Arlington Heights, Ill.: Harlan Davidson, 1994), 61. For the role of public speaking in building Sumner's reputation, see especially ibid., 86–93.

22. Michael Les Benedict, "The Party, Going Strong: Congressional Elections in the Mid-Nineteenth Century," *Congress and the Presidency* 9 (Winter 1981–82): 37–68, revised and republished in this volume; Silbey, *The American Political Nation*, 141–58; Silbey, "Parties and Politics in Mid-Nineteenth-Century America," in Joel Silbey, *The Partisan Imperative: The Dynamics of American Politics Before the Civil War* (New York: Oxford University Press, 1985), 33–49. Glenn C. Altschuler and Stuart M. Blumin have attempted to debunk the notion that mid-nineteenth-century Americans were strongly partisan and active in "Limits of Political Engagement in Antebellum America: A New Look at the Golden Age of Participatory Democracy," *Journal of American History* 84 (December 1997): 855–85. In my view, Harry L. Watson, a leading political historian of the Jacksonian era, responded persuasively in "Humbug! Bah! Altschuler and Blumin and the Riddle of the Antebellum Electorate," ibid., 886–93. Altschuler and Blumin search for, and fail to find, what they call "participatory democracy." For them, the test of political engagement is participation in the process beyond mere voting. But "participation" is not the same as "salience." Judging by turnout, politics was more *salient* for nineteenth-century Americans—that is, people cared more and paid greater attention—than most Americans do today. Even many of those for whom politics has the most profound meaning would likely fail Altschuler's and Blumin's test of participation.

1. Preserving the Constitution: The Conservative Basis of Radical Reconstruction

1. Don E. Fehrenbacher, *The Slaveholding Republic: An Account of the United States Government's Relations to Slavery*, ed. Ward M. McAfee (New York: Oxford University Press, 2001).

2. For antebellum racism in the North, see Leon F. Litwack, *North of Slavery: The Negro in the Free States, 1790–1860* (Chicago: University of Chicago Press, 1961); John Hope Franklin and Alfred A. Moss, Jr., *From Slavery to Freedom: a History of African Americans*, 7th ed. (New York: McGraw-Hill, 1994), 148–70. James Brewer Stewart provides a sophisticated analysis of the development of northern racism in "Modernizing 'Difference': The Political Meanings of Color in the Free States, 1776–1840," in *Race and the Early Republic: Racial Consciousness and Nation-Building in the Early Republic*, ed. Michael A. Morrison and James Brewer Stewart (Lanham, Md.: Rowman & Littlefield, 2002), 113–34. For the way in which black servitude encouraged white racism, see David R. Roediger's seminal *The Wages of Whiteness: Race and the Making of the American Working Class*, rev. ed. (London and New York: Verso, 1999) and Anthony Gronowicz, *Race and Class Politics in New York City Before the Civil War* (Boston: Northeastern University Press, 1998).

3. The notorious *Dred Scott* case, *Scott v. Sandford*, 60 U.S. (19 How.) 393 (1857), is the foremost example. In it, the Supreme Court ruled that even if their states recognized their citizenship, free persons of African descent were not citizens of the United States and entitled to none of the privileges and immunities of United States citizens. It also ruled that Congress had no power to ban slavery in United States territories (that is, American territories not yet admitted to statehood), but clearly implied that it did have the authority to establish slave codes there. In *Prigg v. Pennsylvania*, 41 U.S. (16 Pet.) 539 (1842), *Jones v. Van Zandt*, 46 U.S. (5 How.) 215 (1847), and *Ableman v. Booth*, 62 U.S. (21 How.) 506 (1859), the Court sustained an expansive interpretation of Congress's power to enforce the Fugitive Slave clause of the Constitution, even though the clause was directed to the states and did not explicitly delegate any power to Congress to

enforce it. At the same time, the Court ignored the obvious inconsistencies between the draconian federal Fugitive Slave Acts and the Bill of Rights. In *Barron v. Baltimore,* 32 U.S. (7 Pet.) 243 (1833), the Court ruled that the Bill of Rights did not apply to the states, thus freeing the states to pass laws severely circumscribing the rights of their free black inhabitants and restricting the rights of their white citizens to oppose slavery. Yet in *Prigg v. Pennsylvania* and *Ableman v. Booth,* noted above, the Court interpreted the Fugitive Slave clause of the Constitution to restrict the power of states to protect the rights of their citizens against slave catchers.

The other departments of the federal government likewise interpreted the Constitution to authorize and even mandate the exercise of federal power on slavery's behalf, while until the 1850s state and lower federal courts struck down state actions designed to circumscribe it. See Fehrenbacher, *The Slaveholding Republic;* Donald G. Nieman, *Promises to Keep: African-Americans and the Constitutional Order, 1776 to the Present* (New York: Oxford University Press, 3–29; Leonard L. Richards, *The Slave Power: The Free North and Southern Domination, 1780–1860* (Baton Rouge: Louisiana State University Press, 2000); and, for state and lower federal courts, Robert M. Cover, *Justice Accused: Antislavery and the Judicial Process* (New Haven, Conn.: Yale University Press, 1975).

4. Fehrenbacher, *The Slaveholding Republic,* 295–304.

5. While all historians and constitutional scholars recognize the magnitude of the change, the concept of a constitutional transformation has been articulated most profoundly by the constitutional theorist Bruce Ackerman in *We the People,* vol. 2: *Transformations* (Cambridge, Mass.: Harvard University Press, 1998), 99–252. So too Robert J. Kaczorowski. See his "Revolutionary Constitutionalism in the Era of the Civil War and Reconstruction," *New York University Law Review* 61 (November 1986): 863–940, and "To Begin the Nation Anew: Congress, Citizenship, and Civil Rights After the Civil War," *American Historical Review* 92 (February 1987): 45–68. As will become clear below, Kaczorowski draws specific conclusions about Republican understandings of this change with which I strongly disagree.

6. Eric Foner, *Reconstruction: America's Unfinished Revolution, 1863–1877* (New York: Harper & Row, 1988).

7. William Gillette stresses racism in *Retreat from Reconstruction, 1869–1879* (Baton Rouge: Louisiana State University Press, 1979). So do C. Vann Woodward in "Seeds of Failure in Radical Race Policy," in *New Frontiers of the American Reconstruction,* ed. Harold M. Hyman (Urbana: University of Illinois Press, 1966), 125–47, and John Hope Franklin in part two ("The Old Order Changeth Not") of *Racial Equality in America* (Chicago: University of Chicago Press, 1976), 37–74. Foner, by no means insensitive to the role of racism, stresses the retreat from radical free-labor ideology among northern elites in his *Reconstruction,* 460–564. I make a similar argument, focusing on the rise of laissez-faire ideology, in "Reform Republicans and the Retreat from Reconstruction," in *The Facts of Reconstruction: Essays in Honor of John Hope Franklin,* ed. Eric Anderson and Alfred A. Moss, Jr. (Baton Rouge: Louisiana State University Press, 1991), 53–78, republished in this volume. Heather Cox Richardson nicely combines the two perspectives in *The Death of Reconstruction: Race, Labor, and Politics in the Post–Civil War North, 1865–1901* (Cambridge, Mass.: Harvard University Press, 2001), as does Nancy Cohen, *The Reconstruction of American Liberalism, 1865–1914* (Chapel Hill: University of North Carolina Press, 2002), 23–85.

8. A recent exception has been Claudine L. Ferrell, whose *Reconstruction* (Westport, Conn.: Greenwood Press, 2003), a brief textbook with documents, gives full weight to Americans' commitment to federalism as a factor in Reconstruction. It is no coincidence that Ferrell's dissertation director was the eminent constitutional historian Harold

M. Hyman, whose students (including myself) have been most attentive to the role of federalism in Reconstruction.

9. C. Herman Pritchett, *The American Constitution*, 2d ed. (New York: McGraw-Hill, 1968), 712. See especially Robert J. Kaczorowski, *The Politics of Judicial Interpretation: The Federal Courts, Department of Justice and Civil Rights, 1866–1876* (Dobbs Ferry, N.Y.: Oceana Publications, 1985), and Frank J. Scaturro, *The Supreme Court's Retreat from Reconstruction: A Distortion of Constitutional Jurisprudence* (Westport, Conn.: Greenwood Press, 2000). Other examples are too numerous to list all of them. For some, see Richard L. Aynes, "Constricting the Law of Freedom: Justice Miller, the Fourteenth Amendment, and the *Slaughter-House* Cases," *Chicago Kent Law Review* 70 (1994): 627–88; Eugene Gressman, "The Unhappy History of Civil Rights Legislation," *Michigan Law Review* (June 1952): 1323–58; Robert J. Harris, *The Quest for Equality: The Constitution, Congress, and the Supreme Court* (Baton Rouge: Louisiana State University Press, 1960), 58, 82–91; John R. Howard, *The Shifting Wind: The Supreme Court and Civil Rights from Reconstruction to Brown* (Albany: State University of New York Press, 1999), 35–116; Loren Miller, *The Petitioners: The Story of the Supreme Court of the United States and the Negro* (New York: Pantheon Books, 1966), 83–182; Howard N. Meyer, *The Amendment That Refused to Die* (Lanham, Md.: Madison Books, 2000).

10. Kaczorowski, "To Begin the Nation Anew: Congress, Citizenship, and Civil Rights After the Civil War"; Kaczorowski, "Revolutionary Constitutionalism in the Era of the Civil War and Reconstruction."

11. In *Equal Justice Under Law: Constitutional Development, 1835–1875* (New York: Harper & Row, 1982), 299–301, Harold M. Hyman and William M. Wiecek insightfully point out the ambiguity in the meaning of civil rights before the Civil War, with most rights grounded in localities and slight consideration paid to defining and protecting "national" rights. The problem for Republicans was that emancipation meant that state and local definitions of ordinary rights now had national implications. Would Americans tolerate the transfer of primary responsibility for protecting these rights from states and localities to the national government?

12. See Robert H. Bork, "Neutral Principles and Some First Amendment Problems," *Indiana Law Journal* 47 (Fall 1971): 1–35; Edwin M. Meese III, "A Jurisprudence of Original Intention," in The Federalist Society, *The Great Debate: Interpreting Our Written Constitution* (Washington, D.C.: The Federalist Society, 1989), 31–41; Meese, "Interpreting the Constitution," reprinted in *Interpreting the Constitution: The Debate Over Original Intent*, ed. Jack N. Rakove (Boston: Northeastern University Press, 1990), 13–21.

13. For example, Raoul Berger, *Government by Judiciary: The Transformation of the Fourteenth Amendment* (Cambridge, Mass.: Harvard University Press, 1977) (see pages 1–3 for an explicit commitment to the binding authority of "original intent"); Kaczorowski, "Revolutionary Constitutionalism in the Era of the Civil War and Reconstruction"; Earl Maltz, *Civil Rights, the Constitution, and Congress* (see ix–xii for a similar view of the authority of "original understanding"); William E. Nelson, *The Fourteenth Amendment: From Political Principle to Judicial Doctrine* (Cambridge, Mass.: Harvard University Press, 1988); Michael Kent Curtis, *No State Shall Abridge: The Fourteenth Amendment and the Bill of Rights* (Durham, N.C.: Duke University Press, 1986).

14. For a somewhat longer discussion, see Michael Les Benedict, "Constitutional History and Constitutional Theory: Reflections on Ackerman, Reconstruction, and the Transformation of the American Constitution," *Yale Law Journal* 108 (June 1999): 2017–23.

15. Bruce Ackerman discounts the notion that the "grasp-of-war theory" provided the basis for Republican Reconstruction, as I argue below, as "bad history" (115). What he really means is that it is a *bad legal theory* to explain the events of Reconstruction. That may be so, but as I demonstrate below, it was the theory upon which Republicans

operated. Ackerman seems to think it important to his argument about the nature of constitutional transformations that Republicans understood and accepted his theory. I don't see why. I find Ackerman's elucidation of the theoretical implications of what Republicans did compelling, whether contemporaries were aware of the legal implications of their actions or not.

Robert J. Kaczorowski likewise argues that Republicans clearly understood the full theoretical implications of what they were doing during Reconstruction, and advocated the revolutionary change that could follow. Either Kaczorowski believes that a broad reading of the Fourteenth Amendment must rely on the original intent or understanding of those who framed and ratified it, or he simply wants to undercut the effectiveness of conservative arguments that the framers intended a narrower conception. He is compelled to interpret the statements of the contemporary actors in a way that sustains the proposition that they conceived the Civil War constitutional revolution in the same way a late-twentieth-century constitutional nationalist and advocate of equal rights would; every claim for federal power is treated as evidence that its author meant "primary" power to define and protect American rights regardless of what the states did rather than "corrective" power to cure state infringements of rights or failures to protect them. For example, Kaczorowski relies on House Judiciary Committee James F. Wilson's declaration regarding the Civil Rights Act of 1866 (889–90): "If the States would all observe the rights of our citizens, there would be no need of this bill.... But, sir, the practice of the States leaves us no avenue of escape, and we must do our duty by supplying the protection which the States deny." Kaczorowski interprets this statement as signaling the intention to transfer primary authority over civil rights to the federal government. Surely it could instead be interpreted as a call for a federal corrective power. The terms of the Civil Rights Act itself suggest the latter by making it a crime for persons to deny rights under the color of state law and providing that citizens who were denied rights in the state courts could transfer their cases to the federal courts. Moreover, it left the specifications of citizens' rights to the states, requiring only that all persons have the same rights as white persons. U.S. Statutes at Large, 14 (1866): 27.

It may be, as Kaczorowski argues, that the *legal* consequence of Republicans' legislation and the Fourteenth Amendment was to authorize the federal government to exercise the primary responsibility for defining and protecting rights. But the *historical* fact was that most Republicans did not advocate that proposition, and the actual language of the Civil Rights Act and the Fourteenth Amendment reflected their reluctance to do so. This in turn created the *historical* context in which federal judges would later interpret the Civil War constitutional amendments. What is astonishing is that Kaczorowski accuses me of reaching conclusions based on "logical reasoning from an assumed premise" rather "than a close adherence to the sources" (869 n. 19). I invite anyone to compare the direct evidence I present in the discussion below to Kaczorowski's consistent interpretation of the plain language of his sources to fit his premise.

In stressing Republicans' conservative rhetoric during Reconstruction, I do not intend to buttress arguments based on original intent for a narrow reading of the Fourteenth Amendment today. First, Civil War–era Americans were engaged in popular constitutionalism. Their constitutional arguments were aimed at justifying what they were doing and establishing a framework for future legislative action, not at making a record for future judges. Second, finding a clear "original intent" requires a winnowing out of the complexities and inconsistencies that characterize the actual historical situation. In the real, historical world, the meaning of legislation and constitutional amendments is worked out over time; it is not established by the authority of the framers. Third, from a legal perspective, original intent or understanding, when it can be discerned through an appropriate legal analysis of the historical record, is in my view only one source of authority, not the controlling authority.

16. Pamela Brandwein, *Reconstructing Reconstruction: The Supreme Court and the Production of Historical Truth* (Durham, N.C.: Duke University Press, 1999), 57.

17. William Archibald Dunning, *Essays on the Civil War and Reconstruction and Related Topics* (New York: Macmillan, 1904), 63–135; John W. Burgess, *Reconstruction and the Constitution, 1866–1876* (New York: Charles Scribner's Sons, 1902).

18. Howard K. Beale, *The Critical Year: A Study of Andrew Johnson and Reconstruction* (New York: Harcourt, Brace, 1930), 214–15. See also Robert Selph Henry, *The Story of Reconstruction* (Indianapolis: Bobbs-Merrill, 1938), 184; and James G. Randall and David Donald, *The Civil War and Reconstruction* (Boston: D. C. Heath, 1961), 633. Milton Lomask entitled one of his chapters "The Subversion of the Federal System." Lomask, *Andrew Johnson: President on Trial* (New York: Farrar, Strauss, 1960). The work on Reconstruction that appeared between the late 1920s and the 1950s barely mentioned the constitutional aspects of the struggle. As Eric L. McKitrick points out, most historians simply presumed Andrew Johnson's position to be the constitutional one. McKitrick, *Andrew Johnson and Reconstruction* (Chicago: University of Chicago Press, 1960), 93.

19. Alfred H. Kelly, "Comment on Harold M. Hyman's Paper," in *New Frontiers of the American Reconstruction*, ed. Harold M. Hyman (Urbana: University of Illinois Press, 1966), 40–58; McKitrick, *Johnson and Reconstruction*, 117–19; William R. Brock, *An American Crisis: Congress and Reconstruction, 1865–1867* (New York: St. Martin's, 1963), 271–73.

20. See Phillips S. Paludan, *A Covenant with Death: The Constitution, Law, and Equality in the Civil War Era* (Urbana: University of Illinois Press, 1975); Patricia Allan Lucie, *Freedom and Federalism: Congress and Courts, 1861–1866* (New York: Garland, 1986); as well as this essay, of course. Hyman's initial view is reflected in his essay "Reconstruction and Political-Constitutional Institutions: The Popular Expression," in *New Frontiers of the American Reconstruction*, 1–39. Although his students influenced Hyman to take a narrower view of the constitutional implications of Reconstruction, his thesis that the Civil War emancipated the Constitution from crabbed prewar interpretations still permeates his epic *A More Perfect Union: The Impact of the Civil War and Reconstruction on the Constitution* (New York: Knopf, 1973).

21. Francis Lieber to Martin Russell Thayer, February 3, 1864, Francis Lieber Papers, Huntington Library, San Marino, Calif. The letter is quoted in Thomas Sargeant Perry, *Life and Letters of Francis Lieber* (Boston: J. R. Osgood, 1882), 339–41. Thaddeus Stevens was the most important statesman to accept this view. James Albert Woodburn, *The Life of Thaddeus Stevens: A Study in American Political History, Especially in the Period of the Civil War and Reconstruction* (Indianapolis: Bobbs-Merrill, 1913), 207–38. See also John A. Bingham's comments in the *Congressional Globe*, 39 Cong., 1 Sess., 1292 (March 9, 1866); R.F.E., "The Right to Confiscate and Emancipate," *Monthly Law Reporter* 24 (September 1862): 646; J. H. A., "Legal Miscellany: Martial Law," *American Law Register* 9 (June 1861): 498–511; D. [Theodore W. Dwight?], "Writ of Habeas Corpus," ibid. (October 1861): 705–17; Sidney George Fisher, *The Trial of the Constitution* (Philadelphia: Lippincott, 1862), 63–64, 199; Grosvenor P. Lowrey, *The Commander in Chief: A Defence Upon Legal Grounds of the Proclamation of Emancipation, and an Answer to Ex-Judge Curtis' Pamphlet Entitled "Executive Power"* (New York: G. P. Putnam, 1862); Oliver Wendell Holmes, *Oration Delivered Before the City Authorities of Boston on the Eighty-Seventh Anniversary of the National Independence of America* (Philadelphia: n.p., 1863), 26–27; Matthew Hale Carpenter, *Letter on Martial Law* (New York: n.p., 1865), 3–4.

22. Daniel Agnew, *Our National Constitution: Its Adaptation to a State of War or Insurrection* (Philadelphia: C. Sherman and Son, 1863), 11; Joel Parker, *Habeas Corpus and Martial Law: A Review of the Opinion of Chief Justice Taney, in the Case of John Merryman* (Philadelphia: J. Campbell, 1862); Jehu Baker, *The Rebellion: Speech Delivered in Hall of Representatives, Springfield, Ill., Feb. 4, 1863* (Belleville, Ill.: Belleville Advocate

Book and Job Office, 1863); Oliver P. Morton's speech, April 11, 1863, in Loyalist National League, *The Sumter Anniversary, 1863: Opinions of Loyalists Concerning the Great Questions of the Times* (New York: C. S. Wescott, 1863), 40–50, especially 47–48; Lyman Trumbull's defense of the constitutionality of confiscation in the *Congressional Globe*, 38 Cong., 1 Sess., 3306 (June 27, 1864); and also *Argument of Hon. Lyman Trumbull in the Supreme Court of the United States, Mar. 4, 1868, in the Matter of Ex Parte William H. McCardle, Appellant* (Washington, D.C.: Government Printing Office, 1868), 24.

23. James W. Grimes to Trumbull, October 14, 1861, Lyman Trumbull Papers, Manuscript Division, Library of Congress (hereafter LC), Washington, D.C.; *Congressional Globe*, 39 Cong., 1 Sess., 2446 (May 8, 1866). Grimes made his statement during debate over the proposed national quarantine against cholera in 1866. The history of that legislation provides an excellent illustration of Congress' constitutional conservatism immediately after the Civil War. Michael Les Benedict, "Contagion and the Constitution: Quarantine Agitation from 1859 to 1866," *Journal of the History of Medicine and Allied Sciences* 25 (April 1970): 177–93. See also comments of Bingham and William P. Fessenden, *Congressional Globe*, 39 Cong., 1 Sess., 27–28 (December 12, 1865), 1292 (March 9, 1866).

24. For full, traditional discussions, see Dunning, *Essays on the Civil War*; Burgess, *Reconstruction and the Constitution*. For a concise summary, see McKitrick, *Johnson and Reconstruction*, 97–117. Burgess did not differentiate between the state suicide and the forfeit rights theories, which Dunning attributed to Charles Sumner and Samuel S. Shellabarger, respectively. Dunning too noted the similarity and wrote that the forfeit rights theory gradually came to resemble the state suicide theory. Dunning, *Essays on the Civil War*, 122.

25. Even the presidential theory, which was generally accepted by Democrats as well as President Johnson, prescribed that the southern states' functions as states in the Union were suspended. See Johnson's message to Congress, December 4, 1865, in *A Compilation of the Messages and Papers of the Presidents, 1789–1902*, ed. James D. Richardson, 20 vols. (New York: Bureau of National Literature, 1897–1911), 8:3555–56.

26. Boston *Evening Journal*, June 27, 1865. See also Wendell Phillips's objections to recognizing the restoration of Louisiana to the Union in February 1865: recognize the state government there as legitimate, he warned, and "we have put up a fence between the Federal Government and the State Government. . . . Put up the fence between you and Louisiana or South Carolina, and the Federal law runs to it, not over it." Wendell Phillips, "The Immediate Issue: A Speech of Wendell Phillips at the Annual Meeting of the Massachusetts Anti-Slavery Society at Boston," in *Equality Before the Law Claimed and Defended*, ed. George Luther Stearns (Boston: Rand & Avery, 1865), 31. See also Thaddeus Stevens, *Reconstruction: Speech of the Hon. Thaddeus Stevens, Delivered in the City of Lancaster, September 7th, 1865* (Lancaster, Pa.: Examiner and Herald Printing, 1865), 3, 7; Fernando C. Beaman, *Congressional Globe*, 39 Cong., 1 Sess., 1018 (February 24, 1866); William Whiting, *The Return of the Rebellious States to the Union: A Letter from Hon. Wm. Whiting to the Union League of Philadelphia* (Philadelphia: C. Sherman and Son, 1864), 3–4; Carl Schurz, "The Logical Results of the War," in *Speeches, Correspondence, and Political Papers of Carl Schurz*, ed. Frederic Bancroft, 6 vols. (New York: G. P. Putnam's Sons, 1913), 1: 378–80; Alpheus Crosby, *The Present Position of the Seceded States and the Rights and Duties of the General Government in Respect to Them: An Address to the Phi Beta Kappa Society of Dartmouth College, July 19, 1865* (Boston: Rand & Avery, 1865), 12; T. W. Higginson, "Fair Play the Best Policy," *Atlantic Monthly*, 15 (May 1865), 628; Count A. de Gasparin, *Reconstruction: A Letter to President Johnson*, trans. Mary L. Booth (New York: Loyal Publication Society, 1865), 13.

27. *Congressional Globe*, 39 Cong., 1 Sess., 72 (December 18, 1865).

28. Stevens, *Reconstruction*, 3.

29. Ibid., 3–4.

30. *Congressional Globe*, 39 Cong., 2 Sess., 250 (January 3, 1867). Among the most prominent proponents of the territorial policy were George W. Julian, Benjamin F. Butler, James M. Ashley, and William D. Kelley. George S. Boutwell advocated this policy for some of the rebel states. See George W. Julian, "Dangers and Duties of the Hour—Reconstruction and Suffrage," *Speeches on Political Questions* (New York: Hurd and Houghton, 1872), 287–88; Benjamin F. Butler, *Butler's Book: Autobiography and Personal Reminiscences of Major-General Benj. F. Butler* (Boston: A. M. Thayer, 1892), 960–61; George S. Boutwell, "Reconstruction: Its True Basis," *Speeches and Papers Relating to the Rebellion and the Overthrow of Slavery*, 2 vols. (Boston: Little, Brown, 1867), 2:389–90. Several Radical congressmen proposed legislation in 1867 to create territorial governments in the area once controlled by the Confederacy—for example, Hezekiah S. Bundy's Texas territorial government bill (H.R. 223), Julian's bill to establish territorial governments in the rebellious states (H.R. 894), and Henry D. Washburne's bill to reestablish civil governments in the rebellious states (H.R. 985). House of Representatives bill file, 39 Cong., Records of the United States House of Representatives (Record Group 233), National Archives, Washington, D.C.

31. Woodbury Davis, "Political Problems and Conditions of Peace," *Atlantic Monthly* 12 (August 1863): 254. William Whiting, solicitor of the war department, told Gideon Welles that "[h]e denied that a majority, or the whole people [of a southern state] . . . could establish or reestablish a government and continue to be or to become a member of the Union after having been in rebellion, except by consent or permission." Gideon Welles, *Diary of Gideon Welles: Secretary of the Navy Under Lincoln and Johnson*, ed. Howard K. Beale, vol. 2 (New York: Norton, 1960), 85 (July 25, 1864).

32. *New York Times*, June 24, 1865. During the war Richard Henry Dana was one of the most conservative Republican officeholders in Massachusetts, strongly supporting Lincoln's emancipation policy against radical criticism. In 1868 Dana ran as a conservative Republican candidate for Congress against the great Radical Benjamin F. Butler. Samuel Shapiro, *Richard Henry Dana, Jr., 1815–1882* (East Lansing: Michigan State University Press, 1961), 124–27, 141–53.

33. Collis P. Huntington to Hugh McCulloch, October 19, 1865, Hugh McCulloch Papers, LC; O. J. Hollister, *The Life of Schuyler Colfax* (New York: Funk & Wagnalls, 1887), 286; Francis Fessenden, *Life and Public Services of William Pitt Fessenden*, 2 vols. (Boston: Houghton Mifflin, 1907), 2: 386–88; William Lawrence, *Congressional Globe*, 39 Cong., 2 Sess., 1083 (February 7, 1867); Schurz, "Logical Results of the War," 405–406. See also *The Diary of Edward Bates, 1859–1866*, ed. Howard K. Beale (Washington, 1933), 543, which indicates the currency of the grasp-of-war doctrine, although Bates himself rejected it. McKitrick refers to Shellabarger's speech of January 8, 1866, in the House, which enunciated the forfeit-rights theory, as embodying the solution to the constitutional problem that Republicans accepted. McKitrick offers little evidence to substantiate this claim and probably relies on Dunning and Burgess, who held that Republican policy appeared to conform to the forfeit rights theory more closely than to any other. McKitrick, *Johnson and Reconstruction*, 113–17; Burgess, *Reconstruction and the Constitution*, 60; Dunning, *Essays on the Civil War*, 112. Actually, as McKitrick implies, Shellabarger's speech dealt primarily with the status of the rebel states, touching only vaguely on the source of congressional power over them. The concept of forfeit rights nicely complemented the grasp-of-war doctrine, because according to that doctrine, southern political organizations had no rights beyond those guaranteed by the laws of war until Congress recognized the restoration of peace. There were two major differences between Shellabarger's version of the forfeit rights theory and that incorporated into the grasp-of-war doctrine. First, as already noted, Shellabarger barely came to grips with the problem of congressional power over the South, concentrating almost exclusively on the

status problem. The grasp-of-war theory carried the concept of forfeit rights forward by explaining just where Congress' power came from—the continued existence of the state of war. Second, Shellabarger's version hinted at civilian control of the South, insofar as it discussed the contours of congressional power at all. The grasp-of-war doctrine manifestly called for continued military government under the national government's war powers. The Reconstruction legislation that Republicans finally passed did provide for military rather than civilian government. In fact, Republicans chose this alternative rather than a plan for civilian government in the South that Shellabarger himself proposed. See Michael Les Benedict, *A Compromise of Principle: Congressional Republicans and Reconstruction, 1863–1869* (New York: Norton, 1974), 228–39.

34. *New York Times*, June 24, 1865.

35. Bigelow to Dana, August 8, 1865, and Dana to Bigelow, October 25, 1865, in John Bigelow, *Retrospections of an Active Life*, 4 vols. (New York: Baker & Taylor, 1909), 3:144–45, 205–209.

36. Quoted in Charles Francis Adams Jr., *Richard Henry Dana: A Biography*, 2 vols. (Boston: Houghton Mifflin, 1891), 2:330–31.

37. Matthew Hale Carpenter, *The Powers of Congress: The Constitutionality of its Acts on Reconstruction: Speech of Hon. Matt. H. Carpenter at Chicago, Ill., Aug. 12, 1868* (Washington, D.C.: Union Republican Congressional Committee, 1868), 3; John A. Rawlins, "Address of General Rawlins, Delivered at Galena, Illinois, June 14, 1867," in James Harrison Wilson, *The Life of John A. Rawlins: Lawyer, Assistant Adjutant-General, Chief of Staff, Major General of Volunteers, and Secretary of War* (New York: Neale, 1916), 491–93; [Charles Sumner], "Our Domestic Relations; Or, How to Treat the Rebel States," *Atlantic Monthly* 12 (Oct.1863): 525–26; William Whiting, *Address of Hon. William Whiting, Before the Boston Highlands Grant Club, Aug. 5, 1868* (Boston: A. Williams, 1868), 7; Oliver P. Morton, *Congressional Globe*, 40 Cong., 2 Sess., 723–24 (January 24, 1868); Benjamin F. Wade, ibid., 38 Cong., 1 Sess., 3450–51 (July 1, 1864). See also Charles O. Lerche Jr., "Congressional Interpretations of the Guarantee of a Republican Form of Government During Reconstruction," *Journal of Southern History* 15 (May 1949): 192–211.

38. See Richard Yates's comments, *Congressional Globe*, 40 Cong., 2 Sess., 2746 (June 1, 1868) and Sumner, ibid., 3 Sess., 903 (February 5, 1869).

39. Ibid., 40 Cong., 1 Sess., 193 (March 18, 1867), 656–57 (July 15, 1867).

40. William D. Kelley proposed a bill that no state could adopt a new constitution that left citizens without a vote owing to race, color, or previous condition of servitude. Ibid., 512 (July 8, 1867). The bill died in committee. John M. Broomall proposed a bill in 1867 to enfranchise African Americans in all the states. After long debate in 1868, the House dropped the matter. Ibid., 591 (July 11, 1868), 621 (July 12, 1867), 2 Sess., 1939 (March 17, 1868), 1954–72 (March 18, 1868). Henry Wilson and Charles Sumner proposed similar bills in 1868–69, but they were defeated in the Senate Judiciary Committee, which proposed a constitutional amendment instead. When Sumner proposed his bill as a substitute for the amendment, only eight Republicans joined him. Ibid., 5 (December 7, 1868), 38, 43 (December 10, 1868), 378 (January 15, 1869), 1041 (February 9, 1869).

41. Lerche, "Congressional Interpretations of the Guarantee of a Republican Form of Government During Reconstruction," 198–99. See for instance the report of the Joint Committee on Reconstruction on the conditions for being restored to normal relations in the Union: "The first step towards that end would necessarily be the establishment of a republican form of government by the people." U.S. Congress, *Report of the Joint Committee on Reconstruction at the First Session Thirty-Ninth Congress* (Washington, D.C.: Government Printing Office, 1866), xiv.

42. Ibid., xi.

43. Ibid., xii–xiii.

44. *Congressional Globe*, 39 Cong., 1 Sess., 1033 (February 26, 1866), 1054–67 (February 27, 1866), 1083–95 (February 28, 1866). Although he would later argue that he meant to authorize the federal government to protect the rights of Americans against deprivation from any source, *Congressional Globe*, 42 Cong., 1 Sess., appendix, 84–85 (March 31, 1871), during the debate on his measure, Bingham consistently referred to the state actions that his proposal was designed to counteract. See also the comments of Thaddeus Stevens, the senior House member of the Reconstruction Committee, which reported the language to the floor, *Congressional Globe*, 39 Cong., 1 Sess., 1063 (February 17, 1866). Michael P. Zuckert denies that the decision to postpone consideration of Bingham's original version of the citizenship section of the Fourteenth Amendment was a repudiation of its positively worded language. Zuckert, "Congressional Power Under the Fourteenth Amendment—The Original Understanding of Section Five," *Constitutional Commentary* 3 (Winter 1986): 123–56. It is true, as Zuckert stresses, that Bingham himself agreed to the postponement. But its mover, another influential Republican member of the Reconstruction Committee, made clear that he had opposed the measure there. Conservative Republicans were vocal opponents. In light of President Johnson's veto of the first Republican Reconstruction legislation, the party above all needed unity, and the measure was postponed to avoid open divisions at so delicate a juncture. See Benedict, *A Compromise of Principle*, 159–61. Thus the failing of the measure was not that so many Republicans opposed it as to put its passage at risk, but rather that it was too divisive in its original, positively worded form. Bingham's reworking, which merely reflected what he and other Republicans intended all along, enabled nearly all Republicans to unite on the measure.

45. *Boston Daily Advertiser*, May 24, 1866, summarizing the speech explicating the Amendment by its manager in the upper chamber, Senator Jacob M. Howard.

46. Schurz, "Logical Results of the War," 378. See also the endorsement by the arch-conservative Jacob D. Cox: "If these rights are in good faith protected by State laws and State authorities, there will be no need of federal legislation on the subject, and the power will remain in abeyance." Quoted in Charles Fairman, "Does the Fourteenth Amendment Incorporate the Bill of Rights? The Original Understanding," *Stanford Law Review* 2 (December 1949): 96. There is substantial scholarly disagreement over the scope Republicans intended for the citizenship section of the Fourteenth Amendment. Historians and legal scholars have demonstrated that the range of rights that Republicans intended to guarantee to citizens was far wider than the Supreme Court admitted in the *Slaughter-House Cases* and wider than scholars had believed until recently. It is well accepted now that the section's terms referred to a vague but broad mass of rights, privileges, and immunities that guaranteed the full liberty of American citizens. At minimum these terms related to cogent, systematic constitutional doctrines developed by antislavery leaders during the thirty-five years preceding the Fourteenth Amendment's passage. See Howard Jay Graham, *Everyman's Constitution: Historical Essays on the Fourteenth Amendment, the "Conspiracy Theory," and American Constitutionalism* (Madison: State Historical Society of Wisconsin, 1968), 152–241, 266–94, 295–336; and John P. Frank and Robert F. Munro, "The Original Understanding of 'Equal Protection of the Laws,'" *Columbia Law Review* 50 (February 1950): 131–69. A growing number of constitutional scholars argue that the Amendment was meant to incorporate some or all of the Bill of Rights, reversing the long-standing consensus on that subject. See Curtis, *No State Shall Abridge*; Akhil Reed Amar, "The Bill of Rights and the Fourteenth Amendment," *Yale Law Journal* 101 (April 1992): 1193–1284; Richard L. Aynes, "On Misreading John Bingham and the Fourteenth Amendment," *Yale Law Journal* 103 (October 1993): 57–104; Aynes, "Charles Fairman, Felix Frankfurter, and the Fourteenth Amendment," *Chicago Kent Law Review* 70 (1995): 1197–1273; Bryan H. Wildenthal, "The Lost Compromise: Reassessing the Early Understanding in Court and Congress on Incorpo-

ration of the Bill of Rights in the Fourteenth Amendment," *Ohio State University Law Journal* 61 (2003): 1051–1173. Significantly, Earl M. Maltz, who generally argues for a constricted interpretation of the Fourteenth Amendment and Reconstruction legislation, concludes that the framers intended that the Amendment incorporate the Bill of Rights. Maltz, *Civil Rights, the Constitution, and Congress*, 113–18.

But this does not answer the question whether the national government acquired power through the Fourteenth Amendment to legislate directly to protect those rights irrespective of state action. Although some scholars have argued differently, it appears from the entire tenor of the constitutional discussion of 1865–66 that Republicans did not intend to change the locus of police power from state to national government, even where the police power protected fundamental civil rights. A number of scholars argue that, at least by 1871 when Congress passed the Force Act, Republicans believed that the national government could intervene both when states affirmatively violated protected citizens' rights by legislation and when they violated these rights more subtly by maladministration or nonadministration. See Alfred Avins, "The Ku Klux Klan Act of 1871: Some Reflected Light on State Action and the Fourteenth Amendment," *St. Louis University Law Journal* 11 (Spring 1967): 331–81; Alfred Avins, "Racial Segregation in Public Accommodations: Some Reflected Light on the Fourteenth Amendment from the Civil Rights Act of 1875," *Western Reserve Law Review* 18 (May 1967): 1251–83; Laurent B. Frantz, "Congressional Power to Enforce the Fourteenth Amendment against Private Acts," *Yale Law Journal* 73 (July 1964): 1353–84; Robert J. Harris, *The Quest for Equality: The Constitution, Congress and the Supreme Court* (Baton Rouge: Louisiana State University Press, 1960), 44–53; Zuckert, "Congressional Power under the Fourteenth Amendment," 139–43. Robert J. Kaczorowski argues forcefully that the Fourteenth Amendment granted the national government direct and primary power to protect civil rights in his article "Revolutionary Constitutionalism in the Era of the Civil War and Reconstruction." Classic similar arguments are Graham, *Everyman's Constitution*, 295–36, and Frank and Munro, "The Original Understanding of 'Equal Protection of the Laws,'" 163–64. The debate between Bingham, James A. Garfield, and John F. Farnsworth over the Force Act in the House of Representatives offers valuable insights into the question. See the *Congressional Globe*, 42 Cong., 1 Sess., appendix, 81–85, 115–16 (March 31, 1871), 151–54 (April 4, 1871). Howard Jay Graham chronicles another valuable debate, this one between Trumbull and Matthew Hale Carpenter, but Graham simply accepts Carpenter's interpretation of the Fourteenth Amendment, although Trumbull served in the Senate, which passed the amendment, while Carpenter did not. Graham, *Everyman's Constitution*, 323–31. For a clear indication of how state-centered Republicans understood the constitutional amendment as they passed and ratified it, see the compendia of Republican arguments in Fairman, "Does the Fourteenth Amendment Incorporate the Bill of Rights?" especially 41–134. The evidence is all the more impressive because Fairman was dealing with another point entirely.

47. Fairman, "Does the Fourteenth Amendment Incorporate the Bill of Rights?"

48. For a detailed chronicle of the concerns and controversies that led to the formulation of the first Reconstruction plan, see Benedict, *A Compromise of Principle*, 134–87.

49. Trumbull would be among the seven Republican senators voting against convicting President Johnson in his impeachment trial. In 1872 he became a leader of the dissident Liberal Republican movement. By 1876 he had returned to the state rights–oriented Democratic Party, which he had left over the slavery issue in the 1850s. See Mark M. Krug, *Lyman Trumbull, Conservative Radical* (New York: A. S. Barnes, 1965).

50. *Congressional Globe*, 39 Cong., 1 Sess., 211–12 (January 12, 1866). For Trumbull's discussions of constitutional justifications for the Freedmen's Bureau bill, see ibid., 420 (January 25, 1866), 938–39, 942 (February 20, 1866); Fessenden, ibid., 365 (January 23,

1866); William M. Stewart, ibid., 297 (January 18, 1866); Samuel W. Moulton, ibid., 631 (February 8, 1866); Thomas D. Eliot, ibid., 656 (February 5, 1866).

51. Ibid., 323 (January 19, 1866), 364–66 (January 23, 1866). See especially ibid., 323, for a good illustration of the differences between those who, like Fessenden, believed national war powers stood outside the Constitution and those who, like Trumbull, believed the Constitution sanctioned those powers.

52. Ibid., 211–12 (January 12, 1866), 474 (January 29, 1866). The specified rights were "to make and enforce contracts, to sue, be parties, and give evidence, to inherit, purchase, lease, sell, hold, and convey real and personal property, and to full and equal benefit of all laws and proceedings for the security of person and property, and . . . [to] be subject to like punishment, pains, and penalties, and to none other."

53. Politically, Trumbull still supported Johnson at the time he framed the Civil Rights bill, and he intended it as a measure to insure cooperation between Republican conservatives and centrists and the president, who he believed had advocated civil rights for freed slaves in his message to Congress. With the Civil Rights bill enacted and the president cooperating with Congress, he believed most Republicans would accept the southern state governments erected under his authority. See Trumbull's speech in Chicago, summer 1866, Trumbull scrapbook, Lyman Trumbull Papers, Illinois State Historical Library, Springfield; Welles, *Diary*, 2: 489 (April 19, 1866); Trumbull, *Congressional Globe*, 39 Cong., 1 Sess., 322 (January 19, 1866), 1760 (April 4, 1866); *Washington Chronicle*, January 10, 1866, 1; Boston *Evening Journal*, January 17, 1866, 2; January 18, 1866, 2. See also newspaper correspondence from "Herman," Trumbull scrapbook, Trumbull Papers. On constitutional questions not involving Reconstruction, Trumbull joined other Republican constitutional conservatives and Democrats in voting against proposals to expand the functions of the national government. See the votes on proposals for a nationwide quarantine to protect against cholera, *Congressional Globe*, 39 Cong., I Sess., 2586, 2589 (May 15, 1866); to facilitate interstate commerce and communications, ibid., 2870, 2876 (May 29, 1866); to repair levees on the Mississippi River, ibid., 4083 (July 21, 1866).

54. *Congressional Globe*, 39 Cong., 1 Sess., 476 (January 29, 1866). Also see ibid., 600 (February 2, 1866). Other Republicans interpreted the measure the same way. See the conservative Stewart's justification for supporting the measure, ibid., 1785 (April 5, 1866); and Jacob D. Cox to Johnson, March 22, 1866, Andrew Johnson Papers, LC. Both Cox and Stewart had supported Johnson's policy up to this time, including his veto of the Freedmen's Bureau bill. This interpretation is in flat disagreement with that expounded by the Supreme Court in *Jones v. Alfred H. Mayer Co.*, 392 U.S. 409 (1968); Robert L. Kohl in "The Civil Rights Act of 1866, Its Hour Come Round at Last: *Jones v. Alfred H. Mayer Co.*," *Virginia Law Review* 55 (March 1969): 272–300; Robert J. Kaczorowski, "The Enforcement Provisions of the Civil Rights Act of 1866: A Legislative History in Light of *Runyon v. McCrary*," *Yale Law Journal* 98 (January 1989): 565–95; Kaczorowski, "To Begin the Nation Anew"; Barry Sullivan, "Historical Reconstruction, Reconstruction History, and the Proper Scope of Section 1981," *Yale Law Journal* 98 (January 1989): 541–64. Both the opinion and the articles are long on inference but short on evidence. See note 15 for criticism of Kaczorowski's interpretation of evidence. The Supreme Court in the *Jones* case cites the provisions of the Freedmen's Bureau bill as evidence for interpreting the meaning of the Civil Rights bill. But, as the Court recognizes, Trumbull left the key word "prejudice" out of the Civil Rights bill when defining the conditions under which discrimination in civil rights was illegal. To one familiar with Trumbull's extreme conservatism in constitutional matters, the reason is clear: The Freedmen's Bureau bill, a war measure, was justified under Congress's war powers, which were in Trumbull's opinion limited only by the law of nations. Therefore a provision against denial of rights based on personal prejudice was constitutionally justifiable. The Civil

Rights bill he justified under peacetime provisions of the Constitution. That legislation would be permanent, and Trumbull intended no permanent extension of federal power of this magnitude.

In defending the Supreme Court's decision, Robert L. Kohl argues that the Civil Rights bill was framed in response to extralegal as well as legal discrimination against black men in the South. Barry Sullivan makes the same point. Neither gives hard evidence to this effect, relying instead on the fact that testimony before the Joint Committee on Reconstruction indicated that such discrimination existed. Sullivan argues that the language specifying agencies through which civil rights might be violated could not have been meant to be exhaustive in light of the private discrimination the bill must have been intended to combat, reasoning that seems circular to me. Kohl assumes that the prohibition on discrimination in civil rights due to "custom" in the Civil Rights bill must have been intended to combat this type of discrimination. But Trumbull framed the section involved before the Reconstruction Committee had received any testimony, and the bill was reported not from the Reconstruction Committee but from the Judiciary Committee. This does not mean that Trumbull could not have had such discrimination in mind; he had access to Freedmen's Bureau correspondence, which offered testimony similar to that the Reconstruction Committee heard. It only means that it is not certain that he had it in mind. Given this uncertainty, it would be helpful to have clear indications from Trumbull that he did indeed intend to combat extralegal prejudice. But his statements, such as the one quoted in the text, imply a contrary view. Moreover, Trumbull later opposed legislation operating directly on extralegal criminal conspiracies to violate citizens' rights. See his arguments on the Ku Klux Klan Act of 1871, *Congressional Globe*, 42 Cong., 1 Sess., 578–79 (April 11, 1871). This may indicate no more than that Trumbull had changed his mind along with his politics (by 1871 he was in open revolt against the Republican Party), but it will take a more thorough study than those offered so far to prove it. An analysis of every argument made in Congress in favor of passing the Civil Rights bill shows eleven instances in which congressmen characterized it primarily as abrogating discriminatory state laws or procedures; six that indicate that some Republicans may have believed the law would protect citizens when states failed to protect their rights although the laws themselves were not overtly discriminatory (in only two of these instances did speakers clearly indicate this understanding); and only four statements which could possibly be interpreted to mean that the law would give the national government original power to protect rights regardless of the state's complicity in the denial—and three of these are not at all clear. Aimed primarily at state legislation or procedures: Howard, ibid., 39 Cong., 1 Sess., 503, 504 (January 30, 1866), Lane, 602–03 (February 2), Trumbull, 474, 475 (January 29), 600, 605 (February 2), 1758, 1759 (April 4), Williams, 573 (February 1), Wilson, 603 (February 2), Stewart, 1785 (April 5), Bingham, 1291, 1293 (March 9), Broomall, 1263 (March 8), Cook, 1123, 1124 (March 1). Aimed at state inaction in protecting rights: Trumbull, ibid., 475 (January 29, 1866), 600 (February 2), 1758, 1761 (April 4) (questionable), Bingham, 1291 (March 9) (questionable), Broomall, 1263 (March 8) (very questionable), Cook, 1123 (March 1) (questionable). Complete national power to protect civil rights, regardless of state complicity: Howard, ibid., 503, 504 (January 30, 1866) (very questionable), Trumbull, 475 (January 29) (questionable), 500 (January 30), 1757 (April 4) (questionable).

The foregoing does not mean that Republicans were willing to leave southern blacks at the mercy of southern whites. Republicans believed governments were obligated to enforce their laws. The assumption that if states were required to protect all citizens equally they would do so permeated the debates of 1866. Slavery had been essentially a legal institution, created and protected by state law. Republicans' experience with slavery led them to emphasize the state's part in its perpetuation, and the passage of the so-called Black Codes in 1865 and 1866 reinforced this habit of mind. Moreover, northern

Republicans had firsthand experience with their own racist communities, in which African Americans were generally subject to private discrimination but protected in basic rights. See Paul Finkelman, "Prelude to the Fourteenth Amendment: Black Legal Rights in the Antebellum North," *Rutgers Law Journal* 17 (Spring and Summer 1986): 415–82. They did not have a century of tragic experience with the refusal of southern state and local governments to protect black citizens in theoretically equal rights. Nonetheless, as the preceding citations indicate, some Republicans did believe that the national government could intervene to protect rights where the states failed to do so. Trumbull put this bluntly in a discussion of the Freedmen's Bureau bill: "It shall be understood that it is the policy of the Government that the rights of the colored men are to be protected by the States if they will, but by the Federal Government if they will not." Even here the context of his remarks indicates that Trumbull still believed removal of discriminatory state laws and protection of rights amounted to the same thing. Ibid., 322 (January 19, 1866).

55. Benjamin B. Kendrick, ed., *The Journal of the Joint Committee of Fifteen on Reconstruction, 39th Congress 1865–1867* (New York: Columbia University Press, 1914), 124–29.

56. Augustus Brandegee, *Congressional Globe*, 39 Cong., 2 Sess., 1076 (February 7, 1867); Bingham, ibid., 1082 (February 7, 1867).

57. Ibid., 1083 (February 7, 1867).

58. Edward McPherson, ed., *The Political History of the United States During the Period of Reconstruction (from April 15, 1865 to July 15, 1870),* 2d ed. (Washington: Solomons & Chapman, 1875), 191–92. Detailed accounts of the passage of the Reconstruction Act may be found in Benedict, *A Compromise of Principle*, 210–43; Brock, *An American Crisis*, 153–211; Donald, *Politics of Reconstruction*, 53–82; and McKitrick, *Johnson and Reconstruction*, 448–85.

59. Dana to Charles Francis Adams, Jr., April 14, 1867, quoted in Adams, *Dana*, 2: 334–35.

60. See Jacob M. Howard, *Congressional Globe*, 39 Cong., 2 Sess., 1365 (February 15, 1867); Shellabarger, ibid., 1102 (February 8, 1867); Garfield, ibid., 1104; John A. Kasson, ibid., 1105; Abner C. Harding, ibid., 1098–99; Stewart, ibid., 1364 (February 15, 1867); Trumbull, *Argument in Ex Parte McCardle*, 14, 20–26; James A. Rawley, *Edwin D. Morgan 1811–1883: Merchant in Politics* (New York: Columbia University Press, 1955), 226. In an outline of a speech on Reconstruction, Fessenden vigorously asserted that the Reconstruction Acts were passed under Congress's war powers alone. The speech is filed under 1868, but I have found no record of its actual delivery. William Pitt Fessenden Papers, LC.

61. *Congressional Globe*, 39 Cong., 2 Sess., 1184 (February 12, 1867). According to John Sherman there was "a clear, easy, and right way for these States to be restored to their full power in the Government. All that it demands of the people of the southern States is to extend to all their male citizens . . . the elective franchise." Ibid., 1462 (February 16, 1867).

62. [E. L. Godkin], "Universal Suffrage and Universal Amnesty," *New York Nation*, November 29, 866, 430. See also William Sprague, *Congressional Globe*, 38 Cong., 2 Sess., 960 (February 21, 1865); "Reconstruction," *North American Review* 100 (April 1865): 553; Joseph Medill to McCulloch, June 10, 1865, McCulloch Papers; Henry Winter Davis, *Speeches and Addresses Delivered in the Congress of the United States, and on Several Public Occasions* (New York: Harper & Bros., 1867), 579–81; "Correspondence: Winter Davis on Reconstruction," *New York Nation*, November 30, 1865, 681; John Stuart Mill to "Judge Dickson," quoted in *Littel's Living Age* 87 (October 7, 1865): 47–48; de Gasparin, *Reconstruction*, 37–38; J. L. Haynes to Nathaniel P. Banks, January 11, 1866, Nathaniel P. Banks Papers, Illinois State Historical Library, Springfield; Morton in the *Congressional*

Globe, 40 Cong., 2 Sess., 725 (January 24, 1868); John Covode to Edwin M. Stanton, n.d. [summer 1865], John Covode Papers, LC. See also James G. Blaine and others, "Ought the Negro to Be Disfranchised? Ought He to Have Been Enfranchised?" *North American Review* 128 (March 1879): 230, 246; and Carl Schurz, *The Reminiscences of Carl Schurz*, 3 vols. (New York: McClure, 1908), 3:246.

63. [Carl Schurz], "The True Problem," *Atlantic Monthly* 19 (March 1867): 377.
64. "What the South Needs First," *New York Nation*, January 18, 1866.
65. Charles D. Drake, *Congressional Globe*, 40 Cong., 2 Sess., 2629 (May 28, 1868).
66. Ibid., 2744 (June 1, 1868).
67. Ibid., 2659 (May 29, 1868).
68. Ibid., 2746 (June 1, 1868).
69. Ibid., 2603 (May 27, 1868).
70. Morton, ibid., 2603 (May 27, 1868). See also Roscoe Conkling's and John B. Henderson's arguments against permanent conditions, ibid., 2663–67 (May 29, 1863) and 2603 (May 27, 1868); Trumbull, ibid., 2699 (May 30, 1868); Frederick T. Frelinghuysen, ibid., 2692 (May 30, 1868); Joseph S. Fowler, ibid., 2743–44 (June 1, 1868); and Bingham, ibid., 2211 (March 29, 1868). Judicial authority was split on the question at issue. The weight of opinion held that all fundamental conditions were presumed met when Congress admitted a state into the Union and that no *in futuro* condition could limit state authority in areas of jurisdiction the United States Constitution delegated to the states. That was the view articulated in *Permoli v. First Municipality*, 3 Howard 589 (1845) and affirmed in *Strader et al. v. Graham*, 10 Howard 82 (1850). The only contrary authority was the decision in *Spooner v. McConnell et al.*, 22 Federal Cases 939 (No. 13, 245) (C.C.D. Ohio, 1838). In the 1880s the Supreme Court firmly established the conservatives' position in *Escabana Co. v. Chicago*, 107 U.S, 678 (1882); *Huse v. Glover*, 119 U.S. 543 (1886); and *Sands v. Manistee River Improvement Co.*, 123 U.S. 288 (1887). In 1910 and 1911, the courts ruled *in futuro* conditions to grants of statehood unconstitutional in cases directly in point. A condition requiring Oklahoma to bar the sale of liquor in former Indian territory for twenty-one years was overturned in *U.S. ex rel. Friedman et al. v. U.S. Express Co.*, 180 Federal Reporter 1006 (D.C.W.D. Ark. 1910). The Supreme Court ruled a condition requiring Guthrie to remain Oklahoma's capital until 1913 unconstitutional in *Coyle v. Oklahoma*, 221 U.S. 559 (1910).
71. *Congressional Globe*, 40 Cong., 2 Sess., 2701 (May 30, 1868).
72. *New York Tribune*, December 1, 1868.
73. *Congressional Globe*, 40 Cong., 3 Sess., 491 (January 21, 1869), 728 (January 29, 1869). Julian and Rep. James M. Ashley's proposals of positively worded black-suffrage constitutional amendments (House Resolution Nos. 371 and 381) were not printed in the *Congressional Globe*. They can be found in the Resolution file, 40 Cong., Records of the United States House of Representatives, National Archives.
74. Willard Warner, *Congressional Globe*, 40 Cong., 3 Sess., 862 (February 3, 1869). For more thorough discussions of the Fifteenth Amendment as a defeat for more radical Republicans, see Benedict, *A Compromise of Principle*, 325–36, and Xi Wang, *The Trial of Democracy: Black Suffrage and Northern Republicans, 1860–1910* (Athens: University of Georgia Press, 1997), 39–48.
75. Henry Brooks Adams, "The Session," *North American Review* 91 (July 1870): 42–43; [James Parton], "The Pressure Upon Congress," *Atlantic Monthly* 25 (February 1870), 155.
76. *Speeches of Carl Schurz*, 1:419; Reuben Fenton, *Issues of the Campaign: Speech of Gov. Reuben E. Fenton, at Jamestown, September 19th, 1868* (n.p., 1868), 5. There are myriad Republican speeches, all emphasizing the peace theme in the Edward M. McPherson scrapbooks on the campaign of 1868, Edward M. McPherson Papers, LC.

77. *Congressional Globe*, 41 Cong., 2 Sess., 643 (January 21, 1870), 502 (January 14, 1870). When first proposed in the Senate, the conditions had been defeated by overwhelming margins. Ibid., 416 (January 13, 1870), 464, 466 (January 14, 1870).

78. Ibid, 2820, 2821, 2823, 2825, 2829 (April 19, 1870), 1770 (March 8, 1870), 4796 (June 21, 1870).

79. Ibid., appendix, 151 (April 4, 1871).

80. See Avins, "The Ku Klux Klan Act of 1871"; Alfred Avins, "The Civil Rights Act of 1875: Some Reflected Light on the Fourteenth Amendment and Public Accommodations," *Columbia Law Review* 66 (May 1966): 873–915; Harris, *Quest for Equality*, 44–52.

81. The so-called abandonment of southern Republicans after 1877 actually was a presidential promise not to respond to requests for federal intervention on behalf of Republican contestants in disputed elections. President Grant and Congress had exercised that authority to fulfill the federal government's obligation to guarantee republican forms of government to the states under Article IV. Republican administrations continued to attempt to enforce federal laws guaranteeing civil and political rights. See Robert M. Goldman, *"A Fair Ballot and a Free Count": The Department of Justice and the Enforcement of Voting Rights in the South, 1877–1893* (New York: Garland, 1990).

82. See Michael Les Benedict, "Preserving Federalism: Reconstruction and the Waite Court," *Supreme Court Review* 1978: 39–80.

83. Brooks D. Simpson, *The Reconstruction Presidents* (Lawrence: University Press of Kansas, 1998), 235. Grant's observations appeared originally in John Russell Young, *Around the World with President Grant* (New York: American News Company, 1879), 362–63.

2. The Rout of Radicalism: Republicans and the Elections of 1867

1. Beale, *The Critical Year: A Study of Andrew Johnson and Reconstruction* (New York: Frederick Ungar, 1930).

2. See, for example, Henry Adams to Charles Francis Adams, April 3, 1867, alluding to Charles's concern that events indicated that Americans were disposed to abrogate the Constitution in the Reconstruction crisis. *The Letters of Henry Adams*, ed. J. C. Levenson et al. (Cambridge, Mass.: Harvard University Press, 1982), 1:557.

3. Eric L. McKitrick, *Andrew Johnson and Reconstruction* (Chicago: University of Chicago Press, 1960). LaWanda and John H. Cox, *Politics, Principle, and Prejudice, 1865–1866: Dilemma of Reconstruction America* (Glencoe, Ill: Free Press, 1963), and W. R. Brock, *An American Crisis: Congress and Reconstruction, 1865–1867* (New York: St. Martin's, 1963) had stressed the moderation of Republicans' initial policy. See also Michael Les Benedict, *A Compromise of Principle: Congressional Republicans and Reconstruction, 1863–1869* (New York: Norton, 1974), 135–87, which contrasted the "Conservative Reconstruction" of 1866 with the "Radical Reconstruction" that followed.

4. McKitrick, *Johnson and Reconstruction*, 476–85; Donald, *The Politics of Reconstruction, 1863–1867* (Baton Rouge: Louisiana State University Press, 1965), 53–82; Brock, *An American Crisis*, 175–203; Larry G. Kincaid, "The Legislative Origins of the Military Reconstruction Act, 1865–1867" (Ph.D. dissertation, Johns Hopkins University, 1968); Benedict, *A Compromise of Principle*, 210–43.

5. Eric Foner, *Reconstruction: America's Unfinished Revolution, 1863–1877* (New York: Harper & Row, 1988), 313–16; David Herbert Donald, Jean H. Baker, and Michael F. Holt, *The Civil War and Reconstruction* (New York: Norton, 2001), 568–69; Claudine Ferrell, *Reconstruction* (Westport, Conn.: Praeger, 2003), 40; James M. McPherson, *Ordeal by Fire: The Civil War and Reconstruction* (New York: Knopf, 1982), 571–72.

6. Sumner urged his measure as a necessity in a long letter to Theodore Tilton, editor of the radical *Independent*. Tilton published the letter in his newspaper and endorsed Sumner's position. Sumner's proposition received further support from the

Border State Convention, meeting in Baltimore early in September 1867. As the only national Republican meeting of 1867, it was given wide publicity by the party press. It was presided over by Tennessee congressman Horace Maynard. Many leading border-state Republicans attended, including Congressman Robert T. Van Horn, former Senator John A. J. Creswell, and Tennessee leader (soon to be U.S. Representative) Roderick R. Butler. *The Independent*, May 2, 1867; Edward M. McPherson scrapbook: Campaign of 1867, 1:68–73, in McPherson Mss., Library of Congress; *New York Times*, September 13, 1867.

7. *Roberts v. Boston*, 5 Cushing 198 (1849). Sumner proposed his educational requirement as an amendment to the first Supplementary Reconstruction Act, but it had been defeated by a coalition of Democrats and conservative Republicans. *Congressional Globe*, 40 Cong. 1 Sess., 165–70 (March 16, 1867). He renewed his efforts at the July 1867 session, called to modify the Reconstruction laws to prevent presidential interference. Again the Democrats and conservative Republicans defeated him. Ibid., 581 (July 11, 1867).

8. *New York Tribune*, May 8, 1867. Thomas Wentworth Higginson, the society's president, seconded the demand for land reform at the same meeting. *The Independent*, May 2, 1867, p. 4. Stevens expressed his views on reconstruction in letters to Edward M. McPherson, widely published in the nation's press. They and comments on them may be found in the *National Anti-Slavery Standard*, May 4, 1867; June 22, 1867; *Centreville Indiana True Republican*, July 4, 1867; *Boston Commonwealth*, March 23 and March 30, 1867; *Gettysburg Star and Herald*, quoted in the *New York Times*, May 29, 1867. Butler's endorsement of confiscation came in a letter to a Republican campaign meeting in Washington, D.C., reported ibid., June 7, 1867.

9. Michael Les Benedict, *The Impeachment and Trial of Andrew Johnson* (New York: Norton, 1973), 52–60.

10. The Reconstruction Act, as originally reported from the Joint Committee on Reconstruction, was merely a military government bill, providing no means for restoration at all. After a bitter battle, conservative Republicans succeeded in adding provisions to enable southerners to organize new civil governments entitled to restoration. See Brock, *An American Crisis*, 188–203; Donald, *Politics of Reconstruction*, 70–82; Benedict, *A Compromise of Principle*, 223–39.

11. *New York Times*, September 2, 1867.

12. Kirk H. Porter and Donald Bruce Johnson, *National Party Platforms, 1840–1956* (Urbana: University of Illinois Press, 1956), 39.

13. *Boston Daily Advertiser*, June 13, 1867; *Cincinnati Commercial*, June 15, 1867.

14. *Boston Evening Journal*, May 24, 1867; Wilson in *The Independent*, May 9 and June 6, 1867; *Cincinnati Commercial*, July 8, 1867; *Boston Daily Advertiser*, July 4, 1867. Greeley traveled to Richmond to conciliate southern whites. See his speech there, reported in his *New York Tribune*, May 17, 1867. Greeley was also influenced in part by political considerations in joining a group of northerners in raising bail money for Jefferson Davis. See the *New York Tribune*'s comment on May 31, 1867. For enthusiastic reports of white southern acceptance of the Republican party, see ibid., May 20, 21, 28, 1867; General John Pope to Robert C. Schenck, May 20, 1867, Schenck Mss., Rutherford B. Hayes Library, Fremont, Ohio; John Sherman to William Tecumseh Sherman, August 9, 1867, quoted in John Sherman and William Tecumseh Sherman, *The Sherman Letters: Correspondence between General and Senator Sherman from 1837 to 1891*, ed. Rachel Sherman Thorndike (New York: Charles Scribner's Sons, 1894), 292–94.

15. *New York Times*, May 2, 1867,

16. *National Anti-Slavery Standard*, August 17, 1867. See Thaddeus Stevens's attack on conservative Republicans in a letter published in the *Gettysburg Star and Herald*, quoted in the *New York Times*, May 29, 1867; Stevens's speech before the American Anti-

Slavery Society, quoted in the *New York Tribune*, May 8, 1867; *National Anti-Slavery Standard*, March 30, April 6, and October 26, 1867; Wendell Phillips's attack on Greeley, discussed in Glyndon C. Van Deusen, *Horace Greeley: Nineteenth Century Crusader* (New York: Hill & Wang, 1964), 352–56, and Greeley's reply in the *New York Tribune*, May 24, 1867; Zachariah Chandler's biting attack on conservative Republicans in a campaign speech at Ashtabula, Ohio, in the McPherson scrapbook: Campaign of 1867, 2:135–36, McPherson Mss.; Sumner's assault on conservative Republican Senators Fessenden, George F. Edmunds, and Roscoe Conkling in an interview with James Redpath, quoted in the *Boston Daily Advertiser*, September 4, 1867.

17. In the House of Representatives, leading radicals had opposed reestablishing the rank of Lieutenant General of the Army for him. Stevens, George S. Boutwell, James A. Garfield, William D. Kelley, George W. Julian, and Henry Winter Davis had tried to prevent it but failed. *Congressional Globe*, 38 Cong., 1 Sess., 427–31 (February 7, 1864); T. Harry Williams, *Lincoln and the Radicals* (Madison: University of Wisconsin Press, 1941), 334–37; William Frank Zornow, *Lincoln and the Party Divided* (Norman: University of Oklahoma Press, 1954), 87–88, 94.

18. William B. Hesseltine, *Ulysses S. Grant, Politician* (New York: Dodd, Mead, 1935), 61; William S. McFeely, *Grant: A Biography* (New York: Norton, 1981), 239–41, 249–52, 255; Badeau to E. B. Washburne, October 20, 1865. Washburne Mss.; Rawlins to Mrs. Rawlins, August 30 and September 1, 1866, quoted in James Harrison Wilson, *The Life of John A. Rawlins, Lawyer, Assistant Adjutant-General, Chief of Staff, Major General of Volunteers, and Secretary of War* (New York: Neale, 1916), 334–36; Orville H. Browning, *Diary of Orville Hickman Browning*, ed. James G. Randall (Springfield: Trustees of the Illinois State Historical Library, 1938), 2:103–104. In his study of Grant during Reconstruction, Brooks Simpson takes a more nuanced view, concluding that Grant's position moved in tandem with that of such centrist Republicans as Lyman Trumbull, from a desire to conciliate Johnson to ever greater concern that he was putting the fruits of victory at risk. Until 1868 he kept his concerns to himself and close confidants, permitting Johnson-backers to claim his sympathy and dismaying radical Republicans. Simpson, *Let Us Have Peace: Ulysses S. Grant and the Politics of War and Reconstruction, 1861–1868* (Chapel Hill: University of North Carolina Press, 1991), 135–76.

19. *The Independent*, August 29, 1867. See also Phillips in the *National Anti-Slavery Standard*, August 24, 1867; *New York Tribune*, August 15, 1867.

20. Curtin to E. B. Washburne, October 17, 1867, Washburne Mss.; *New York Herald*, July 6, 1867; Thurlow Weed Barnes, *Memoir of Thurlow Weed* (Boston: Houghton Mifflin, 1884), 457–58; Glyndon G. Van Deusen, *Thurlow Weed: Wizard of the Lobby* (Boston: Little, Brown, 1947), 327–28; Hesseltine, *Grant*, 91–92; *New York Times*, October 17, November 10, 27, 1867.

21. Greeley to Chandler, August 25, 1867, Chandler Mss. Greeley attacked Grant and his New York supporters in his *New York Tribune*, August 15, 1867.

22. Curtin, in Pennsylvania, found he could not convince Republican leaders to endorse Grant as part of their 1867 campaign effort. Curtin to E. B. Washburn, October 17, 1867. Washburne Mss. Republican Congressman Godlove S. Orth reported that Indiana Republicans were lukewarm to the prospect of Grant's nomination. William Henry Smith reported the same about Ohio radicals. The *New York Tribune* mobilized the radical wing of the New York party behind Chase. Charles Sumner openly criticized Grant's reticence on the issues. Orth to Schuyler Colfax [Spring 1867], Orth Mss., Indiana State Library, Indiana Division, Indianapolis; Smith to James H. Barrett, April 25, 1867, Smith Mss., Ohio Historical Society, Columbus; *New York Tribune*, October 15, 1867; Sumner in the *Boston Daily Advertiser*, September 4, 1867; Phillips before the American Anti-Slavery Society, quoted in the *New York Tribune*, May 8, 1867; *National Anti-Slavery*

Standard, August 3, 1867; James G. Blaine, *Twenty Years of Congress: From Lincoln to Garfield* (Norwich, Conn.: Henry Bill, 1884–1886), 2:531.

23. Forney to Sumner, July 10, 1867, Sumner Mss., Houghton Library, Harvard University.

24. During the 1866 elections, conservatives had worked hard to restrain their Radical allies in the effort to defeat Johnson and the Democrats. Not only had Republican legislation been conservative, but on the stump they had also emphasized its conservatism and reasonableness, at least implying that if southerners ratified the Fourteenth Amendment, their states would be restored to normal relations in the Union. They had abandoned efforts to enfranchise blacks or to disband the governments in the South erected by presidential authority. Radicals had played a slight role in the campaign. Not until the southern state legislatures rejected the Fourteenth Amendment did Republicans decide they could go farther than they had indicated they would during the 1866 canvass. See Benedict, *A Compromise of Principle*, 196–213; McKitrick, *Johnson and Reconstruction*, 442–54; Hans L. Trefousse, *The Radical Republicans: Lincoln's Vanguard for Racial Justice* (New York: Knopf, 1969), 348–51.

25. Blaine to Israel Washburn, September 12, 1867, quoted in Gaillard Hunt, *Israel, Elihu and Cadwallader Washburn: A Chapter in American Biography* (New York: Macmillan, 1925), 122–23. The letter seems to have been dated earlier than one would expect, in light of Blaine's confidence that Republicans were not to succeed at the polls. However, it is dated after the Maine elections, in which Republicans had done less well than they had the previous year.

26. Although Massachusetts Democrats and conservative Republicans treated the results as a repudiation of Republican radicalism, historian Dale Baum argues persuasively that it was the prohibition issue that led to the Republican reverses. Baum, *The Civil War Party System: The Case of Massachusetts, 1848–1876* (Chapel Hill: University of North Carolina Press, 1984), 122–44.

27. The statistics are from the *New York Tribune Almanac, 1868* (New York: New York Tribune, 1868).

28. *New York Times*, September 2, 1867.

29. Smith to S. R. Reid, October 3, 1867; Smith to Murat Halstead, October 2, 1867, Smith Mss., Rutherford B. Hayes Library; Schuyler Colfax to John A. J. Creswell, September 28, 1867, Colfax Mss., Hayes Library; John Sherman to William Tecumseh Sherman, August 9, 1867, quoted in *The Sherman Letters*, 292–94; Rutherford B. Hayes, *Diary and Letters of Rutherford B. Hayes, Nineteenth President of the United States*, ed. Charles Richard Williams (Columbus, Ohio: The Ohio State Archaeological and Historical Society, 1922–26), 3:48 (October 6, 1867). The election statistics are from the *Tribune Almanac, 1868*.

30. *Chicago Times*, quoted in the *Cincinnati Commercial*, October 12, 1867.

31. Adams to Charles Francis Adams Jr., April 3, 1867, in *Letters of Henry Adams*, 528.

32. Blaine to Israel Washburn, September 12, 1867, quoted in Hunt, *Washburn*, 122–23.

33. Banks to Mrs. Banks, November 13, 1867, Banks Mss., Essex Institute, Salem, Mass. Henry Adams was typically more restrained. He called the results in Massachusetts a "distinct and dignified reprimand" of the state's radical senators Sumner and Wilson, who had blocked the appointment of his brother John Quincy as Boston collector of customs. Henry Adams to Charles Francis Adams Jr., November 16, 1867, *Letters of Henry Adams*, 557–58.

34. Sherman to Colfax, October 20, 1867, Colfax Mss., Rush Rhees Library, University of Rochester; Wade in an interview published in the *Cincinnati Commercial*, quoted in the *New York Times*, November 8, 1867.

35. Binney to John A. Andrew, September 13, 1867, Andrew Mss., Massachusetts Historical Society; Wade to Chandler, October 10, 1867, Chandler Mss.

36. *The Independent*, October 24 and November 14, 1867.

37. *Congressional Globe*, 40 Cong., 2 Sess., 67–68 (December 7, 1867). The impeachment resolution that finally did pass came in February 1868, when the president apparently violated a law of Congress—the Tenure of Office Act.

38. Clemenceau, *American Reconstruction, 1865–1870, and the Impeachment of President Johnson*, ed. Fernand Baldensperger, trans. Margaret MacVeagh (New York: Dial Press, 1926), 118.

39. *Cincinnati Commercial*, October 21, 1867.

40. W. Ralph Thayer to Washburne, October 10, 1867; Curtin to Washburne, October 17, 1867; John Cochrane to Washburne, November 9, 1867; John Meredith Read to Washburne, November 7, 1867; E. H. Rollins to Washburne, October 11, 1867, Washburne Mss.; William Pitt Fessenden to James W. Grimes, October 20, 1867, Fessenden Mss., Bowdoin College Library; E. D. Morgan to C. E. Bishop, November 17, 1867, Morgan Mss., New York State Library, Albany; Henry J. Raymond to Hugh McCulloch, October 11, 1867, McCulloch Mss., LC; *New York Times*, October 17, 1867.

41. *New York Times*, November 8, 1867.

3. A New Look at the Impeachment of Andrew Johnson

1. Eleanor Bushnell, *Crimes, Follies, and Misfortunes: The Federal Impeachment Trials* (Urbana: University of Illinois Press, 1992).

2. Michael Les Benedict, *The Impeachment and Trial of Andrew Johnson* (New York: Norton, 1973), 180.

3. James C. Durham, "Impeachment: Historical Development and Recent Prospects," *Wichita State University Bulletin* 52 (May 1976): 8. Durham was characterizing both the Johnson impeachment and the earlier Jeffersonian Republican impeachment of Supreme Court Justice Samuel Chase.

4. Charles L. Black Jr., *Impeachment: A Handbook* (New Haven, Conn.: Yale University Press, 1974), 51–52.

5. Irving Brant, *Impeachment: Trials and Errors* (New York: Knopf, 1972), 4; Raoul Berger, *Impeachment: The Constitutional Problems* (Cambridge, Mass.: Harvard University Press, 1973), 295. For similar assessments, see Claude Bowers, *The Tragic Era: The Revolution After Lincoln* (Boston: Houghton, Mifflin, 1929); Lloyd Paul Stryker, *Andrew Johnson: Profile in Courage* (New York: Macmillan, 1929); John Fort Milton, *The Age of Hate: Andrew Johnson and the Radicals* (New York: Coward, McCann, 1930); Milton Lomask, *Andrew Johnson: President on Trial* (New York: Farrar, Straus, 1960).

6. David Miller DeWitt, *Impeachment and Trial of Andrew Johnson, Seventeenth President of the United States: A History* (New York: Macmillan, 1903).

7. Eric L. McKitrick, *Andrew Johnson and Reconstruction* (Chicago: University of Chicago Press, 1960), 506. See David Donald, "Why They Impeached Andrew Johnson," *American Heritage* 8 (December 1956): 21–25, 102–3; Hans L. Trefousse, *The Radical Republicans: Lincoln's Vanguard for Racial Justice* (New York: Knopf, 1969); Berger, *Impeachment*.

8. John F. Kennedy, *Profiles in Courage* (New York: Harper, 1956), 126–51.

9. Raoul Berger, *Impeachment*, 295, 252.

10. Black, *Impeachment*, 29, 33–36, 39–40.

11. John R. Labovitz, *Presidential Impeachment* (New Haven, Conn.: Yale University Press, 1978), 126.

12. See, for example, Paul Fenton, "The Scope of Impeachment Power," *Northwestern University Law Review* 65 (November–December 1970): 719–58; Ronald Rotunda, "An Essay on the Constitutional Parameters of Federal Impeachment," *Kentucky Law*

Journal 76, no. 3 (1987–88): 707–32; Michael J. Gerhardt, *The Federal Impeachment Process: A Constitutional and Historical Analysis*, 2d ed. (Chicago: University of Chicago Press, 2000), 103–11. Michael J. Gerhardt, currently the dean of legal experts on impeachment, refers to "an apparent consensus" among legal scholars on the paradigmatic impeachment for abuse of power—a "serious injury to the constitutional order" connected to the impeached official's formal duties." Gerhardt, "The Lessons of Impeachment History," *George Washington Law Review* 67 (March 1999): 617.

13. Michael Les Benedict, *The Impeachment and Trial of Andrew Johnson*; Hans L. Trefousse, *Impeachment of a President: Andrew Johnson, the Blacks, and Reconstruction* (Knoxville: University of Tennessee Press, 1975); James Sefton, *Andrew Johnson and the Uses of Constitutional Power* (Boston: Little, Brown and Co., 1980), 164–69; Brooks D. Simpson, *The Reconstruction Presidents* (Lawrence: University Press of Kansas, 1998), 100–130. Eric Foner offers a balanced view of the Johnson impeachment in his standard synthesis *Reconstruction: America's Unfinished Revolution, 1863–1877* (New York: Harper & Row, 1988), 333–37. See also textbooks such as Michael Perman, *Emancipation and Reconstruction, 1862–1879*, 2d ed. (Arlington Heights, Ill.: Harlan Davison, 2003), 68–72; David Herbert Donald et al., *The Civil War and Reconstruction* (New York: Norton, 2001), 566–73; Claudine Ferrell, *Reconstruction* (Westport, Conn.: Praeger, 2003), 40–43; James M. McPherson, *Ordeal by Fire: The Civil War and Reconstruction*, 2d ed. (New York: Knopf, 1982), 521–29, all of which reflect the influence of my work and that of Hans Trefousse, noted above. Legal scholars too have since displayed a new respect for the Johnson impeachment. See, for example, Labovitz, *Impeachment*, 47–89; Bruce Ackerman, *We the People*, vol. 2: *Transformations* (Cambridge, Mass.: Harvard University Press, 1998); 207–30; Keith Whittington, *Constitutional Construction: Divided Powers and Constitutional Meaning* (Cambridge, Mass.: Harvard University Press, 1999), 113–57.

14. Noel B. Gerson, *The Trial of Andrew Johnson* (Nashville, Tenn.: Thomas Nelson, 1977); Chester G. Hearn, *The Impeachment of Andrew Johnson* (Jefferson, N.C.: McFarland & Co., 2000). Conceding flaws in Johnson's character and political acumen, Gene Smith's account of the impeachment still bears more resemblance to prerevisionist histories. Smith, *High Crimes and Misdemeanors: The Impeachment and Trial of Andrew Johnson* (New York: William Morrow, 1977). Chief Justice William H. Rehnquist's description of the Johnson impeachment, part two of *Grand Inquests: The Historic Impeachments of Justice Samuel Chase and President Andrew Johnson* (New York: William Morrow, 1992), is virtually void of interpretative judgment.

15. Cass I. Sunstein, "Impeaching the President," *University of Pennsylvania Law Review* 147 (December 1998): 295. Sunstein cited Chief Justice William H. Rehnquist's popular history of the Johnson impeachment as his authority, ignoring twenty years of historiography and legal scholarship with which he was almost certainly familiar. Likewise, historian Sean Wilentz told members of the House Judiciary Committee that "historians have looked behind the language at the actual facts of the case as well as at the political context of the time. And in general, they have concluded that the impeachment effort against Johnson was a drastic departure from what the framers intended, one that badly weakened the presidency for decades." Wilentz, "Transcript: Statement of Professor Sean Wilentz, House Judiciary Committee Hearing, December 8, 1998," CNN.com <http://www.cnn.com/ALLPOLITICS/stories/1998/12/08/transcripts/wilentz.html>. Bruce Ackerman blamed the Johnson impeachment for "a massive shift towards a British-style system of parliamentary government." Ackerman, "What Ken Starr Neglected to Tell Us," *New York Times*, September 14, 1998. Ackerman repeated his observation in his testimony before the House Judiciary Committee, December 7, 1998, reprinted in *P.S.: Political Science & Politics* 32 (March 1999): 31. However, in his testimony Ackerman distinguished the Clinton impeachment from the Johnson impeachment, which was a

response to presidential conduct that "amounted to an assault on the very foundation of our democracy." Ibid.

16. Adam Cohen, "An Impeachment Long Ago: Andrew Johnson's Saga," *Time*, December 21, 1998; Robert A. Jordan, "Wanted: An Edmund G. Ross to Save Us from Ourselves," *Boston Globe*, December 13, 1998.

17. Michael Fellman et al., *This Terrible War: The Civil War and Its Aftermath* (New York: Longman, 2003), 310–14.

18. See W. R. Brock, *An American Crisis: Congress and Reconstruction, 1865–1867* (New York: St. Martin's, 1963); LaWanda and John H. Cox, *Politics, Principle, and Prejudice, 1865–1866: Dilemma of Reconstruction America* (New York: Free Press, 1963); McKitrick, *Andrew Johnson and Reconstruction*; Kenneth M. Stampp, *The Era of Reconstruction, 1865–1877* (New York: Knopf, 1965); and Trefousse, *The Radical Republicans*.

19. *New York Tribune*, February 15, 17, 18, 1867. Unpublished testimony before the Select Committee . . . on a Corrupt Bargain with the President, 39 Congress, Record Group 233, National Archives, Washington, D.C.

20. *New York Times*, January 6, 7, 1867. Bingham was the second-ranking House Republican member of the Joint Committee on Reconstruction and author of the civil rights section of the Fourteenth Amendment; Washburne was the senior Republican in the House and also a member of the Reconstruction Committee.

21. *Congressional Globe*, 39 Cong., 2 Sess., 319–21 (January 7, 1867), 443–46 (January 14, 1867), 807–8 (January 28, 1867), 991 (February 4, 1867).

22. *New York Times*, March 7, 1867; *Boston Evening Journal*, March 6 and 7, 1867; Senator James W. Grimes to Mrs. Grimes, March 12, 1867, quoted in William Salter, *The Life of James W. Grimes, Governor of Iowa, 1854–1858; Senator of the United States, 1859–1869* (New York: Appleton, 1876), 323; Senator John Sherman to William T. Sherman, March 7, 1867, quoted in Rachel S. Thorndike, ed., *The Sherman Letters: Correspondence Between General Sherman and Senator Sherman from 1837 to 1891* (New York: Charles Scribner's Sons, 1894), 289–90; Francis Fessenden, *Life and Public Service of William Pitt Fessenden*, 2 vols. (Boston: Houghton Mifflin, 1907), 2:128.

23. After a hard-fought struggle, Congress adjourned over the summer of 1867 with a provision allowing it to reconvene if a quorum was present on the first Wednesday in July. Behind the scenes, Representative Robert C. Schenck, generally allied with the more radical Republicans, and Senator Edmund D. Morgan, a conservative Republican, co-chairmen of the Republican Congressional Campaign Committee, were delegated the responsibility of deciding whether Congress need meet. All had agreed that a July meeting was unlikely. *Congressional Globe*, 40 Cong., 16 Sess., (March 7, 1867), 303–8, 315–20 (March 23, 1867), 321–22, 331, 334 (March 25, 1867), 352–60 (March 26, 1867), 387–91 (March 27, 1867), 401–8, 419–20, 425–27 (March 28, 1967), 438–41, 446–54 (March 29, 1867); Zachariah Chandler, speaking at Ashtabula, Ohio, in McPherson scrapbook: Campaign of 1867, 2:135–36, in the Edward McPherson Mss., Library of Congress (hereafter LC).

24. *Boston Daily Advertiser*, July 4, 1867; *Congressional Globe*, 40 Cong., 1 Sess., 480 (July 3, 1867), 481–99 (July 5, 1867), 565–67 (July 10, 1867), 587–90 (July 11, 1867), 732–35 (July 19, 1867).

25. These differing concepts were developed in three major exchanges during the critical year preceding the great trial. The first was an indirect exchange in the *American Law Register* in March and September, 1867, between Professor Theodore W. Dwight of Columbia College Law School and Representative (formerly Judge) William Lawrence of Ohio, a member of the House Judiciary Committee; the second clash came in the Judiciary Committee's majority and minority reports on the impeachment resolution of November–December 1867; and the third was embodied in the speeches that Represen-

tative George S. Boutwell and Judiciary Committee Chairman Wilson, as ranking signers respectively of the majority and minority reports, delivered on the floor of the House in defense of their positions. Dwight, "Trial by Impeachment," *American Law Register* 15 (March 1867): 257–83; Lawrence, "The Law of Impeachment," ibid. (September 1867): 641–80; *House Report No. 7*, 40 Cong., 1 Sess., 1–59 (Majority), 59–105 (Republican minority), 105–11 (Democratic minority); *Congressional Globe*, 40 Cong., 2 Sess., appendix 54–62 (December 5, 6, 1867; Boutwell), 62–65 (December 6, 1867; Wilson). Charles Mayo Ellis wrote a less influential article, endorsing what would become the radical position, "The Causes for Which a President Can Be Impeached," *Atlantic Monthly* 19 (January 1867): 88–92. The arguments echoed those forwarded in earlier impeachments, precedents upon which participants on both sides drew, described in Brant, *Impeachment*, 46–83, 122–32; Lynn W. Turner, "The Impeachment of John Pickering," *American Historical Review* 54 (April 1949): 485–507; and Richard B. Lillich, "The Chase Impeachment," *American Journal of Legal History* 4 (January 1960): 49–72.

26. See Benedict, *Impeachment and Trial*, 26–36; Berger, *Impeachment*, 53–102, and especially 305–6, where Berger challenges the citations of Theodore Dwight, the leading legal spokesman for the conservative position; David Y. Thomas, "The Law of Impeachment in the United States," *American Political Science Review* 21 (May 1908): 378–95; Alexander Simpson Jr., *A Treatise on Federal Impeachments* (Philadelphia: n.p., 1916), 30–50; C. X. Potts, "Impeachment as a Remedy," *St. Louis Law Review* 12 (1927): 23–25; Andrew C. McLaughlin, *A Constitutional History of the United States* (New York: D. Appleton-Century, 1935), 320–24; Samuel P. Weaver, *Constitutional Law and Its Administration* (Chicago: Callaghan and Co., 1946), 167; Edward S. Corwin, *The Constitution of the United States of America: Analysis and Interpretation* (Washington, D.C.: U.S. Government Printing Office, 1952), 502–4; Brant, *Impeachment*, 23. See also the recent analysis of impeachment cited in note 12.

27. Lawrence, "The Law of Impeachment," 647.

28. Pomeroy, *An Introduction to the Constitution of the United States* (New York: Hurd and Houghton, 1868), 491–92.

29. William Rawle, *A View of the Constitution of the United States of America*, 2d. ed. (Philadelphia: P. H. Nicklin, 1829), 211–12; Alexander Hamilton, The Federalist No. 81, in Hamilton, James Madison, and John Jay, *The Federalist on the New Constitution, Written in the Year 1788* . . . (Washington, D.C.: Jacob Gideon, Jr., 1818), 501–11, especially 505; William Alexander Duer, *Outlines of Constitutional Jurisprudence of the United States* (New York: Collins and Hannay, 1833), 89–91, and Duer, *A Course of Lectures on Constitutional Jurisprudence, Delivered Annually in Columbia College*, 2d ed. (Boston: Little, Brown, 1856), 76–78; Joseph Story, *Commentaries on the Constitution*, 2d ed., 2 vols. (Boston: Little and Brown, 1851), 1:553–58; James Kent, *Commentaries on American Law*, ed. George F. Comstock, 11th ed., 3 vols. (Boston: Little, Brown, 1867), 1: 302, 367n; Timothy Farrar, *The Manual of the Constitution of the United States of America* (Boston: Little, Brown, 1867), 436–37.

30. *United States Statutes at Large*, 13 (1865): 507–9. The peculiar wording of the Freedmen's Bureau act referred to the provision of the Confiscation Act, which limited confiscation of southern property to the lifetime of the rebel owner. This provision had been added at the insistence of President Lincoln in 1862, but in 1865 congressional Republicans evidenced their intentions to proceed with land reform when each house passed a bill that repealed the lifetime limitation. However, since no single bill passed both houses, the repeal did not go into effect.

A large literature indicates how close Republicans came during the war to inaugurating a real land reform in the South. LaWanda Cox, "The Promise of Land to the Freedmen," *Mississippi Valley Historical Review* 55 (December 1958): 413–40; Paul W. Gates, "Federal Land Policy in the South, 1866–1888," *Journal of Southern History* 6 (August

1940): 303–30; John A. Carpenter, *The Sword and the Olive Branch: Oliver Otis Howard* (Pittsburgh, Pa.: University of Pittsburgh Press, 1964), 106–7. For experimental land reforms and the pressure leading to creation of the Freedmen's Bureau with its land-reform potential, see John C. Sproat, "Blueprint for Radical Reconstruction," *Journal of Southern History* 23 (February 1957), 25–44; Willie Lee Rose, *Rehearsal for Reconstruction: The Port Royal Experiment* (New York: Bobbs-Merrill, 1964); George R. Bentley, *A History of the Freedmen's Bureau* (Philadelphia: University of Pennsylvania Press, 1955), 16–49; William S. McFeely, *Yankee Stepfather: General O. O. Howard and the Freedmen* (New Haven, Conn.: Yale University Press, 1968), 45–64.

31. For Johnson's order, see *Message from the President Relative to Pardons and Abandoned Property, House Executive Document No. 99*, 39 Cong., 1 Sess. See also *House Report No. 30*, 40 Cong., 2 Sess. For Johnson's pardon and amnesty policy, see Jonathan T. Dorris, *Pardon and Amnesty Under Lincoln and Johnson: The Restoration of the Confederates to Their Right and Privileges* (Chapel Hill: University of North Carolina Press, 1953), 227–33. For the effects, see Paul Cimbala, "The Freedmen's Bureau, the Freedmen, and Sherman's Grant in Reconstruction Georgia," *Journal of Southern History* 56 (February 1990): 597–632; Oliver Otis Howard, *Autobiography of Oliver Otis Howard*, 2 vols. (New York: Baker and Taylor, 1908), 2:234–36; Carpenter, *The Sword and the Olive Branch*, 106–9; William S. McFeely, *Yankee Stepfather*, 111–17.

32. Hans L. Trefousse, "Andrew Johnson and the Freedmen's Bureau," in *The Freedmen's Bureau and Reconstruction: Reconsiderations*, ed. Paul A. Cimbala and Randall M. Miller (New York: Fordham University Press, 1999), 29–45.

33. Hugh McCulloch, *Men and Measures of Half a Century* (New York: Charles Scribner's Sons, 1888), 227, 386; Gideon Welles, *Diary of Gideon Welles—Secretary of the Navy Under Lincoln and Johnson*, 3 vols., ed. Howard K. Beale (New York: Norton, 1960), 2:318–19 (June 20, 1865), 357–58 (August 11, 1865); *Senate Executive Document No. 3*, 39 Cong., 1 Sess. (December 18, 1865); Testimony on Impeachment, *House Report No. 7*, 40 Cong., 1 Sess., appendix, 604–11, 661–63; Message from the President Relative to the Oath of Office, *House Executive Document No. 81*, 39 Cong., 1 Sess. (April 6, 1866); Letter of the Secretary of the Treasury, *Senate Executive Document No. 38*, 39 Cong., 1 Sess. (April 6, 1866). Of the seven provisional governors Johnson appointed, only two clearly could have taken the test oath had he required it of them.

34. United States Department of Justice, *Opinions of the Attorneys General of the United States* 12 (1867): 182–206.

35. Sickles to the Adjutant General, June 19, 1867, Edwin M. Stanton Mss., LC.

36. Benedict, *A Compromise of Principle*, 253–55.

37. General Ulysses S. Grant to Pope, September 9, 1867. Headquarters of the Army, letters sent, Record Group 108, National Archives, Washington, D.C. For the implications of the removals in their political context, see Benjamin P. Thomas and Harold M. Hyman, *Stanton: The Life and Times of Lincoln's Secretary of War* (New York: Knopf, 1962), 533–60; Martin E. Mantell, *Johnson, Grant, and the Politics of Reconstruction* (New York: Columbia University Press, 1973), 34–36; Brooks D. Simpson, *Let Us Have Peace: Ulysses S. Grant and the Politics of War and Reconstruction* (Chapel Hill: University of North Carolina Press, 1991), 177–91. For the lead up to Sheridan's and Sickles's removals and the implications for Reconstruction in Louisiana, Texas, and North Carolina, see Joseph G. Dawson III, *Army Generals and Reconstruction: Louisiana, 1862–1877* (Baton Rouge: Louisiana State University Press, 1982), 46–59; Roy Morris, *Sheridan: The Life and Wars of General Phil Sheridan* (New York: Crown, 1992), 285–94; William L. Richter, *The Army in Texas During Reconstruction, 1865–1870* (College Station: Texas A&M University Press, 1987), 294–314; James Roy Morrill III, "North Carolina and the Administration of Brevet Major General Sickles," *North Carolina Historical Review* 42 (Summer 1965): 291–305.

38. *U.S. Statutes at Large* 14 (1867): 430. See Benedict, *The Impeachment and Trial of Andrew Johnson*, 46-49, 51-52.

39. Whittington, *Constitutional Construction*, 113-57.

40. *Congressional Globe*, 40 Cong., 1 Sess., 791-92 (November 25, 1867), 2 Sess., 61-62 (December 5, 1867), 65-67 (December 6, 1867), 67-69 (December 7, 1867), appendix, 54-56 (December 5-6, 1867); James A. Garfield to Burke A. Hinsdale, December 5, 1867, quoted in *Garfield-Hinsdale Letters: Correspondence Between James Abram Garfield and Berke Aaron Hinsdale*, ed. Mary L. Hinsdale (Ann Arbor: University of Michigan Press, 1949), 117-18; William Pitt Fessenden to Francis Fessenden, December 1, 1867, William P. Fessenden Mss., Bowdoin College Library, Brunswick, Maine; *National Anti-Slavery Standard*, December 14, 1867.

41. *The Independent*, December 12, 1867.

42. *New York Times* quoting the *National Anti-Slavery Standard*, December 13, 1867; *The Independent*, December 12, 1867. Blaine recalled that the failure of the impeachment resolution "led to no little recrimination inside the ranks of the party" in his *Twenty Years of Congress*, 2 vols. (Norwich, Conn.: Henry Bill, 1884-86), 2:347; likewise, radical George W. Julian in *Political Recollections, 1840-1872* (Chicago: Jansen, McClurg and Co., 1884), 312-13, and his report in the *Centreville Indiana True Republican*, December 19, 1867. (The paper was published by his brother Isaac.)

43. General John Schofield, commander of the district embracing Virginia, remained in place. He had little sympathy for Republican policy, executing it, he later wrote, in such a way as to "save that State from the great evils suffered by sister States." Schofield, *Forty-Six Years in the Army* (New York: Century, 1897), 397. See also James L. McDonough, "John Schofield as Military Dictator of Reconstruction in Virginia," *Civil War History* 15 (September 1969): 237-56; Richard Lowe, *Republicans and Reconstruction in Virginia, 1856-1870* (Charlottesville: University Press of Virginia, 1991), 75-76.

44. Howard to Edgar Ketchum, December 30, 1867, Howard Mss., Bowdoin College Library, Brunswick, Maine.

45. Foster Blodgett to John Sherman, December 30, 1867, Sherman Mss., LC. (This was a circular letter sent to many congressmen.) John C. Underwood to Elihu B. Washburne, December 9, 16, 1868; George Ely to Washburne, February 9, 1868; W. H. Gibbs to Washburne, January 15, 1868, Washburne Mss., LC; B. W. Norris to [the Republican congressional Campaign Committee], January 4, 1868; Ed. I. Costello to T. L. Tullock, January 17, 1868, files of the Select Committee on Reconstruction, 40-41 Cong., R. G. 233, National Archives, Washington, D.C. (file 40A-F29.8 and 40A-F29.23, respectively). *House Miscellaneous Documents* 43, 54, and 57, 40 Cong., 2 Sess.

46. *Boston Commonwealth*, January 4, 1867. See also the *Chicago Tribune*, December 30, 1867; Horace White to Elihu B. Washburne, January 16, 1868, Washburne Mss.

47. The four were Alabama, Virginia, Mississippi, and Texas, although Republicans repealed part of the Reconstruction law to facilitate Alabama's restoration. Moreover, in the second state to vote upon a new constitution, Arkansas, pro-Reconstruction forces won by a margin of only 1,400 out of 55,000 votes. Not until impeachment discouraged white southerners and forced Johnson to cease interference did Republican margins of victory become comfortable in those states that finally complied with the law: Edward McPherson, ed., *The Political History of the United States of America During the Period of Reconstruction*, 2d ed. (Washington, D.C.: Solomons & Chapman, 1875).

48. See Boutwell's prophecy to this effect, *Congressional Globe*, 40 Cong., 2 Sess., 595 (January 17, 1868).

49. Ibid.

50. Justin S. Morrill to Jewett, May 4, 1866, quoted in William B. Parker, *The Life and Public Services of Justin Smith Morrill* (Boston: Houghton Mifflin, 1924), 229-30; George S. Boutwell, *Reminiscences of Sixty Years in Public Affairs*, 2 vols. (New York:

McClure, Phillips and Co., 1902), 2:79, 107–12; Charles Sumner to John Bright, September 3, 1866, quoted in Edward I.. Pierce, *Memoir and Letters of Charles Sumner*, 4 vols. (Boston: Roberts Brothers, 1893), 4:298–99; Samuel F. Miller to David Davis, October 12, 1866. Davis Mss., LC; Testimony on impeachment, *House Report No. 7*, 40 Cong., 1 Sess., appendix, 45–51, 833–34; Adam Badeau, *Grant in Peace: From Appomattox to Mount McGregor—A Personal Memoir* (Hartford, Conn.: S. S. Scranton and Co., 1887), 51; John A. Krout, ed., "Henry J. Raymond on the Republican Caucuses of July, 1866," *American Historical Review* 33 (July 1928): 835–42; *New York Times*, July 16, 1866; *Chicago Tribune*, July 16, 17, 1866; August 28, 1866; September 1, 14, 15, 1866; October 10, 11, 1866; *New York Tribune*, September 12, 13, 18, 20, 1866; *Boston The Right Way*, August 18, 1866; September 22, 1866; *The Independent*, October 25, 1866.

51. John Sherman, speech at Cincinnati, quoted in Edward McPherson scrapbook, Elections of 1867, 2:111. McPherson Mss., L.C.; Carl Schurz to Mrs. Margarethe Meyer Schurz, August 31, November 9, 1867, quoted in *Intimate Letters of Carl Schurz, 1841–1869*, ed. Joseph Schafer (Madison: Wisconsin State Historical Society, 1928), 392–93, 412–16; John Binny to William Pitt Fessenden, September 10, 1867, Fessenden Mss., LC; *Boston Daily Advertiser*, August, 29, 1867; September 2, 1867; *New York Times*, September 17, 1867; October 1, 1867; *Chicago Tribune*, September 27, 1867; October 1, 3, 11, 1867; *Boston Evening Traveller*, October 5, 1867; *National Anti-Slavery Standard*, October 27, 1866; "The Conspiracy at Washington," *Atlantic Monthly* 20 (November 1867): 633–38. William A. Russ Jr. indicates that these rumors were produced by Republicans for political effect, although he himself points out that the "statements of rebel and Copperhead papers which called upon the President to use force are legion." Russ, "Was There Danger of a Second Civil War During Reconstruction?" *American Historical Review* 25 (June 1938): 39–58 (quoted at 43).

52. Schurz, *Reminiscences of Carl Schurz*, 3 vols. (New York: McClure, 1908), 3:252. It is clear by Schurz's bemused tone that by the time he wrote of these fears he no longer remembered how real they then appeared.

53. W. T. Sherman to Ellen Ewing Sherman, January 13, 1868, W. T. Sherman Mss., Notre Dame Archives, South Bend, Ind. The letter is excerpted in *Home Letters of General Sherman*, ed. Mark A. DeWolfe Howe (New York: Charles Scribner's Sons, 1909), 364–65.

54. Notes of Col. William G. Moore, February 17, 1868, in the Andrew Johnson Mss., LC.

55. W. T. Sherman to Johnson, January 31, February 14, 1868, in *The Sherman Letters: Correspondence Between General and Senator Sherman from 1837 to 1891*, ed. Rachel Sherman Thorndike (New York: Charles Scribner's Sons, 1894), 300–304; Sherman to Ellen Ewing Sherman, January 30, 1868, W. T. Sherman Mss., Notre Dame Archives (excerpts quoted in *Home Letters of General Sherman*, 369–70); Sherman to Thomas Ewing Sr., February 13, 1868, ibid., 370–74; Johnson to Grant, February 6, 1868; Johnson to Sherman, February 19, 1868, Headquarters of the Army, Letters Received, Record Group 108, N.A.; W. T. Sherman to John Sherman (letter), February 14, 1868; W. T. Sherman to Grant, February 14, 1868; W. T. Sherman to John Sherman (telegram), February 14, 1868, in *The Sherman Letters*, 305–6.

56. *Congressional Globe*, 40 Cong., 2 Sess., 1340 (February 22, 1868).

57. During the trial, Johnson's counsel argued that Stanton was not protected under the general provisions of the Tenure of Office Act. The House and Senate had originally disagreed over whether the tenure of department heads should be protected under the bill—the House insisting upon protection, the Senate insisting that the president's power to replace Cabinet members should remain untrammeled. The conference committee on the bill decided to obfuscate rather than compromise the issue, providing that the terms of department heads would run one month beyond the term of the president

who appointed them, during which time they could be removed only with the consent of the Senate. The House conferees had confidently announced that this language was "in fact an acceptance by the Senate of the position of the House." Ibid., 39 Cong., 2 Sess., 1340 (February 19, 1867). Representatives did not know that the Senate conferees had told their colleagues the opposite. Ibid., 1514–18 (February 18, 1867). Moreover, the president had appeared to acknowledge that Stanton was covered when he suspended Stanton in August 1867, naming Grant interim secretary of war, as the act required. In December, Johnson had sent a message to the Senate, once more as the law required, offering justifications for Stanton's removal. When the Senate rejected Johnson's presentation, Stanton retook possession of the War Office, again in conformity with the law. All this seemed to have settled the question of whether Stanton was covered by the act.

58. *Congressional Globe*, 40 Cong., 2 Sess., 1386 (February 24, 1868). See also the remarks of Representatives Rufus P. Spalding, ibid., 1340 (February 22, 1868); Ebon C. Ingersoll, ibid., 1358 (February 32); Austin Blair, ibid., 1367–68 (February 22); James K. Moorhead, ibid., appendix, 137 (February 24); Frederick E. Woodbridge, ibid., 1387–88, and Luke P. Poland, ibid., 1394 (February 24).

59. Ibid, 1368 (February 22, 1868).

4. The Party, Going Strong: Congress and Elections in the Mid-Nineteenth Century

1. Warren E. Miller and J. Merrill Shanks, *The New American Voter* (Cambridge, Mass.: Harvard University Press, 1996).

2. William H. Flanigan and Nancy H. Zingale, *Political Behavior of the American Electorate*, 10th ed. (Washington, D.C.: CQ Press, 2002), 68 (Table 3–1).

3. Ibid., 121–26.

4. Paul S. Herrnson, *Congressional Elections: Campaigning at Home and in Washington*, 4th ed. (Washington, D.C.: CQ Press, 2004), 6–8.

5. John F. Bibby, *Politics, Parties, and Elections*, 5th ed. (Belmont, Calif.: Wadsworth, 2003), 38–40.

6. Larry J. Sabato and Bruce Larson, *The Party's Just Begun: Shaping Political Parties for America's Future*, 2d ed. (New York: Longman, 2002), 112. See Harold D. Clarke and Marianne C. Stewart, "The Decline of Parties in the Minds of Citizens," *Annual Review of Political Science* 1 (1998): 357–78.

7. Matthew Crenson and Benjamin Ginsburg, "Party Politics and Personal Democracy," in *American Political Parties: Decline or Resurgence?* ed. Jeffrey E. Cohen, Richard Fleisher, and Paul Kantor (Washington, D.C.: CQ Press, 2001), 78–99.

8. Indeed, something profound may have happened in the later 1960s and early 1970s—a fundamental restructuring and ideological polarization of the party system that led to divided government mistaken as dealignment. See Arthur Paulson, *Party Realignment and Party Revival: Understanding American Electoral Politics at the Turn of the Twenty-First Century* (Westport, Conn.: Praeger, 2000). Paulson posits that the realignment of existing parties led to the decay that most observers recorded, preparing the way for the revitalization of parties that we witness today. See also Jeffrey M. Stonecash, Mark D. Brewer, and Mack D. Mariani, *Diverging Parties: Social Change, Realignment, and Party Polarization* (Boulder, Colo.: Westview Press, 2003).

9. David S. Broder, *The Party's Over: The Failure of Politics in America* (New York: Harper & Row, 1972). For scholarly statements, see also Byron E. Shafer, "Anti Party Politics," *The Public Interest* 63 (1981): 95–111; Ruth K. Scott and Ronald J. Hrebener, *Parties in Crisis* (New York: John Wiley, 1979); Paul A. Beck, "The Dealignment Era in America," in *Electoral Change in Advanced Industrial Democracies*, ed. Russell J. Dalton et al. (Princeton, N.J.: Princeton University Press, 1984), 240–66; Joel H. Silbey, "The Rise and Fall of American Political Parties, 1790–1993," in *The Parties Respond: Changes in American Parties and Campaigns*, ed. L. Sandy Maisel, 2d ed. (Boulder, Colo: West-

view, 1994), 3–20; Martin R. Wattenberg, *The Decline of the Parties, 1951–1996* (Cambridge, Mass. Harvard University Press, 1998). As late as 2001, William Flanigan and Nancy Zingale still characterized the current political era as one of dealignment in *Political Behavior in the American Electorate*, 73.

10. Marc Heatherington, "Resurgent Mass Partisanship: The Role of Elite Polarization," *American Political Science Review* (November 2001): 619–31.

11. Stonecash, Brewer, and Mariani, *Diverging Parties*; Richard Fleisher and Jon R. Bond, "Evidence of Increasing Polarization Among Ordinary Citizens," in *American Political Parties*, 55–77; Lawrence C. Dodd and Bruce I. Oppenheimer, "Congress and the Emerging Order: Conditional Party Government or Constructive Partisanship?" in *Parties Reconsidered*, 6th ed., ed. Lawrence C. Dodd and Bruce I. Oppenheimer (Washington, D.C.: CQ Press, 1997), 390–413; A. James Reichley, "The Future of the American Two-Party System at the Beginning of a New Century," in *The State of the Parties: The Changing Role of Contemporary American Parties*, 4th ed., ed. John C. Green and Rich Farmer (Lanham, Md.: Rowman & Littlefield, 2003), 19–37. Others recognize a resurgence of partisanship but note crosscurrents and obstacles to a true revival. Jeffrey E. Cohen and Paul Kantor, "Decline and Resurgence in the American Party System," ibid., 243–63.

The political-science literature holds that few Americans have consistent ideologies. Party identification enables them to sort political information and determine their own positions efficiently. This implies that partisanship will be strongest when the parties themselves give clear cues about differences and their importance. See Heatherington, "Resurgent Mass Partisanship." Increasing partisanship in Congress, not only in the form of greater party cohesion but of increasing polarization, is one present source of such cues. See Barbara Sinclair's study of congressional Democrats "Parties in Congress: New Roles and Leadership Trends," in *The Parties Respond*, 2d ed., 299–318; Nicol C. Rae and Colton C. Campbell, "Party Politics and Ideology in the Contemporary Senate," in *The Contentious Senate: Partisanship, Ideology, and the Myth of Cool Judgment*, ed. Colton C. Campbell and Nicol C. Rae (Lanham, Md.: Rowman & Littlefield, 2001), 1–18; Joseph Cooper and Garry Young, "Partisanship, Bipartisanship, and Crosspartisanship in Congress Since the New Deal," in Dodd and Oppenheimer, *Parties Reconsidered*, 246–73; and the essays in Jon R. Bond and Richard Fleisher, *Polarized Politics: Congress and the President in a Partisan Era* (Washington, D.C.: CQ Press, 2000). There has been a parallel development among party activists in general. Walter J. Stone et al., "Party Polarization: The Reagan Revolution and Beyond," in *The Parties Respond*, 2d ed., 69–99.

At the same time and probably in consequence, there has been a reordering of parties generally along ideological lines, making Republicans more consistently conservative and Democrats more consistently liberal. Paulson, *Realignment and Party Revival*, 148–68. And analysts have noted a decline in ticket-splitting among voters, a sign of the growing importance of party identification in voter's decisions. David C. Kimball, "A Decline in Ticket Splitting and the Increasing Salience of Party Labels," in *Models of Voting in Presidential Elections: The 2000 Presidential Election*, ed. Herbert F. Weisberg and Clyde Wilcox (Stanford, Calif.: Stanford University Press, 2004), 161–79.

12. Angus Campbell et al., *Elections and the Political Order* (New York: John Wiley, 1966); Paul F. Lazarsfeld et al., *The People's Choice : How the Voter Makes Up His Mind in a Presidential Campaign*, 3d ed. (New York: Columbia University Press, 1968); David H. McKay, "The United States in Crisis: A Review of the American Political Science Literature," *Government and Opposition* 14 (Summer 1979): 373–85; Norman H. Nie, Sidney Verba, and John R. Petrocik, *The Changing American Voter* (Cambridge, Mass.; Harvard University Press, 1979); Gerald M. Pomper, *Voter's Choice: Varieties of American Electoral Behavior* (New York: Dodd, Mead, 1975), 18–41. On ideology and mass public

opinion: Philip E. Converse, "The Nature of Belief Systems in Mass Publics," in *Ideology and Discontent*, ed. David E. Apter (New York: Free Press, 1964), 206–61; Converse, "Public Opinion and Voting Behavior," in *The Handbook of Political Science*, 9 vols., ed. Fred I. Greenstein and Nelson W. Polsby (Reading, Mass.: Addison Wesley, 1975), 4:75–169; Norman H. Nie, "Mass Belief Systems Revisited: Political Change and Attitude Structure," *Journal of Politics* 36 (August 1974): 540–87; James A. Stimson, "Belief Systems: Constraint, Complexity, and the 1972 Election," *American Journal of Political Science* 19 (August 1975): 393–417. The major challenge to the notion that during the 1960s and 1970s voters had only superficial knowledge of party and candidate positions on issues was Pomper, *Voter's Choice*, esp. 166–85. Nie, Verba, and Petrocik observed growing congruence between voters' position on issues and their voting behavior, replacing reliance on party as a voting cue; *The Changing American Voter*, 156–73.

13. Donald E. Stokes and Warren E. Miller, "Party Government and the Saliency of Congress," *Public Opinion Quarterly* 26 (Winter 1962): 531–46; Barbara C. Hinckley et al., "Information and the Vote: A Comparative Election Study," *American Politics Quarterly* 2 (April 1974): 131–58; Patricia Hurley and Kim Quaile Hill, "The Prospects for Issue-Voting in Contemporary Congressional Elections," *American Politics Quarterly* 8 (October 1980): 425–48. By the 1980s the issue was no longer whether there was a decline in partisanship but whether the decline was the result of apathy or positive antipathy toward the parties. See Martin R. Wattenberg, *The Decline of American Political Parties, 1951–1980* (Cambridge, Mass.: Harvard University Press, 1984); Thomas M. Konda and Lee Sigelman, "Public Evaluations of the American Parties," *Journal of Politics* 49 (August 1987): 814–29.

14. See, for examples, David W. Brady, Joseph Cooper, and Patricia A. Hurley, "The Decline of Party in the U.S. House of Representatives, 1887–1968," *Legislative Studies Quarterly* 4 (August 1979): 381–407; Melissa P. Collie and David W. Brady, "The Decline of Partisan Voting in the House of Representatives," in *Congress Reconsidered*, ed. Lawrence C. Dodd and Bruce I. Oppenheimer, 3d ed. (Washington, D.C.: Congressional Quarterly Press, 1985), 276–87; Samuel C. Patterson and Gregory A. Caldeira, "Party Voting in the United States Congress," *British Journal of Political Science* 17 (January 1988): 111–31.

15. David R. Mayhew, *Congress: The Electoral Connection* (New Haven, Conn.: Yale University Press, 1960). See also Charles O. Jones, "The Role of the Campaign in Party Politics," in *The Electoral Process*, ed. M. Kent Jennings and L. Harmon Ziegler (Englewood Cliffs, N.J.: Prentice-Hall, 1966), 21–41; Paul S. Herrnson, *Congressional Elections: Campaigning at Home and in Washington* (Washington: CQ Press, 1995); J. E. Jackson, *Constituencies and Leaders in Congress: Their Effects on Senate Voting Behavior* (Cambridge, Mass.: Harvard University Press, 1974); John W. Kingdon, *Congressmen's Voting Decisions*, 2d ed. (New York: Harper & Row, 1981), 110–45; David A. Leuthold, *Electioneering in a Democracy: Campaigns for Congress* (New York: John Wiley, 1968); Glenn R. Parker, *Characteristics of Congress: Patterns in Congressional Behavior* (Englewood Cliffs, N.J.: Prentice-Hall, 1989). A number of studies of congresspeople made the same points—for example, Charles L. Clapp, *The Congressman: His Work as He Sees It* (Washington: Brookings Institution, 1963); David E. Price, *The Congressional Experience: The View from the Hill* (Boulder, Colo.: Westview, 1992); Donald G. Tacheron and Morris K. Udall, *The Job of the Congressman: An Introduction to Service in the U.S. House of Representatives* (Indianapolis: Bobbs-Merrill, 1966). Stonecash, Brewer, and Mariani summarize the candidate-centered view of congressional elections in the process of challenging it in *Diverging Parties*, 131–43.

16. Peverill Squire, "Candidates, Money, and Voters: Assessing the State of Congressional Elections Research," *Political Research Quarterly* 48 (December 1995): 891–917; Martin P. Wattenberg, "From a Partisan to a Candidate-Centered Electorate," in *The*

New American Political System, ed. Anthony King (Washington, D.C.: AEI Press, 1990), 139–74.

17. Clapp, *The Congressman*, 150–58, 286–90, 313–20; Mayhew, *Congress*, 99–105; Parker, *Characteristics of Congress*, 184–90; Randall B. Ripley, *Party Leaders in the House of Representatives* (Washington, D.C.: Brookings Institution, 1967), 73–77, 145–48; Leroy N. Rieselbach, *Congressional Politics: The Evolving Legislative System* (Boulder, Colo.: Westview, 1995), 163–92.

18. Wattenberg, *The Decline of American Political Parties*, 125–31.

19. John H. Aldrich, *Why Parties? The Origin and Transformation of Party Politics in America* (Chicago: University of Chicago Press, 1995); John F. Bibby, "State Party Organizations: Strengthened and Adapting to Candidate-Centered Politics and Nationalization," in *The Parties Respond: Changes in American Parties and Campaigns*, ed. L. Sandy Maisel, 4th ed. (Boulder, Colo.: Westview, 2002), 19–46; Bibby, *Politics, Parties, and Elections in America*, 38–40.

20. Joel H. Silbey, *The American Political Nation, 1838–1893* (Stanford, Calif.: Stanford University Press, 1991), 125–40. See also Keith Ian Polakoff, *The Politics of Inertia: The Election of 1876 and the End of Reconstruction* (Baton Rouge: Louisiana State University Press, 1973), 3–12; Mark Wahlgren Summers, *Party Games: Getting, Keeping and Using Power in Gilded Age Politics* (Chapel Hill: University of North Carolina Press, 2004), 19–53.

21. The Rice index of party likeness is found by subtracting the percentage of one party's members voting for a measure from the percentage of the other party's members voting for it, always subtracting the smaller number from the larger. The difference is subtracted from 100 and then multiplied by 100. Thus a roll call on which the parties split 75–25 percent and 25–75 percent respectively would have an index of likeness equal to that on a roll call on which they split 90–10 and 40–60 respectively (that is, 50.00). An index equaling less than 50 marks a rather large disagreement. See Lee F. Anderson et al., *Legislative Roll Call Analysis* (Evanston, Ill.: Northwestern University Press, 1966), 44–45; Michael Les Benedict, *A Compromise of Principle: Congressional Republicans and Reconstruction, 1863–1869* (New York: Norton, 1974), 46–48.

These figures differ somewhat from those offered by Jerome M. Clubb, William H. Flanigan, and Nancy Zingale, *Partisan Realignment: Votes, Parties, and Government in American History* (Beverly Hills, Calif.: Sage, 1980), 231, 236. There are two reasons. First, the authors based their figures on all votes on substantive legislation. While Clubb, Flanigan, and Zingale's method is satisfactory for the purpose they have in mind—a comparison of party division in Congress over time—it is less accurate as a measure of party division in individual Congresses, because it does not account for the large series of identical and similar votes on amendments to legislation, or even filibuster votes, which can run into the dozens. So long as these are randomly distributed among Congresses, it will not skew their comparison of Congresses over time.

However, a second potential problem is more serious. The ICPR data, which is based on the Congressional Directory, generally identifies congressmen by their party affiliation when first elected. In the large House, with its high nineteenth-century turnover, this is not very serious. But in the smaller Senate, with its longer terms, it may affect the findings significantly, as by 1862 several senators elected as Democrats attended the Republican caucus and Whig senators had divided between the parties. If Clubb, Flanigan, and Zingale did not correct for this, it would explain why their Rice indices of "unlikeness" are so much lower than mine and also explain why changes in party division in the House correlated with distance from the year of partisan realignment while changes in the Senate did not).

22. Jerome M. Clubb and Santa A. Traugott, "Partisan Cleavage and Cohesion in the House of Representatives, 1861–1874," *Journal of Interdisciplinary History* 7 (Winter

1977): 382–83. Indices of cohesion and likeness reflected higher levels of partisanship in the Senate after a low point in the 41st and 42d Congresses, which followed the Reconstruction crisis. See William G. Shade et al., "Partisanship in the United States Senate: 1869–1901," *Journal of Interdisciplinary History* 4 (Autumn 1973): 185–205.

23. Carl Schurz, *Speeches, Correspondence, and Political Papers of Carl Schurz*, ed. Frederic Bancroft, 6 vols. (New York: G. P. Putnam's Sons, 1913), 1:423. See also Benedict, *A Compromise of Principle*, 323–34.

24. Senator Daniel D. Pratt, quoted in the *Cincinnati Daily Commercial*, June 9, 1870.

25. Michael Les Benedict, "Factionalism and Representation: Some Insight from the Nineteenth-Century United States," *Social Science History* 9 (Fall 1985): 361–98; Benedict, "The Politics of Reconstruction," in *American Political History: The State of the Discipline*, ed. John F. Marszalek and Wilson D. Miscamble (Notre Dame, Ind.: University of Notre Dame Press, 1997), 54–107, both revised and republished in this volume.

26. Akerman to Foster Blodgett, November 8, 1871, Akerman Letterbooks, Alderman Library, University of Virginia, Charlottesville.

27. The foregoing suggests that there may be two different ways in which increased partisan division may occur in Congress. There may be increased polarization across all issues, which is what is usually presumed to occur in times of strong partisanship; but increased polarization may also be due to increased attention to selected issues—even a single issue—of great party salience. That is certainly true of the Thirty-Ninth through Forty-Fourth Congresses, as tables 4.1 and 4.2 indicate. It is interesting to note that Clubb, Flanigan, and Zingale found an extremely high index of party "unlikeness" in the Fifty-first House, an extreme deviation from the pattern of declining partisan division they found from the 1860s through the 1890s. That strong division is also reflected in their Senate figures, although it does not deviate from so clear a pattern. This was the Congress (1889–91) that considered the Force bill of 1890, the last Republican attempt to protect black voting rights in the South. Likewise, the declining partisan division Clubb, Flanigan, and Zingale found was reversed in the late 1870s, when a great partisan confrontation took place over repeal of laws permitting the national government to protect voting rights in the South; *Partisan Realignment*, 231, 236 (tables 7.5 and 7.6).

28. Republican caucuses framed the first Reconstruction resolutions, the Fourteenth Amendment, and the Reconstruction Act of 1867, the key pieces of Republican Reconstruction legislation. The Senate Republican caucus limited and directed business in the critical first session of the Fortieth Congress; the House caucus determined the process by which members considered impeachment. See Michael Les Benedict, *The Impeachment and Trial of Andrew Johnson* (New York: Norton, 1975), 25–26, 140–42, 185–86, 235–36, 238, 245, 253; Benedict, *A Compromise of Principle*, 23–24, 52, 550. The Republican caucus arranged the process by which Republicans reached a compromise on the bitterly contested currency issue, the Resumption Act of 1875, one of the most important fiscal laws of the nineteenth century and one of the few laws of the 1860s and 1870s equal in importance to those concerning Reconstruction. See Irwin Unger, *The Greenback Era: A Social and Political History of American Finance, 1865–1879* (Princeton, N.J.; Princeton University Press, 1964), 253–56 and 234–53 for background.

29. Benedict, *A Compromise of Principle*, 34–35.

30. Besides tables 4.1 and 4.2 herein, see Glenn M. Linden, "Radicals and Economic Policies: The Senate, 1861–1873," *Journal of Southern History* 32 (May 1966): 189–99; Linden, "Radicals and Economic Policies: The House of Representatives, 1861–1863," *Civil War History* 13 (March 1967): 51–65; Terry L. Seip, *The South Returns to Congress: Men, Economic Measures, and Intersectional Relationships, 1868–1879* (Baton Rouge: Louisiana State University Press, 1983).

31. See Howard K. Beale, *The Critical Year: A Study of Andrew Johnson and Reconstruction* (New York: Frederick Ungar, 1930), an assessment of the congressional elec-

tions of 1866; Benedict, *A Compromise of Principle*, 188–209 and 257–78, for the elections of 1866 and 1867; Charles H. Coleman, *The Election of 1868: The Democratic Effort to Regain Control* (New York: Columbia University Press, 1933) for the election of 1868; Earle Dudley Ross, *The Liberal Republican Movement* (New York: Rumford Press, 1919), 152–77, and William Gillette, "Election of 1872," in *History of American Presidential Elections*, ed. Arthur M. Schlesinger Jr. et al. (Philadelphia: Chelsea House, 1971), 4:1313–75, esp. 1322–27, for the election of 1872. For the election of 1876, see Paul Leland Haworth, *The Hayes-Tilden Disputed Presidential Election of 1876* (Cleveland, Ohio: Burrows Brothers, 1906), 40–44; Roy Morris Jr., *Fraud of the Century: Rutherford B. Hayes, Samuel Tilden, and the Stolen Election of 1876* (New York: Simon and Schuster, 2003), 119–20, 130–31, 141, 145–46; and William Gillette, *Retreat from Reconstruction, 1869–1879* (Baton Rouge: Louisiana State University Press, 1979), 300–311.

32. See, for examples, Ronald P. Formisano, *The Birth of Mass Political Parties: Michigan, 1827–1861* (Princeton, N.J.: Princeton University Press, 1966); Melvyn Hammarberg, *The Indiana Voter: The Historical Dynamics of Party Allegiance During the 1870s* (Chicago: University of Chicago Press, 1977); Michael F. Holt, *The Political Crisis of the 1850s* (New York: John Wiley, 1978); Paul Kleppner, *The Third Electoral System, 1853–1892: Parties, Voters, and Political Culture* (Chapel Hill: University of North Carolina Press, 1979); Richard Franklin Bensel, *The American Ballot Box in the Mid-Nineteenth Century* (New York: Cambridge University Press, 2004).

33. For a general overview of the relationship between nativism and related issues, such as temperance and Sabbatarianism, to the rise of the Republican Party, see William E. Gienapp, *The Origins of the Republican Party, 1852–1856* (New York: Oxford University Press, 1987); Tyler Anbinder, *Nativism and Slavery: The Northern Know-Nothings and the Politics of the 1850s* (New York: Oxford University Press, 1992); and Michael F. Holt, "Making and Mobilizing the Republican Party, 1854–1860," in *The Birth of the Grand Old Party: The Republicans' First Generation*, ed. Robert F. Engs and Randall M. Miller (Philadelphia: University of Pennsylvania Press, 2002), 29–59. All these studies explain how Republicans were able to attract the support of nativists and Protestant moralists with an ideology that stressed support for liberty and republicanism and opposition to "the Slave Power" rather than appeals to nativism and what we would now call "culture-war" issues.

Studies of the issues in specific states reinforce the point. Although temperance reform played a large role in the organization of the anti-Democratic coalition in Wisconsin, for example, by 1856 "the party's gravediggers buried its connection with the issue," after discovering "that the Maine law issue could loose a flood of opposition" in the heavily German state. Frank L. Byrne, "Maine Law Versus Lager Beer: A Dilemma of Wisconsin's Young Republican Party," *Wisconsin Magazine of History* 42 (Winter 1958–59): 119–17. The same was true in Iowa, where Germans also made up a large proportion of the population. Dan Elbert Clark, "The History of Liquor Legislation in Iowa, 1846–1861," *Iowa Journal of History and Politics* 6 (January 1908): 55–87. Although Democrats tried to keep the issue alive—a clear indication of whom they thought it benefited—there was little temperance agitation during the Civil War and Reconstruction years. Asa Earl Martin, "The Temperance Movement in Pennsylvania Prior to the Civil War," *Pennsylvania Magazine of History and Biography* 49 (April 1925): 226–30; Clark, "History of Liquor Legislation in Iowa," 339–62; Robert R. Dykstra, *Bright Radical Star: Black Freedom and White Supremacy on the Hawkeye Frontier* (Ames: Iowa State University Press, 1993), 222–23. John A. Krout, "The Maine Law in New York Politics," *New York History* 17 (July 1936): 271. Even in Maine, home of the "Maine law," Republican regulars worked to keep temperance crusader Neal Dow from committing the party to his cause. Frank L. Byrne, *Prophet of Prohibition: Neal Dow and His Crusade* (Madison: University of Wisconsin Press, 1961), 66–68, 111–15.

Likewise, appeals to nativism, important in the realignment of 1854–56, were quickly relegated to obscurity once the Republicans had established their basic constituency and had begun to look beyond it for the votes needed to gain power. In Ohio, Republicans in the late 1850s began "systematically weeding out" old Know-Nothings from leadership ranks to conciliate Germans. Jed Dannenbaum, "Immigrants and Temperance: Ethnocultural Conflict in Cincinnati, 1845–1860," *Ohio History* 77 (Spring 1978): 138. See also F. I. Herriott, "The Germans of Iowa and the 'Two Year' Amendment of Massachusetts," *Deutsch-Amerikanische Geschichtungsblaetter* 13 (1913): 202–308; Charles Wilson Emery, "The Iowa Germans in the Election of 1860," in *Ethnic Voters and the Election of Lincoln*, ed. Frederick C. Luebke (Lincoln: University of Nebraska Press, 1971), 16–45; James M. Bergquist, "People and Politics in Transition: the Illinois Germans, 1850–1860," ibid., 204–15; Michael F. Holt, *Forging a Majority: The Formation of the Republican Party in Pittsburgh, 1848–1860* (New Haven, Conn.: Yale University Press, 1969), 286–92; Carl F. Brand, "History of the Know-Nothing Party in Indiana," *Indiana Magazine of History* 18 (September 1922): 281–98; Dale Baum, "Know-Nothingism and the Republican Majority in Massachusetts: The Political Realignment of the 1850s," *Journal of American History* 64 (March 1978): 959–86.

34. Colfax to Francis Preston Blair, Sr., July 17, 1856, quoted in Gienapp, *Origins of the Republican Party*, 370. Abbreviations as in original.

35. Edward McPherson, *Political History of the United States of America During the Period of Reconstruction*, 2d ed. (New York: Solomons and Chapman, 1875).

36. For the method for deriving individual behavior from aggregate statistics and the assumptions that must be made to justify its use, see W. P. Shively, "Ecological Inference: The Use of Aggregate Data to Study Individuals," *American Political Science Review* 63 (December 1969): 1183–96; J. Morgan Kousser, "Ecological Correlation and the Analysis of Past Politics," *Journal of Interdisciplinary History* 4 (Fall 1973): 237–92. These figures are estimates, accurate to the degree that voting groups behaved the same way over all counties. Therefore some estimates are less than 0 percent and more than 100 percent. These are given in parentheses in table 4.4.

37. George W. Julian, *Political Recollections, 1840–1872* (Chicago: Jansen, McClung and Co., 1884), 116–17.

38. Henry Watterson, *"Marse Henry": An Autobiography*, 2 vols. (New York: George H. Doran, 1919), 2:22.

39. William D. Kelley, *Speeches, Addresses and Letters on Industrial and Financial Questions* (Philadelphia: Henry C. Baird, 1872; repr. New York: Greenwood, 1969), 399.

40. Garfield to Harmon Austin, June 21, 1868, quoted in Theodore Clarke Smith, *The Life and Letters of James Abram Garfield*, 2 vols. (New Haven, Conn.: Yale University Press, 1925), 1:433.

41. David Turpie, *Sketches of My Own Times* (Indianapolis: Bobbs-Merrill, 1903), 109, 194, 232.

42. Alfred Conkling, *Life and Letters of Roscoe Conkling, Orator, Statesman, Advocate* (New York: C. C. Webster, 1889), 75.

43. Edward Winslow Martin, *The Life and Public Services of Schuyler Colfax* (New York: United States Publishing, 1868), 13.

44. William Dean Howells, *Sketch of the Life and Character of Rutherford B. Hayes* (New York: Hurd and Houghton, 1876), 98–99.

45. See Smith, *Garfield*, 1:547–62; Allan Peskin, *Garfield: A Biography* (Kent, Ohio: Kent State University Press, 1978), 375–83.

46. Sumner to Charles Francis Adams, December 15, 1850, quoted in Edward L. Pierce, *Memoir and Letters of Charles Sumner*, 4 vols. (Boston: Roberts Brothers, 1893), 3:233; ibid., 231–44; David Donald, *Charles Sumner and the Coming of the Civil War* (New York: Knopf, 1961), 189–202.

47. *The Diary of James A. Garfield*, vol. 2: *1872–1874*, ed. Harry James Brown and Frederick D. Williams (East Lansing: Michigan State University Press, 1967), 167 (April 2, 1873).

48. In 1871, for example, Hayes flirted with the idea of permitting dissident Republicans to join with Democrats to elect him to the United States Senate over the nominee of the Republican caucus. *Diary and Letters of Rutherford B. Hayes, Nineteenth President of the United States*, ed. Charles R. Williams, 5 vols. (Columbus: Ohio Archaeological and Historical Society, 1922–26), 3:210–11. Ostensibly, Hayes decided he could not in good conscience encourage Republicans to bolt their regular nomination. In fact, he risked defeat and ostracism from a party with which he was dissatisfied on ethical grounds. See also Hayes's professed indifference to the result of the 1875 gubernatorial and 1876 presidential contests, and contrast it to the obvious evidence of his passionate interest. Ibid., 268–85, 289–422. See also the more detailed presidential diary edited by T. Harry Williams, *Hayes: Diary of a President, 1875–1881* (New York: David McKay, 1964) for similar inconsistencies.

49. Chase to Gerritt Smith, April 2, 1868, quoted in Robert Bruce Warden, *An Account of the Private Life and Public Services of Salmon P. Chase* (Cincinnati: Wilstach, Baldwin and Co., 1874), 683.

50. Some of these are in collections and are thus easily available. See, for example, James G. Blaine, *Political Discussions, Legislative, Diplomatic, and Peculiar, 1856–1886* (Norwich, Conn.: Henry Bill, 1887), 48–54, 61–71, 95–103, 119–24; George S. Boutwell, *Speeches and Papers Relating to the Rebellion and the Overthrow of Slavery* (Boston: Little, Brown, 1867), 347–55; James A. Garfield, *The Works of James Abram Garfield*, ed. Burke Aaron Hinsdale, 2 vols. (Boston: James R. Osgood, 1883), 1:216–42, 390–407, 610–31; George W. Julian, *Speeches on Political Questions* (New York: Hurd and Houghton, 1872), 399–414.

51. Garfield, "Political Issues of 1870," in Garfield, *Works*, 1:610–11.

52. Julian, "The Seymour Democracy and the Public Lands," in *Speeches*, 399–414.

53. Garfield, "Political Issues of 1868," in Garfield, *Works*, 1:399–407.

54. Ibid., 407.

55. See also Blaine, "Presidential Election of 1864—Lincoln against McClellan," in Blaine, *Political Discussions*, 54.

56. John J. Coleman, "Party Images and Candidate-Centered Campaigns in 1996: What's Money Got to Do With It?" in *The State of the Parties: The Changing Role of Contemporary American Parties*, 3d ed., ed. John C. Green and Daniel M. Shea (Lanham, Md.: Rowman & Littlefield, 1999), 337–54.

57. *Toledo Daily Blade*, September 6, 1866.

58. Patrick W. Riddleberger, *1866: The Critical Year Revisited* (Carbondale: Southern Illinois University Press, 199), 217–23.

59. Paul T. David, *Party Strength in the United States, 1872–1970* (Charlottesville: University of Virginia Press, 1972), 16.

60. William H. Flanigan and Nancy H. Zingale, *Political Behavior in Midterm Elections* (Washington, D.C.: CQ Press, 2000), 36 (table 3–1).

61. Nelson W. Polsby, "The Institutionalization of the U.S. House of Representatives," *American Political Science Review* 62 (March 1968): 144–68; H. Douglas Price, "The Congressional Career—Then and Now," in *Congressional Behavior*, ed. Nelson W. Polsby (New York: Random House, 1971), 14–27; Morris P. Fiorina et al., "Historical Change in House Turnover," in *Congress in Change: Evolution and Reform*, ed. Norman J. Ornstein (New York: Praeger, 1975), 24–49; Garrison Nelson, "Change and Continuity in the Recruitment of U.S. House Leaders, 1789–1975," ibid., 155–83.

62. See John M. Dobson, *Politics in the Gilded Age: A New Perspective on Reform* (New York: Praeger, 1972), 25–34; Leonard D. White, *The Jacksonians: A Study in Admin-*

istrative History, 1829–1861 (New York: Macmillan, 1954), 332–43; White, *The Republican Era, 1869–1901: A Study in Administrative History* (New York: Macmillan, 1958), esp. 10–14.

63. Robert Marcus, *Grand Old Party: Political Structure in the Gilded Age, 1880–1896* (New York: Oxford University Press, 1971), 6–10.

64. Anthony Downs, *An Economic Theory of Democracy* (New York: Harper & Row, 1957). Mayhew specifically rejected the Downs formulation in *Congress: The Electoral Connection*.

5. Factionalism and Representation: Some Insight from the Nineteenth-Century United States

1. Joel Silbey, *A Respectable Minority: The Democratic Party in the Civil War Era, 1860–1868* (New York: Norton, 1977); Michael Perman, *The Road to Redemption: Southern Politics, 1869–1879* (Chapel Hill: University of North Carolina Press, 1984).

2. Michael Les Benedict, *A Compromise of Principle: Congressional Republicans and Reconstruction, 1863–1869* (New York: Norton, 1974); Robert D. Marcus, *Grand Old Party: Political Structure in the Gilded Age, 1880–1896* (New York: Oxford University Press, 1971). Other studies of mid-nineteenth-century politics that attend to intraparty factionalism are much too numerous to list here. Many will be cited later. See also the bibliography in Duane Lockard, *Politics of State and Local Government*, 2d ed. (New York: Macmillan, 1969), 513–25.

3. The standard history of the era notices factionalism, and every modern history of Reconstruction stresses its contribution to the collapse of southern Republicanism. Eric Foner, *Reconstruction: America's Unfinished Revolution, 1863–1877* (New York: Harper & Row, 1988), 348–51; Richard H. Abbott, *For Free Press and Equal Rights: Republican Newspapers in the Reconstruction South*, ed. John W. Quist (Athens: University of Georgia Press, 2004); Michael W. Fitzgerald, *The Union League Movement in the Deep South: Politics and Agricultural Change During Reconstruction* (Baton Rouge: Louisiana State University Press, 1989), 72–112. In his afterword to *Southern Black Leaders of the Reconstruction Era*, ed. Howard N. Rabinowitz (Urbana: University of Illinois Press, 1982), August Meier notes that "cleavages and factionalism among the Negroes . . . [come] up in nearly every essay in this volume" (399). See also Fitzgerald, *Urban Emancipation: Popular Politics in Reconstruction Mobile, 1860–1890* (Baton Rouge: Louisiana State University Press, 2002); Sarah Woolfolk Wiggins, *The Scalawag in Alabama Politics, 1865–1881* (University: University of Alabama Press, 1977); Jerrell H. Shofner, *Nor Is It Over Yet: Florida in the Era of Reconstruction, 1863–1877* (Gainesville: University Presses of Florida, 1974); Canter Brown Jr., *Ossian Bingley Hart: Florida's Loyalist Reconstruction Governor* (Baton Rouge: Louisiana State University Press, 1997), 190–222; Carl H. Moneyhon, *Texas After the Civil War: The Struggle of Reconstruction* (College Station: Texas A&M University Press, 2004); Elizabeth Studley Nathans, *Losing the Peace: Georgia Republicans and Reconstruction, 1865–1871* (Baton Rouge: Louisiana State University Press, 1968); Joel Gray Taylor, *Louisiana Reconstructed, 1863–1877* (Baton Rouge: Louisiana State University Press, 1974); William C. Harris, *The Day of the Carpetbagger: Republican Reconstruction in Mississippi* (Baton Rouge: Louisiana State University Press, 1978); Thomas Holt, *Black Over White: Negro Political Leadership in South Carolina During Reconstruction* (Urbana: University of Illinois Press, 1977); Dale Baum, *The Shattering of Texas Unionism: Politics in the Lone Star State During the Civil War Era* (Baton Rouge: Louisiana State University Press, 1998); Richard Lowe, *Republicans and Reconstruction in Virginia, 1856–1870* (Charlottesville: University Press of Virginia, 1991), and works cited herein.

4. The main exceptions are Felice A. Bonadio, *North of Reconstruction: Ohio Politics, 1865–1870* (New York: New York University Press, 1970), and Dale Baum, *The Civil*

War Party System: The Case of Massachusetts, 1848–1876 (Chapel Hill: University of North Carolina Press, 1984), esp. 101–21, 145–82. Two old studies of New York state politics pay close attention to factionalism: Sidney David Brummer, *Political History of New York State During the Period of the Civil War* (New York: Columbia University Press, 1911), and Homer Adolph Stebbins, *A Political History of the State of New York, 1865–1869* (New York: Columbia University Press, 1913).

State political histories have gone out of fashion. The main survey dates to the mid-1970s, and the authors of the essays in that compilation paid surprisingly little attention to the ubiquitous phenomenon. James C. Mohr, *Radical Republicans in the North: State Politics During Reconstruction* (Baltimore: Johns Hopkins University Press, 1976). For overviews of factionalism in northern states in the context of the growth of the dissident liberal Republican movement, see Matthew T. Downey, "The Rebirth of Reform: A Study of Liberal Reform Movements, 1865–1872" (Ph.D. dissertation, Princeton University, 1963) and Jacqueline Balk Tusa, "Power, Priorities, and Political Insurgency: The Liberal Republican Movement, 1869–1872" (Ph.D. dissertation, Pennsylvania State University, 1970).

5. V. O. Key, *Southern Politics in State and Nation* (New York: Knopf, 1949). See, for examples of southern state studies in the Key mode, John H. Fenton, *Politics in the Border States: A Study of Political Organization and Political Change Common to the Border States—Maryland, West Virginia, Kentucky, and Missouri* (New Orleans: Hauser Press, 1957); Leon Epstein, *Politics in Wisconsin* (Madison: University of Wisconsin Press, 1958); Malcolm E. Jewell and Everett W. Cunningham, "Democratic Factionalism," in *Kentucky Politics*, ed. Jewell and Cunningham (Lexington: University of Kentucky Press, 1968), 121–79; Duane Lockard, *New England State Politics* (Princeton, N.J.: Princeton University Press, 1959); David L. Martin, "Alabama: Personalities and Factionalism," in *Interest Group Politics in the Southern States*, ed. Ronald J. Hrebenar and Clive S. Thomas (Tuscaloosa: University of Alabama Press, 1992), 249–67; Allan P. Sindler, *Huey Long's Louisiana: State Politics, 1920–1952* (Baltimore: Johns Hopkins University Press, 1956).

In 1986 David R. Mayhew published a state-by-state analysis of party organization, noting a few states with "persistent factionalism" and attending to the subject in all of them. Mayhew, *Placing Parties in American Politics: Organization, Electoral Settings, and Government Activity in the Twentieth Century* (Princeton, N.J.: Princeton University Press, 1986). Successors tend to discuss more formal organizational structure of parties and their new role as providers of services to candidates. There is virtually no attention to the role of candidates as promoters of continuing factional organizations. Analysis of factions has been replaced by the study of interest groups. Factions are in effect subsumed in "interest groups." See, for example, Virginia Gray and Russell L. Hanson, eds., *Politics in the American States: A Comparative Analysis*, 8th ed. (Washington, D.C.: CQ Press, 2004).

6. Belle Zeller, ed., *American State Legislatures: A Report* (New York: Crowell, 1954), 112–213 (quoted at 192).

7. For attention to factionalism in the national parties, see especially Seymour Martin Lipset, ed., *Emerging Coalitions in American Politics* (San Francisco: Institute for Contemporary Studies, 1978) and Lipset, ed., *Party Coalitions in the 1980s* (San Francisco: Institute for Contemporary Studies, 1981). See also Paul Allen Beck, "The Changing American Party Coalitions," in *The State of the Parties: The Changing Role of Contemporary American Parties*, ed. John C. Green and Daniel M. Shea (Lanham, Md.: Rowman & Littlefield, 1999), 28–49; John F. Bibby, "Party Networks: National-State Integration, Allied Groups and Issue Activists," ibid., 69–85; Nicol C. Rae, *Southern Democrats* (New York: Oxford University Press, 1994); Rae, "Party Factionalism, 1946–1996," in *Partisan Approaches to Postwar American Politics*, ed. Byron Shafer et al. (New York: Chatham House, 1998), 41–74; John C. Green and James L. Guth, "Controlling the Mischief of

Faction: Party Support and Coalition Building Among Party Activists," in *Politics, Professionalism, and Power: Modern Party Organization and the Legacy of Ray C. Bliss*, ed. John C. Green (Lanham, Md.: University Press of America, 1994), 234–64.

8. Malcolm E. Jewell and David M. Olson, *American State Political Parties and Elections* (Homewood, Ill.: Dorsey, 1978), 52.

9. Ibid., rev. ed. (Homewood, Ill.: Dorsey, 1982), 52–67. In *State Politics, Parties, and Policy*, which has succeeded *American State Political Parties and Elections*, Jewell and his new coauthor Sarah McCally Morehouse allude to Key's various insights but no longer categorize parties according to their degree of factionalism. Jewell and Morehouse, *State Politics, Parties, and Policy* (Lanham, Md.: Rowman & Littlefield, 2003), 27–52.

10. John J. McGlennon, "Factionalism Transformation in the Two-Party South: It's Getting Harder to Pick a Fight," in *Southern Political Party Activists: Patterns of Conflict and Change, 1991–2001*, ed. John A. Clark and Charles L. Prysby (Lexington: University Press of Kentucky, 2004), 91–106; Charles L. Prysby and John A. Clark, "Conclusion: Patterns of Change Between and Within Party Organizations," ibid., 199–203.

11. Harold W. Stanley, "Party Activists in the South," in *Southern State Party Organizations and Activists*, ed. Charles D. Hadley and Lewis Bowman (Westport, Conn.: Praeger, 1995), 208.

12. Paul Allen Beck and Paul Lapatto, "The End of Southern Distinctiveness," in *Contemporary Southern Political Attitudes and Behavior: Studies and Essays*, ed. Laurence W. Moreland et al. (New York: Praeger, 1982), 160–82.

13. For example, Nicol C. Rae's *Southern Democrats* (New York: Oxford University Press, 1994) was not about factionalism among Democrats in the South but between southern Democrats and their northern counterparts. Analysts of southern politics speak of "cleavages" that characterize a "traditionalist" political system, taking the terms of their analysis from Daniel Elazar's distinction among "moralistic," "individualistic," and "traditionalistic" political cultures. Daniel J. Elazar, *American Federalism: A View from the States* (New York: Crowell, 1966), 86–94. See, for example, Dale Krane and Stephen D. Shaffer, "Culture and Politics in Mississippi: It's Not Just Black and White," in *Mississippi Government & Politics: Modernizers Versus Traditionalists* (Lincoln: University of Nebraska Press, 1992), 3–23. In Hrebenar and Thomas's *Interest Group Politics in the Southern States*, published in 1992, many essays mention past and continued factionalism as an important context for understanding the subject, but only one, Martin's "Alabama: Personalities and Factionalism" makes a special point of the relationship between factionalism and public policy.

14. Rae, *Southern Democrats*, 6.

15. See, for example, Leon D. Epstein's 1993 "Overview of Research on Party Organizations," in *Machine Politics, Sound Bites, and Nostalgia: On Studying Political Parties*, ed. Michael Margolis and John C. Green (Lanham, Md.: University Press of America, 1993), 1–6, which lamented the lack of attention to extraparty organizations that were replacing "the old machines" (2). That inattention soon ended, and studies of organized pressure groups proliferated, while analysis of individual political ambition and local intraparty factionalism has almost disappeared.

16. Elizabeth M. Brumfiel, "Factional Competition and Political Development in the New World: An Introduction," in *Factional Competition and Political Development in the New World*, ed. Elizabeth M. Brumfiel and John W. Fox (New York: Cambridge University Press, 1994), 4.

17. J. Boissevain, "Factionalism," *International Encyclopedia of the Social and Behavioral Sciences*, ed. Neil S. Smelser and Paul B. Baltis (Amsterdam: Elsevier, 2001), 8:5237. The work referred to as "definitive" is *A House Divided? Anthropological Studies in Fac-*

tionalism, ed. M. Silverman and R.F. Salisbury (St. Johns: Institute of Social and Economic Research, Memorial University of Newfoundland, 1977).

18. Raphael Zariski, "Party Factions and Comparative Politics: Some Preliminary Observations," *Midwest Journal of Political Science* 4 (February 1960): 27–51; Zariski, "Party Factions and Comparative Politics: Some Empirical Findings," in *Faction Politics: Political Parties and Factionalism in Comparative Perspective*, ed. Frank P. Belloni and Dennis C. Beller (Santa Barbara, Calif.: ABC-Clio, 1978), 19–38. See generally the essays in Beller and Belloni, eds., *Faction Politics*; Jeremy Boissevain, *Friends of Friends: Networks, Manipulators and Coalitions* (Oxford, Eng.: Basil Blackwell, 1974); Brumfiel and Fox, eds., *Factional Competition and Political Development in the New World*; Christopher Clapham, ed., *Private Patronage and Public Power: Political Clientelism in the Modern State* (London: Frances Pinter, 1982); S. N. Eisenstadt and L. Roniger, *Patrons, Clients, and Friends: Interpersonal Relations and the Structure of Trust in Society* (Cambridge, England: Cambridge University Press, 1984); Luis Roniger and Ayse Gunes-Ayata, *Democracy, Clientelism, and Civil Society* (Boulder, Colo.: Lynne Rienner, 1994); Steffen W. Schmidt et al., eds., *Friends, Followers, and Factions: A Reader in Political Clientelism* (Berkeley: University of California Press, 1977), 506–10; Silverman and Salisbury, *A House Divided?*

19. Key's central interests are suggested by the titles of some of his other books: *Politics, Parties, and Pressure Groups* (New York: Thomas Y. Crowell, 1942); *The Responsible Electorate: Rationality in Presidential Voting, 1936–1960* (Cambridge, Mass.: Harvard University Press, 1966); *A Primer of Statistics for Political Scientists* (New York: Crowell, 1966).

20. For example, Earl Black and Merle Black, "Successful and Durable Democratic Factions in Southern Politics," in *Contemporary Southern Political Attitudes and Behavior*, 99–120; Bradley C. Cannon, "Factionalism in the South: A Test of a Theory and a Revision of V. O. Key, Jr.," *American Political Science Review* 22 (November 1978): 833–48; M. T. Echols and Austin Ranney, "The Impact of Intraparty Competition Reconsidered: the Case of Florida," *Western Political Quarterly* 24 (December 1976): 142–53; Allan P. Sindler, "Bi-Factional Rivalry as an Alternative to Two-Party Competition in Louisiana," *American Political Science Review* 44 (September 1955): 641–62; Raymond Tatalovich, "Friends and Neighbors Voting in Mississippi, 1943–1973," *Journal of Politics* 37 (August 1976): 807–814; J. R. Van Wingen, "Localism, Factional Fluidity, and Factionalism: Louisiana and Mississippi Gubernatorial Contests," *Social Science History* 8 (Winter 1984): 34–41.

21. Key, *Southern Politics in State and Nation*, 10–16; Key, *American State Politics: An Introduction* (New York: Knopf, 1963), 109–11.

22. Key, *Southern Politics in State and Nation*, 310–11.

23. Ibid., 12.

24. See, for example, Hugh A. Bone, *American Politics and the Party System*, 4th ed. (New York: McGraw-Hill, 1971), 107–9; Fred I. Greenstein, *The American Party System and the American People*, 2nd ed. (Englewood Cliffs, N.J.: Prentice Hall, 1970), 70–77; Jewell and Olson, *American State Political Parties and Elections*, rev. ed., 56–67; and Duane Lockard, *The Politics of State and Local Government*, 2d ed. (New York: Macmillan, 1969), 173–81.

25. M. I. Ostrogorski, *Democracy and the Organization of Political Parties*, 2 vols. (New York: Macmillan, 1922; orig. pub. in English 1902); Ostrogorski, *Democracy and the Party System in the United States: A Study in Extra-Constitutional Government* (New York: Macmillan, 1921); Robert Michels, *Political Parties: A Sociological Study of the Oligarchical Tendencies of Modern Democracy* (New York: Collier, 1959; orig. pub. 1915); Gaetano Mosca, *The Ruling Class* (New York: McGraw-Hill, 1939); Maurice Duverger, *Political Parties: Their Organization and Activity in the Modern State* (New York: John

Wiley and Sons, 1954); Giovanni Sartori, *Parties and Party Systems: A Framework for Analysis*, 2 vols. (New York: Cambridge University Press, 1976).

26. Ibid., 1:97.

27. Key, *Southern Politics in State and Nation*, 406–23; Sartori, *Parties and Party Systems*, 97–104.

28. See the work cited in note 7.

29. For example, Gary W. Cox, *Making Votes Count: Strategic Coordination in the World's Electoral Systems* (New York: Cambridge University Press, 1997).

30. See the works cited in note 18.

31. Christopher Clapham, "Clientelism and the State," in *Private Patronage and Public Power: Political Clientelism in the Modern State*, ed. Christopher Clapham (London: Frances Pinter, 1982), 1–35; Carl H. Lande, "Introduction: The Dyadic Basis of Clientelism," in *Friends, Followers, and Factions*, 506–10; Norman K. Nicholson, "The Factional Model and the Study of Politics," *Comparative Political Studies* 5 (October 1972): 291–314; John Duncan Powell, "Peasant Society and Clientelist Politics," *American Political Science Review* 64 (June 1970): 411–25; Alex Weingrod, "Patrons, Patronage, and Political Parties," *Comparative Studies in Society and History* 10 (July 1968): 377–400.

32. Sartori, *Parties and Party Systems*, 1: 105.

33. Laswell, "Factions," *Encyclopedia of the Social Sciences* (New York: Macmillan, 1930–1935), 5:51.

34. Alan S. Zuckerman, *The Politics of Faction: Christian Democratic Rule in Italy* (New Haven, Conn.: Yale University Press, 1979), 33–37. See also Mosca, *The Ruling Class*, 259; Haruhiro Fukui, "Japan: Factionalism in a Dominant Party System," in *Faction Politics*, 65–69; K.G. Machado, "Continuity and Change in Philippine Factionalism," ibid., 213–15.

35. Zeller, *American State Legislatures*, 190–91.

36. Marie-France Toinet and Ian Glenn, "Clientelism and Corruption in the 'Open' Society: The Case of the United States," in *Private Patronage and Public Power*, 194.

37. Beller and Belloni, "The Study of Factions," in *Faction Politics*, 6. See also F. G. Bailey, "The Definition of Factionalism," in *A House Divided?*, 21–36, which aims "to take account of the shady connotations" (21). "There is . . . in factionalism an element of shame," he writes (24).

38. For examples, Sartori, *Parties and Party Systems*, 1:106; Belloni, "Factionalism, the Party System, and Italian Politics," in *Faction Politics*, 100–102.

39. Luis Roniger, "The Comparative Study of Clientelism and the Changing Nature of Civil Society in the Contemporary World," in *Democracy, Clientelism, and Civil Society*, 1–18.

40. Key, *Southern Politics in State and Nation*, 16n.

41. Black and Black, "Successful Durable Democratic Factions in Southern Politics," 102.

42. For examples, see the works cited in note 20.

43. Austin Ranney, *Curing the Mischiefs of Faction: Party Reform in America* (Berkeley: University of California Press, 1975). For Ranney's discussion of primaries, see pp. 121–34. See also John M. Dobson, *Politics in the Gilded Age: A New Perspective* (New York: Praeger, 1972); Richard Hofstadter, *The Age of Reform: From Bryan to F.D.R.* (New York: Knopf, 1961), 254–69; Morton J. Keller, *Affairs of State: Public Life in Late Nineteenth Century America* (Cambridge, Mass.: Harvard University Press, 1977), 272–73.

44. John F. Bibby, "State Party Organizations: Strengthened and Adapting to Candidate-Centered Politics and Nationalization," in *The Parties Respond*, ed. L. Sandy Maisel, 4th ed. (Boulder, Colo.: Westview, 2002), 19–46; Stephen A. Salmore, *Candidates, Parties, and Campaigns: Electoral Politics in America*, 2d ed. (Washington, D.C.: CQ Press, 1989); Salmore and Barbara G. Salmore, "The Transformation of State Electoral Poli-

tics," in *The State of the States*, 3d ed., ed. Carl E. Van Horne (Washington, D.C.: CQ Press, 1993), 51–76; Martin P. Wattenberg, *The Rise of Candidate-Centered Politics: Presidential Elections of the 1980s* (Cambridge, Mass.: Harvard University Press, 1991).

45. Key, *Southern Politics in State and Nation*, 16n.

46. Nelson W. Polsby, "Coalition and Faction in American Politics," in *Emerging Coalitions in American Politics*, 108.

47. There are no histories of particular factions in nineteenth-century American politics, and most political histories tend to concentrate on policy issues, with little appreciation for factionalism. For a somewhat more extended discussion of New York Republican factionalism, see Benedict, *A Compromise of Principle*, 61–63, and the works cited therein. See also James C. Mohr, *The Radical Republicans and Reform in New York During Reconstruction* (Ithaca: Cornell University Press, 1973) and Harry J. Carman and Reinhard H. Luthin, *Lincoln and the Patronage* (New York: Columbia University Press, 1943).

48. For Bryant and the Republican Party in Georgia, see Ruth Currie-McDaniel, *Carpetbagger of Conscience: A Biography of John Emory Bryant* (Athens: University of Georgia Press, 1987); Olive Hall Shadgett, *The Republican Party in Georgia from Reconstruction through 1900* (Athens: The University of Georgia Press, 1964); and Nathans, *Losing the Peace*.

49. Jonathan M. Bryant, *How Curious a Land: Conflict and Change in Greene County, Georgia, 1850–1885* (Chapel Hill: University of North Carolina Press, 1996), 122–45.

50. For the most concise account, see Carl H. Moneyhon, *The Impact of the Civil War and Reconstruction on Arkansas: Persistence in the Midst of Ruin* (Baton Rouge: Louisiana State University, 1994), 257–61. For fuller accounts, see George H. Thompson, *Arkansas and Reconstruction: The Influence of Geography, Economics, and Personality* (Port Washington, N.Y.: Kennikat Press, 1976), 77–169; Orval T. Driggs Jr., "The Issues of the Powell Clayton Regime, 1868–1871," *Arkansas Historical Quarterly* 8 (Spring 1949): 1–75; John M. Harrell, *The Brooks and Baxter War* (St. Louis: Slawson, 1893); Everett Swinney, "United States v. Powell Clayton: Use of the Federal Enforcement Act in Arkansas," *Arkansas Historical Quarterly* 26 (Summer 1967): 143–54.

51. Patrick W. Riddleberger, *George Washington Julian, Radical Republican: A Study in Nineteenth Century Politics and Reform* (Indianapolis: Indiana Historical Bureau, 1966); Mary Elizabeth Seldon, "George W. Julian: Political Independent," in *Gentlemen from Indiana: National Party Candidates, 1836–1940*, ed. Ralph D. Gray (Indianapolis: Indiana Historical Bureau, 1977), 31–54; William Dudley Foulke, *Life of Oliver P. Morton, Including His Most Important Speeches*, 2 vols. (Indianapolis: Bowen-Merrill, 1899); George W. Julian, *Political Recollections, 1840–1872* (Chicago: Jensen, McClurg and Co., 1884).

52. Leo Hershkowitz, *Tweed's New York: Another Look* (Garden City, N.Y.: Anchor Press, 1977), 47–85; Jerome Mushkat, *Fernando Wood: A Political Biography* (Kent, Ohio: Kent State University Press, 1990), 1–115; Mushkat, *The Reconstruction of the New York Democracy, 1861–1874* (Rutherford, N.J.: Farleigh-Dickinson University Press, 1981), 15–32.

53. Michael Les Benedict, "Vallandigham: Constitutionalist and Copperhead," *Timeline* 3 (February–March 1986): 16–25; Frank L. Klement, *The Limits of Dissent: Clement L. Vallandigham and the Civil War* (Lexington: University of Kentucky Press, 1970).

54. F. G. Bailey, *Stratagems and Spoils: A Social Anthropology of Politics* (New York: Schocken Books, 1969).

55. Leonard White, *The Jacksonians: A Study in Administrative History, 1829–1861* (New York: Macmillan, 1954), 300–46, 394–99; White, *The Republican Era: A Study in Administrative History, 1869–1901* (New York: Macmillan, 1958), 20–67; Carman and

Luthin, *Lincoln and the Patronage.* For a good sense of the clientelistic nature of the federal job market, see Cindy Sondik Aron, *Ladies and Gentlemen of the Civil Service: Middle-Class Workers in Victorian America* (New York: Oxford University Press, 1987), 96–106.

56. Foulke, *Morton*, 1:152–53.
57. *Centreville Indiana True Republican*, November 30, 1865.
58. *U.S. Senate Executive Journal* 15 (1867): 136.
59. The Julian-Morton rivalry can best be followed in their rival newspaper organs from 1865 to 1872, Julian's *Centreville Indiana True Republican* and later his *Richmond Radical*, and Morton's *Indianapolis Journal*.
60. Michael C. Robinson, "Illinois Politics in the Post–Civil War Era: The Liberal Republican Movement, A Test Case" (Ph.D. dissertation, University of Wyoming, 1973), 8–23. Events can be followed best in the Lyman Trumbull papers, LC. For the role of Trumbull and other Republican centrists in trying to maintain harmony with Johnson, see Benedict, *A Compromise of Principle*, 134–87. Trumbull's biographer Ralph J. Roske was not sensitive to Logan's flirtation with Johnson but recognized that Trumbull's allies took advantage of his break with the president over the Civil Rights Act. See Roske, *His Own Counsel: The Life and Times of Lyman Trumbull* (Reno: University of Nevada Press, 1979), 131.
61. For the long-running tensions among Illinois factions at the city and state level, consult Don E. Fehrenbacher, *Chicago Giant: A Biography of "Long John" Wentworth* (Madison, Wis.: American History Research Center, 1957); Joseph Logsdon, *Horace White, Nineteenth Century Liberal* (Westport, Conn.: Greenwood, 1971); Marc Krug, *Lyman Trumbull: Conservative Radical* (New York: A. S. Barnes, 1965).
62. Felice A. Bonadio, *North of Reconstruction: Ohio Politics, 1865–1870* (New York: New York University Press, 1970). Over all, local factional divisions among Ohio Republicans must be followed in local Ohio newspapers and the personal papers of Salmon P. Chase at the Library of Congress and the Cincinnati Historical Society; those of James A. Garfield, John Sherman, James A. Garfield, and Benjamin F. Wade at the Library of Congress; and the Rutherford B. Hayes Collection in the Hayes Memorial Library, Fremont, Ohio. Chase's papers are available on microfilm: *Salmon P. Chase Papers*, ed. John Niven et al. (Frederick, Md.: University Publications of America, 1987). As are Garfield's: *James A. Garfield Papers* (Washington, D.C.: Library of Congress Photoduplication Service, 1970). And Hayes's: *The Rutherford B. Hayes Papers* (Fremont, Ohio: Rutherford B. Hayes Presidential Center, 1982).
63. Bonadio, *North of Reconstruction*, 100–104.
64. Wiggins, *The Scalawag in Alabama Politics*, 57–58.
65. Benedict, *A Compromise of Principle*, 60–63.
66. Ibid., 66–69; Bonadio, *North of Reconstruction*, 141–66.
67. John Niven, *Salmon P. Chase: A Biography* (New York: Oxford University Press, 1995), 427–32; David F. Hughes, "Salmon Portland Chase: Chief Justice" (Ph.D. dissertation, Princeton University, 1963), 138–50; Thomas Graham Belden and Marva Robbins Belden, *So Fell the Angels* (Boston: Little, Brown, 1956), 197–217; Edward Perzel, "Alexander Long, Salmon P. Chase, and the Election of 1868," *Bulletin of the Cincinnati Historical Society* 23 (January 1965): 3–10; Mushkat, *Reconstruction of the New York Democracy*, 133–37.
68. George H. Morgan to William Allen, June 20 and 30, 1875, Allen papers, LC; George L. Miller to Manton Marble, March 20, 1876; S. L. M. Barlow to Marble, May 10, 1876; August Belmont to Marble, June 12 and 19, 1876, Manton Marble papers, ibid. Detailed reports about New York factional opposition to Tilden are in letters to James F. Bayard from March to June 1876, in the Bayard papers, ibid. For opposition to Tilden's renomination, see Bayard to Barlow, November 24, 1878, S. L. M. Barlow papers,

Huntington Library, San Marino, Calif.; August Belmont to Horatio Seymour, April 19, 1879, Miscellaneous Mss., Seymour, New York Historical Society New York; Bigelow, Diary, November 17, 1878, quoted in John Bigelow, *Retrospections of an Active Life* (New York: Baker and Taylor, 1909), 4:397.

69. Krug, *Trumbull*, 157–72; Horace White, *The Life of Lyman Trumbull* (Boston: Houghton Mifflin, 1913), 139–48; Carman and Luthin, *Lincoln and the Patronage*, 20–26.

70. *Charlotte Republican*, quoted in Mary Karl George, *Zachariah Chandler: A Political Biography* (East Lansing: Michigan State University, 1969), 199–200.

71. There is no full explication of the customary rights surrounding patronage. For some of the rules and political consequences, see Rienow and Rienow, *Of Snuff, Sin, and the Senate*, 28–29, 39–108; White, *The Republican Era*, 26–27, 31–32; Joseph P. Harris, *The Advice and Consent of the Senate: A Study of the Confirmation of Appointments by the United States Senate* (Berkeley: University of California Press, 1953), 65–87; and Carl Russell Fish, *The Civil Service and the Patronage* (Cambridge, Mass.: Harvard University Press, 1904), 173–77.

72. Martin Ridge, *Ignatius Donnelly: Portrait of a Politician* (Chicago: University of Chicago Press, 1962), 106–26; Howard F. Gillette, "Corrupt and Contented: Philadelphia's Political Machine, 1865–1887" (Ph.D. dissertation, Yale University, 1970), 92–99; Erwin Stanley Bradley, *Simon Cameron, Lincoln's Secretary of War: A Political Biography* (Philadelphia: University of Pennsylvania Press, 1966), 309–14.

73. Wilmer C. Harris, *Public Life of Zachariah Chandler, 1851–1875* (Lansing, Mich.: 1917), 64.

74. Donald Barr Chidsey, *The Gentleman from New York: A Life of Roscoe Conkling* (New Haven, Conn.: Yale University Press, 1935); David M. Jordan, *Roscoe Conkling of New York: Voice in the Senate* (Ithaca, N.Y.: Cornell University Press, 1971), 150–51, 153–54.

75. Bradley, *Cameron*, 109–14.

76. Benedict, *A Compromise of Principle*, 62–63.

77. Thomas S. Barclay, *The Liberal Republican Movement in Missouri, 1865–1871* (Columbia: University of Missouri Press, 1926); Downey, "The Rebirth of Reform," 267–82; Norma L. Peterson, *Freedom and Franchise: The Political Career of B. Gatz Brown* (Columbia: University of Missouri Press, 1965), 178–204; Hans L. Trefousse, *Carl Schurz: A Biography* (New York: Fordham University Press, 1998), 182–204.

78. Wiggins, *Scalawag in Alabama Politics*, 79–82; Richard N. Current, *Those Terrible Carpetbaggers: A Reinterpretation* (New York: Oxford University Press, 1988), 273–74.

79. Ibid., 189–92; Harris, *The Day of the Carpetbagger*, 406–80; Lillian A. Pereyra, *James Lusk Alcorn: Persistent Whig* (Baton Rouge: Louisiana State University Press, 1966), 131–76.

80. Current, *Those Terrible Carpetbaggers*, 246–55; Taylor, *Louisiana Reconstructed*, 156–313.

81. Bonadio, *North of Reconstruction*, 14.

82. Lowe, *Republicans and Reconstruction in Virginia*, 164–82; Jack P. Maddex, *The Virginia Conservatives, 1867–1869: A Study in Reconstruction Politics* (Chapel Hill: University of North Carolina Press, 1970), 67–85.

83. See, generally, William M. Cash, "Alabama Republicans During Reconstruction" (Ph.D. dissertation, University of Alabama, 1973), 275–374; Fitzgerald, *The Union League Movement*, 72–86; Wiggins, *The Scalawag in Alabama Politics*; Current, *Those Terrible Carpetbaggers*, 153–71, 271–76.

84. For example, Nicholson, "The Factional Model and the Study of Politics"; Weingrod, "Patrons, Patronage, and Political Parties"; Luis Roniger, *Hierarchy and Trust in Modern Mexico and Brazil* (New York: Praeger, 1990), 3. Rene Lemarchand observes, "It is primarily where social change has lagged substantially behind political moderniza-

tion that clientelistic forms of dependency have been most resilient." Lemarchand, "Comparative Political Clientelism: Structure, Process and Optic," in *Political Clientelism, Patronage, and Development*, ed. S. N. Eisenstadt and Rene Lemarchand (Beverly Hills, Calif.: Sage, 1981), 19. Eisenstadt and others stress the connection to societies characterized by "maternal religious" images, "an emphasis on mediators and the various conceptions of honor." Eisenstadt and Roniger, "The Study of Patron-Client Relations and Recent Developments in Sociological Theory," ibid., 284. While some parts of the nineteenth-century United States may have manifested these characteristics, factions appeared in American parties everywhere.

85. Ibid., 277.

86. William Nisbet Chambers, *Political Parties in the New Nation: The American Experience, 1776–1809* (New York: Oxford University Press, 1963).

87. For the already classic discussion, see Gordon S. Wood, *The Radicalism of the American Revolution* (New York: Knopf, 1992).

88. Although Oliver E. Allen does not expressly place Tammany Hall's operations within the framework of factional clientelism in *The Tiger: The Rise and Fall of Tammany Hall* (Reading, Mass.: Addison-Wesley, 1993), 80–117, he describes clearly how it dished out contracts and took kickbacks, doled out jobs in exchange for political support, directed resources to poor immigrant communities, and was courted by bankers, industrialists, and others needing government favors. For a similar description of the Republican machine in 1870s Philadelphia, see Peter McCaffery, *When Bosses Ruled Philadelphia: The Emergence of the Republican Machine, 1867–1933* (University Park: Pennsylvania State University, 1993), 17–46.

89. James C. Scott, "Political Clientelism: A Bibliographical Essay," in *Friends, Followers, and Factions*, 493–94, 502–3. Indeed, when students of clientelism assess its existence in the United States, they turn to urban political machines as the prime, if not only, example. For example, Terry Nicholas Clark, "Clientelism, U.S.A.: The Dynamics of Change," in *Democracy, Clientelism, and Civil Society*, ed. Luis Roniger and Ayse Gunes-Ayata (Boulder: Lynne Rienner, 1994), 121–44.

90. Fitzgerald, *Urban Emancipation*, 168–97.

91. Russell Duncan, *Freedom's Shore: Tunis Campbell and the Georgia Freedmen* (Athens: University of Georgia Press, 1986), 20–28.

92. Holt, *Black Over White*.

93. For Douglass as patron of the capital's black middle class, see William S. McFeely, *Frederick Douglass* (New York: Norton, 1991), 291. According to his leading biographer, Washington "became a minority group boss." Louis R. Harlan, *Booker T. Washington: The Making of a Black Leader, 1856–1901* (New York: Oxford University Press, 1982), 254. Historians refer to the "Tuskegee Machine"—"an intricate, nationwide web of institutions in the black community that were conducted, dominated, or strongly influenced" by Washington. Ibid., 254. See Arnold Cooper, "The Tuskegee Machine in Action: Booker T. Washington's Influence on Utica Institute, 1903–1915," *Journal of Mississippi History* 48 (November 1986): 283–95; Carl S. Matthews, "The Decline of the Tuskegee Machine, 1915–1925: The Abdication of Political Power," *South Atlantic Quarterly* 75 (Autumn 1976): 460–69; August Meier, "Booker T. Washington and the Negro Press: With Special Reference to the Colored American," *Journal of Negro History* 38 (January 1953): 67–90; Kevern Verney, *The Art of the Possible: Booker T. Washington and Black Leadership in the United States, 1881–1925* (New York: Routledge, 2001), 69, 79–80, 95–109, 114–18.

94. Italian immigrant *padrones* served primarily as job brokers and have a bad reputation as exploiters of labor, but they often were local leaders who served as mediators between immigrants and the larger culture. See Luciano J. Lorizzo and Salvatore Modello, *The Italian Americans* (New York: Twayne, 1971), 138–58. As small businessmen

who served as go-betweens, handling money and interactions with government, they might also be called *cicerones*. For the variety of people who exercised Italian immigrant "community leadership" and often developed personal political followings, see Lawrence Frank Pisani, *The Italian in America: A Social Study and History* (New York: Exposition Press, 1957), 127–38.

95. Fitzgerald, "The Mainspring of It All," chapter 5 of *Urban Emancipation*, 168–97; Lawrence N. Powell, "The Politics of Livelihood: Carpetbaggers in the Deep South," in *Region, Race, and Reconstruction: Essays in Honor of C. Vann Woodward*, ed. J. Morgan Kousser and James M. McPherson (New York: Oxford University Press, 1982), 315–48.

96. N. M. Blake, *William Mahone of Virginia: Soldier and Political Insurgent* (Richmond, Va.: Garrett and Massie, 1935), 97–140. The best source of information on Mahone's role in Virginia politics is the Mahone papers in the William R. Perkins Library, Duke University, Durham, North Carolina.

97. Mark Wahlgren Summers, *Railroads, Reconstruction and the Gospel of Prosperity: Aid Under the Radical Republicans, 1865–1877* (Princeton, N.J.: Princeton University Press, 1984), 240–42; Nathans, *Losing the Peace*, 189–90, 208–14; Darrell C. Roberts, *Joseph E. Brown and the Politics of Reconstruction* (University: University of Alabama Press, 1973), 91–94; Joseph Howard Parks, *Joseph E. Brown of Georgia* (Baton Rouge: Louisiana State University Press, 1977), 449–62; Thomas E. Schott, *Alexander H. Stephens: A Biography* (Baton Rouge: Louisiana State University Press, 1988), 485–86.

98. Mohr, *Radical Republicans and Reform in New York During Reconstruction*, 10–12, 111–12, 124, 160–64, 188–89; Edwin Bruce Thompson, *Matthew Hale Carpenter: Webster of the West* (Madison: State Historical Society of Wisconsin, 1954), 202–204, 212–32; Leland L. Sage, *William Boyd Allison: A Study in Practical Politics* (Iowa City: State Historical Society of Iowa, 1956), 71–118; Edward Younger, *John A. Kasson: Politics and Diplomacy from Lincoln to McKinley* (Iowa City: State Historical Society of Iowa, 1955), 194–277; Stanley P. Hirshson, *Grenville M. Dodge: Soldier, Politician, Railroad Pioneer* (Bloomington: Indiana University Press, 1967), 124–204.

99. For Scott's efforts generally, see C. Vann Woodward, *Reunion and Reaction: The Compromise of 1877 and the End of Reconstruction* (Boston, Mass.: Little, Brown, 1966), 68–100. The relationship between Scott's lobbying effort and factional politics can be best seen in private correspondence, such as that of House speaker Samuel J. Randall at the University of Pennsylvania, Philadelphia. For its effect on the House speakership race in 1875, see Margaret Susan Thompson, *The "Spider Web": Congress and Lobbying in the Age of Grant* (Ithaca, N.Y.: Cornell University Press, 1985), 294–97. In Georgia, dissident Democrats Alexander H. Stephens and William H. Felton were allied with Scott's Texas & Pacific interest, while the dominant faction favored the interests of Scott's rival, Collis P. Huntington. Robert William Pitman, "The Public Career of Dr. William H. Felton" (Ph.D. dissertation, University of North Carolina, 1952), 48–50. In Tennessee, dissident Democrat Andrew J. Kellar lambasted party leaders for failing to give the Texas & Pacific a proper support. *Memphis Daily Avalanche*, January 11, 15, 22; March 22; April 13, 24, 25; June 27, 1876. Compare these editorials with that appearing August 3, 1876, in the *Nashville Weekly American*, the organ of the leader of the dominant wing of the state's Democratic Party, Isham G. Harris.

100. *Testimony Before the Select Committee Concerning the Whiskey Frauds*, 1876; H. V. Boynton, "The Whiskey Ring," *North American Review* 123 (October 1876): 280–327; A. G. Harris, "The Whiskey Frauds of Grant's Administration" (M.A. thesis, Ohio State University, 1942); Thompson, *Carpenter*, 234–42.

101. For the resources controlled by customs house officials, see White, *The Republican Era*, 118–29. For a good example of their political importance, see George Frederick Howe, *Chester A. Arthur: A Quarter-Century of Machine Politics* (New York: Frederick Ungar, 1935), 48–60.

102. White, *The Republican Era*, 196–208.
103. Ibid., 208–21.
104. Michael Les Benedict, "Laissez Faire and Liberty: A Re-Evaluation of the Meaning and Origins of Laissez-Faire Constitutionalism," *Law and History Review* 3 (Fall 1985): 293–331; John G. Sproat, *"The Best Men": Liberal Reformers in the Gilded Age* (New York: Oxford University Press, 1968), 142–242. For the ideas of the liberal reformers generally, see part 1 of Nancy Cohen, *The Reconstruction of American Liberalism, 1865–1914* (Chapel Hill: University of North Carolina Press, 2002).
105. George C. Worth to Austin Blair, May 25, 1872, quoted in George, *Chandler*, 193.
106. Edward L. Godkin to Charles Eliot Norton, April 23, 1867, quoted in Rollo Ogden, *Life and Letters of Edward Lawrence Godkin*, 2 vols. (New York: Macmillan, 1907), 1:299–300.
107. Nordhoff to Carl Schurz, December 21, 1870. Schurz papers, LC.
108. John M. Dobson, *Politics in the Gilded Age: A New Perspective* (New York: Praeger, 1972), 186. For insight into the way reformers maneuvered for position in the Republican party, see the letters from Henry Adams to Charles Milnes Gaskell and Henry Cabot Lodge from 1869 to 1872 and 1875–1876, printed in *The Letters of Henry Adams*, vol. 2: *1868–1885*, ed. J. C. Levenson et al. (Cambridge, Mass.: Harvard University Press, 1982).
109. Michels, *Political Parties*, 185–87, 205–14, 377–92; C. W. Cassinelli, "The Law of Oligarchy," *American Political Science Review* 67 (September 1973): 773–84. See C. K. Ansell, "Oligarchy (Iron Law)," *The International Encyclopedia of Social and Behavioral Sciences*, ed. Neil J. Smelser and Paul B. Baltes (New York: Elsevier, 2002), 16:10, 853–55. Related to Michel's ideas are concepts of institutionalization and bureaucratization articulated by Ostrogorski, Max Weber, and Robert K. Merton. See Joseph R. Gusfield, "Social Movements: The Study of Social Movements," *International Encyclopedia of Social Science*, ed. David L. Sills (New York: Free Press, 1968), 14:448–49; Merton, "Moisei I. Ostrogorski," ibid., 11:347–51; E. Friedberg, "Organizations, Sociology of," *International Encyclopedia of the Social and Behavioral Sciences*, 16:10,968–73; and Merton, *Social Theory and Social Structure*, rev. ed. (Glencoe, Ill.: Free Press, 1957), 195–206.
110. *Springfield Weekly Republican*, December 22, 1871.
111. Morton J. Keller, *Affairs of State*, 275; see also Downey, "Rebirth of Reform," 76–127; Ari Hoogenboom, "Civil Service Reform and Public Morality," in *The Gilded Age*, ed. H. Wayne Morgan, rev. ed. (Syracuse, N.Y.: Syracuse University Press, 1970), 77–95.
112. Tusa, "Power, Priorities, and Political Insurgency"; Bonadio, *North of Reconstruction*, 167–91; Robinson, "Illinois Politics in the Civil War Era."
113. George William Curtis, "Machine Politics and the Remedy," in *Orations and Addresses of George William Curtis*, ed. Charles Eliot Norton, 3 vols. (New York: Harper and Brothers, 1894), 2:149.
114. [Henry Adams], "The Session," *North American Review* 108 (April 1869): 617. Reform journals, such as the *Nation*, the *North American Review*, and *Harper's Weekly* repeated this theme endlessly from 1867 through the 1870s. See Michael Les Benedict, "Reform Republicans and the Retreat from Reconstruction," *The Facts of Reconstruction: Essays in Honor of John Hope Franklin*, ed. Alfred A. Moss and Eric Anderson (Baton Rouge: Louisiana State University Press, 1991), 53–78, revised and republished in this volume.
115. For example, Nathan, "An Analysis of Factionalism of Chinese Party Politics," in *Faction Politics*, 397; Roback and James, "Party and Factions in the United States," ibid., 340. American political scientists consistently identify ideological groupings as factions, without considering the connection between individual political ambition and adoption of ideological positions. See the works cited in note 7. I do not wish to suggest here

that this shift away from patron-client relationships is necessarily tied to modernization, although that seems to be the predominant view in the social-science literature, at least until recently (see Brumfiel, "Factional Competition and Political Development in the New World: An Introduction," 3–13). A couple of years' stay in Japan has convinced me that clientelism can persist in modern societies.

116. Ranney, *Curing the Mischiefs of Faction*, 134–42. Present analysts compare amateur "purists" among party activists to professional "pragmatists" See, for example, Marjorie Randon Hershey, *Party Politics in America*, 11th ed. (New York: Pearson, Longman, 2005).

117. *Congressional Globe*, 40 Cong., 3 Sess., 708 (January 29, 1869) (Sen. Samuel C. Pomeroy, R-Kans.); Ibid., 39 Cong., 2 Sess., 287 (January 4, 1867) (Rep. Josiah Grinnell, R-Iowa).

118. *New York Tribune*, April 5, 1867.

119. J. A. Wheelock to Ignatius Donnelly, October 9, 1865, Donnelly papers, Minnesota Historical Society, St. Paul.

120. John Sherman, Speech at Cincinnati, July 15, 1864, quoted in the *New York Times*, July 21, 1864, p. 2; Horace Greeley to Zachariah Chandler, August 25, 1867, Chandler papers, LC.

121. *Congressional Globe*, 39 Cong., 2 Sess., 290 (January 5, 1867) (Rep. Rufus Spalding, R-Ohio).

122. Aaron F. Perry to Jacob D. Cox, 22 December 1865, Cox papers, Oberlin College Archives, Oberlin, Ohio.

123. Silbey, *A Respectable Minority*, 115–39.

124. Perman, *The Road to Redemption*, 23–25.

125. Mohr, *Radical Republicans and Reform in New York*, 115–18; John Niven, "Connecticut: Slow Progress in the Land of Steady Habits," in *Radical Republicans in the North: State Politics during Reconstruction*, ed. James C. Mohr (Baltimore: Johns Hopkins University Press, 1976), 26–29; Richard N. Current, "Wisconsin: Shifting Strategies to Stay on Top," ibid., 150–54.

126. *Boston Commonwealth*, January 27, 1866.

127. Henry J. Raymond to Hugh McCulloch, October 11, 1867, McCulloch papers, LC.

128. See "The Rout of Radicalism: Republicans and the Elections of 1867" in this volume.

129. *Cincinnati Commercial*, October 21, 1867.

130. *New York Times*, December 30, 1867.

131. *Indianapolis Journal*, August 2, 1867.

132. Richard H. Abbott, "Massachusetts: Maintaining Hegemony," in *Radical Republicans in the North*, 18–22.

133. Reginald Charles McGrane, *William Allen: A Study in Western Democracy* (Columbus: Ohio State Archaeological and Historical Society, 1925), 250–57. For Democratic divisions over financial policy in 1875 and 1876, see Irwin Unger, *The Greenback Era: A Social and Political History of American Finance, 1865–1879* (Princeton, N.J.: Princeton University Press, 1964), 289–93, 302–5, 308–11. Gretchen Ritter surveys Democratic disagreements over the financial question in the latter half of the nineteenth century in *Goldbugs and Greenbacks: The Antimonopoly Tradition and the Politics of Finance in America, 1865–1896* (New York: Cambridge University Press, 1997), 41–47.

134. J. E. Cooley to Tilden, October 20, 1875, quoted in John Bigelow, ed., *Letters and Literary Memorials of Samuel J. Tilden*, 2 vols. (New York: Harper & Brothers, 1908), 1:388.

135. *Nation*, August 1, 1867.

136. Henry Adams to John G. Palfrey, February 19, 1869, Palfrey papers, Houghton Library, Harvard University, Cambridge, Mass.

137. Edward Atkinson to David A. Wells, July 17, 1871, David A. Wells papers, LC.

138. *Boston Commonwealth*, June 3, 1876. For more on the factional nature of post–Civil War reform Republicanism, see "Reform Republicans and the Retreat from Reconstruction" in this volume.

139. Actual credit for inventing the phrase goes to liberal Democratic Senator Paul Wellstone of Minnesota.

140. For examples, Silbey, *A Respectable Minority*, and Perman, *The Road to Redemption*.

141. For example, Benedict, *A Compromise of Principle*.

6. The Politics of Reconstruction

1. Joel H. Silbey, *A Respectable Minority: The Democratic Party in the Civil War Era, 1860–1868* (New York: Norton, 1977). See also local studies, such as Jonathan M. Bryant's wonderful *How Curious a Land: Conflict and Change in Greene County, Georgia, 1850–1885* (Chapel Hill: University of North Carolina Press, 1996).

2. William Gillette, *Retreat from Reconstruction, 1869–1879* (Baton Rouge: Louisiana State University Press, 1979); James Ford Rhodes, *The History of the United States from the Compromise of 1850 to the Final Restoration of Home Rule at the South in 1877*, vol. 6: *1866–1872* (New York: Macmillan, 1906), and vol. 7: *1872–1877* (New York: Macmillan, 1906). The revisionist studies of the 1960s barely attended to the subject. See for example, John Hope Franklin, *Reconstruction: After the Civil War* (Chicago: University of Chicago Press, 1961); Rembert W. Patrick, *The Reconstruction of the Nation* (New York: Oxford University Press, 1967); Kenneth M. Stampp, *The Era of Reconstruction, 1865–1877* (New York: Knopf, 1965).

3. David W. Blight, *Race and Reunion: The Civil War in American Memory* (Cambridge, Mass.: Harvard University Press, 2001); Nancy Cohen, *The Reconstruction of American Liberalism, 1865–1914* (Chapel Hill: University of North Carolina Press, 2002); Heather Cox Richardson, *The Death of Reconstruction: Race, Labor, and Politics in the Post–Civil War North, 1865–1901* (Cambridge, Mass.: Harvard University Press, 2001).

4. Ronald P. Formisano, *The Birth of Mass Politics: Michigan as a Case Study* (Princeton, N.J.: Princeton University Press, 1971); Michael F. Holt, *Forging a Majority: The Formation of the Republican Party in Pittsburgh, 1848–1860* (New Haven, Conn.: Yale University Press, 1969); Holt, *The Political Crisis of the 1850s* (New York: Wiley, 1978).

5. Paul Kleppner, *The Third Electoral System, 1853–1892: Parties, Voters, and Political Cultures* (Chapel Hill: University of North Carolina Press, 1979); Melvyn Hammarberg, *The Indiana Voter: The Historical Dynamics of Party Allegiance during the 1870s* (Chicago: University of Chicago Press, 1977).

6. Kleppner, *The Third Electoral System*, 8.

7. It should be noted that some practitioners of the new political history challenged the interpretation that issues related to ethnicity explained Civil War–era voting behavior. See, for example, Dale Baum, *The Civil War Party System: The Case of Massachusetts, 1858–1876* (Chapel Hill: University of North Carolina Press, 1984), 24–54; Stephen C. Hansen, *The Making of the Third Party System: Voters and Parties in Illinois, 1850–1876* (Ann Arbor, Mich.: UMI Research Press, 1980), 59–102; Stephen E. Maizlish, *The Triumph of Sectionalism: The Transformation of Ohio Politics, 1844–1856* (Kent, Ohio: Kent State University Press, 1983).

8. For works stressing the racist elements of the antislavery movement and Republicanism, see Robert F. Durden, "Ambiguities in the Anti-Slavery Crusade of the Republican Party," in *The Antislavery Vanguard: New Essays on the Abolitionists*, ed. Martin

Duberman (Princeton, N.J.: Princeton University Press, 1965), 362–94; Eric Foner, "Politics and Prejudice: The Free Soil Party and the Negro, 1849–1852," *Journal of Negro History* 50 (October 1965): 239–56; Eugene Berwanger, *The Frontier Against Slavery: Western Anti-Negro Prejudice and the Slavery Extension Controversy* (Urbana: University of Illinois Press, 1967); and Larry Gara, "Slavery and the Slave Power: A Crucial Distinction," *Civil War History* 15 (March 1969): 5–18.

9. C. Vann Woodward, "Seeds of Failure in Radical Race Policy," in Woodward, *American Counterpoint: Slavery and Racism in the North-South Dialogue* (Boston: Little, Brown, 1971), 163–83.

10. William Gillette, *The Right to Vote: Politics and the Passage of the Fifteenth Amendment* (Baltimore: Johns Hopkins University Press, 1965); Gillette, *Retreat from Reconstruction*, 190–96, 197–279.

11. See, for example, Daniel Feller et al., *The Terrible War: The Civil War and Its Aftermath* (New York: Longman, 2003), 354–57.

12. Margaret S. Thompson, *The "Spider Web": Congress and Lobbying in the Age of Grant* (Ithaca, N.Y.: Cornell University Press, 1985).

13. C. Vann Woodward, *Reunion and Reaction: The Compromise of 1877 and the End of Reconstruction* (rev. ed., New York: Oxford University Press, 1991); Michael Les Benedict, "Southern Democrats in the Crisis of 1876–1877: A Reconsideration of *Reunion and Reaction*," *Journal of Southern History* 46 (November 1980): 508–9, revised and republished in this volume.

14. Eric Foner, *Reconstruction, 1863–1877: America's Unfinished Revolution* (New York: Harper & Row, 1988), 486–87; Keith Ian Polakoff, *The Politics of Inertia: The Election of 1876 and the End of Reconstruction* (Baton Rouge: Louisiana State University Press, 1973), 127–20, 134–40.

15. Joel Silbey, *The American Political Nation, 1938–1893* (Stanford, Calif.: Stanford University Press, 1991), 194. See also Foner, *Reconstruction*, 486–87.

16. Michael Les Benedict, "The Rout of Radicalism: Republicans and the Elections of 1867," *Civil War History* 18 (December 1872): 334–44, revised and republished in this volume.

17. *New York Tribune*, July 6, 1875; *Nation*, July 15, 1875; Alfred Yapla [?] to William Allen, March 30, 1875, Allen Mss., Library of Congress (hereafter LC); Charles Francis Adams Jr. to Carl Schurz, August 14, 1875, Schurz Mss., LC; Zachariah Chandler to James G. Blaine, August 15, 1875, Blaine Mss., LC; Samuel J. Randall to George W. Morgan, August 17, 1875, Vertical file, Western Reserve Historical Society, Cleveland, Ohio.

18. Gillette, *Retreat from Reconstruction*, 159; Foner, *Reconstruction*, 562–63.

19. Eric Foner, *Nothing But Freedom: Emancipation and Its Legacy* (Baton Rouge: Louisiana State University Press, 1983), 45–47.

20. Albion W. Tourgee, *A Fool's Errand* (New York: Fords, Howard and Hulbert, 1880).

21. James F. Sefton, *The United States Army and Reconstruction, 1865–1877* (Baton Rouge: Louisiana State University Press, 1967), 236. Brooks D. Simpson writes eloquently of the limits of the possible in his assessment of the southern policies of *The Reconstruction Presidents* (Lawrence: University Press of Kansas, 1998), 209–36.

22. Holden's fellow North Carolina Republicans Oliver H. Dockery, John Pool, Tod R. Caldwell, and others were experienced Whig politicians. Edgar Estes Folk, "W. W. Holden and the North Carolina Standard, 1843–1848: A Study in Political Journalism," *North Carolina Historical Review* 19 (January 1942): 22–47; Folk, "W. W. Holden and the Election of 1858," ibid., 21 (October 1944): 294–318; James L. Lancaster, "The Scalawags of North Carolina, 1850–1868" (Ph.D. dissertation, Princeton University, 1974); Horace W. Raper, *William W. Holden: North Carolina's Political Enigma* (Chapel Hill: University of North Carolina Press, 1985); William C. Harris, *William Woods Holden: Firebrand of*

North Carolina Politics (Baton Rouge: Louisiana State University Press, 1987). So were Alabama ex-Congressman Alexander White and Lewis E. Parsons, whom Andrew Johnson had appointed Alabama's provisional governor in 1865. Robert M. Patton, whom Alabamans had elected to replace Parsons, Republican Governor David P. Lewis, and Samuel F. Rice had been active Democrats. Alabama's Republican Senator Willard Warner had been a Republican legislator in Ohio. William M. Cash, "Alabama Republicans During Reconstruction: Personal Characteristics, Motivations, and Political Activity of Party Activists, 1867–1880" (Ph.D. dissertation, University of Alabama, 1973); Sarah Woolfolk Wiggins, *The Scalawag in Alabama Politics, 1865–1881* (Tuscaloosa: University of Alabama Press, 1991); Richard N. Current, *Those Terrible Carpetbaggers: A Reinterpretation* (New York: Oxford University Press, 1988), 34–35, 68–69. James Lusk Alcorn of Mississippi and William G. Brownlow of Tennessee, both of whom would serve as Republican governors and senators, were experienced Whigs; Andrew Jackson Hamilton, who joined the Republicans while serving as provisional governor in Texas, had been an active Democratic ally of unionist Sam Houston. Lillian A. Pereya, *James Lusk Alcorn: Persistent Whig* (Baton Rouge: Louisiana State University Press, 1966); Thomas B. Alexander, "Whiggery and Reconstruction in Tennessee," *Journal of Southern History* 16 (August 1950): 291–305; John L. Waller, *Colossal Hamilton of Texas: A Biography of Andrew Jackson Hamilton, Militant Unionist and Reconstruction Governor* (El Paso: Texas Western Press, 1968). See generally James Alex Baggett, "The Scalawags: Southern Dissenters in the Civil War and Reconstruction" (Baton Rouge: Louisiana State University, 2003).

23. Brown to Bullock, December 3, 1868, Hargrett Collection, University of Georgia.

24. Eric Foner, *Free Soil, Free Labor, Free Men: The Ideology of the Republican Party Before the Civil War* (New York: Alfred A. Knopf, 1970), 11–39; Louis Gerteis, "Slavery and Hard Times: Morality and Utility in American Antislavery Reform," *Civil War History* 29 (December 1983): 316–31; Donald K. Pickens, "The Republican Synthesis and Thaddeus Stevens," *Civil War History* 31 (March 1985): 57–73. See also Gabor S. Boritt, *Lincoln and the Economics of the American Dream* (Memphis, Tenn.: Memphis State University Press, 1978).

25. Frederick F. Low to Cornelius Cole, October 25, 1871, Cornelius Cole Mss., UCLA Library, Los Angeles, Calif.

26. Frederick Law Olmsted, *A Journey in the Seaboard Slave States, in the Years 1853–1854 with Remarks on Their Economy*, 2 vols. (New York: G. P. Putnam's Sons, 1904 [1856]), 1:239.

27. Union Congressional Republican Committee, *The Policy of Congress in Reference to the Restoration of the Union*, printed in the *Boston Evening Journal*, May 29, 1867 (supplement). For the general conviction among its critics that slavery condemned society to economic and cultural backwardness, see Richard N. Current, *Northernizing the South* (Athens: University of Georgia Press, 1983), 33–35, 40–41, 54–57; Robert William Fogel and Stanley L. Engerman, *Time on the Cross: The Economics of American Negro Slavery*, 2 vols. (Boston: Little, Brown, 1974), 1:158–90; Foner, *Free Soil, Free Labor, Free Men*, 40–51; Ronald G. Walters, *The Antislavery Appeal: American Abolitionism After 1830* (Baltimore: Johns Hopkins University Press, 1976), 111–28.

28. "Occasional" (John W. Forney) in the *Philadelphia Press*, February 4, 1870.

29. *New York Tribune* March 11, 1869; *New York Times* August 17, 1869.

30. *Wilmington* (N.C.) *Post*, July 1867, quoted in James A. Padgett (ed.), "Reconstruction Letters from South Carolina," *North Carolina Historical Review* 20 (January 1943): 81. For other examples, see the *Little Rock Republican*, November 3, 1868; April 2, 6, 1869.

31. There is a large literature on intrastate sectionalism in the South, stressing a variety of sources of conflict and an important although smaller literature on conflict over

taxation. See Charles S. Sydnor, *The Development of Southern Sectionalism, 1819–1848* (Baton Rouge: Louisiana State University Press, 1948), 275–93; Ralph A. Wooster, *Politicians, Planters, and Plain Folk: Courthouse and Statehouse in the Upper South, 1850–1860* (Knoxville: University of Tennessee Press, 1975), 2–21; George C. Rable, "Taxes and Slavery in the Ante Bellum South," *Journal of Southern History* 26 (May 1960): 180–214; Lewy Dorman, *Party Politics in Alabama from 1850 to 1860* (Wetumpka: Alabama State Department of Archives and History, 1935), 96–98, 222; Lucien E. Roberts, "Sectional Factors in the Movements for Legislative Reapportionment and Reduction in Georgia, 1777–1860," in *Studies in Georgia History and Government*, ed. James C. Bonner and Lucien E. Roberts (Athens: University of Georgia Press, 1940), 94–122; Peter Wallenstein, "'More Unequally Taxed than any People in the Civilized World': The Origins of Georgia's Ad Valorem Tax System," *Georgia Historical Quarterly* 69 (Winter 1985): 459–87; Michael P. Johnson, *Towards a Patriarchal Republic: The Secession of Georgia* (Baton Rouge: Louisiana State University Press, 1977), 85–90; Shugg, *Origins of Class Struggle in Louisiana*, 121–34; Percy Lee Rainwater, *Mississippi: Storm Center of Secession, 1856–1861* (Baton Rouge: Louisiana State University Press, 1938), 6–12; Edwin Arthur Miles, *Jacksonian Democracy in Mississippi* (Chapel Hill: University of North Carolina, 1960), 18–32; Richard Aubrey McLemore, ed., *A History of Mississippi*, 2 vols. (Hattiesburg: University and College Press of Mississippi, 1973), 1: 249–50, 266–74, 284–85, 295–96, 369–71; James Byrne Ranck, *Albert Gallatin Brown: Radical Southern Nationalist* (New York: Appleton-Century, 1937), 4–10; Jonas Viles, "Sections and Sectionalism in a Border State [Missouri]," *Mississippi Valley Historical Review* 21 (June 1934): 3–22; Thomas E. Jeffrey, "Beyond 'Free Suffrage': North Carolina Parties and the Convention Movement of the 1850s," *North Carolina Historical Review* 62 (October 1985): 387–419; Jeffrey, "Internal Improvements and Political Parties in Antebellum North Carolina, 1836–1860" *North Carolina Historical Review* 55 (1978): 111–56; Jeffrey, "National Interests, Local Issues, and the Transformation of Antebellum North Carolina Politics," *Journal of Southern History* 50 (February 1984): 43–74; Joseph Carlyle Sitterson, "Economic Sectionalism in Ante-Bellum North Carolina," *North Carolina Historical Review* 16 (April 1939): 134–46; Marc W. Kruman, *Parties and Politics in North Carolina, 1836–1865* (Baton Rouge: Louisiana State University Press, 1983), 88–103, 189–96; John L. Inscoe, *Mountain Masters, Slavery and the Sectional Crisis in Western North Carolina* (Knoxville: University of Tennessee Press, 1989); William A. Schaper, "Sectionalism and Representation in South Carolina, A Sociological Study," *Annual Report of the American Historical Association for 1900*, 2 vols. (Washington, D.C.: Government Printing Office, 1901), 1:237–464; Laura A. White, "The National Democrats in South Carolina, 1852–1860," *South Atlantic Quarterly* 28 (October 1929): 374–76; Jonathan M. Atkins, *Parties, Politics, and the Sectional Conflict in Tennessee, 1832–1861* (Knoxville: University of Tennessee Press, 1997), 14–21, 215–61; Stanley John Folmsbee, *Sectionalism and Internal Improvements in Tennessee, 1796–1845* (Philadelphia: n.p., 1939), esp. 54–56, 116–19, 148–53, 162–76, 208–209, 216–35; Mary Emily Robertson Campbell, *The Attitude of Tennesseans Towards the Union, 1847–1861* (New York: Vantage Press, 1961), 34–35, 38–40, 175, 198–212; Eric Russell Lacy, *Vanquished Volunteers: East Tennessee Sectionalism from Statehood to Secession* (Johnson City: East Tennessee State University Press, 1965); Carl H. Moneyhon, *Republicanism in Reconstruction Texas* (Austin: University of Texas Press, 1980), 12–16; Weston J. McConnell, *Social Cleavages in Texas: A Study of the Proposed Division of the State* (New York: Columbia University Press, 1925), 15–39; D. W. Meinig, *Imperial Texas: An Interpretive Essay in Cultural Geography* (Austin: University of Texas Press, 1969), 38–62; Roger A. Griffin, "Intrastate Sectionalism in the Texas Governor's Race of 1853," *Southwestern Historical Quarterly* 76 (Fall, 1972): 142–60; Charles Henry Ambler, *Sectionalism in Virginia from 1776 to 1861* (Chicago: University of Chicago Press, 1910); Alison Freehling, *Drift Toward Dissolution: The Virginia Slavery Debate of 1831–1832* (Baton Rouge: Louisiana State University, 1982), 36–81, 122–69, 235–41; Freehling, "Editorial Revolution, Virginia, and the Coming of Civil War: A Review Essay," *Civil War History* 16 (March 1969): 64–72.

32. David M. Potter, *Lincoln and His Party in the Secession Crisis* (New Haven, Conn.: Yale University Press, 1942), 235–39; Potter, "Why the Republicans Rejected Both Compromise and Secession," in *The Crisis of the Union: 1860–1861*, ed. George Harmon Knoles (Baton Rouge: Louisiana State University Press, 1965), 99–102. The conviction that southern unionists were duped or dragged into war is evident in the histories of secession that appeared during and immediately after the war—for example, Horace Greeley, *The American Conflict: A History of The Great Rebellion in the United States of America, 1860–'64*, 2 vols. (Hartford, Conn.: O .D. Case & Co., 1864), 1: 350–51; Benson J. Lossing, *Pictorial History of the Civil War in the United States of America* (Philadelphia: George W. Childs, 1866), 1:36–40; Henry Wilson, *The Rise and Fall of the Slave Power in America*, 3 vols. (Boston: Houghton Mifflin, 1872–77), 1:127–46. See Richard H. Abbott, *The Republican Party and the South, 1855–1877* (Chapel Hill: University of North Carolina Press, 1986), 20–21, 43–44; William C. Harris, "Lincoln and Wartime Reconstruction in North Carolina, 1861–1863," *North Carolina Historical Review* 63 (April 1986): 149–68.

33. For unionism in the Civil War South in general: Paul D. Escott, *After Secession: Jefferson Davis and the Failure of Confederate Nationalism* (Baton Rouge: Louisiana State University Press, 1978), 94–134, 196–225; William S. Freehling, *The South vs. the South: How Anti-Confederate Southerners Shaped the Course of the Civil War* (New York: Oxford University Press, 2001); John C. Inscoe and Robert C. Kenzer, eds., *Enemies of the Country: New Perspectives on Unionists in the Civil War South* (Athens: University of Georgia Press, 2001); Charles W. Ramsdell, *Behind the Lines in the Southern Confederacy* (New York: Greenwood, 1944); Georgia Lee Tatum, *Disloyalty in the Confederacy* (Chapel Hill: University of North Carolina Press, 1934); Charles H. Wesley, *The Collapse of the Southern Confederacy* (New York: Russell and Russell, 1937), 47–73, 74–104; Wilfred Buck Yearns, *The Confederate Congress* (Athens: University of Georgia Press, 1960), 71–83; Stephen E. Ambrose, "Yeoman Discontent in the Confederacy," *Civil War History* 8 (September 1962): 259–68; Richard E. Beringer, "The Unconscious 'Spirit of Party' in the Confederate Congress," *Civil War History* 18 (December 1972): 315–23. In particular states: Hugh C. Bailey, "Disaffection in the Alabama Hill Country, 1861," *Civil War History* 4 (June 1988): 183–93; Margaret M. Storey, "Civil War Unionists and the Political Culture of Loyalty in Alabama, 1860–1861," *Journal of Southern History* 69 (February 2003): 71–106; M. Shannon Mallard, "'I Had No Comfort to Give the People': Opposition to the Confederacy in Civil War Mississippi," *North & South* 6, no. 4 (2003): 78–86; Michael K. Honey, "The War Within the Confederacy: White Unionists of North Carolina," *Prologue* 18 (Summer 1986): 75–93; Horace Raper, *William W. Holden: North Carolina's Political Enigma* (Chapel Hill: University of North Carolina Press, 1985), 45–58; Martha L. Turner, "The Cause of the Union in East Tennessee," *Tennessee Historical Quarterly* 40 (Winter 1981): 366–80; Henry T. Shanks, "Disloyalty to the Confederacy in Southwestern Virginia, 1861–1865," *North Carolina Historical Review* 21 (April 1944): 118–35.

34. Wendell Phillips, "The State of the Country," in Phillips, *Speeches, Lectures, and Letters* (Boston: Lee & Shepard, 1884), 532–33.

35. Duncan Russell, *Entrepreneur for Equality: Governor Rufus Bullock, Commerce, and Race in Post–Civil War Georgia* (Athens: University of Georgia Press, 1994), 42–44.

36. *Atlanta New Era* March 13, 1868, quoted in Mark W. Summers, *Railroads, Reconstruction, and the Gospel of Prosperity: Aid Under the Radical Republicans, 1865–1877* (Princeton, N.J.: Princeton University Press, 1984), 26; Thomas B. Settle, "Notes of a Speech Delivered in Rockingham County . . . March, 1867," in the Thomas Settle Papers, Southern Historical Collection, University of North Carolina, Chapel Hill; Charles D.

Drake, *Immediate Emancipation in Missouri,* in Drake, *Union and Antislavery Speeches* (Cincinnati: Applegate & Co., 1864), 282–88; Richard G. Lowe, "The Republican Party in Antebellum Virginia," *Virginia Magazine of History and Biography* 81 (July 1973): 266, 269–70; E. Russ Williams, Jr., "John Ray: Forgotten Scalawag," *Louisiana Studies* 13 (Fall 1974): 244, 246; Roger P. Leemhuis, *Robert L. Orr and the Sectional Conflict* (Washington, D.C.: University Press of America, 1979), 107–108; Ross A. Webb, *Benjamin Helms Bristow* (Lexington: University Press of Kentucky, 1969), 72–73, 87–88.

37. Mississippi Republican platform of 1869, in Edward McPherson, ed., *Political History of the United States During the Period of Reconstruction* (Washington, D.C.: Solomons & Chapman, 1875), 481. From 1867 to 1869 equal taxation planks appeared in Republican platforms in Alabama, Arkansas, Mississippi, South Carolina, and Virginia. Ibid., 251, 253, 481, 485; *Appleton's Annual Cyclopedia* (1867), 26, 695, 758. For examples of Republican use of the tax issue in Arkansas, see E. W. Gantt's and Thomas Boles's election speeches published in the *Little Rock Republican,* September 4 and November 2, 1868, respectively, and the *Republican's* editorial of June 15, 1869,

38. *Appleton's Annual Cyclopedia* (1867), 460, 695.

39. Francis L. Cardozo, *Address Before the Grant Council of the Union Leagues . . . July 27, 1870,* published as Edward F. Sweat, ed., "Document—The Union Leagues and the South Carolina Election of 1870," *Journal of Negro History* 41 (April 1976): 209; Joel Williamson, *After Slavery: The Negro in South Carolina During Reconstruction* (Chapel Hill: University of North Carolina Press, 1965), 148–59.

40. Constitution of Alabama (1868), Art. 9, sec. 1; Constitution of Arkansas (1868), Art. 10, sec. 2; Constitution of Florida (1868), Art. 13, sec. 1; Constitution of Louisiana (1868), Title 6, article 118; Constitution of Mississippi (1869), Art. 7, sec. 20; Constitution of North Carolina (1868), Art. 5, sec. 1, 3, Art. 7, sec. 9; Constitution of South Carolina (1868), Art. 2, sec. 33; Constitution of Virginia (1869), Art. 10, sec. 1, 4.

41. Constitution of Alabama (1868), Art. 14; Constitution of Arkansas (1868), Art. 12, sec. 1, 3; Constitution of Florida (1868), Art. 10; Constitution of Georgia (1868), Art. 7, sec. 5135; Constitution of North Carolina (1868), Art. 10, sec. 1, 3; Constitution of South Carolina, Art. 2, sec. 32; Constitution of Virginia (1869), Art. 11, sec. 1. See Kenneth Edson St. Clair, "Debtor Relief in North Carolina During Reconstruction," *North Carolina Historical Review* 18 (July 1941): 215–35; Robert J. Haws and Michael V. Namorato, "Race, Property, and Economic Consequences of Reconstruction," *Vanderbilt Law Review* 32 (January, 1979): 319–22; Jack B. Scroggs, "Carpetbagger Constitutional Reform in the South Atlantic States, 1867–1868," *Journal of Southern History* 27 (November 1961): 479–80.

42. Harold Woodman, "Post–Civil War Southern Agriculture and the Law," *Agricultural History* 53 (January 1979): 318–37; Joel Williamson, *After Slavery: The Negro in South Carolina During Reconstruction, 1861–1877* (Chapel Hill: University of North Carolina Press, 1965), 171–72.

43. *Vicksburg Republican* April 28, 1868, quoted in Summers, *Radical Reconstruction and the Gospel of Prosperity,* 15.

44. *Philadelphia Press,* October 9, 1869; George Frisbie Hoar, "Are the Republicans in to Stay?" *North American Review* 149 (November 1889): 621.

45. *Little Rock Republican,* May 25, 1869.

46. Elisha M. Pease to James G. Tracy, May 24, 1869, Pease papers, Austin Public Library. See Duncan Russell's description of Republican Governor Rufus B. Bullock's desperate effort to enact an economic development program in Georgia. Duncan, *Entrepreneur for Equality,* 98–121.

47. George M. Welker to William W. Holden, May 11, 1869, Holden Mss., Duke University.

48. Joseph E. Brown, *Speech of Ex-Gov. Joseph E. Brown, of Georgia, Delivered in Milledgeville, Ga., June 6th, 1867, on the Present Situation and Future Prospects of the Country* (N.p., [1867]), 1.

49. *Banker's Magazine* 24 (January 1870): 547. For general information about banking, currency, credit, and finances in the postwar period, see William J. Schultz and M. R. Caine, *Financial Development of the United States* (New York: Prentice-Hall, Inc., 1937), 312–62; Milton Friedman and Anna Jacobson Schwartz, *A Monetary History of the United States, 1867–1960* (Princeton, N.J.: Princeton University Press, 1963), 15–88; Edward C. Kirkland, *Industry Comes of Age: Business, Labor, and Public Policy, 1860–1897* (New York: Holt, Rinehart and Winston, 1961), 13–42; John A. James, *Money and Capital Markets in Postbellum America* (Princeton, N.J.: Princeton University Press, 1978), 22–29; Richard Sylla, "Federal Policy, Banking Market Structure, and Capital Mobilization in the United States, 1863–1913," *Journal of Economic History* 29 (December 1969): 657–86. For the banking and financial situation in the South, see George L. Anderson, "The South and the Problem of Post–Civil War Finance," *Journal of Southern History* 9 (May 1943): 181–85; Roger L. Ransom and Richard Sutch, *One Kind of Freedom: The Economic Consequences of Emancipation* (Cambridge: Cambridge University Press, 1977), 106–25. Notes of credit, with slaves as collateral, were a central form of circulating financial media in the South. Emancipation depreciated their value and eliminated this form of collateralized note in the future. See Richard Holcombe Kilbourne Jr., *Debt, Investment, and Slaves: Credit Relations in East Feliciana Parish, Louisiana, 1825–1885* (Tuscaloosa: University of Alabama Press, 1995). Modern financial experts recognize that deposits in commercial banks augment currency in the nation's money supply. Sixty percent of these deposits were in the national banks and therefore, like currency, concentrated in the northeastern and mid-Atlantic states. Friedman and Schwartz, *Monetary History of the U.S.*, 17.

50. Theodore C. Peters, *A Report Upon Conditions of the South, with Regard to Its Need for a Cotton Crop and Its Financial Wants in Connection Therewith as Well as the Safety of Temporary Loans* (Baltimore: H. A. Robinson, 1867), 8; *Alabama State Journal* (Montgomery), March 11, 1869.

51. Until the mid-1870s, Republicans' opponents in the South often referred to Republicans as "Radicals" and to themselves as "Conservatives," rather than Democrats. The custom reflected the fact that southerners of both Whig and Democratic backgrounds organized the opposition to Republican Reconstruction policy from 1865 to 1868.

52. Ibid., June 24, 1869.

53. For examples, see Henry Wilson's speech at New Orleans in May 1867, *Boston Evening Journal*, May 30, 1867; Horace Greeley's address at Richmond, Va., *New York Tribune*, May 17, 1867; ibid., May 20, 28 1867; *Cincinnati Commercial*, July 5, 1867; Daniel R. Goodloe, *Letter of Daniel R. Goodloe to Hon. Charles Sumner, on the Situation of Affairs in North Carolina* (N.p., [1868]), 14–15; Wiggins, *The Scalawag in Alabama Politics*, 27–34.

54. *Nation*, October 15, 1868.

55. Henry Clay Warmoth, *War, Politics and Reconstruction: Stormy Days in Louisiana* (New York: Macmillan, 1930), 75.

56. There are not many histories of public policy in the South from an African American perspective. For an illuminating local study that indicates how African Americans responded to the varying pressures for conciliation and forceful pursuit of group interests, see Michael W. Fitzgerald, *Urban Emancipation: Popular Politics in Reconstruction Mobile, 1860–1890* (Baton Rouge: Louisiana State University Press, 2002). See also Thomas Holt, *Black Over White: Negro Political Leadership in South Carolina during Reconstruction* (Urbana: University of Illinois Press, 1977), 122–51. Historians tend to

read the reluctance of conservative white Republicans fully to endorse black equality as a product of their racism. No doubt personal racism played a role, but historians ought to consider as well conservative and moderate Republicans' awareness of the depth of racism among the whites whose support they hoped to attract. Read in that light, for example, Jonathan M. Bryant's chronicle of the twisting political course of Robert L. McWhorter, *How Curious a Land: Conflict and Change in Greene County, Georgia, 1850–1885* (Chapel Hill: University of North Carolina Press, 1996), 122–25, 134–37, 142–44, 181, and Christopher Waldrep's account of the course of Charles E. Furlong, Vicksburg's white Republican leader, in "Black Political Leadership: Warren County, Mississippi," in *Local Matters: Race, Crime, and Justice in the Nineteenth-Century South*, ed. Christopher Waldrep and Donald G. Nieman (Athens: University of Georgia Press, 1991), 225–49.

57. For insight into the importance of fairly administered legal institutions to enforce contracts, see Laura F. Edwards, "The Problem of Dependency: African Americans, Labor Relations, and the Law in the Nineteenth-Century South," *Agricultural History* 72 (Spring 1998): 313–40; Donald G. Nieman, *To Set the Law in Motion: The Freedmen's Bureau and the Legal Rights of Blacks, 1865–1868* (Millwood, N.Y.: KTO Press, 1979), 179–89; and Nieman, "African American Communities, Politics, and Justice: Washington County, Texas, 1865–1890," in *Local Matters*, 201–24. See also William A. Blair, "Justice Versus Law and Order: The Battles Over the Reconstruction of Virginia's Minor Judiciary, 1865–1870," *Virginia Magazine of History and Biography* 103 (April 1995): 155–80; Bryant, *How Curious a Land*, 9–11; and Kenneth M. Hamilton, "White Wealth and Black Repression in Harrison County, Texas: 1865–1868," *Journal of Negro History* 84 (Fall 1999): 351–54.

58. Although historians generally have recognized that planters were desperate to maintain their recourse to force to compel the freed people to labor, they have been slow to recognize what is clear from planters' own complaints—that they would be forced to pay what they considered to be impossibly high wages if they competed for black labor. The result of the new ability of African Americans to resist coercion was the establishment of the sharecropping system, which provided important advantages over wage labor until Democrats altered its legal context after regaining power in the 1870s. See generally Harold D. Woodman, *New South, Old South: The Legal Foundations of Credit and Labor Relations in the Postbellum Agricultural South* (Baton Rouge: Louisiana State University Press, 1995); Robert Higgs, *Competition and Coercion: Blacks in the American Economy, 1865–1914* (Cambridge: Cambridge University Press, 1977), 40–53; Roger L. Ransom and Richard Sutch, "The Impact of the Civil War and Emancipation on Southern Agriculture," *Explorations in Economic History* 12 (January 1975): 1–28; and Wesley Allen Riddle, "The Origins of Black Sharecropping," *Mississippi Quarterly* 49 (Winter 1995): 53–71.

Local studies indicate the way a free-labor contractual regime, protecting the mobility of labor, empowered black workers. See Ronald L. F. Davis, *Good and Faithful Labor: From Slavery to Sharecropping in the Natchez District, 1860–1890* (Westport, Conn.: Greenwood, 1982), 78–115; Charles L. Flynn, *White Land, Black Labor: Caste and Class in Late Nineteenth-Century Georgia* (Baton Rouge: Louisiana State University Press, 1983), 57–83; Thavolia Glymph, "Freedpeople and Ex-Masters," in *Essays on the Postbellum Southern Economy*, ed. Thavolia Glymph and John J. Kushma (College Station, Tex.: Texas A.& M. University Press, 1985), 48–72; Robert Tracy McKenzie, "Freedom and the Soil in the Upper South: The Reorganization of Tennessee Agriculture, 1865–1880," *Journal of Southern History* 59 (February 1993): 63–84; John C. Rodrigue, "Labor Militancy and Black Grassroots Political Mobilization in the Louisiana Sugar Region, 1865–1868," *Journal of Southern History* 67 (February 2001): 115–42; Ralph Shlomowitz, "'Bound' or 'Free'? Black Labor in Cotton and Sugarcane Farming, 1865–1880," *Journal of Southern History* 50 (November 1984): 569–96; and Michael S. Wayne, *The Reshaping of Plantation*

Society: The Natchez District, 1860–1880 (Baton Rouge: Louisiana State University Press, 1983), 45–52, 116–42.

59. William C. Hine, "Black Politicians in Reconstruction Charleston," *Journal of Southern History* 49 (November 1983): 555–84; Holt, *Black Over White*, 43–71; Holt, "Negro State Legislators in South Carolina During Reconstruction," in *Southern Black Leaders of the Reconstruction Era*, ed. Howard N. Rabinowitz (Urbana: University of Illinois Press, 1982), 223–46; David C. Rankin, "The Origins of Negro Leadership in New Orleans during Reconstruction," ibid., 155–89; Richard L. Hume "Negro Delegates to the State Constitutional Conventions of 1867–1869," ibid., 129–53; August Meier, "Afterword: New Perspectives on the Nature of Black Political Leadership During Reconstruction," ibid., 393–406. For examples of ambitious blacks who immigrated from the North during Reconstruction, see the essays on Aaron A. Bradley, Benjamin A. Boseman, and George T. Ruby, ibid., 281–308, 335–62, 363–92. See also Russell Duncan, *Freedom's Shore: Tunis Campbell and the Georgia Freedmen* (Athens: University of Georgia Press, 1986); Peggy Lamson, *The Glorious Failure: Black Congressman Robert Brown Elliott and the Reconstruction in South Carolina* (New York: Norton, 1973); Victor Ullman, *Martin R. Delaney: The Beginnings of Black Nationalism* (Boston: Beacon Press, 1971); and Bettye J. Gardner, "William H. Foote and Yazoo County Politics, 1866–1883," *Southern Studies* 21 (Winter 1982): 398–407.

60. Occasionally, African American politicians were frank about their reliance upon political offices for financial support. See, for example, Rapier to Henry K. Thomas, September 8, 1869, Rapier Mss., Howard University, Washington, D.C., and Martin Delaney's request for a job from South Carolina Governor Robert K. Scott, quoted in Victor Ullman, *Martin Delaney: The Beginnings of Black Nationalism* (Boston: Beacon, 1971), 420. Blanche K. Bruce parlayed his earnings from political office into substantial wealth. See William C. Harris, "Blanche K. Bruce of Mississippi: Conservative Assimilationist," in *Southern Black Leaders*, 6–8. See also Lamson, *Elliott*, 273–74; Euline W. Brock, "Thomas W. Cardozo: Fallible Black Reconstruction Leader," *Journal of Southern History* 47 (May 1981): 183–206; Russell Duncan, *Freedom's Shore: Tunis Campbell and the Georgia Freedmen* (Athens: University of Georgia Press, 1986); Holt, *Black over White*, 112. See Foner, *Reconstruction*, 361–62.

61. Michael Les Benedict, "Factionalism and Representation: Some Insight from the Nineteenth-Century United States," *Social Science History* 9 (Fall 1985): 361–98, revised and republished in this volume.

62. Perman, *The Road to Redemption*, 22–56; Lawrence A. Powell, "The Politics of Livelihood: Carpetbaggers in the Deep South," in *Race, Region, and Reconstruction: Essays in Honor of C. Vann Woodward*, ed. J. Morgan Kousser and James M. Patterson (New York: Oxford University Press, 1982), 315–48; James L. Garner, *Reconstruction in Mississippi* (New York: Columbia University Press, 1901), 136; Thomas H. Holt, *Black Over White*, 112; Tunnell, *Crucible of Reconstruction: War, Radicalism, and Race in Louisiana, 1862–1877* (Baton Rouge, Louisiana State University Press, 1984), 148–49. Michael Fitzgerald describes the deteriorating reports that the Dun Credit Agency's Mobile agent sent back about the wealthy storeowner Frederick Bromberg after he became an active Republican in 1867. He had, the agent reported, "destroyed his bus[iness] utterly by taking violent radical principles into his head." Fitzgerald, *Urban Emancipation*, 110–111.

63. Unnamed black speaker in Mobile, Alabama, quoted in *Appleton's Annual Cyclopedia* (1867), 18; Edward Shaw quoted in Armstead L. Robinson, "Beyond the Realm of Social Consensus: New Meanings of Reconstruction for American Historian," *Journal of American History* 68 (September 1981): 291.

64. McPherson, *Political Reconstruction*, 374. These are the states in which voters were reported by race.

65. To some degree, factional disagreements over how to approach white southerners and to reward black Republicans separated "scalawags" (native southern Republicans) from "carpetbaggers" (northern-born southern Republicans). For insight, see Wiggins, *The Scalawag in Alabama Politics*.

66. Charles H. Lewis to Senator Henry Wilson, November 19, 1867, Wilson Mss., LC. In Louisiana, white Republican organizers reported that moderate Union men "are apprehensive that they will be thrown overboard by the negroes." "That will ruin us," they warned. Thomas B. Waters to Robert W. Taliaferro, May, 25, 1867, quoted in Tunnell, *Crucible of Reconstruction*, 128. Unionist leader Michael Hahn, who had served as governor of Abraham Lincoln's reconstructed Louisiana government in 1865, echoed the complaint. "Instead of extending the Republican fold, old citizens of Union and Republican proclivities were ostracized and only new comers were placed in positions of power and emolument." Hahn, quoted in Richard N. Current, *Three Carpetbag Governors* (Baton Rouge: Louisiana State University, 1967), 49. U.S. Marshall J. P. M. Epping, who likewise warned against alienating southern whites, stormed out of the 1867 convention of the South Carolina Union League, blasting "demagogues and renegades . . . having in view only their own selfish interests, [who] keep prating and howling about rebellion and slavery." William C. Hine, "Frustration, Factionalism, and Failure: Black Political Leadership and the Republican Party in Reconstruction Charleston, 1865–1877" (Ph.D. dissertation, Kent State University, 1979), 67. North Carolina Unionist and U.S. Marshal Daniel R. Goodloe complained that the Reconstruction Act "was a signal for a scrub-race for office among demagogues. . . . Whoever made the loudest professions of devotion to black men's rights . . . was the soundest patriot. Life-long devotion to the Union . . . went for nothing." Goodloe, *The Marshalship in North Carolina* (N.p., 1869), 6. For the frustrated efforts of one influential South Carolinian to establish a Republican Party that could appeal to whites, see Roger P. Leemhuis, *James L. Orr and the Sectional Conflict* (Washington, D.C.: University Press of America, 1979).

67. "Political Conditions in South Carolina," *Atlantic Monthly* 39 (February 1877): 177–94. The complex relationship between black and white Republican leaders is illuminated by the essays in Rabinowitz's *Southern Black Leaders of the Reconstruction Era*. In his concluding essay, August Meier emphasizes black dependence on white connections, but he recognizes that the relationship "was a two-way street." Meier, "Afterword," 398.

68. Judge Daniel L. Russell to Thomas Settle, September 16, 1874, quoted in *Maverick Republican in the Old North State: A Political Biography of Daniel L. Russell*, ed. Jeffrey J. Crow and Robert F. Durden (Baton Rouge: Louisiana State University Press, 1977), 29. See generally Current, *Those Terrible Carpetbaggers*. In Alabama, for example, more moderate Republicans allied with Governor William H. Smith and Senator Willard Warner struggled for influence with more radical Republicans allied with Senator George E. Spencer, who emerged triumphant when his faction secured control of federal patronage in 1870. Wiggins, *The Scalawag in Alabama Politics*. In Mississippi, native southern Governor James Lusk Alcorn and his moderate allies battled Senator Adelbert Ames, who had come to the state as military commander in 1869. William C. Harris, *Day of the Carpetbagger: Republican Reconstruction in Mississippi* (Baton Rouge: Louisiana State University Press, 1979), 413–19, 459–80. In Louisiana, northern immigrant Governor Henry Clay Warmoth urged moderation in contrast to his rival, fellow immigrant William Pitt Kellogg, and his allies among the federal officeholders. Joe Gray Taylor, *Louisiana Reconstructed, 1863–1877* (Baton Rouge: Louisiana State University, 1974), 209–52; Ted Tunnell, *Crucible of Reconstruction*, 136–72; Current, *Three Carpetbag Governors*, 49–56. In Florida, it was Governor Harrison Reed, another postwar arrival, against Senator Thomas W. Osborn and his allies among federal officeholders, who among other things rejected Reed's conciliatory program, which included opposition to further civil-rights legislation. Canter Brown, Jr., "Carpetbagger Intrigues, Black Leadership, and a South-

ern Loyalist Triumph: Florida's Gubernatorial Election of 1872," *Florida Historical Quarterly* 72 (January 1994): 277–78; Jerrell H. Shofner, *Nor Is It Over Yet: Florida in the Era of Reconstruction, 1863–1877* (Gainesville: University of Florida Press, 1974), 198–224; Current, *Three Carpetbag Governors*, 20–26. South Carolina seems to have been an exception. There the Customs House faction of the party, centered in Charleston and environs and allied with conservative Republican Senator Frederick A. Sawyer, consistently bolted from the party to form fusion movements with the Democrat/Conservatives. Holt, *Black Over White*, 119; Hine, "Frustration, Factionalism, and Failure."

69. Ames to Senator Justin S. Morrill, October 20, 1871, Morrill Mss., LC. Ames became governor of Mississippi in 1873, defeating Alcorn who ran as a reform Republican with Conservative backing. Harris, *Day of the Carpetbagger*, 459–80. In Louisiana, the conservative Warmoth lost control of the Republican Party to Senator William Pitt Kellogg and his allies in the New Orleans customs house and other federal offices. In 1872, Kellogg was elected governor in Louisiana, defeating a coalition of Democrat/Conservatives backed by Warmoth. Taylor, *Louisiana Reconstructed*, 209–52; Tunnell, *Crucible of Reconstruction*, 170–71. In Florida, Senator Thomas W. Osborne's federal officeholder wing of the party almost succeeded in ousting conservative Republican Governor Harrison Reed through impeachment. But, in contrast to events elsewhere, Republicans then turned to a moderate native Unionist, Ossian B. Hart, as their gubernatorial candidate. Brown, "Carpetbagger Intrigues," 275–301; Brown, *Ossian Bingley Hart*, 190–281.

In South Carolina, the formerly conservative Governor Robert K. Scott responded to black criticism of his passivity in the face of the Ku Klux Klan. Moving toward the left, he retained control of the party and secured reelection in 1870. The Conservative *Charleston News and Courier* reported events as follows: "The governor, in order to make his election sure, has appealed to all the passions of the colored men—hugged them to his bosom, appointed them to office . . . pandered to their prejudices, all for the simple purpose of driving out of the party every decent white man in it, and ruling alone" (March 4, 1870). Having secured his reelection, Scott alienated many black leaders by moving back toward conservatism. Franklin J. Moses Jr., a Scott ally who nonetheless criticized Scott's retreat, won the gubernatorial nomination and then defeated a bolting Republican ticket, organized by the conservative Republican Senator Frederick A. Sawyer and supported by Democrat/Conservatives. See Joel Williamson, *After Slavery: The Negro in South Carolina During Reconstruction, 1861–1877* (Chapel Hill: University of North Carolina Press, 1965), 190–98, 206–208, 259–66; Lamson, *Glorious Failure*, 80–173. In Texas, Governor Edmund J. Davis and Senator Morgan C. Hamilton seized control of the party from Hamilton's more conservative brother, Andrew J. Hamilton, by promising vigorous action to counteract anti-black and anti-Republican violence. See Carl H. Moneyhon, *Texas After the Civil War: The Struggle of Reconstruction* (College Station: Texas A&M University Press, 2004), 87–187; John L. Waller, *Colossal Hamilton of Texas: A Biography of Andrew Jackson Hamilton, Militant Unionist and Reconstruction Governor* (El Paso: Texas Western Press, 1968), 122–40.

Events in Arkansas and North Carolina, where African Americans made up smaller proportions of the population, followed a different course. There Republicans advocating liberality toward ex-Confederates remained powerful within the party. Persistent factionalism in both states enabled Conservative/Democrats to regain power. For Arkansas, see Thomas S. Staples, *Reconstruction in Arkansas, 1862–1872* (New York: Columbia University Press, 1923); Justin M. Harrell, *The Brooks and Baxter War* (St. Louis: Slawson Printing Co., 1893); Carl H. Moneyhon, *The Impact of the Civil War and Reconstruction on Arkansas: Persistence in the Midst of Ruin* (Baton Rouge: Louisiana State University Press, 1994). For North Carolina, see Raper, *Holden*, 105–223; Harris, *Holden*, 200–312.

For the general story of the triumph of more radical Republican factions in the South, see Perman, *The Road to Redemption*, 22–56.

70. Foner, *Reconstruction*, 350–56; Perman, *Road to Redemption*, 139–41. For these developments in Mississippi, see Harris, *Day of the Carpetbagger*, 437–52; for South Carolina, see Holt, *Black Over White*, 105–10; Williamson, *After Slavery*, 258–62.

71. Goodloe, *Letter of Daniel R. Goodloe to Hon. Charles Sumner*, 10; Goodloe, *The Marshalship in North Carolina*, 6. The quoted material is taken from both of these published letters.

72. Davis Tillson to Jacob D. Cox, November 23, 1867, Cox Mss., Oberlin College, Oberlin, Ohio. See also Judge Richard Busteed to Senator William Pitt Fessenden, March 11, 1868, Fessenden Mss., Western Reserve Historical Society, Cleveland, Ohio; Michael Hahn to Elihu B. Washburne, October 21, 1868, Washburne Mss., LC; J. P. M. Epping to James L. Orr, May 1867, quoted in Hine, "Frustration, Factionalism, and Failure," 67.

73. For the effect of the economic collapse of 1873 on southern Republicans' economic program, see Summers, *Railroads, Reconstruction, and the Gospel of Prosperity*, 268–98. Michael Perman describes the new stress on retrenchment of expenditures in the South after 1873 without expressly linking the change to the economic downturn. See Perman, *The Road to Redemption*, 143–48.

74. For southern whites' perception that it was they who were fighting for liberty against tyranny, and the public policies that led to it, see Michael Les Benedict, "The Problem of Constitutionalism and Constitutional Liberty in the Reconstruction South," in *An Uncertain Tradition: Constitutionalism and the History of the South*, ed. Kermit L. Hall and James W. Ely (Athens: University of Georgia Press, 1989), 225–49, revised and republished in this volume.

75. Historians have paid slight attention to the differences among Democrats in the Reconstruction South. The best source is Perman's *The Road to Redemption*, 149–77, which describes what Perman calls "the forked road to redemption." But Perman does not stress enough the importance of the federal threat of intervention to maintaining the moderate Democratic position.

76. The correlations between party support and the ethnocultural variables are not reciprocal for Democrats and Republicans, because the party variables are based on the proportion of the eligible electorate voting Republican or Democratic, rather than on the two-party vote. The ethnocultural variables are based on the 1870 census unless otherwise noted.

77. Dale Baum, *The Civil War Party System: Massachusetts as a Test Case, 1852–1876* (Chapel Hill: University of North Carolina Press, 1985), 125–35; Kleppner, *The Third Electoral System*, 131–39.

78. Michael Les Benedict, *A Compromise of Principle: Congressional Republicans and Reconstruction, 1863–1869* (New York: Norton, 1975), 188–209.

79. The median estimated voter turnout in the northern and border states was 61.2 percent in 1866, compared to 56.4, 57.9, and 57.3 percent for the congressional elections of 1862, 1870, and 1874.

80. In the 1864 elections the Republicans had gained forty-seven congressmen over their number of Republicans in the previous Congress. In the 1866 elections they lost only six, which they gained back in the presidential election of 1868. In the succeeding off-year congressional elections of 1870, 1874, and 1878, the Republicans would lose fifteen, ninety-five, and ten seats respectively.

81. Akerman to Thomas L. Tullock, June 23, 1876, Ackerman Mss., Alderman Library, University of Virginia, Charlottesville.

82. *Richmond Dispatch*, August 30, 1876.

83. Ibid., July 25, 1876.

84. Vincent P. De Santis, *Republicans Face the Southern Question: The New Departure Years, 1877–1897* (Baltimore: Johns Hopkins University Press, 1959), 66–103.
85. *New York Herald*, March 31, 1879.
86. Joel Silbey, *A Respectable Minority*, 181–87, 200–202. There is no study of the struggle between Bourbon and liberal Democrats leading to the "New Departure" movement of 1871. It may be followed by reading such Democratic and independent Democratic organs as the *New York World, New York Herald, Chicago Times,* and the *Cincinnati Enquirer*. Jerome Mushkat discusses the New Departure movement in New York in *The Reconstruction of the New York Democracy, 1861–1874* (Rutherford, N.J: Farleigh Dickinson University Press, 1981), 173–75, 191–92.
87. The Tenure of Office Act kept federal officers in place until their successors were confirmed, thus making every sitting officer beholden to his senator, no matter who had been most influential in securing his nomination originally. Senators established a custom of "senatorial courtesy" by which any senator could block the confirmation of a nominee offensive to him. Not only did this enable senators both to protect sitting allies, but it also meant that any aspiring officeholder and his patron had to secure at least the acquiescence of his senator to an appointment. Of course, this system operated only when the president and senator were of the same party. Thus, it was Republican senators rather than Democrats who established predominance in their state parties during the late 1860s and the 1870s.
88. Benedict, "Factionalism and Representation," 373–74; Morton Kellar, "The Triumph of Organizational Politics," chapter 7 of *Affairs of State: Public Life in the Late Nineteenth Century* (Cambridge, Mass.: Harvard University Press, 1977), 238–83.
89. Robert Michels, *Political Parties: A Sociological Study of the Oligarchical Tendencies of Modern Democracy,* trans. Eden and Cedar Paul (New York: Hearst's International Library, 1915). This rule is widely accepted in the political science literature. See E. Spencer Wellhoffer and Timothy M. Hennessey, "Political Party Development: Institutionalization, Leadership Recruitment, and Behavior," *American Journal of Political Science* 18 (February 1974): 135–65; Joseph R. Gusfield, "Social Movements: The Study of Social Movements," *International Encyclopedia of the Social Sciences,* 16 vols. (New York: Free Press, 1968), 14: 445–52; Robert K. Merton, "Bureaucratic Structure and Personality," in Merton, *Social Theory and Social Structure,* rev. ed. (Glencoe, Ill.: Free Press, 1957), 195–206.
90. *Nation*, August 1, 1867. For a fuller discussion of the role dissident, reform-oriented Republicans played in undermining support for Reconstruction, see Michael Les Benedict, "Reform Republicans and the Retreat from Reconstruction," in *The Facts of Reconstruction: Essays in Honor of John Hope Franklin,* ed. Alfred Moss and Eric Anderson (Baton Rouge: Louisiana State University Press, 53–78), revised and republished in this volume. See also Foner, *Reconstruction,* 488–99.
91. For an insightful discussion of the politics of "corruption" in the Reconstruction era, see Mark Summers, *The Era of Good Stealings* (New York: Oxford University Press, 1993).
92. See Mark Summers, "The Press Gang: Corruption and the Independent Press in the Grant Era," *Congress & the Presidency* 17 (Spring 1990): 29–44.
93. Foner, *Reconstruction,* 518. See also Cohen, *The Reconstruction of American Liberalism,* 61–85; Richardson, *The Death of Reconstruction,* 83–121, 183–224.
94. Silbey, *The American Political Nation,* 224–30.
95. Stanley Coben, "Northeastern Business and Radical Reconstruction: A Re-Examination," *Mississippi Valley Historical Review* 46 (June 1959): 67–90; Peter Kolchin, "The Business Press and Reconstruction, 1865–1868," *Journal of Southern History* 33 (May 1967): 183–96; Harold Francis Williamson, *Edward Atkinson: The Biography of an American Liberal, 1827–1905* (Boston: Old Corner Book Store, 1934). Currency issues

were crucial in alienating much of the Republican financial community from radical Republicans. Leading radicals, such as Benjamin F. Butler, Thaddeus Stevens, and Benjamin F. Wade, opposed contracting the money supply and returning to a specie-based currency. Northeastern business and financial interests bitterly condemned their position. Benedict, *A Compromise of Principle*, 262–65. See also Robert P. Sharkey, *Money, Class, and Party: An Economic Study of Civil War and Reconstruction* (Baltimore: Johns Hopkins University Press, 1959).

96. For the relationship between the "equal-rights, no special privileges" element of free-labor ideology and laissez-faire moralism, see Michael Les Benedict, "Laissez-Faire and Liberty: A Re-Evaluation of the Meaning and Origins of Laissez-Faire Constitutionalism," *Law and History Review* 3 (Fall 1985): 361–98.

97. Albert G. Riddle, *The Life, Character, and Public Services of James A. Garfield* (Cleveland, Ohio: W. W. Williams, 1881), 298.

98. David W. Blight's influential *Race and Reunion* makes much the same point, showing how the desire for reconciliation between North and South eroded northerners' memory of what the war was about, to the detriment of African Americans' rights. See also Nina Silber, *The Romance of Reunion: Northerners and the South, 1865–1900* (Chapel Hill: University of North Carolina Press, 1993), 124–58.

99. Stanley P. Hirshson, *Farewell to the Bloody Shirt: Northern Republicans and the Southern Negro, 1877–1893* (Bloomington: Indiana University Press, 1962), 190–250.

7. Salmon P. Chase and Constitutional Politics

1. *New York Tribune*, May 8, 1873.

2. See Bray Hammond, *Banks and Politics in America From the Revolution to the Civil War* (Princeton, N.J.: Princeton University Press, 1957), 718–34; Leonard P. Curry, *Blueprint for Modern America: Nonmilitary Legislation of the First Civil War Congress* (Nashville, Tenn.: Vanderbilt University Press, 1968), 181–206; Heather Cox Richardson, *The Greatest Nation of the Earth: Republican Economic Policies During the Civil War* (Cambridge, Mass.: Harvard University Press, 1997).

3. Albert Bushnell Hart, *Salmon Portland Chase* (Boston: Houghton Mifflin, 1899), 435.

4. The two biographies were prepared by bitter rivals—Jacob W. Schuckers, Chase's longtime friend and personal secretary, who wrote with the blessing of Chase's imperious daughter Kate, and Robert Bruce Warden, to whom the chief justice had turned over much of his correspondence, diaries, and memoirs toward the end of his life. Written in the nineteenth-century "life and letters" genre, both books were filled with hundreds of pages of personal correspondence, public addresses, and documents. Warden was able to add extracts from Chase's diaries and journals. Short on analysis of any kind, they have provided primary source material for generations of historians. See Jacob William Schuckers, *The Life and Public Services of Salmon P. Chase, U.S. Senator and Governor of Ohio* (New York: D. Appleton, 1874); Robert Bruce Warden, *An Account of the Private Life and Public Services of Salmon P. Chase* (Cincinnati: Wilstach, Baldwin and Co., 1874). Chase's reputation remained significant enough at the turn of the twentieth century to warrant the editor of *The American Statesmen* series to assign Chase's biography to one of the nation's leading historians, Albert Bushnell Hart. Hart, *Chase*, cited in note 3. Old-fashioned in style but very accessible to a public that still remembered wartime events, it was the last biography of Chase to appear for eighty-eight years.

5. T. Harry Williams, *Lincoln and the Radicals* (Madison: University of Wisconsin Press, 1941), 294–313; James G. Randall called the radical Republicans "Vindictives" in his standard textbook *The Civil War and Reconstruction* (Boston: D. C. Heath, 1937). See also Claude G. Bowers, *The Tragic Era: The Revolution After Lincoln* (Boston: Houghton Mifflin, 1929); George Fort Milton, *The Age of Hate: Andrew Johnson and the Radicals*

(New York: Coward, McCann, 1930); and William M. Zornow, *Lincoln and the Party Divided* (Norman: University of Oklahoma Press, 1954).

6. Donnal V. Smith, *Chase and Civil War Politics* (Columbus, Ohio: F. J. Heer, 1931). Thomas and Marva Belden's engaging and ironic *So Fell the Angels* probably made matters worse, wickedly detailing the un-Victorian (or all-too-Victorian) relationship among Chase, Kate, and her wealthy, corrupt husband, Senator William Sprague. Thomas Graham Belden and Marva Robins Belden, *So Fell the Angels* (Boston: Little, Brown, 1956).

7. Hans L. Trefousse, *The Radical Republicans: Lincoln's Vanguard for Racial Justice* (New York: Knopf, 1968). See also Eric L. McKitrick, *Andrew Johnson and Reconstruction* (Chicago: University of Chicago Press, 1960); John Hope Franklin, *Reconstruction: After the Civil War* (Chicago: University of Chicago Press, 1961); Kenneth M. Stampp, *The Era of Reconstruction, 1865–1877* (New York: Knopf, 1965); Michael Les Benedict, *A Compromise of Principle: Congressional Republicans and Reconstruction, 1863–1869* (New York: Norton, 1974).

8. Frederick J. Blue, *Salmon P. Chase: A Life in Politics* (Kent, Ohio: Kent State University Press, 1987); John Niven, *Salmon P. Chase: A Biography* (New York: Oxford University Press, 1995).

9. John Niven, ed., *The Salmon P. Chase Papers* [microform] (Frederick, Md.: University Publications of America, 1987); Niven, *The Salmon P. Chase Papers*, 5 vols. (Kent, Ohio: Kent State University Press, 1993–1998).

10. See Michael Les Benedict, "The Party, Going Strong: Congressional Elections in the Mid-Nineteenth Century," *Congress and the Presidency* 9 (Winter 1981–82): 37–60, revised and republished in this volume.

11. Miller to William P. Ballinger, October 15, 1876, quoted in Charles Fairman, *Mr. Justice Miller and the Supreme Court, 1862–1890* (Cambridge, Mass.: Harvard University Press, 1939), 251–52.

12. Warden, *Chase*, 683.

13. Ibid., 693.

14. The following biographical sketch is based on Blue's and Niven's biographies.

15. See Eric Foner's chapter on Chase and the antislavery constitutional argument in *Free Soil, Free Labor, Free Men: The Ideology of the Republican Party before the Civil War* (New York: Oxford University Press, 1970), 73–102, and William M. Wiecek, *The Sources of Antislavery Constitutionalism in America* (Ithaca, N.Y.: Cornell University Press, 1977), 202–27.

16. Arthur M. Bestor, "State Sovereignty and Slavery: A Reinterpretation of Proslavery Constitutional Doctrine, 1846–1860," *Journal of the Illinois State Historical Society* 54 (Summer 1961): 162–67.

17. *U.S. Statutes at Large* 1 (1793): 302; ibid. 9 (1850): 462. This is the legal form for citing the *U.S. Statutes at Large*.

18. Chase's constitutional views are best articulated in Salmon P. Chase, *Speech of Salmon P. Chase, in the Case of the Colored Woman, Matilda, Who was Brought Before the Court of Common Please of Hamilton County, Ohio, by Writ of Habeas Corpus; March 11, 1837* (Cincinnati: Pugh & Dodd, 1837) (hereafter Chase, Speech in the Matilda Case); Chase, *Reclamation of Fugitives from Service; An Argument for the Defendant, Submitted to the Supreme Court of the United States . . . in the Case of Warton Jones vs. John Van Zandt* (Cincinnati, Ohio: R. P. Donogh, 1847); and in his speech "Union and Freedom, Without Compromise," in the *Congressional Globe*, 31 Cong., 1 Sess., appendix, 468–80 (Mar. 26–27, 1850).

19. The lead cases were *Somerset v. Stewart*, 4 Douglas 300, 99 Eng. Rep. 891 (K.B. 1785), decided by the great English jurist Lord Mansfield, and *Commonwealth v. Aves*, 18

Pickering (Mass.) 193 (1836), decided by the influential Massachusetts chief justice Lemuel Shaw.

20. Foner, *Free Soil, Free Labor, Free Men*, 83.
21. Chase, *Speech in the Matilda Case*, 19.
22. Ibid., 20.
23. 41 U.S. (16 Pet.) 539 (1842).
24. See Paul Finkelman, "Prigg v. Pennsylvania and Northern State Courts: Antislavery Use of a Proslavery Decision," *Civil War History* 25 (1979): 5.
25. See Campbell, *The Slave Catchers: Enforcement of the Fugitive Slave Law, 1850–1860* (Chapel Hill: University of North Carolina Press, 1968), 110–86, for a discussion both of northern interference with slavecatching and efforts at federal prosecution of obstructionists. For other descriptions of litigation surrounding the seizure and rescue of fugitive slaves, see Allen Sharp and Johannes Williams, "Free at Last: How the Powell Fugitive Slave Family Became and Stayed Free," *Supreme Court Historical Quarterly* 17, no. 1 (1996): 7–15; Stephen Middleton, "Law and Ideology in Ohio and Kentucky: The Kidnapping of Jerry Phinney," *Filson Club History Quarterly* 67 (July 1993): 347–72; Middleton, "The Fugitive Slave Crisis in Cincinnati, 1850–1860: Resistance, Enforcement, and Black Refugees," *Journal of Negro History* 72 (Winter/Spring 1987): 20–32.

Not until *Ableman v. Booth*, 62 U.S. (21 How.) 506 (1859), did the Supreme Court rule that states could not issue writs of habeas corpus to interfere with the seizure and transport of alleged runaways under the Fugitive Slave Act. The facts are illustrative of the obstacles slavecatchers faced and the way slaveholders used federal power to counteract them. The owner of an alleged runaway secured a certificate from the U.S. commissioner for fugitive slaves in Milwaukee, Wisconsin. The slave-owner and a deputy marshal seized the alleged slave and incarcerated him in the county jail, despite the Wisconsin law prohibiting local officials from enforcing the Fugitive Slave Law. Booth, a local abolitionist and Republican leader, secured a writ of habeas corpus from a county judge. The marshal, supported by the local sheriff, denied the applicability of the writ to a prisoner in federal custody and refused to produce him. A mob then broke into the jail and released the prisoner, who made good his escape. Booth and others in the crowd were then indicted for violating the Fugitive Slave Act by abetting the rescue. Wisconsin judges again issued writs of habeas corpus, this time on behalf of Booth and his friends, which the state supreme court sustained on appeal. The court refused to return the writ of error issued by the United States Supreme Court. But when the Supreme Court vacated the state court order anyway, an evenly divided state supreme court backed down. Booth spent ten months in jail before being pardoned on the eve of the Civil War. Campbell, *The Slavecatchers*, 157–61.

26. *Congressional Globe*, 33 Cong., 2 Sess., appendix, 211 (February 15, 1855).
27. See the removal provisions (section 3) of the Civil Rights Act of 1866, 14 Stat. 27 (1866), and the Removal Act of 1875, 18 Stat. 470 (1875).
28. *Congressional Globe*, 33 Cong., 2 Sess., appendix, 211 (February 15, 1855).
29. *Congressional Globe*, 31 Cong., 1 Sess., appendix 477 (March 27, 1850).
30. Chase to Lincoln, June 13, 1859, in Chase, *Papers*, 3:14.
31. Lincoln to Chase, June 20, 1859, in Roy P. Basler, ed., *The Collected Works of Abraham Lincoln*, 8 vols. (New Brunswick, N.J.: Rutgers University Press, 1953), 3:386 (hereafter Lincoln, *Collected Works*). The different spellings of "its" are given as they appeared in the original.
32. Ibid., 131–32.
33. Lincoln, "First Inaugural Address," ibid., 264.
34. This was the language of the resolutions of a mass convention of Chase's antislavery Democrats in 1851, quoted in Chase, *Speech . . . Delivered at Toledo, May 30, 1851, Before a Mass Convention of the Democracy of North-Western Ohio*, 8.

35. Ibid., 4.
36. Ibid., 1.
37. John S. Benson, *The Judicial Record of the Late Chief Justice Chase* (New York: Baker, Voorhis & Co., 1882), 36. The essay originally appeared in the October 1873 number of *Harper's Monthly*.
38. William D. Pederson and Norman W. Provizer, eds., *Great Justices of the U.S. Supreme Court: Ratings and Case Studies* (New York: Peter Lang, 1993), 13–23.
39. Jesse Choper, ed., *The Supreme Court and Its Justices* (Chicago: American Bar Association, 1987).
40. Felix Frankfurter, *The Commerce Clause Under Marshall, Taney, and Waite* (Chapel Hill: University of North Carolina Press, 1937).
41. David F. Hughes, "Salmon P. Chase: Chief Justice" (Ph.D. dissertation, Princeton University, 1963).
42. Harold M. Hyman, *The Reconstruction Justice of Salmon P. Chase: In re Turner and Texas v. White* (Lawrence: University Press of Kansas, 1997). David P. Currie attends to the Chase court in his *The Constitution in the Supreme Court*, in which he offers close analyses of the quality of the Court's legal reasoning, almost devoid of historical context. David P. Currie, *The Constitution in the Supreme Court: The First Hundred Years, 1789–1888* (Chicago: University of Chicago Press, 1985). Much better is the discussion in William Wiecek's brief history of the Supreme Court *Liberty under Law: The Supreme Court in American Life* (Baltimore, Md.: Johns Hopkins University Press, 1988). The most complete, coherent, and best-contextualized study of Chase as chief justice remains David F. Hughes's doctoral dissertation, aspects of which he summarized in an excellent law review article, "Salmon P. Chase: Chief Justice," *Vanderbilt Law Review* 18 (March 1965): 569. A series of insightful essays and comments on Chase, published in the "Chase Centennial Issue" of the *Northern Kentucky Law Review* 21 (Fall 1993), augments earlier work.
43. George Hoadly, *Address at Music Hall, Cincinnati, Ohio, on the Occasion of the Removal of the Remains of Salmon P. Chase to Spring Grove Cemetery, Thursday, October 14, 1886* (Cincinnati: Robert Clarke & Co., 1887), 21. Like his mentor, Hoadly switched parties in the decade following the Civil War. Although elected governor as a Democrat, he was a prime mover behind the passage of Ohio's equal accommodations act, enacted with primarily Republican support after the Supreme Court ruled the federal Civil Rights Act of 1875 unconstitutional. See David A. Gerber, *Black Ohio and the Color Line, 1860–1915* (Urbana: University of Illinois Press, 1976), 236–43.
44. Hart, *Chase*, 325.
45. Charles Warren, *The Supreme Court in United States History*, 3 vols. (Boston: Little, Brown & Co., 1924), 3:130, 131.
46. Ibid., 140–219. See James Ford Rhodes, *History of the United States from the Compromise of 1850 to the Final Restoration of Home Rule at the South in 1877*, 7 vols. (New York: Macmillan, 1904), 6: 11–13.
47. Warren, *Supreme Court in U.S. History*, 3:204.
48. Ibid., 214. See generally 140–219.
49. Randall, *The Civil War and Reconstruction*, 802–6; James G. Randall and David Donald, *The Civil War and Reconstruction*, 2d ed. (Boston: D. C. Heath, 1961), 643–46; Alfred H. Kelly, *The American Constitution: A History* (New York: Norton, 1963), 477–81; W. R. Brock, *An American Crisis: Congress and Reconstruction, 1865–1867* (New York: St. Martin's, 1963), 264.
50. James W. Burgess, *Reconstruction and the Constitution, 1866–1876* (New York: Charles Scribner's Sons, 1902), 157–94; David Miller Dewitt, *The Impeachment and Trial of Andrew Johnson, Seventeenth President of the United States: A History* (New York: Macmillan, 1903). Among early historians of Reconstruction, the exception was William A.

Dunning, who, despite his hostility toward Republican Reconstruction policy, wrote a balanced account in "The Impeachment and Trial of President Johnson," in Dunning, *Essays on the Civil War and Reconstruction, and Related Topics* (New York: Macmillan, 1898), 253–303.

51. Rhodes, *History of the United States*, 6:118.
52. Hart, *Chase*, 360.
53. Charles Fairman, *Reconstruction and Reunion, 1864–1888: Part One* (Vol. 6 of *The Oliver Wendell Holmes Devise History of the Supreme Court of the United States*) (New York: Macmillan, 1971). The volume is marred by repetition and inclusion of extraneous material. It is useful more as a compendium of information and analysis of specific events and cases than as a cogent overview.
54. Wiecek, *Liberty Under Law*, 88.
55. Stanley I. Kutler, *Judicial Power and Reconstruction Politics* (Chicago: University of Chicago Press, 1968), 65. See also William M. Wiecek, "The Reconstruction of Federal Power," *American Journal of Legal History* 13 (October 1969): 333–59; Wiecek, *Liberty Under Law*, 84–93. Although Bernard Schwartz seems ambivalent about the new understanding in his *A History of the Supreme Court* (New York: Oxford University Press, 1993), 154–55, he no longer refers to "the fallen state of the Supreme Court," as he did in his *A Basic History of the Supreme Court* (Huntington, N.Y.: Robert E. Krieger, 1979 [1968]), 48.
56. Robert J. Kaczorowski, "The Chase Court and Fundamental Rights: A Watershed in American Constitutionalism," *Northern Kentucky Law Review* 1 (1993): 21–190. See also Eugene Gressman, "The Unhappy History of Civil Rights Legislation," *Michigan Law Review* 50 (June 1952): 1323–58; Robert J. Harris, *The Quest for Equality: The Constitution, Congress, and the Supreme Court* (Baton Rouge: Louisiana State University Press, 1960), 82–83; Loren Miller, *The Petitioners: The Story of the Supreme Court of the United States and the Negro* (New York: Pantheon, 1966), 102–9; Howard N. Meyer, *The Amendment That Refused to Die* (Boston: Beacon, 1973), 75–83; Walter F. Murphy, "Slaughter-House, Civil Rights, and Limits on Constitutional Change," *American Journal of Jurisprudence* 32, no. 1 (1987): 1–22; and Richard L. Aynes, "Constricting the Law of Freedom: Justice Miller, the Fourteenth Amendment, and the Slaughter-House Cases," *Chicago Kent Law Review* 70, no. 2 (1994): 627–88.
57. Kaczorowski, "The Chase Court and Fundamental Rights," 172–73, 182–83.
58. Charles Richard Williams, ed., *Diary and Letters of Rutherford Birchard Hayes*, 5 vols. (Columbus: Ohio State Archeological and Historical Society, 1922–1926), 3:242.
59. Examples abound in Niven's edition of Chase's correspondence.
60. William Strong to William M. Evarts, Sept. 10, 1874, quoted in Fairman, *Reconstruction and Reunion*, 1477.
61. The Circassian, 69 U.S. (2 Wall.) 135 (1865); The Baigorry, ibid., 474 (1865); The Andromeda, ibid., 481 (1865); The Josephine, 70 U.S. (3 Wall.) 83 (1866); The Bermuda, ibid., 514 (1866).
62. The Springbok, 72 U.S. (5 Wall.) 1 (1867); The Peterhoff, ibid., 28 (1867); The Dashing Wave, ibid., 170 (1867); The Volent, ibid., 179 (1867); The Sir William Peel, ibid., 517 (1867); The Sea Witch, ibid., 242 (1868).
63. Quoted in Hughes, "Chase," 326.
64. *U.S. Statutes at Large* 14 (1866): 27.
65. Chase to Stephen J. Field, April 39, 1866, quoted in Schuckers, *Chase*, 526–27.
66. Ibid., 527.
67. Chase to Henry W. Hilliard, April 27, 1866, quoted ibid., 528; Niven, *Chase*, 383.
68. Chase to Wendell Phillips, May 1, 1866, quoted in Warden, *Chase*, 649.
69. In re Turner, 24 Fed. Cas. 339 (No. 14,247) (C.C.D. Md. 1867).

70. Chase to George William Curtis, August 8, 1867, Chase Mss., LC.
71. Reconstruction Act, ibid. 15 (1867): 2; First Supplementary Reconstruction Act, *U.S. Statutes at Large* 14 (1867): 428.
72. Fairman, *Reunion and Reconstruction*, 324.
73. After two years of refusing to hold court in his circuit, he went to Raleigh, North Carolina, to explain that he had done so because he was unwilling to sit in areas where the military was supreme. *New York Times*, June 7, 1867.
74. Benedict, *A Compromise of Principle*, 260. Chase's refusal to attend circuit court while military authority remained supreme in his circuit was the primary cause of the delay, along with delays sought by counsel. See Fairman, *Reunion and Reconstruction*, 175–76, 607–12.
75. *Chase's Circuit Court Decisions* 136 (C.C.D.N.C. 1867).
76. Ibid., 141–42.
77. Michael Les Benedict, "The Rout of Radicalism: Republicans and the Elections of 1867," *Civil War History* 18 (December 1972): 334–44, revised and republished in this volume.
78. Michael Les Benedict, *The Impeachment and Trial of Andrew Johnson* (New York: Norton, 1973), 115–22 and 126–67; Fairman, *Reconstruction and Reunion*, 1: 521–27.
79. Blue, *Chase*, 285–300.
80. Chase to J. Glancy Jones, May 17, 1867, Chase Mss., LC.
81. Chase to H. Cummins, December 6, 1867, Chase Mss., LC.
82. See the letters reproduced in Schuckers, *Chase*, 575–588.
83. Chase to Gerritt Smith, April 2, 1868, quoted in Warden, *Chase*, 683.
84. Benedict, *A Compromise of Principle*; Joel Silbey, *A Respectable Minority; The Democratic Party in the Civil War Era, 1860–1868* (New York: Norton, 1977), 133–35; Jerome Mushkat, *The Reconstruction of the New York Democracy, 1861–1874* (Rutherford, N.J.: Farleigh Dickinson Press, 1981), 85–142.
85. Chester M. Destler, "The Origins and Character of the Pendleton Plan," *Mississippi Valley Historical Review* 24 (September 1937): 171–84; George L. Anderson, "The South and Problems of Post–Civil War Finance," *Journal of Southern History* 9 (May 1943): 181–95.
86. Silbey, *A Respectable Majority*, 189–206; Mushkat, *Reconstruction of the New York Democracy*, 133–35; Felice A. Bonadio, *North of Reconstruction: Ohio Politics, 1865–1870* (New York: New York University Press, 1970), 158–59; Coleman, *The Election of 1868*, 146–49.
87. Schuckers, *Chase*, 561–62; Blue, *Chase*, 68–73, 84–88; Reinhard H. Luthin, "Chase's Political Career Before the Civil War," *Mississippi Valley Historical Review* 29 (March 1943): 520–22.
88. Bonadio, *North of Reconstruction*, 144–46; Luthin, "Chase's Political Career Before the Civil War," 534; Hughes, "Salmon P. Chase: Chief Justice," 40–41.
89. Coleman, *Election of 1868*, 82, 113–16.
90. Warden, *Chase*, at 702–16; Blue, *Chase*, at 285–300.
91. *New York Herald*, July 7, 1869. The demonstration was described ibid., July 6, 1869. There is no study of Chase's role as the representative of Democratic–New Departure sentiments in 1869 and 1870. For indications of it, see Chase to William N. [?] Boyd, April 3, 1869; Chase to George [?] H. Hill, January 7, 1870; Chase to Thomas H. Yeatman, January 12, 1870, all in the Chase Letterbooks, Chase Mss., LC; *Charleston Daily Courier*, June 2, 1869; *New York Herald*, June 22, 1869; *Boston Commonwealth*, July 20, 1869.
92. Charles I. Grady to Chase, Mar. 29, 1872, Chase Mss., LC. Little has been written about Chase's part in the early development of Liberal Republicanism. Michael Perman alludes to his 1872 Republican presidential ambitions in *The Road to Redemption: South-*

ern Politics, 1869–1879 (Chapel Hill: University of North Carolina Press, 1984), 14. See also the *National Antislavery Standard*, June 26, 1869; *Philadelphia Press*, July 31, 1869 (quoting the *Baltimore American*); *Richmond Dispatch*, July 31, 1869 (quoting the *Baltimore Gazette*).

93. Case of Jefferson Davis, *Chase's Circuit Court Decisions*, 124.
94. *New York Tribune*, November 26, 1868.
95. Hughes, "Salmon P. Chase: Chief Justice," 278–81.
96. Caesar Griffin's Case, *Chase's Circuit Court Decisions*, 364 (C.C.D.Va. 1869).
97. Ibid., 421.
98. U.S. v. Morrison, *Chase's Circuit Court Opinions*, 521, 525 (C.C.D.S.C. 1869).
99. Ibid., xiii–xiv.
100. *New York Herald*, June 22, 1869.
101. 74 U.S. (7 Wall.) 700 (1869).
102. For Lincoln's powerful statements of the argument, see his *First Inaugural Address*, in Samuel D. Richardson, ed., *A Compilation of the Messages and Papers of the Presidents*, 20 vols. (New York: Bureau of National Literature, 1897), 7:3206–13, and his message to the special session of Congress, July 4, 1865, ibid., 3228–29.
103. Texas v. White, 74 U.S. at 724–25 (1869).
104. Ibid., 725.
105. Ibid., 729.
106. Ibid., 725.
107. 74 U.S. (7 Wall.) 1 (1869).
108. Ibid., 76.
109. Ibid., 77.
110. Collector v. Day, 78 U.S. (11 Wall.) 113 (1871).
111. Ibid., 124.
112. Ibid., 126.
113. 80 U.S. (13 Wall.) 581 (1871). A look at table 2 indicates suggests how unpredictable Chase's vote would have been.
114. 83 U.S. (16 Wall.) 36 (1873).
115. Ibid., 78.
116. Ibid.
117. For the role commitment to federalism played in limiting what the Supreme Court would permit in the way of federal enforcement of civil and political rights, see Michael Les Benedict, "Preserving Federalism: Reconstruction and the Waite Court," *Supreme Court Review* 1978: 39–80, and Robert J. Kaczorowski, *The Politics of Judicial Interpretation: The Federal Courts, Department of Justice and Civil Rights, 1866–1876* (New York: Oceana Press, 1985).
118. 73 U.S. (6 Wall.) 766 (1868).
119. U.S. v. Padelford, 76 U.S. (9 Wall.) 531 (1870).
120. U.S. v. Klein, 80 U.S. (13 Wall.) 128 (1872).
121. Johnson Reports, iv.
122. Ibid., 167 (C.C.D.Va. 1868).
123. 84 U.S. (7 Wall.) 700 (1869).
124. Thorington v. Smith, 75 U.S. (8 Wall.) 1 (1869).
125. Fairman, *Reunion and Reconstruction*, 601–607. Had the judge succeeded, other Republican federal judges would surely have emulated him.
126. Johnson Reports, v.
127. 74 U.S. (7 Wall.) 229 (1868).
128. Ibid., 252.
129. Ibid., 249.
130. Hepburn v. Griswold, 75 U.S. (8 Wall.) 603 (1869).

131. Knox v. Lee, 79 U.S. (12 Wall.) 457 (1871). The story is told in detail in Fairman, *Reconstruction and Reunion*, 677–775.

132. Veazie Bank v. Fenno, 8 Wall. (75 U.S.) 333 (1869).

8. The Problem of Constitutionalism and Constitutional Liberty in the Reconstruction South

1. Daniel H. Chamberlain, "Reconstruction in South Carolina," *Atlantic Monthly* 87 (1901): 484.

2. Kenneth M. Stampp, *The Era of Reconstruction, 1865–1877* (New York: Knopf, 1965), 170.

3. Charles William Ramsdell, *Reconstruction in Texas* (New York: Columbia University Press, 1910), 227; Cal Ledbetter, Jr., "The Constitution of 1868: Conqueror's Constitution or Constitutional Continuity?" *Arkansas Historical Quarterly* 44, no. 1 (1985): 34–35.

4. In Arkansas, the transfer of power precipitated civil war. Louisianans rose in open insurrection, temporarily overthrowing the Republican state government, in September 1874. From then until 1877 they forcefully took control of town and parish governments and offices, finally coercing Republicans to surrender power under threat of violence after the disputed election of 1876. In South Carolina, Conservatives backed their claim to victory in the disputed election of 1876 with armed force; Republican rivals had to surrender to it when President Rutherford B. Hayes informed them that he would not intervene to prevent violence. See John M. Harrell, *The Brooks and Baxter War: A History of the Reconstruction Period in Arkansas* (St. Louis, Mo.: Slawson Printing Co., 1893); Joe Gray Taylor, *Louisiana Reconstructed, 1863–1877* (Baton Rouge: Louisiana State University Press, 1974), 267–313, 480–505; and Richard Zuczek, *State of Rebellion: Reconstruction in South Carolina* (Columbia: University of South Carolina Press, 1996), 188–205 (Zuczek titles the relevant chapter "The Revolution of '76").

5. Conservatives captured control of the state legislature in 1872 in a campaign marked by some amount of violence. In advance of the gubernatorial election of 1873, they gutted the militia law by refusing appropriations, thus depriving the Republican governor of a force to protect Republican voters (or intimidate Democratic ones, depending on the politics of the observer). More important, they provided only one day for the election, in apparent contravention of the four-day requirement imposed by the state constitution. Consequently, the defeated Republicans refused to concede the legitimacy of the election and prepared to resist the claims of the Conservative governor-elect by both force and law. They conceded defeat when President Ulysses S. Grant refused to send troops to maintain order, in effect refusing to protect the Republican claimants from the superior military force of the Conservatives. Ramsdell, *Reconstruction in Texas*, 313–17; John L. Waller, *Colossal Hamilton of Texas: A Biography of Andrew Jackson Hamilton, Militant Unionist and Reconstruction Governor* (El Paso: Texas Western Press, 1968), 136–39.

6. The historian of Mississippi Reconstruction entitled his chapter on the transfer of power "Revolution." William C. Harris, *The Day of the Carpetbagger: Republican Reconstruction in Mississippi* (Baton Rouge: Louisiana State University Press, 1979), 650–90. See also Harry P. Owens, "Notes and Documents—The Eufaula Riot of 1874," *Alabama Review* 16 (July 1963): 224–37; Melinda H. Hennessey, "Reconstruction Politics and the Military: The Eufaula Riot of 1874," *Alabama Historical Quarterly* 38 (Summer 1976): 112–25; Loren Schweringer, *James T. Rapier and Reconstruction* (Chicago: University of Chicago Press, 1978), 133–50; and Walter L. Fleming, *Civil War and Reconstruction in Alabama* (New York: Columbia University Press, 1905), 771–96. In Florida, a campaign preceded by several years of violence led to a disputed result. Both sides contemplated the use of force, but the Conservatives won a court decision in which the

Republicans decided to acquiesce. Jerrell H. Shofner, *Nor Is It Over Yet: Florida in the Era of Reconstruction, 1863–1877* (Gainesville: University of Florida Press, 1973), 225–42, 295–98, 309–39.

7. Elizabeth Studley Nathans, *Losing the Peace: Georgia Republicans and Reconstruction, 1865–1871* (Baton Rouge: Louisiana State University Press, 1968), 127–46; Horace W. Raper, *William W. Holden: North Carolina's Political Enigma* (Chapel Hill: University of North Carolina University Press, 1985), 155–98; Allen W. Trelease, *White Terror: The Ku Klux Klan Conspiracy and Southern Reconstruction* (New York: Harper & Row, 1971), 226–42.

8. Tennessee law disfranchised large numbers of ex-Confederates. The Republican governor, DeWitt Clinton Senter, running for reelection with Conservative support against a rival Republican, secured victory for himself and Conservative control of the state legislature by ordering registrars not to challenge the votes cast by those disfranchised. Thomas B. Alexander, *Political Reconstruction in Tennessee* (Nashville: University of Tennessee Press, 1950), 217–26; James C. Parker, "Tennessee Gubernatorial Elections: I. 1869: The Victory of the Conservatives," *Tennessee Historical Quarterly* 33 (Spring 1974): 34–48.

9. Jack P. Maddex, *The Virginia Conservatives, 1867–1879: A Study in Reconstruction Politics* (Chapel Hill: University of North Carolina Press, 1970), 67–85; Caroline F. Putnam to Benjamin F. Butler, November 14, 1869, in the *National Anti-Slavery Standard*, December 4, 1869; Address of the Republican State Convention, Held in Richmond, Virginia, on the 24th and 25th of November, 1869, *Senate Miscellaneous Document No. 3*, 41 Cong., 2 Sess.; petition from Isaac P. Baldwin et al., January 11, 1870, Senate Judiciary Committee Papers, Record Group 46, National Archives, Washington, D.C.

10. Taylor, *Louisiana Reconstructed*, 304–7.

11. Congress responded after a critical delay by rescinding the state's restoration to normal relations in the Union. The Republican governor's attempt to recover from the disaster by postponing the next scheduled elections divided his own party, and the demoralized and divided Republicans were easily defeated. Nathans, *Losing the Peace*, 147–212.

12. Raper, *Holden*, 199–218.

13. Harris, *Day of the Carpetbagger*, 691–98; Richard N. Current, *Three Carpetbag Governors*, 91–92.

14. Nathans, *Losing the Peace*, 220–22.

15. For examples of the problems raised by partisan returning boards, see William Gillette, *Retreat from Reconstruction, 1869–1879* (Baton Rouge: Louisiana State University Press, 1979), 110–11, 121–23, 315, 324–29; Shofner, *Nor Is It Over Yet*, 285–87, 307–13; and Taylor, *Louisiana Reconstructed*, 241–46, 491–93.

16. Nathans, *Losing the Peace*, 185–89.

17. For the overwhelmingly dominant view of white southerners as historical "bad guys," see Eric Foner's *Reconstruction*, the synthesis of revisionist Reconstruction scholarship. When I first suggested an empathetic (not *sympathetic*, let me make clear) account of conservative white southerners' attitudes toward Reconstruction at one of the symposia on Emancipation and Its Aftermath that LaWanda Cox, Hans Trefousse, Eric Foner, and others organized in New York in the 1970s and 1980s, a colleague (and good friend) got laughs by ostentatiously sliding his chair several feet away from mine.

18. Zebulon B. Vance, "Reconstruction in North Carolina," in *Why the Solid South? or, Reconstruction and Its Results*, ed. Hilary A. Herbert et al. (Baltimore, Md.: R. H. Woodward, 1890), 70.

19. James A. Renshaw, "Liberty Monument," *Louisiana Historical Quarterly* 3 (1920): 259–78.

20. It was restored to a less prominent position in 1993. For insight, see Sanford Levinson, "Silencing the Past: Public Monuments and the Tutelary State," *Report from*

the Institute for Philosophy and Public Policy 16 (Summer/Fall 1996): 6–11; David Wasserman, "Commemoration and Renewal," ibid., 12–13.

21. Henry Winter Davis, "Lessons of the War," in Davis, *Speeches and Addresses Delivered in the Congress of the United States, and on Several Public Occasions* (New York: Harper Brothers, 1867), 580.

22. George S. Boutwell, "Reconstruction: Its True Basis," in Boutwell, *Speeches and Papers Relating to the Rebellion and the Overthrow of Slavery*, 2 vols. (Boston: McClure, Phillips, and Co., 1867), 2:406. I have reversed the order of the sentences.

23. For a fuller discussion of this point, see Michael Les Benedict, "Preserving the Constitution: The Conservative Basis of Radical Reconstruction," *Journal of American History* 61 (June 1974): 65–90, revised and republished in this volume.

24. *Congressional Globe*, 39 Cong., 1 Sess., 74 (December 18, 1865).

25. George W. Julian, "Dangers and Duties of the Hour—Reconstruction and Suffrage," in Julian, *Speeches on Political Questions* (New York: Riverside Press, 1872), 269–70.

26. George W. Julian, *Political Recollections, 1840–1872* (Chicago: Jansen, McClurg and Co., 1884), 306. See Michael Les Benedict, *A Compromise of Principle: Congressional Republicans and Reconstruction, 1863–1869* (New York: Norton, 1974), 137.

27. John A. Bingham, in the *Congressional Globe*, 39 Cong., 2 Sess., 1211 (February 13, 1867). The conservative Republican Senate majority leader, William Pitt Fessenden, also tried to abort any Reconstruction measure spelling out how southerners must proceed. Benedict, *A Compromise of Principle*, 237–38.

28. Benedict, "Preserving the Constitution," 82–83.

29. Of course, the most apparent problem is that in the Lockean system all individuals must agree to enter into society; it is difficult to justify the ability of the majority to impose its will on those who refuse. The southern use of conventions to legitimize secession led to a reaction in the North against the view that they represented the organic people. But the more limited, legalistic view of conventions was fully articulated only in 1867, with the appearance of John A. Jameson's *The Constitutional Convention: Its History, Powers, and Mode of Proceeding* (New York: Charles Scribner, 1867). See Harold M. Hyman, *A More Perfect Union: The Impact of the Civil War and Reconstruction upon the Constitution* (New York: Knopf, 1973), 41–49, 119–23.

30. Reconstruction Act, *U.S. Statutes at Large* 14 (1867): 428–29; Supplementary Reconstruction Act, *U.S. Statutes at Large* 15 (1867): 14–16.

31. The calculations on which William A. Russ based his conclusion that huge numbers of southerners were disfranchised are seriously deficient, in that they ignore the casualties inflicted by the war and attribute failure to register to vote during Reconstruction entirely to disfranchisement. Russ, "Registration and Disfranchisement under Radical Reconstruction," *Mississippi Valley Historical Review* 21 (September 1934): 163–80. Nonetheless, it is clear that many tens of thousands were ineligible to vote under the Reconstruction Acts. Gen. Edward R. S. Canby, commander of the second military district under the acts, estimated totals of 11,686 whites ineligible to vote in North Carolina and 8,244 in South Carolina, respectively 9 percent and 14 percent of the white electorate early in 1867. Registered Voters in Rebel States, *Senate Executive Document No. 53*, 42 Cong., 2 Sess., 3–7. The army estimated that 10,500 Georgians were disfranchised, about 9 percent of the electorate. Ibid., 8.

32. One cannot tell the effect simply by seeing whether constitutions were ratified by a larger majority than the number disfranchised. The fact of disfranchisement may have affected strategy and élan in ways that multiplied its effect.

33. Benedict, *A Compromise of Principle*, 315–20.

34. Resolutions of Alabama Conservatives, as quoted in *Appleton's Annual Cyclopedia*, 1868, 15.

35. William M. Fishback, "Reconstruction in Arkansas," in *Why the Solid South?*, 297.

36. Michael Perman, *Reunion Without Compromise: The South and Reconstruction, 1865–1868* (New York: Cambridge University Press, 1973), 304–48.

37. Edward McPherson, *Political History of the United States of America during the Period of Reconstruction*, 2d ed. (Washington, D.C.: Solomons and Chapman, 1875), 374.

38. Donald W. Davis, "Ratification of the Constitution of 1868—Record of the Votes," *Louisiana History* 6 (Summer 1965): 301–5.

39. William M. Cash, "Alabama Republicans During Reconstruction: Personal Characteristics, Motivations, and Political Activity of Party Activists, 1867–1880" (Ph.D. dissertation, University of Alabama, 1973), 102.

40. Margaret Davidson Sizemore, "Frederick G. Bromberg of Mobile: An Illustrious Character, 1837–1928," *Alabama Review* 29 (April 1976): 111.

41. Vance, "Reconstruction in North Carolina," 77.

42. Harold M. Hyman and William M. Wiecek discuss constitutional trends in the nation in *Equal Justice Under Law: Constitutional Development, 1835–1875* (New York: Harper & Row, 1982), 356–57. Harris has recorded a similar judgment on the Mississippi Constitution. Harris, *Day of the Carpetbagger*, 158–59. The Reconstruction constitutions may be consulted conveniently in *Sources and Documents of United States Constitutions*, ed. William F. Swindler, 10 vols. (Dobbs Ferry, N.Y.: Oceana Publications, 1973–88).

43. As initially proposed, the constitutions of Virginia and Mississippi also included disfranchisement sections, but in deference to Conservative and moderate Republican opposition, national Republicans arranged for those sections to be voted on separately, and they were defeated. Maddex, *The Virginia Conservatives*, 67–85; Harris, *Day of the Carpetbagger*, 199–217, 257.

44. Petition of John A. Winston et al., Petitions and Memorials File, 40th Cong., House of Representatives, Record Group 233, National Archives.

45. As quoted in *Appleton's Annual Cyclopedia*, 1868, 510.

46. For a fuller discussion of the following description of laissez-faire constitutionalism, see Michael Les Benedict, "Laissez-Faire and Liberty: A Re-Evaluation of the Origins of Laissez-Faire Constitutionalism," *Law and History Review* 3 (Fall 1985): 293–331. For the way laissez-faire ideas were incorporated into American constitutional law, see Howard Gillman, *The Constitution Besieged: The Rise and Decline of Lochner-Era Police Powers Jurisprudence* (Durham, N.C.: Duke University Press, 1993).

47. Vernon L. Parrington, *Main Currents in American Thought*, 3 vols. (New York: Harcourt, Brace, 1927–30), 1:359.

48. Philip N. Nicholas, in *Proceedings and Debates of the Virginia State Convention of 1829–30* (Richmond, Va.: S. Shepherd and Co., 1830), 367.

49. Jack R. Pole, *Political Representation in England and the Origins of the American Republic* (New York: St. Martin's, 1966), 31; Jack P. Greene, "'Slavery or Independence': Some Reflections on the Relationship Among Liberty, Black Bondage, and Equality in Revolutionary South Carolina," *South Carolina Historical Magazine* 80 (July 1979): 207; Edmund S. Morgan, "Slavery and Freedom: The American Paradox," *Journal of American History* 59 (June 1972): 5–29; Dickson D. Bruce, Jr., *The Rhetoric of Conservatism: The Virginia Convention of 1829–30 and the Conservative Tradition in the South* (San Marino, Calif.: Huntington Library, 1982), 75–76; Chilton Williamson, "American Suffrage and Sir William Blackstone," *Political Science Quarterly* 68 (December 1953): 552–57.

50. Benedict, "Laissez-Faire and Liberty," 306–7; Michael E. McGerr, *The Decline of Popular Politics: The American North, 1865–1928* (New York: Oxford University Press, 1986), 48.

51. Kirk H. Porter, *A History of Suffrage in the United States* (Chicago: University of Chicago Press, 1918), 62–111.
52. *Congressional Globe*, 39 Cong., 2 Sess., 83 (December 12, 1866).
53. Durbin Ward, "Against the Fifteenth Amendment," in Ward, *Life, Speeches and Orations of Durbin Ward* (Columbus, Ohio: A. H. Smith, 1888), 166.
54. Oliver Otis Howard, *Report of the . . . Commissioner Bureau of Refugees, Freedmen, and Abandoned Lands to the Secretary of War, Oct. 20, 1869* (Washington, D.C.: U.S. Government Printing Office, 1869), 13.
55. Thaddeus Stevens, in the *Congressional Globe*, 39 Cong., 1 Sess., 74 (December 18, 1865); George W. Julian, "Dangers and Duties of the Hour—Reconstruction and Suffrage," in Julian, *Political Speeches*, 268–69.
56. Juhl [Julius J. Fleming], in the *Charleston (S.C.) News and Courier*, July 22, 1865, reprinted in *The Juhl Letters to the Charleston Courier: A View of the South, 1865–1871*, ed. John Hammond Moore (Athens: University of Georgia Press, 1974), 22.
57. James L. Kemper, *Letter from Governor Kemper on the Petersburg Charter* (Richmond, Va.: n.p., 1874), 2.
58. William Henry Trescot to Wilson, September 8, 1867, in Gaillard Hunt, "Letter of William Henry Trescot," *American Historical Review* 15 (April 1910): 579.
59. E. A. Trescot to William Henry Trescot, April 7, 1867, typescript, William Henry Trescot Papers, Caroliniana Library, University of South Carolina, Columbia.
60. James M. Willcox to Susannah Willcox, July 20, 1868, J. M. Willcox Papers, Perkins Library, Duke University, Durham, N.C.
61. *A Compilation of Messages and Papers of the Presidents of the United States*, ed. James D. Richardson, 10 vols. (Washington, D.C.: Government Printing Office, 1896–99), 6:478, 566.
62. Kemper, *Letter on the Petersburg Charter*, 3.
63. Michael Perman, *The Road to Redemption: Southern Politics, 1869–1879* (Chapel Hill: University of North Carolina Press, 1984).
64. Remonstrance of South Carolina Democrats, as quoted in *Appleton's Annual Cyclopedia*, 1868, 697.
65. As quoted in the *New York Times*, August 9, 1867.
66. Gathright illustrated his charge with the example of schools in Noxumbee County, where it would cost $40,000 to build schoolhouses, "and not twenty-five white children in that county can be benefited, while the colored Population pays almost no part of this tax." *Hinds County Gazette*, October 12, 1870, as quoted in Stuart Grayson Noble, *Forty Years of the Public Schools in Mississippi* (New York: Columbia University Press, 1918), 14.
67. Remonstrance of South Carolina Democrats, as quoted in *Appleton's Annual Cyclopedia*, 1868, 697. I have reversed the order of the sentences.
68. *Jackson Daily Clarion*, November 4, 1869; ibid., May 19, 1868.
69. "Memorial of the Citizens of Louisiana," Senate Judiciary Committee Papers, 40th Cong., Record Group 46, National Archives.
70. *Montgomery Advertiser*, January 7, 1868.
71. William C. Hines, "Frustration, Factionalism, and Failure: Black Political Leadership and the Republican Party in Reconstruction Charleston, 1865–1877" (Ph.D. dissertation, Kent State University, 1979), 185.
72. Lawrence N. Powell, "The Politics of Livelihood: Carpetbaggers in the Deep South," in *Region, Race, and Reconstruction: Essays in Honor of C. Vann Woodward*, ed. J. Morgan Kousser and James M. McPherson (New York: Oxford University Press, 1982), 315–47; Mark W. Summers, *Railroads, Reconstruction, and the Gospel of Prosperity: Aid Under the Radical Republicans, 1865–1877* (Princeton, N.J.: Princeton University Press, 1984), 126–28.

73. *Jackson Weekly Clarion*, June 2, 1870; ibid., November 23, 1871.

74. We badly need a sophisticated study of fiscal policy and management in the Reconstruction South. Traditional accounts rely on what may be doctored Conservative and Democratic accounts, stress increased property taxes without noting that taxes on slave property had been eliminated, do not try to adjust tax rates for low tax assessments or payment in depreciated state scrip and bonds, and fail to take into account a host of other factors. One can find the traditional horror story of debt and high taxation recounted in the Dunningite studies cited in note 4 and in C. Mildred Thompson, *Reconstruction in Georgia: Economic, Social, Political, 1865–72* (New York: Columbia University Press, 1915), 207–34; and Simpkins and Woody, *South Carolina During Reconstruction*, 175–79. Revisionist histories have been more sympathetic, but they still chronicle a rather dismal tale. See Harris, *Day of the Carpetbagger*, 295–300; Taylor, *Louisiana Reconstructed*, 187–208, 265–67; Summers, *Railroads, Reconstruction, and the Gospel of Prosperity*, esp. 158–59, 196–208, 280–85; and J. Mills Thornton, "Fiscal Policy and the Failure of Reconstruction in the Lower South," in *Region, Race, and Reconstruction*, 349–94.

75. Horace Greeley, *Mr. Greeley's Letters from Texas and the Lower Mississippi; Address to the Farmers of Texas, and His Speech on His Return to New York, June 12, 1871* (New York: Tribune Office, 1871), 51.

76. Thornton, "Fiscal Policy and the Failure of Reconstruction," 351.

77. Harris, *Day of the Carpetbagger*, 299.

78. *Report of the Auditor of the State of Alabama for . . . 1873* (Montgomery, Ala.: J.G. Stokes, 1873), 108–9.

79. William Pitt Kellogg, *Annual Message of His Excellency, Wm. Pitt Kellogg, to the General Assembly of Louisiana, Session of 1874* (New Orleans: Republican Office, 1874). Thornton reports that interest payments equaled 22 percent of South Carolina's disbursements in 1876 and 32 percent of Florida's. Thornton, "Fiscal Policy and the Failure of Reconstruction," 384.

80. Carl H. Moneyhon, *Texas After the Civil War: The Struggle of Reconstruction* (College Station: Texas A&M University Press, 2004), 152–53.

81. Thornton, "Fiscal Policy and the Failure of Reconstruction," 382–85.

82. Edward King, "The Great South: The South Carolina Problem," *Scribner's Monthly* 8 (June 1874): 139.

83. W. W. Boyce to Schurz, May 8, 1874, Schurz Papers, LC.

84. *Alexandria Caucasian*, August 1, 1874.

85. *Natchez Democrat*, January 15, 1875, as quoted in Harris, *Day of the Carpetbagger*, 645.

86. *Jackson Weekly Clarion*, March 11, 1875.

87. For example, Gillette, *Retreat from Reconstruction*, 190–96, 197–279; Robert F. Durden, *James Shepard Pike: Republicanism and the American Negro, 1850–1882* (Durham, N.C.: Duke University Press, 1957); and Patrick W. Riddleburger, "The Break in the Radical Ranks: Liberals vs. Stalwarts in the Election of 1872," *Journal of Negro History* 44 (April 1959): 136–57.

88. Richardson, *The Death of Reconstruction: Race, Labor, and Politics in the Post–Civil War North, 1865–1901* (Cambridge, Mass.: Harvard University Press, 2001), 83–121.

89. Francis Parkman, "The Failure of Universal Suffrage," *North American Review* 127 (July–August 1878): 20; J. Francis Fisher, as quoted in Simon Sterne, *On Representative Government and Personal Reputation* (Philadelphia: J. B. Lippincott, 1871), 74; Simon Sterne, *Suffrage in Cities* (New York: G. P. Putnam's Sons, 1878), 26. See Benedict, "Laissez-Faire and Liberty," 306–7; and McGerr, *The Decline of Popular Politics*, 45–50.

90. *New York Times*, May 8, 1876.

91. *Nation*, December 7, 1871; "Socialism in South Carolina," ibid., April 16, 1874.

92. Benjamin F. Butler, *The Negro in Politics: Review of the Recent Legislation for His Protection* . . . (Lowell, Mass.: Marden & Rowell, 1871), 11.

93. *Beauregard and Wesson (Miss.) Times*, September 3, 1874, as quoted in Harris, *Day of the Carpetbagger*, 637–38.

94. S. R. Cockrill to Andrew Johnson, January 9, 1868, Johnson Papers, LC. (emphasis added).

95. Benjamin F. Perry, "Gov. Perry's Address to his Constituency," in Perry, *Biographical Sketches of Eminent American Statesmen with Speeches, Addresses and Letters* (Philadelphia: Free Press, 1887), 214.

96. George W. Blount to Matthew W. Ransom, August 8, 1874, Ranson Papers, Southern Historical Collection, University of North Carolina, Chapel Hill.

97. William Y. Thompson, *Robert Toombs of Georgia* (Baton Rouge: Louisiana State University Press, 1966), 242.

98. S. B. French to Samuel J. Tilden, November 21, 1875, Tilden Papers, New York Public Library.

99. For a discussion of the Redeemer constitutions, see Perman, *The Road to Redemption*, 193–220. The constitutions themselves may be found in Swindler, *Sources and Documents*. For northern constitutions in the 1870s and 1880s, see Hyman and Wiecek, *Equal Justice Under Law*, 356–57; and Morton Keller, *Affairs of State: Public Life in Late Nineteenth Century America* (Cambridge, Mass.: Harvard University Press, 1977), 319–20.

9. Reform Republicans and the Retreat from Reconstruction

1. Eric Foner, *Reconstruction: America's Unfinished Revolution* (New York: Harper & Row, 1988).

2. William Gillette, *Retreat from Reconstruction, 1869–1879* (Baton Rouge: Louisiana State University Press, 1979); Heather Cox Richardson, *The Death of Reconstruction: Race, Labor, and Politics in the Post–Civil War North, 1865–1901* (Cambridge, Mass.: Harvard University Press, 2001). The last prior books on post-1868 national Reconstruction policy were volumes 6 and 7 of John Ford Rhodes's majestic *The History of the United States from the Compromise of 1850 to the Final Restoration of Home Rule at the South in 1877* (New York: Macmillan, 1906).

3. For an overview of historians' assessments of southern Republicans, see Carl H. Moneyhon, "The Failure of Southern Republicanism, 1867–1876," in *The Facts of Reconstruction: Essays in Honor of John Hope Franklin*, ed. Eric Anderson and Alfred A. Moss, Jr. (Baton Rouge: Louisiana State University Press, 1991), 99–119. For the role of white southern violence, see Michael Perman, "Counter Reconstruction: The Role of Violence in Southern Redemption," ibid., 121–40. Perman's *The Road to Redemption: Southern Politics, 1869–1879* (Chapel Hill: University of North Carolina Press, 1984) remains the standard account of the failure of Reconstruction in the South.

4. David Donald et al., *The Civil War and Reconstruction*, 3d ed. (New York: Norton, 2001), 619; James McPherson, *Ordeal by Fire: The Civil War and Reconstruction*, 2 ed. (New York: Knopf, 1992), 545–47, 560–65; David W. Blight, *Race and Reunion: The Civil War in American Memory* (Cambridge, Mass.: Harvard University Press, 2001), 122–28; Foner, *Reconstruction*, 488–99; Patrick W. Riddleberger, "The Radicals' Abandonment of the Negro During Reconstruction," *Journal of Negro History* 45 (April 1960): 88–102; Hans L. Trefousse, *Radical Republicans: Lincoln's Vanguard for Racial Justice* (New York: Knopf, 1969), 454–63.

5. Eric Foner, *Politics and Ideology in the Age of the Civil War* (New York: Oxford University Press, 1980), 125–27, 144; Foner, *Reconstruction*, 475–84, 512–24, 582–87. See

W. E. Burghardt Du Bois, *Black Reconstruction: An Essay Toward a History of the Part which Black Folk Played in the Attempt to Reconstruct Democracy in America, 1860–1880* (New York: Russell & Russell, 1935); David Montgomery, *Beyond Equality: Labor and the Radical Republicans, 1862–1872* (New York, 1967).

6. Richardson, *The Death of Reconstruction*; Nancy Cohen, *The Reconstruction of American Liberalism, 1865–1914* (Chapel Hill: University of North Carolina Press, 2002), 61–85.

7. Cohen, *The Reconstruction of American Liberalism*, 29–30.

8. Cohen's *Reconstruction of American Liberalism* bids well to become the standard account of these elite reformers' ideas, but John G. Sproat's *"The Best Men": Liberal Reformers in the Gilded Age* (New York: Oxford University Press, 1968) remains the best account of their activities. For an excellent discussion of their attitudes toward and impact on the political process, see Michael E. McGerr, *The Decline of Popular Politics: The American North, 1865–1928* (New York: Oxford University Press, 1986), 42–68. Their role in Gilded Age politics is also discussed in H. Wayne Morgan, *From Hayes to McKinley: National Party Politics, 1877–1896* (Syracuse, N.Y.: Syracuse University Press, 1969). Matthew Thomas Downey offers an excellent assessment of their ideas in "The Rebirth of Reform: A Study of Liberal Reform Movements, 1865–1871" (Ph.D. dissertation, Princeton University, 1963).

9. George M. Fredrickson, *The Inner Civil War: Northern Intellectuals and the Crisis of the Union* (New York: Harper & Row, 1965), 113–29; Cohen, *Reconstruction of American Liberalism*, 23–29, 61–68. Sproat, in his influential study of the reformers, stresses too much their "moderation" during Reconstruction. In the war years and the early years of Reconstruction, the reformers generally took more radical positions than moderate leaders in the Republican Party.

10. Ibid., 200–201; Sproat, *The Best Men*, 29–44; William Gillette, *Retreat from Reconstruction*, 366–68; Riddleberger, "Radical Abandonment of the Negro During Reconstruction"; Robert F. Durden, *James Shepherd Pike: Republicanism and the American Negro, 1850–1882* (Durham, N.C.: Duke University Press, 1957). Among recent analysts, Richardson describes the construction of "the un-American Negro." Richardson, *The Death of Reconstruction*, 183–224. Cohen refers to a "new insidious racism . . . gaining influence among those who had once advocated Radical Reconstruction." Cohen, *The Reconstruction of American Liberalism*, 77.

11. Garfield to D. G. Swain, July 26, 1865, Garfield-Swain Letters, Western Reserve Historical Society, Cleveland, Ohio; Cameron in the *Congressional Globe*, 41 Cong., 2 Sess., 1544 (February 24, 1870).

12. Ibid., 38 Cong., 1 Sess., 133 (January 7, 1864). I have reversed the phrases. Stevens, among the most radical of Republicans, had also conceded, "I do not know that ever shall I come across men of dark color of the same intelligence as white men," although he added that "I have seen some that I thought not much inferior to most of us."

13. Ignatius Donnelly Diary, January 14, 1866, Donnelly Papers, Minnesota Historical Society, St. Paul; *Sacramento Union*, March 6, 1863. See also Schuyler Colfax ("I never believed in negro equality. . . . But God forgive me if . . . I would endeavor to grind down lower the oppressed race."), quoted in the *Boston Evening Transcript*, November 8, 1866; Thomas T. Davis in the *Congressional Globe*, 38 Cong., 2 Sess., 155 (January 7, 1865); John F. Farnsworth, ibid., 1 Sess., 2979 (June 15, 1864); Timothy Otis Howe, ibid., 39 Cong., 1 Sess., 438 (January 26, 1866); *Leslie's Illustrated Newspaper*, December 25, 1869. Hans L. Trefousse, "Ben Wade and the Negro," *Ohio Historical Quarterly* 58 (April 1959): 161–76. As the *New York Tribune* put it, "Human rights do not depend on the equality of Man or Races, but are wholly independent of them." *New York Tribune*, October 6, 1862.

14. Charles Francis Adams, Jr., *Charles Francis Adams, 1835–1915: An Autobiography* (Boston: Houghton Mifflin, 1916), 179. For the worship of science and the growth of the notion of social science, see Luther L. Bernard and Jessie Bernard, *Origins of American Sociology: The Social Science Movement in the United States* (New York: Thomas Y. Crowell, 1943), esp. 45–55, 461–523; Fredrickson, *The Inner Civil War*, 199–277; Thomas L. Haskell, *The Emergence of Professional Social Science: The American Social Science Association and the Nineteenth-Century Crisis of Authority* (Urbana: University of Illinois Press, 1977), 65–90; William E. Nelson, *The Roots of American Bureaucracy, 1830–1900* (Cambridge Mass.: Harvard University Press, 1981), 80–111; Dorothy Ross, *The Origins of American Social Science* (New York: Cambridge University Press, 1991), 53–64 .

15. Amasa Walker, *The Science of Wealth*, 7th ed. (Boston: Little, Brown, 1874), 3–4, originally published in 1866; Gamaliel Bradford, "The Treasury Reports," *North American Review* 110 (January 1870): 109. See also Richard T. Ely, *Ground Under Our Feet: An Autobiography* (New York: Macmillan, 1938), 58; Sproat, *The Best Men*, 141–68.

16. Sidney Fine, *Laissez Faire and the General Welfare State: A Study of Conflict in American Thought, 1865–1901* (Ann Arbor: University of Michigan Press, 1956), 123.

17. Rollo Ogden, *Life and Letters of Edwin Lawrence Godkin*, 2 vols. (New York: Macmillan, 1907), 1:11. See also Edwin L. Godkin, "The Economic Man," in Godkin, *Problems of Modern Democracy: Political and Economic Essays of Edwin Lawrence Godkin*, ed. Morton Keller (Cambridge, Mass.: Harvard University Press, 1966), 156–79, originally published in the *North American Review* in 1891.

18. Simon Newcomb, "The Let-Alone Principle," *North American Review* 110 (January 1807): 1–33.

19. Fine, *Laissez Faire and the General Welfare State*, 65; Arthur Latham Perry, *Elements of Political Economy*, 5th ed. (New York: Charles Scribner, 1870), 80–81.

20. Godkin quoted in Irwin Unger, *The Greenback Era: A Social and Political History of American Finance, 1865–1879* (Princeton, N.J.: Princeton University Press, 1964), 121. Despite his scientism, E. L. Godkin's biographers agree that his judgments on public issues were always based primarily upon his moral values. Edward C. Kirkland, *Business in the Gilded Age: The Conservatives' Balance Sheet* (Madison: University of Wisconsin Press, 1952), 29–33; Morton Keller, introduction to Godkin, *Problems of Modern Democracy*, xxix. See R. Jackson Wilson, *In Quest of Community: Social Philosophy in the United States, 1860–1920* (New York: Wiley, 1968), 39–40, for a similar judgment.

21. Francis Parkman, "The Failure of Universal Suffrage," *North American Review* 126 (July–August 1878): 1–20; William Graham Sumner, "State Interference," in *Essays of William Graham Sumner*, ed. Albert G. Keller and Maurice R. Davie, 2 vols. (New Haven, Conn.: Yale University Press, 1934), 2:138–40; Michael Les Benedict, "Laissez Faire and Liberty: A Re-Evaluation of the Meaning and Origins of Laissez-Faire Constitutionalism," *Law and History Review* 3 (Fall 1985): 293–331. Read in this light Sproat, *The Best Men*, 205–42.

22. This was the way the publishers distilled David A. Wells's tract *The Creed of Free Trade* on the pamphlet's cover.

23. Edward Atkinson, "The Inefficiency of Economic Legislation," *Journal of Social Science* 4 (March 1871): 114; Edward Atkinson, *Revenue Reform: An Essay* (Boston: James R. Osgood and Co., 1871), 18.

24. William Graham Sumner, *What Social Classes Owe Each Other* (New Haven: Yale University Press, 1925 [1883]), 11–12; Sumner, "State Interference," in *Essays of William Graham Sumner*, 2: 145–46.

25. Abram S. Hewitt, *Selected Writings of Abram S. Hewitt*, ed. Allan Nevins (New York: Columbia University Press, 1910), 277. Hewitt, like Sumner, was a lifelong Democrat. But he clearly shared reformers' beliefs and attitudes, working for the supremacy of these in the Democratic Party as most reformers did in the Republican. See Allan

Nevins, *Abram S. Hewitt: With Some Account of Peter Cooper* (New York: Harper and Brothers, 1935).

26. Charles Loring Brace, *The Dangerous Classes of New York, and Twenty Years' Work Among Them* (New York: Wynkoop & Hallenbeck, 1872); Simon Sterne, *Suffrage in Cities* (New York: G. P. Putnam's Sons, 1878), 13. See also Parkman, "Failure of Universal Suffrage," 20. Sproat does not discuss the relationship that reformers perceived between urban corruption and threats to liberty, but he describes well their general attitude toward city-dwelling immigrants in *The Best Men*, 250–57. Cohen notes that reformers saw cities as repositories of "the largest body of ill-suited voters," but does not discuss their concerns over urban corruption generally. Cohen, *The Reconstruction of American Liberalism*, 135. See also Downey, "Rebirth of Reform," 113–16.

27. *Nation*, April 9, 1874. See also "The Butler Canvass," *North American Review* 114 (January 1871): 147–70.

28. E. L. Godkin to Charles Eliot Norton, April 13, 1865, in *The Gilded-Age Letters of E. L. Godkin*, ed. William N. Armstrong (Albany, N.Y.: University of New York Press, 1974), 27; Frances Lieber, *Notes on Fallacies Peculiar to American Protectionists*, 4th ed. (New York: American Free Trade League, 1870), 39. See also Benjamin Pierce, "The National Importance of Social Sciences in the United States," *Journal of Social Science* 12 (1880): xii.

29. *Nation*, February 20, 1870; George L. Prentiss, *Our National Bane; or, The Dry Rot in American Politics: A Tract for the Times Touching Civil Service Reform* (New York: D. F. Randolph, 1877), 2. For an insightful assessment of the relationship between the "liberal reform" movement of the 1870s and the era's new, scientific theory of knowledge, see Downey, "Rebirth of Reform," 98–112.

30. Henry Adams to John Gorham Palfrey, February 19, 1869, Palfrey Papers, Houghton Library, Harvard University; Charles Francis Adams Jr., "The Protection of the Ballot in National Elections," *Journal of Social Science* 1 (1869): 91.

31. Henry Adams to Palfrey, February 19, 1869, Palfrey Papers; James Russell Lowell, "A Look Before and After," *North American Review* 108 (January 1869): 259–60 (I have reversed the order of the sentences). See also E. L. Godkin, "Legislation and Social Sciences" *Journal of Social Science* 3 (1871): 115–32. The liberal reformers' elitism is implicit throughout Sproat and Cohen's exegesis of their ideas in *The Best Men* and *The Reconstruction of American Liberalism*, respectively.

32. James Russell Lowell to Joel Benton, January 19, 1876, in *Letters of James Russell Lowell*, ed. Charles Eliot Norton (Cambridge, Mass.: Harvard University Press, 1904), 377–78. This was a common refrain. See also Henry Adams to Palfrey, February 19, 1869, Palfrey Papers; Charles Francis Adams Jr., "The Protection of the Ballot in National Elections," 91–92; William Graham Sumner, "The Challenge of Facts," in *Essays of William Graham Sumner*, 2:119–20; William Graham Sumner, "Politics in America, 1776–1876," *North American Review* 122 (January 1876): 87.

33. Edward Atkinson to David A. Wells, July 17, 1871, David A. Wells Papers, Library of Congress (hereafter LC); Ari Hoogenboom, *Outlawing the Spoils: A History of the Civil Service Reform Movement, 1865–1883* (Urbana: University of Illinois Press, 1961), 11, 51–52, 62–63; Hoogenboom, "Civil Service Reform and Public Morality," in *The Gilded Age*, ed. H. Wayne Morgan (Syracuse, N.Y.: Syracuse University Press, 1970), 77–95; Downey, "Rebirth of Reform," 117–21.

34. Julian M. Sturtevant, *Economics; or, The Science of Wealth* (New York: G. P. Putman's Sons, 1877), 69–75; Francis Bowen, *American Political Economy* (New York: Scribner, 1870), 157–72; Perry, *Elements of Political Economy*, 34–35, 209–35. See also Walter T. K. Nugent, *The Money Question During Reconstruction* (New York: Norton, 1967), 52–58; Unger, *The Greenback Era*, 117–19.

35. John Murray Forbes to Carl Schurz, January 23, 1874, Carl Schurz Papers, LC; Bowen, *American Political Economy*, 315–45; Walker, *Science of Wealth*, 114–213; Sturtevant, *Economics*, 89–90, 96–97; Perry, *Elements of Political Economy*, 248–59; Nugent, *The Money Question During Reconstruction*, 51–58.

36. Bowen, *American Political Economy*, 341.

37. Francis O. French to Elihu B. Washburne, December 31, 1877, Elihu B. Washburne Papers, LC. The letters and writings of the liberal reformers were replete with such moralistic phrases. See, for example, Charles Francis Adams Jr., "The Currency Debate of 1873–1874," *North American Review* 119 (July 1874): 115–16; "The Legal Tender Decision," *Nation*, February 17, 1870; Carl Schurz, "Honest Money," in *Speeches, Correspondence, and Political Papers of Carl Schurz*, ed. Frederic Bancroft, 6 vols. (New York: G. P. Putnam's Sons, 1913), 3:161–214; and Amasa Walker, "Governmental Interference with the Standard of Value," *Bankers' Magazine* 3 (April 1867): 738.

38. John Hay to Whitelaw Reid, September 24, 1875, quoted in William Roscoe Thayer, *The Life and Letters of John Hay*, 2 vols. (Boston: Houghton, Mifflin, 1915), 1:416.

39. Unger, *The Greenback Era*, 81–83, 121–23; Walter T. K. Nugent, *Money and American Society, 1865–1880* (New York: Free Press, 1968), 106–9; Chester McArthur Destler, *American Radicalism, 1865–1901: Essays and Documents* (New York: Octagon Books, 1965), 31–49; Robert P. Sharkey, *Money, Class, and Party: An Economic Study of Civil War and Reconstruction* (Baltimore: Johns Hopkins University Press, 1959), 99–107, 168–69.

40. Sturtevant, *Economics*, 118; Bowen, *American Political Economy*, 480–95; Perry, *Political Economy*, 347–63.

41. Atkinson, *Revenue Reform*, 10. See also Perry, *Political Economy*, 85, 280; Sturtevant, *Economics*, 83; Abraham L. Earle, *Our Revenue System and the Civil Service: Shall They Be Reformed?* 6th ed. (New York: G. P. Putnam's Sons, 1878; orig. pub. 1871); David A. Wells, "The Meaning of Revenue Reform," *North American Review* 113 (July 1871): 145, 148; William Graham Sumner, *Protection and Revenue in 1877: A Lecture Delivered Before the New York Free Trade Club, April 18, 1878* (New York: G. P. Putnam's Sons, 1878), 7; William Graham Sumner, "What Is Free Trade?" in *Essays of William Graham Sumner*, 2:393; James Russell Lowell, "The Place of the Independent in Politics," in *Complete Writings of James Russell Lowell*, vol. 6: *Literary and Political Addresses* (Boston: Houghton, Mifflin, 1886), 217.

42. *Nation*, February 10, 1870.

43. Godkin to Norton, April 13, 1865, in *Gilded-Age Letters of E. L. Godkin*, 27; *Nation*, November 14, 1867; William Graham Sumner, "Republican Government," in *Essays of William Graham Sumner*, 2: 195–96; Sproat, *The Best Men*, 254–55.

44. Henry Reed, "Some Late Efforts at Constitutional Reform," *North American Review* 121 (July 1875): 35; *Nation*, February 10, 1870. William Graham Sumner, the most influential popular American sociologist of the late nineteenth century, consistently warned that efforts to modify the existing social order through legislation risked unforeseen consequences because of unconsidered interaction with general social laws. Appropriately, he named one of his most widely read popular essays "The Absurd Effort to Make the World Over," *Forum* 17 (March 1894): 91–102.

45. *Congressional Globe*, 39 Cong., 2 Sess., 190 (December 19, 1866).

46. Sharkey, *Money, Class, and Party*, 281–83; Montgomery, *Beyond Equality*, 85–89. The relations between Sumner and the reformers may be seen in his correspondence with Edward Atkinson. By April 1868, Atkinson expressed anger at the silence of the New England congressional delegation in the face of the inflationists' pressure, and Sumner answered curtly. Charles Sumner to Edward Atkinson, April 24, 1868, Edward Atkinson Papers, Massachusetts Historical Society, Boston. When Sumner finally came out openly and forcefully for contraction in a major Senate speech, his closest political lieutenant, Edward L. Pierce, wrote him, "You can hardly tell how much easier the work of your

reelection is made by that speech. I was exceedingly anxious to have you make it, and . . . was in great fear that it might not come." Edward L. Pierce to Charles Sumner, July 31, 1868, Charles Sumner Papers, Houghton Library, Harvard University. See David Donald, *Sumner and the Rights of Man* (New York: Knopf, 1970), 346–47. For evidence that there was no ideological connection between radicalism on Reconstruction issues and support for high tariffs and inflation, see Benedict, *A Compromise of Principle*, 40–54.

47. David A. Wells to Edward Atkinson, January 15, 1867, quoted in Herbert Donald Ferleger, *David A. Wells and the American Revenue System, 1861–1870* (New York: Porcupine Press, 1977), 168. See also ibid., 143–75; Stanley Cohen, "Northeastern Business and Radical Reconstruction: A Re-examination," *Mississippi Valley Historical Review* 46 (June 1959): 67–90; Sharkey, *Money, Class, and Party*, 82–88, 107–15.

48. James W. Grimes to Edward Atkinson, September 15, October 14, 1867, Atkinson Papers.

49. David A. Wells to Henry L. Dawes, September 41, 1866, Dawes Papers, LC; David A. Wells to Arthur L. Perry, March 11, 1867, quoted in Ferleger, *Wells*, 181; Benedict, *A Compromise of Principle*, 263.

50. Michael Les Benedict, *The Impeachment and Trial of Andrew Johnson* (New York: Norton, 1973), 66–67, 133–35; Joseph Logsdon, *Horace White, Nineteenth-Century Liberal* (Westport, Conn.: Greenwood, 1971), 151–54.

51. *Boston Advertiser*, June 13, 1867; *Cincinnati Commercial*, June 15, 1867.

52. Lowell, "A Look Before and After," 71; Charles Francis Adams Jr., "Protection of the Ballot," 108–9.

53. *Nation*, October 31, 1867.

54. Edward Atkinson to Hugh McCulloch, August 7, 1867, Hugh McCulloch Papers, LC; *Nation*, July 18, 25, 1867.

55. *Indianapolis Journal*, August 7, 1867; *Nation*, July 18, 1867.

56. Henry Adams to Charles Francis Adams Jr., May 8, 1867, in *Letters of Henry Adams (1858–1891)*, ed. Worthington C. Ford (Boston: Houghton Mifflin, 1930), 128; Horace White to Zachariah Chandler, August 20, 1867, Zachariah Chandler Papers, LC.

57. *Nation*, July 4, 11, 1867; August 1, 15, 1867; September 12, 19, 1867; October 10, 1867; November 14, 1867; *Boston Advertiser*, June 17, 1867.

58. For reformers' political ambitions and desire for appointive office, see Downey, "Rebirth of Reform," 118–11; Geoffrey Blodgett, "Reform Thought and the Genteel Tradition," in *The Gilded Age*, 66; Hoogenboom, "Civil Service Reform and Public Morality," ibid., 77–95; Hoogenboom, *Outlawing the Spoils*, 34–35, 62–63, 77; Edward C. Kirkland, *Charles Francis Adams, Jr., at Bay* (Cambridge, Mass.: Harvard University Press, 1965), 38–41; Samuel Shapiro, *Richard Henry Dana, Jr., 1815–1882* (East Lansing: Michigan State University Press, 1961), 106–63; Ferleger, *Wells*, 220–54.

59. James Russell Lowell to E. L. Godkin, November 5, 1868, quoted in Ogden, *Godkin*, 2: 77; Henry Adams to Charles Francis Adams, Jr., December 9, 1869, quoted in *Letters of Henry Adams*, 1:60; Henry Adams to Charles Milnes Gaskell, December 7, 1869, ibid., 173–74.

60. Ernest Samuels, *Henry Adams: The Major Phase* (Cambridge, Mass.: Harvard University Press, 1964), 193; Amasa Walker to Jacob D. Cox, December 5, 1870, Jacob D. Cox Papers, LC.

61. E. L. Godkin to Charles Eliot Norton, April 13, 1867, quoted in Ogden, *Godkin*, 1: 299–300. One must not be misled by the actual corruption that would be discovered during the Grant administration into thinking that Godkin meant financial peculation at this time. He merely meant the corruption that he thought was inherent in the spoils system and in emphasis on party discipline. For an excellent discussion, see Downey, "Rebirth of Reform," 94–98.

62. Richard Henry Dana to James Russell Lowell, June 12, 1869, quoted in Shapiro, *Dana*, 154; Charles Nordhoff to Carl Schurz, December 21, 1870, in Schurz Papers. See Downey, "Rebirth of Reform," 76–127 for an insightful discussion of the relationship between "reform" and power after the Civil War.

63. *Nation*, August 1, 1867; Andrew D. White, quoted ibid., July 4, 1867.

64. Cohen, *The Reconstruction of American Liberalism*, 111.

65. Edward Atkinson to Hugh McCulloch, May 28, 1867, quoted in Harold Francis Williamson, *Edward Atkinson: The Biography of an American Liberal, 1827–1905* (Boston: Old Corner Book Store, 1934), 81.

66. *Nation*, July 18, 1867.

67. Lowell, "A Look Before and After," 261–66. See also the *New York Times*, November 12, 1868; *Nation*, January 28, 1869.

68. Logsdon, *White*, 119. See also Edward Atkinson to Henry Charles Carey, November 11, 1867, quoted in Williamson, *Atkinson*, 79–80.

69. *Springfield Illinois State Journal*, July 3, 1867; *Springfield Republican*, March 29, 1867; *New York Tribune*, May 20, 28, 1867; *Boston Advertiser*, July 6, 1867; Benedict, *A Compromise of Principle*, 259–60; Paul H. Buck, *The Road to Reunion, 1865–1900* (Boston: Little, Brown, 1937), 90–96, 265–68; McPherson, *Ordeal by Fire*, 563–64, 368–70; Downey, "Rebirth of Reform," 267–71, 364–87, 433–41.

70. *Hinds County Gazette* (Raymond, Miss.), quoted in the *Jackson Weekly Clarion*, June 30, 1873.

71. *Jackson Weekly Clarion*, June 19, November 17, 1871. See also Michael Les Benedict, "The Problem of Constitutionalism and Constitutional Liberty in the Reconstruction South," in *An Uncertain Tradition: Constitutionalism and the History of the South*, ed. Kermit L. Hall and James W. Ely (Athens: University of Georgia Press, 1989), 225–49, revised and republished in this volume.

72. Heather Cox Richardson stresses too much the labor relations aspect of class and race conflict in South Carolina, but nonetheless clearly indicates how white southerners' complaints about "class legislation" resonated with the concerns of northern reformers in her chapter "Black Workers and the South Carolina Government, 1871–1875," in *The Death of Reconstruction*, 83–121.

73. *New York Times*, February 17, 1874.

74. Benedict, *A Compromise of Principle*, 58–69. For a general discussion of nineteenth-century political factionalism and its effect on party positions on issues, see Michael Les Benedict, "Factionalism and Representation: Some Insight from the Nineteenth-Century United States," *Social Science History* 9 (Fall 1985): 361–98, revised and republished in this volume. See also Morton Keller, *Affairs of State: Public Life in Late Nineteenth-Century America* (Cambridge, Mass.: Harvard University Press, 1977), 177–78, Downey, "Rebirth of Reform."

10. Southern Democrats in the Crisis of 1876–77: A Reconsideration of *Reunion and Reaction*

1. Woodward, *Origins of the New South, 1877–1913* (Baton Rouge: Louisiana State University Press, 1951); Woodward, *Tom Watson: Agrarian Rebel* (New York: Macmillan, 1938).

2. Howard K. Beale, *The Critical Year: A Study of Andrew Johnson and Reconstruction* (New York: Frederick Ungar, 1930); Charles A. and Mary R. Beard, *The Rise of American Civilization*, 2 vols. (New York: Macmillan, 1927), 2:98–213; James G. Randall, *The Civil War and Reconstruction* (Boston: D. C. Heath, 1937); William B. Hesseltine, "Economic Factors in the Abandonment of Reconstruction," *Mississippi Valley Historical Review* 22 (September 1935): 191–210.

3. Woodward, *Origins of the New South*, 23–50; Woodward, *Reunion and Reaction: The Compromise of 1877 and the End of Reconstruction* (Boston: Little, Brown, 1951). Woodward carefully clothed his conclusion with caveats, on occasion conceding he was building his case on suppositions (see, for example, *Reunion and Reaction* on Hayes's attitude toward the Texas and Pacific Railroad [117–18] and on Watterson's acceptance of the Electoral Commission Bill [121]) or acknowledging that purely political understandings may have been equal in importance to economic ones (see 117–18, 183), but the total effort clearly left the impression that the Compromise of 1877 was supposed to establish an alliance between sectional representatives of the new business elite.

4. Donald, "Reconstruction," in *Interpreting American History: Conversations with Historians*, ed. John A. Garraty (New York: Macmillan, 1970), 363. Woodward, *Reunion and Reaction*, ix. Paul M. Gaston noted the Beardian origins of *Reunion and Reaction* in "The 'New South,'" in *Writing Southern History: Essays in Historiography in Honor of Fletcher M. Green*, ed. Arthur S. Link and Rembert W. Patrick (Baton Rouge: Louisiana State University Press, 1965), 330, as did Sheldon Hackney, "Origins of the New South in Retrospect," *Journal of Southern History* 38 (May 1972): 196–97.

5. See Jeter A. Iseley's review in the *American Historical Review* 57 (October 1951): 178–79; Arthur E. Kooker in the *Mississippi Valley Historical Review* 38 (March 1952): 717–19. Robert H. Woody was more reserved in his review of *Reunion and Reaction* for the *South Atlantic Quarterly* 52 (January 1953): 129–31, while Dan M. Robison was unconvinced. *Journal of Southern History* 18 (February 1952): 93–95. Allan Peskin found nine leading college history textbooks published in the mid-1960s reflecting Woodward's interpretation. Peskin, "Was There a Compromise of 1877?" *Journal of American History* 40 (June 1973): 64n.

6. Peskin, "Was There a Compromise of 1877?" 63–75; Woodward, "Yes, There Was a Compromise of 1877," *Journal of American History* 60 (June 1973): 215–19; Polakoff, *The Politics of Inertia: The Election of 1876 and the End of Reconstruction* (Baton Rouge: Louisiana State University Press, 1973), 232–314. Woodward's thesis continued to be accepted in contemporary college textbooks, such as Thomas A. Bailey, *The American Pageant: A History of the Republic*, 5th ed. (Lexington, Mass.: D. C. Heath, 1975), 528; Bernard Bailyn et al., *The Great Republic: A History of the American People* (Lexington, Mass.: D. C. Heath, 1977), 811; John M. Blum et al., *The National Experience: A History of the United States*, 4th ed. (New York: Harcourt, Brace, Jovanovich, 1977), 380–83; Richard N. Current et al., *American History: A Survey*, 4th ed. (New York: Knopf, 1974), 442–43; John A. Garraty, *The American Nation: A History of the United States*, 3d ed. (New York: Harper & Row, 1975), 453; Norman A. Graebner et al., *A History of the American People*, 2d ed. (New York: McGraw-Hill, 1975), 444–45; Richard Hofstadter et al., *The United States*, 4th ed. (Englewood Cliffs, N. J.: Prentice-Hall, 1976), 332–33. It was accepted in the leading textbooks and surveys of Reconstruction, such as James G. Randall and David Donald, *The Civil War and Reconstruction* (Lexington, Mass.: D. C. Heath, 1969); Avery O. Craven, *Reconstruction: The Ending of the Civil War* (New York: Holt, Rinehart, and Winston, 1969), 302–4; John Hope Franklin, *Reconstruction: After the Civil War* (Chicago: University of Chicago Press, 1961); Rembert W. Patrick, *The Reconstruction of the Nation* (New York: Oxford University Press, 1967); Kenneth M. Stampp, *The Era of Reconstruction, 1865–1877* (New York: Knopf, 1965); Allen W. Trelease, *Reconstruction: The Great Experiment* (New York: Harper & Row, 1971); Forrest G. Wood, *The Era of Reconstruction, 1863–1877* (New York: Crowell, 1975), as well as Sidney I. Pomerantz's essay "Election of 1876," in *History of American Presidential Elections, 1789–1968*, ed. Arthur M. Schlesinger Jr. and Fred L. Israel, 4 vols. (New York: Chelsea House, 1971), 2:1379–1435. It was incorporated into influential monographic works, such as William W. Rogers, *The One-Callused Rebellion: Agrarianism in Alabama, 1865–1896* (Baton Rouge: Louisiana State University Press, 1970); Jerrell H. Shofner, *Nor Is It Over*

Yet: Florida in the Era of Reconstruction, 1863–1877 (Gainesville: University of Florida Press, 1973); Joe Gray Taylor, *Louisiana Reconstructed, 1863–1877* (Baton Rouge: Louisiana State University Press, 1974); Carl V. Harris, "Right Fork or Left Fork? The Section-Party Alignments of Southern Democrats in Congress, 1873–1897," *Journal of Southern History* 42 (November 1976): 471–506 (challenging Woodward's description of post-1878 southern Democratic behavior but accepting his view of the events of 1876); William C. Harris, *The Day of the Carpetbagger: Republican Reconstruction in Mississippi* (Baton Rouge: Louisiana State University Press, 1979), 548.

Only a few scholars expressed reservations: Joseph F. Wall, *Henry Watterson: Reconstructed Rebel* (New York: Oxford University Press, 1956); Donald, "Reconstruction," 363–64. Thomas B. Alexander expressed surprise to find so few references to economic compromises in the Rutherford B. Hayes papers but did not comment further in his classic "Persistent Whiggery in the Confederate South, 1860–1877," *Journal of Southern History* 27 (August 1961): 324–25.

7. C. Vann Woodward to Michael Les Benedict, February 12, 1979, in the possession of the author.

8. C. Vann Woodward, *Thinking Back: The Perils of Writing History* (Baton Rouge: Louisiana State University Press, 1986), 54. Woodward was the most generous of scholars. We met personally only after my essay appeared, and he was warm and courteous. I was not the only recipient of such generosity of spirit. Howard N. Rabinowitz once mentioned to me that Professor Woodward had helped him professionally in many ways after he had published *Race Relations in the Urban South, 1865–1890* (New York: Oxford University Press, 1978), which had disputed Woodward's conclusion that racial segregation had hardened in the South only in the 1890s.

9. Ibid., 55–57.

10. Surprisingly, Claudine Ferrell, *Reconstruction* (Westport, Conn.: Praeger, 2003), 60–61, seems to reflect most of Woodward's original argument without his later revision. Other surveys and textbooks reflect his revised version. See, for example, David Donald et al., *The Civil War and Reconstruction* (New York: Norton, 2001), 638–39; Michael Fellman et al., *This Terrible War: The Civil War and Its Aftermath* (New York: Longman, 2003), 364–65; Foner, *Reconstruction*, 578, 581; James M. McPherson, *Ordeal by Fire: The Civil War and Reconstruction*, 2d ed. (New York: McGraw-Hill, 1992), 592–93. General American history textbooks likewise have adopted Woodward's revised assessment, sometimes noting scholarly dissent; see Mark H. Carnes and John A. Garraty, *The American Nation: A History of the United States* (New York: Longman, 2003), 441–42; Robert A. Divine et al., *America Past and Present*, 5th ed. (New York: Addison-Wesley, 1999), 505–506; David Goldfield et al., *The American Journey: A History of the United States*, 3d ed. (Upper Saddle River, N.J.: Pearson/Prentice Hall, 2004), 520; John M. Murrin et al., *Liberty, Equality, Power: A History of the American People*, 2d ed. (New York: Harcourt, Brace, 1999), 612–13; Gary B. Nash et al., *The American People: Creating a Nation and a Society*, 6th ed. (New York: Pearson Longman, 2004), 571; Mary Beth Norton et al., *A People and a Nation: A History of the United States*, 5th ed. (Boston: Houghton Mifflin, 1998), 469.

11. Woodward, *Reunion and Reaction*, 22–50, 68–100.

12. Harris, "Right Fork or Left Fork?" See also Irwin Unger, *The Greenback Era: A Social and Political History of American Finance, 1865–1879* (Princeton, N.J.: Princeton University Press, 1964), 340–46; Hannah G. Roach, "Sectionalism in Congress (1870 to 1890)," *American Political Science Review* 19 (August 1925): 520–21; and Terry L. Seip, *The South Returns to Congress: Men, Economic Measures, and Intersectional Relationships, 1868–1879* (Baton Rouge: Louisiana State University Press, 1983), 282–86, 291.

13. Woodward drew upon a wide range of sources that described contacts between southern Democrats and Republicans, as well as general developments during the elec-

toral crisis. But his interpretation of those sources is compelling only in light of the Boynton-Kellar-Smith correspondence, located in the William Henry Smith Papers, William Henry Smith Memorial Library, Indiana Historical Society, Indianapolis—one of only two sources that document the "economic side," as Woodward called it, of the compromise. It will be cited hereafter as the W. H. Smith Papers Ind. A few letters that apparently corroborate the role of the Texas and Pacific lobby are in the General Dodge Letterbooks, Grenville M. Dodge Papers, Iowa State Historical Department, Des Moines, Iowa.

14. Woodward, *Reunion and Reaction*, 28.

15. Woodward interpolated 1870s Democratic factional divisions from Daniel M. Robison's *Bob Taylor and the Agrarian Revolt in Tennessee* (Chapel Hill: University of North Carolina Press, 1935). See Roger L. Hart, *Redeemers, Bourbons, & Populists: Tennessee, 1870–1896* (Baton Rouge: Louisiana State University Press, 1975), 25, which notes Woodward's mistake.

16. *Memphis Ledger*, quoted in the *Memphis Avalanche*, November 24, 1878.

17. Ibid., February 2, 1877. There is no biography of Kellar, who well deserves one. His political course must be traced through the pages of his newspaper, the *Memphis Avalanche*, from 1868 to 1878. He referred regularly to the "Memphis ring of office-seekers," for example ibid., December 3, 1869.

18. Kellar to William Henry Smith, February 17, 1877, W. H. Smith Papers Ind. See also Kellar to Smith February 20, 21, March 15, 1877, William Henry Smith Papers, Ohio Historical Society, Columbus, Ohio, hereafter cited as W. H. Smith Papers Ohio; David M. Abshire, *The South Rejects a Prophet: The Life of Senator D. M. Key, 1824–1900* (New York: Praeger, 1967), 110–11, 114–19, 145–56. For an understanding of Tennessee factional politics in the 1870s see Hart, *Redeemers, Bourbons, & Populists*, 1–55; Robison, *Bob Taylor*; Robison, "The Political Background of Tennessee's War of the Roses," *East Tennessee Historical Society Publications* 5 (January 1933): 125–33; Robert B. Jones, *Tennessee at the Crossroads: The State Debt Controversy, 1870–1883* (Knoxville: University of Tennessee Press, 1977), 1–115; augmented by the *Memphis Avalanche*, *Memphis Appeal*, and Isham G. Harris's organ, the *Nashville American*. As Kellar himself is not often mentioned in these works, one must trace his career in the *Avalanche*. See also the *Memphis Appeal*, November 11, 1876.

Woodward misconceived Arthur S. Colyar's part in Tennessee politics in the same way he did Kellar's. Colyar was a persistent factionalist, declaring and then renouncing independent candidacies so often that the *Nashville American* dubbed him "the Great American Withdrawer." He was until 1877, in the words of Isham G. Harris, "the most chronic case of *independent candidate* I have ever known." Like Kellar, Colyar allied with Andrew Johnson and became a radical proponent of a drastic readjustment of the state debt. Not until the 1880s did he play the role Woodward assigned him. Clyde L. Ball, "The Public Career of Colonel A. S. Colyar, 1870–1877," *Tennessee Historical Quarterly* 12 (March/June 1953): 23–47, 106–28; (September 1953): 213–38 (quotations on 235).

19. Sherman to William T. Sherman, December 10, 1875, William T. Sherman Papers, Manuscript Division, Library of Congress (hereafter LC). Boynton's book was *Sherman's Historical Raid* (Cincinnati: Wilstach, Baldwin, 1875). Actually, Boynton was a fairly well respected muckraker who reflected the journalistic excesses of his day. He is one of the most visible and sympathetically drawn subjects of Mark Wahlgren Summers's *The Press Gang: Newspapers and Politics, 1865–1878* (Chapel Hill: University of North Carolina, 1994), to which readers should turn for more information on his career and character.

20. *Cincinnati Gazette*, November 14, 1876; November 16, 18, 1876; *Washington National Republican*, November 22, 1876; *Cleveland Leader*, November 30, 1876; December 2, 4, 1876; *New York Times*, November 12, 1876.

21. There is no monographic work dealing with struggle between "regulars" and "reformers" for control of the Republican party organization between 1873 and 1876, and literature on the "reformers" themselves does not place their activities in the framework of intraparty factionalism, where much of it belongs. Ari Hoogenboom notes some of the ambiguities of "reform" in the 1870s in his "Civil Service Reform and Public Morality," in The *Gilded Age*, ed. H. Wayne Morgan (Syracuse, N.Y.: Syracuse University Press, 1970), 77–95. For the evidence of the struggle between regulars and reformers for influence with Hayes, see *The Speeches, Correspondence and Political Papers of Carl Schurz*, ed. Frederic Bancroft, 6 vols. (New York, 1913), 3: 280–90, 339–409; Boynton to Bristow, January 4, February 2, 1977; Boynton to William Henry Smith, January 5, 1877 (copy); Murat Halstead to Bristow, January 14, 1877, all in the Benjamin H. Bristow Papers, LC; Richard Smith to John M. Harlan, February 14, 1877, John M. Harlan Papers, LC; John D. DeFrees to Whitelaw Reid, February 19, 1877, Whitelaw Reid Papers, LC; and letters from William E. Chandler, Albert D. Shaw, James M. Comfy, James H. Tyner, and others in the Rutherford B. Hayes Papers, Hayes Memorial Library, Fremont, Ohio.

22. Kellar to Smith, January 2, 1877, W. H. Smith Papers Ohio. Blaine was not an "ultra radical," of course, and cordially hated Butler; Kellar's shaft was aimed at Republican regulars in general.

23. Boynton to Bristow, January 5, 1877, Bristow Papers. See also James M. Comly to Hayes, January 8, 1877, Hayes Papers; Boynton to William Henry Smith, March 17, 1877, W. H. Smith Papers Ohio. Later in 1877 Boynton tried to blackmail Hayes into giving Bristow greater authority over patronage by threatening to publicize Boynton's activities during the electoral crisis. Boynton to William Henry Smith, September 24, 1877; Smith to Hayes, October 3, November 11, 1877; Smith to Kellar, November 3, 1877; Smith to Richard Smith, November 19, 1877, W. H. Smith Papers Ohio; Ross A. Webb, *Benjamin Helm Bristow: Border State Politician* (Lexington: University of Kentucky Press, 1969), 269–74.

24. There was no provision in the statutes giving jurisdiction to the federal courts to adjudicate disputed electoral votes. There were suggestions to turn the matter over to the courts, but none got very far. Polakoff, *Politics of Inertia*, 265–67; David Dudley Field's *quo warranto* bill, *Congressional Record*, 44 Cong., 2 Sess., 2127 (March 2, 1877); Stanley Matthews to Hayes, December 15, 1876, Hayes Papers.

25. Polakoff, *Politics of Inertia*, 220–23, 234–38, 240–42; Paul L. Haworth, *The Hayes-Tilden Disputed Presidential Election of 1876* (Cleveland: Burrows Brothers, 1906), 176–86; Henry Watterson, "The Hayes-Tilden Contest for the Presidency: Inside History of a Great Political Crisis," *Century Magazine* 86 (May 1913): 15, 17.

26. *Memphis Appeal*, December 19, 1876.

27. *Richmond Dispatch*, December 2, 1876. See also the *Raleigh Sentinel*, November 16, 1876; *New Orleans Democrat*, December 12, 1876; *New Orleans Picayune*, December 16, 1876; *Charleston News and Courier*, November 22, 1876; *Nashville Weekly American*, November 23, 1876 (the *Weekly American* was the weekly publication of the *Nashville American*, the leading Democratic newspaper in Tennessee); *Louisville Courier-Journal*, November 24, 27, December 11, 1876; *Atlanta Constitution*, November 30, 1876. Some Democratic organs, such as the *Memphis Appeal*, did insist upon a peaceful solution at first, but they began to hedge when Republican determination became clear, cautioning that Democrats were "for peace, but also for the preservation of liberty and constitutional government. Let the conspirators take warning in time. *They* may force upon the country the dread issue of war." *Memphis Appeal*, December 21, 23, 1876. Earlier the *Appeal* had insisted, "no one proposes armed resistance to any infamy the Radicals may enact." Ibid., December 10, 1876.

28. *Raleigh Sentinel*, November 16, 1876. See also the *Memphis Appeal*, December 29, 1876; *Richmond Dispatch*, December 16, 1876; *Raleigh Sentinel*, November 30, 1876; *New Orleans Democrat*, December 17, 1876; *Louisville Courier-Journal*, December 11, 1876; *Atlanta Constitution*, December 15, 1876.

29. *Charleston News and Courier*, December 6, 1876. See also the *New Orleans Democrat*, December 12, 1876; *Nashville Weekly American*, December 14, 1876.

30. *New Orleans Picayune*, December 16, 1876.

31. For western Democratic calls for firmness, see the *Chicago Times*, December 26, 29, 1876; *Cincinnati Enquirer*, December 4, 7, 8, 12, 1876; *Cleveland Plain Dealer*, December 5, 14, 1876.

32. See for example the descriptions of the elections of 1866 and 1868 in Michael L. Benedict, *A Compromise of Principle: Congressional Republicans and Reconstruction, 1863–1869* (New York: Norton, 1974), 188–209, 322–24; and Charles H. Coleman, *The Election of 1868: The Democratic Effort to Regain Control* (New York: Columbia University Press, 1933), 286–90, 315–31, 375–76. The fear that Democrats were fundamentally hostile to the postwar status quo underlay much of the appeal of the "bloody shirt" issue to northerners.

33. This letter, sent to John M. Fleming by an unidentified writer, November 11, 1876, was printed in the *Nashville Weekly American*, November 23, 1876.

34. Ibid.; George W. Morgan to Tilden, November 18, 1876; January 15, 1877; Morgan to W. C. P. Breckenridge, January 16, 1877; Abram S. Hewitt to the National Democratic Committee, March 3, 1877, all in *Letters and Literary Memorials of Samuel J. Tilden*, ed. John Bigelow, 2 vols. (New York: Harper and Brothers, 1908), 2:490–91, 524–26, 549–53; Bigelow, *Retrospections of an Active Life*, 5 vols. (New York: Baker and Taylor, 1909–13), 4:288; Perry Belmont to James A. Bayard, December 31, 1876, Thomas Francis Bayard Papers, LC; George W. Biddle to Manton Marble, December 5, 1876, Manton Marble Papers, LC; William C. Hudson, *Random Recollections of an Old Political Reporter* (New York: Cupples & Leon, 1911), 69–71; Irving Katz, *August Belmont: A Political Biography* (New York: Columbia University Press, 1968), 225–29; George T. McJimsey, *Genteel Partisan: Manton Marble, 1834–1917* (Ames: Iowa State University Press, 1971), 196–97; Haworth, *Hayes-Tilden Disputed Presidential Election of 1876*, 169–70; Alexander C. Flick, *Samuel Jones Tilden: A Study in Political Sagacity* (New York: Dodd, Mead, 1939), 353–61; Allan Nevins, *Abram S. Hewitt: With Some Account of Peter Cooper* (New York: Harper and Brothers, 1935), 330–34.

35. *New York Times*, November 14, 15, 1876; *New York Tribune*, November 15, 1876, for examples.

36. *Chicago Tribune*, November 25, 1876. See also ibid., November 26, 1876; *New York Times*, November 23, 1876; *New York Tribune*, November 23, 1876; *Cincinnati Gazette*, November 24, 1876; *Cleveland Leader*, November 25, 27, 1876.

37. *Memphis Appeal*, November 24, 1876.

38. *Cincinnati Gazette*, November 28, 1876; *Chicago Times* quoted in the *Atlanta Constitution*, November 25, 1876.

39. John B. Gordon to Samuel L. M. Barlow, January 2, 1877, Samuel L. M. Barlow Papers, Henry E. Huntington Library, San Marino, Calif.; *New Orleans Democrat*, November 26, 1876. (Where more than one source is quoted in the text, the sources will be cited in the order that they are quoted.) See also Gordon to Alfred H. Colquitt, December 24, 1876, quoted in the *New Orleans Picayune*, January 10, 1877 (Gordon's letter was widely reprinted in the southern press); Joseph E. Brown to L. N. Trammell, December 12, 1876, Leander N. Trammell Papers, Emory University, Atlanta, Ga.; *New Orleans Picayune*, January 11, 1877.

40. For Democratic perceptions of Randall's firmness see his correspondence of November and December 1876, Samuel Jackson Randall Papers, University of Pennsyl-

vania, Philadelphia. Randall's rulings on procedure in the first days of Congress and the determination manifested in early caucuses reassured Democrats temporarily. See the *Washington National Republican,* December 5, 1876; *Atlanta Constitution,* December 5, 1876; *Louisville Courier-Journal,* December 7, 1876.

41. Vance to Cornelia Phillips Spencer, November 27, 1876, Cornelia P. Spencer Papers, North Carolina State Department of Archives and History, Raleigh; C. Gibson to Tilden, November 28, 1876. See also George J. Micherns to Tilden, December 13, 1876; J. Duncan Allen to Tilden, December 15, 1876; R. Carter Smith to Tilden, December 15, 1876; J. W. Dungee to Tilden, December 18, 1876; Richard Nugent to Tilden, December 22, 1876, all in Samuel J. Tilden Papers, New York Public Library, New York, N. Y. Similar letters from the South and from dissatisfied northern Democrats were directed to Randall. Augustus H. Garland to Randall, November 17, 1876; Leopold Morse to Randall, December 11, 1876; Richard Vaux to Randall, December 8, 12, 1876; January 13, 1877; W. C. Watson to Randall, December 13, 1876; John J. C. Harvey to Randall, January 16, 1877; George Vickers to Randall, December 14, 1876, Randall Papers. See also August Belmont to Manton Marble, December 11, 1876 (filed under February 11, 1877); L. P. Walker to Marble, December 19, 1876, Marble Papers; J. S. Duckwall to James L. Kemper, December 14, 1876, James L. Kemper Papers, University of Virginia Library, Charlottesville; William M. Brown to Samuel L. M. Barlow, December 13, 18, 1876, Barlow Papers; Edwin Harris to John M. Palmer, December 12, 1876, John M. Palmer Papers, Illinois State Historical Library, Springfield.

42. Who controlled the national administration was of most immediate concern to the Democrats of Louisiana, South Carolina, and Florida, of course. But the campaign of 1876 and the electoral crisis had aroused sectional hostilities to the highest point since 1872. The Republican party remained strong both numerically and organizationally in North Carolina and in parts of Tennessee and Virginia; it probably had a numerical majority in Mississippi. Aggressive national support could threaten Democratic control in those states and certainly preserve Republican dominance in those regions of states— eastern Tennessee and western North Carolina, for example—where it was still paramount in 1876. For Republican strength in the post-Reconstruction South, even after national administrations slackened law-enforcement efforts there, see Vincent P. DeSantis, *Republicans Face the Southern Question: The New Departure Years, 1877–1897* (Baltimore: Johns Hopkins University Press, 1959); Stanley P. Hirshson, *Farewell to the Bloody Shirt: Northern Republicans & the Southern Negro, 1877–1893* (Bloomington: Indiana University Press, 1962); J. Morgan Kousser, *The Shaping of Southern Politics: Suffrage Restriction and the Establishment of the One-Party South, 1880–1910* (New Haven, Conn.: Yale University Press, 1974); Verton M. Queener, "The East Tennessee Republicans in State and Nation, 1870–1900," *Tennessee Historical Quarterly* 11 (June 1943): 99–128; Queener, "The East Tennessee Republicans as a Minority Party, 1870–1896," *East Tennessee Historical Society Publications* 15 (1943): 49–73.

43. L. P. Walker to Manton Marble, December 19, 1876, Marble Papers.

44. *Columbus* (Ga.) *Times,* December 1 [?], 1876, quoted in the *Memphis Avalanche,* December 13, 1876. See also the *La Grange* (Tenn.) *Monitor,* December 9, 1876, and the *Richmond Enquirer,* December 8, 1876, quoted ibid. The anti-Democratic *Avalanche* put its own, rather twisted interpretation upon these excerpts.

45. Woodward, *Reunion and Reaction,* 31–32.

46. *Cincinnati Enquirer,* December 15, 1876; R. B. Bradford to Tilden, December 18, 1876, Tilden Papers.

47. Smith to Hayes, December 7, 1876; Halstead to Hayes, December 10, 1876; William B. Williams to Garfield, December 11, 1876; Garfield to Hayes, December 12, 1876; Dennison to Hayes, December 13, 1876, all in Hayes Papers; *The Diary of James A. Garfield,* ed. Harry J. Brown and Frederick D. Williams, 3 vols. (East Lansing: Michigan

State University Press, 1967–1973), 3:393–94 (December 11, 1876), 394–95 (December 12, 1876).

48. William H. Roberts's testimony, *House Miscellaneous Document No. 31*, 45 Cong., 3 Sess.; *Presidential Election Investigation*, 5 vols. (Washington, Government Printing Office, 1878), 878; cited hereafter as *Presidential Election Investigation*.

49. The chronology of the Smith-Kellar-Boynton relationship can be gleaned from Woodward, *Reunion and Reaction*, 27–28 (quotation on 28). Smith first mentioned Kellar to Hayes in a letter sent December 7, 1876. A letter from Boynton to Bristow dated December 10, 1876, in the Bristow papers at the Library of Congress, makes clear that he broached his ideas to Hayes's friends no earlier than December 11.

50. Boynton to William Henry Smith, December 20, 1876, Hayes Papers.

51. *New York Times*, December 21, 1876. See also *Cincinnati Gazette*, December 11, 13, 14, 18, 1876; *Washington National Republican*, December 18, 1876; *Cincinnati Commercial*, December 20, 22, 1876; *Chicago Tribune*, December 17, 19, 22, 25, 1876. The pro-southern tone of the Republican press after December 15 or so contrasts dramatically with the opinions expressed up to that time and suggests an orchestrated effort to break down Democratic unity rather than an impartial recognition of the fact of southern restraint; the Democratic press certainly took it that way, as I indicate below. Reports of southern frauds and outrages, given front-page treatment through early December, diminished or disappeared from the pages of newspapers closely associated with Hayes. See the *Cincinnati Gazette*, *Columbus Ohio State Journal*, and *Chicago Tribune* over the period.

52. The Kellar interview, which does not name him, is in the *New York Herald*, December 27, 1876. Hill's interview, ibid., December 13, 1876.

53. Kellar to William Henry Smith, December 21, 1876, W. H. Smith Papers Ind.

54. *Nashville Weekly American*, December 22, 1876.

55. *Memphis Appeal*, December 29, 1876. The words were all the more significant coming from one of the journals in the South most opposed to violent resistance to Hayes's election. See also the reports of L. Q. Washington, one of the best-connected southern reporters in Washington. *New Orleans Picayune*, December 27, 1876; and the *Picayune*'s editorial comment, December 16, 1876; *Atlanta Constitution*, December 15, 18, 22, 1876; *Richmond Dispatch*, December 18, 20, 1876; *Louisville Courier-Journal*, December 24, 30, 1876; *Charleston News and Courier*, December 29, 1876; *Richmond Whig*, quoted by the *Chicago Tribune*, December 23, 1876; and the *Augusta Constitutionalist*, *Mobile Register*, and *Savannah Morning News*, all quoted by the *Chicago Tribune*.

56. Hill in the *Atlanta Constitution*, December 24, 1876. See also ibid., December 17, 1876 (Stephens); December 21, 1876 (Hill); *Richmond Dispatch*, December 20, 1876 (Hill); *Louisville Courier-Journal*, December 23, 1876 (an Associated Press story of Lamar's and Stephens's denials carried in many newspapers); January 6, 1877 (Lamar); January 10, 1877 (Hill); *Memphis Appeal*, January 2, 1877 (Young).

57. *New York World* correspondent George W. Adams, quoted in the *Atlanta Constitution*, December 20, 1876; *Cincinnati Enquirer*, December 14, 15, 1876.

58. Hampton to Hayes, December 23, 1876, published in the *New York Times*, December 30, 1876; Hill in the *Atlanta Constitution*, December 24, 1876.

59. L. Q. Washington in the *Louisville Courier-Journal*, January 1, 1877. See also *New Orleans Picayune*, December 31, 1876; Perry Belmont to James A. Bayard, December 31, 1876, Bayard Papers.

60. *New York Times*, January 9, 1877.

61. *Richmond Dispatch*, January 8, 1877. See also the *New Orleans Democrat*, January 15, 1877; *New Orleans Picayune*, January 6, 11, 1877; *Jackson Clarion*, January 7, 9, 1877; *Atlanta Constitution*, January 4, 10, 1877; *Charleston News and Courier*, January 3, 1877.

62. Woodward, *Reunion and Reaction*, 110–12, describes the Jackson Day rallies but exaggerates their size and ignores their context. Watterson, "The Hayes-Tilden Contest

for the Presidency," 15, 17. The organization of the January 8 meetings can be followed in any newspaper of the period. For reports of the most important meetings see the *Louisville Courier-Journal*, January 11, 1877 (Columbus, Ohio); January 9, 1877 (Indianapolis); Washington *National Republican*, January 9, 1877 (Washington, D. C.); *Richmond Dispatch*, January 9, 1877 (Richmond, Va.). For expressions of disappointment by leading Democrats in the meetings see the Diary of George W. Julian, January 21, 1877, George W. Julian Papers, Indiana Division, Indiana State Library; Richard Vaux to Samuel J. Randall, January 13, 1877, Randall Papers; *Louisville Courier-Journal*, January 12, 18, 1877; *Chicago Times*, quoted in the *New Orleans Democrat*, January 13, 1877; and in the *New Orleans Picayune*, January 17, 1877; *Cincinnati Gazette*, January 12, 1877.

63. *Richmond Dispatch*, January 13, 1877; *New Orleans Picayune*, January 11, January 18, 1877; *Louisville Courier-Journal*, January 11, 12, 18, 1877; *Cincinnati Gazette*, January 18, 1877.

64. "H.V.B." in the *Cincinnati Gazette*, January 8, 1877; Boynton to William Henry Smith, January 5, 1877, W. H. Smith Papers, Ohio; Boynton to James M. Comly, January 25, 1877, Hayes Papers.

65. *Louisville Courier-Journal*, December 29, 1876; January 1, 1877; *Cincinnati Enquirer*, December 18, 28, 1876; *New York Graphic*, December 27, 1876, quoted in the *Atlanta Constitution*, January 3, 1877; *New York World*, quoted ibid., December 20, 1876; public letters of Joseph E. Brown and John B. Gordon, ibid., December 31, 1876, and January 8, 1877 (published while Hill was seeking election to the U. S. Senate, these letters were recognized as attacks upon him although not mentioning him by name); *New Orleans Picayune*, December 15, 1876; January 13, 1877; Hewitt to George T. Fry, January 5, 1877; Henry B. Payne to Fry, January 5, 1877; Samuel S. Cox to Fry, January 7, 1877, quoted in the *Atlanta Constitution*, January 14, 1877; Haywood J. Pearce, *Benjamin H. Hill: Secession and Reconstruction* (Chicago: University of Chicago Press, 1928), 289–90; Edward Mayes, *Lucius Q. C. Lamar: His Life, Times, and Speeches, 1825–1893* (Nashville: Publishing House of the Methodist Episcopal Church, South, 1896), 301–2.

66. Boynton to William Henry Smith, December 20, 1876; Hayes to Smith, December 24, 1876. See also Smith to Hayes, December 22, 1876; Boynton to Smith, January 14, 15, 1877, W. H. Smith Papers, Ind. Comly, Boynton, and Garfield discussed the effect endorsement of the Texas and Pacific would have on southern politics after Hayes's inauguration early in January, lamenting the rigidity of Republican opposition to it, but no action was taken, and Garfield still opposed it in the Pacific Railroad committee. Comly to Hayes, January 8, 1877, Hayes Papers; *Diary of James A. Garfield*, 3:398 (December 20, 1876), 399 (December 21, 1876), 414 (January 11, 1877); Garfield to Whitelaw Reid, February 2, 1877, Reid Papers.

67. Boynton to Smith, January 16, 1877, Smith Papers, Ind.

68. Peskin, "Was There a Compromise of 1877?" 69–70; Taylor to Barlow, January 13, 1877. Taylor's note is among the undated material in the Barlow Papers. Dated Saturday, January 13, there is no doubt about the year. See Woodward's account of Scott's efforts in Congress in *Reunion and Reaction*, 222–25, 230–37, which hardly resulted in what Woodward called "brilliant political victories" (237). When Taylor himself took over the job of lobbying the Texas and Pacific through Congress in 1879 he had the same problems and pronounced Scott's chief congressional agents incompetent to do the work. Taylor to Barlow, February 20, 27, March 9, 10, 1879, Barlow Papers.

69. Polakoff offers a perceptive account of how Republicans divided in *Politics of Inertia*, 258–76.

70. *Nashville Weekly American*, January 25, 1877.

71. "The Difficulty of a Settlement," *Nation*, January 4, 1877; "O.O.S." in the *Louisville Courier-Journal*, January 22, 1877. See also the *Nashville Weekly American*, January 18, 1877; *Memphis Avalanche*, February 16, 1877; *Mobile Register*, quoted ibid., February 28,

1877; *Quitman Intelligencer*, quoted ibid., March 27, 1877; Washington correspondent of the *Chicago Times*, quoted in the *Atlanta Constitution*, February 22, 1877; *Richmond Dispatch*, February 20, 1877; *New Orleans Democrat*, March 4, 1877; Henry Watterson in the *Louisville Courier-Journal*, February 20, March 23, 1877; Jesse J. Yeates to W. N. H. Smith, February 23, March 5, 1877; Henry W. Grady in the *Atlanta Constitution*, February 21, 24, 1877; John B. Gordon, ibid., February 27, 1877; Julian Diary, March 11, 1877, Julian Papers; Charles Gibson to Samuel J. Randall, February 25, 1877, Randall Papers. Among the southern newspapers that reluctantly favored the compromise after earlier urging firmness upon northern Democrats were the *Atlanta Constitution*, January 20, 21, 1877; *Richmond Dispatch*, January 19, 20, 1877; *New Orleans Democrat*, January 21, 1877; *Louisville Courier-Journal*, January 18, 20, 1877; *Charleston News and Courier*, January 20, 21, 1877. The *Atlanta Constitution* noted only one southern paper among its exchange opposing the bill; nineteen favored it; January 23, 1877. Reports from Washington indicated that the overwhelming majority of Democrats in Congress accepted it in the same spirit. *Louisville Courier-Journal*, January 20, 1877; January 21, 1877; *Richmond Dispatch*, January 19, 1877; *Cincinnati Enquirer*, January 19, 1877; *New Orleans Democrat*, January 19, 1877; *New Orleans Picayune*, January 20, 1877. See also Richard Taylor to Samuel L. M. Barlow, January 18, 1877, Barlow Papers. Tilden's exact position has been a subject of controversy. He and close political allies later insisted that he had never endorsed the compromise; Hewitt insisted he had. Since Tilden had political reasons for denying responsibility, his account is suspect. See Nevins, *Abram S. Hewitt*, 386-99, for the best secondary account.

72. Of the 154 Democrats voting for the bill, 25 were from the South. *Congressional Record*. 44 Cong., 2 Sess., 1050 (January 26, 1877).

73. Sherman to Hayes, January 18, 1877, Hayes Papers; *Washington National Republican*, January 24, 1877; *Diary of James A Garfield*, 3:419 (January 21, 1877). The evidence of Republican rejection is overwhelming. A *New York Times* newspaper survey found only seven major Republican dailies endorsing the compromise proposal and nineteen opposed. *New York Times*, January 21, 22, 1877. The Hayes, Sherman, William E. Chandler, Garfield papers in the Manuscript Division, Library of Congress and the Morton papers at the Indiana Division, Indiana Slate Library are filled with opposing letters. Although Republican senators favored the proposal by a wide margin, Republican representatives ultimately voted 68 to 33 against it. *Congressional Record*, 44 Cong., 2 Sess., 913, 1050 (January 25, 26, 1877).

74. Boynton's letters indicate that he ceased his campaign to woo southerners when the compromise was accepted. As of January 25 he was concentrating on influencing the Republican personnel of the Electoral Commission. Boynton to James M. Comly, January 25, 1877, Hayes Papers. On February 11 he referred to "the plan we were at work upon before the compromise bill was passed." Comly to William Henry Smith, February 11, 1877, W. H. Smith Papers, Ind. He did not mention southern-northern Democratic division again in his dispatches until February 11.

75. "H.V.B." in the *Cincinnati Gazette*, January 25, 1877; Dodge to Nathaniel O. Dodge, January 17, 1877, Dodge Papers; *Memphis Avalanche*, January 20, 23, 24, 1877. Kellar even criticized Boynton and his paper for his inflexibility. Ibid., February 2, 7, 1877. But in his anonymous interview with the *New York Herald*, Kellar had described his and Boynton's real plans, which required that the joint committee created to find a compromise "be so managed that it shall come to no agreement; but that it shall make no report [to that effect] until the day set for the counting of the vote." At that point the southern Democrats were to join Republicans in resisting House efforts to elect Tilden. *New York Herald*, December 27, 1876.

76. Smith to Hayes, January 23, 1877, Hayes Papers.

77. Boynton to James M. Comly, January 25, 1877, Hayes Papers; Boynton to Bristow, January 21, 1877, Bristow Papers.

78. Boynton to Smith, February 11, 18, 1877. See also Boynton to Smith, February 22, 1877, W. H. Smith Papers Ind.

79. Grenville M. Dodge to Thomas A. Scott, February 20, 1877, Dodge Papers; Kellar to William Henry Smith, February 21, 1877, W. H. Smith Papers Ind.

80. *Louisville Courier-Journal*, February 12, 1877; *Nashville Weekly American*, April 5, 1877; James A. Bayard in the *Atlanta Constitution*, February 13, 1877; *Charleston News and Courier*, February 19, 1877; Benjamin H. Hill Jr., *Senator Benjamin H. Hill of Georgia: His Life, Speeches and Writings* (Atlanta: H. C. Hudgins, 1891), 75–77; John R. Tucker to Henry St. George Tucker, February 25, 1877, Tucker Family Papers, Southern Historical Collection, University of North Carolina Library, Chapel Hill; William R. Morrison to L. H. Hite et al., March 4, 1877, quoted in the *New York World*, March 5, 1877.

81. Sherman to Hayes, February 24, 1877, Hayes Papers. Republicans enthusiastically renewed charges of Democratic irresponsibility and violence. *Washington National Republican*, February 13, 1877; *New York Times*, February 24, 25, 27, 1877; *New York Tribune*, February 24, 28, 1877.

82. Jesse J. Yeates to W. N. H. Smith, February 23, 1877, quoted in *Louisville Courier-Journal*, March 5, 1877.

83. *Charleston News and Courier*, February 20, 1877; *Washington National Republican*, February 20, 24, 1877; *Atlanta Constitution*, February 24, 1877; *New Orleans Picayune*, February 24, 1877. Randall certainly was not influenced to break the filibuster by any relationship with the Texas and Pacific Railroad lobby. Although unfounded rumors suggested he had Scott's support in his losing campaign for the speakership in 1875, Scott bitterly opposed him in 1877. Once again, the Scott lobby was ineffectual. Randall retained his position with no more than ordinary effort. Albert V. House, "The Speakership Contest of 1875: Democratic Response to Power," *Journal of American History* 52 (September 1965): 252–74; Margaret Susan Thompson, *The "Spider Web": Congress and Lobbying in the Age of Grant* (Ithaca, N.Y.: Cornell University Press, 1985), 180–99, 204–8; Chauncey F. Black to Randall, April 7, 15, 27, May 12, 1877; John S. Coyle to Randall, April 9, 1877; Morris K. King to Randall, April 9, 1877; J. M. Keating to Randall, June 4, 1877; Charles Nordhoff to Randall, September 26, 1877, Randall Papers.

84. *Nashville Weekly American*, February 18, 1877; "H.W.G.," in the Atlanta *Constitution*, February 22, 1877; *New Orleans Picayune*, February 26, 1877.

85. Table 10.1 collapses three groups of anti-filibusterers of varying degrees into one "Anti-filibuster" group and two groups of filibusterers into a "Pro-filibuster" group. This process of combination did not affect the voting pattern in any way. *Eta*, the "correlation ratio," is an appropriate measure of correlation between categorical independent variables and dichotomous dependent variables. If the regional categories had no effect on voting patterns, then one would expect the same proportion of yeas and nays among congressmen from each category. In that case *eta* would equal 0. If region completely determined how congressmen voted, then those from some regions would have voted unanimously one way and those from others would have voted unanimously the other way. In that case *eta* would equal 1.00. See Charles M. Dollar and Richard J. Jensen, *Historian's Guide to Statistics: Quantitative Analysis and Historical Research* (New York: Holt, Rinehart, Winston, 1971), 73–79. For the roll calls on which the table is based, see Appendix II.

86. The Holman resolution may be found in the *Congressional Record*, 44 Cong., 1 Sess., 227 (December 15, 1875); the vote to subsidize the repair of the Mississippi levees may be located ibid., 2 Sess., 2232 (March 3, 1877). *Gamma* is a measure of association between ordinal variables—that is, variables whose values can be ordered from highest to lowest but not necessarily at identical intervals. *Gamma* varies from -1.0 to 1.0; the

higher the absolute value, the stronger the association. *A gamma* of 0.0 would connote no association at all. For its computation, see Theodore R. Anderson and Morris Zelditch Jr., *A Basic Course in Statistics with Sociological Applications* (New York: Holt, Rinehart, Winston, 1968), 152–55.

87. Burke's testimony, *Presidential Election Investigation*, 1:962.

88. Ibid., 990 (August 16, 1978). See also *Selected Writings of Abram S. Hewitt*, ed. Allan Nevins (New York: Columbia University Press, 1937), 176–77; Watterson, "The Hayes-Tilden Contest for the Presidency," 18–19. Polakoff's account of the final maneuverings and negotiations is excellent. Polakoff, *Politics of Inertia*, 292–313.

89. Ibid., 306–9; *Diary of James A. Garfield*, 3:448 (February 25, 1877); Murat Halstead to Hayes, February 19, 1877, Hayes Papers; Grenville M. Dodge to Jay Gould, February 20, 1877, Dodge Papers.

90. This is clear from his considerations upon cabinet appointments. Conversing with Comly in January Hayes discussed appointing as secretary of state New York boss Roscoe Conkling's archenemy William M. Evarts; Benjamin F. Butler's foes John Murray Forbes or Alexander H. Rice as postmaster general; and Bristow's chief lieutenant John Marshall Harlan as attorney general. Note of January 1877 in the James M. Comly Papers, Ohio Historical Society; *Hayes: The Diary of a President, 1875–1881*, ed. T. Harry Williams (New York: David McKay, 1964), 69 (January 17, 1877). Abandoning Butler's enemies and Harlan, by late February Hayes determined to appoint to the cabinet Carl Schurz, who, along with Bristow, was the symbol of reform Republicanism. Ibid., 78–79 (February 27, 1877).

91. T. F. Oliver to Ulysses S. Grant, February 17, 1877, Letters Received from the President, General Records of the Department of Justice, Record Group 60, National Archives, Washington, D. C.; William H. Roberts's testimony, *Presidential Election Investigation*, 1:905–8; Edward A. Burke's testimony, ibid., 959.

92. Grant undertook forceful intervention in the South only reluctantly and was perceived as pro-southern and independent of established Republican leaders until at least 1870, and by many until 1871. Roger D. Bridges, "President Grant and the Formation of a Southern Policy, 1869–1877" (unpublished paper presented at the conference "Ulysses S. Grant in Perspective," De Kalb, Illinois, April 1973); Brooks D. Simpson, *The Reconstruction Presidents* (Lawrence: University Press of Kansas, 1998), 139–57.

93. Hayes to Schurz, February 4, 1877, in *Speeches, Correspondence and Political Papers of Carl Schurz*, 3:387. See also William H. Roberts's testimony, *Presidential Election Investigation*, 1:901–3.

94. Edward A. Burke to Francis T. Nicholls, February 27, 1877, copy in William E. Chandler Papers, LC.

95. Henry Watterson, *"Marse Henry": An Autobiography*, 2 vols. (New York: George H. Doran, 1919), 1:312.

96. L.Q.W. [Lucius Quintus Washington], *Louisville Courier-Journal*, April 10, 1877.

97. Numerous petitions and memorials urging compromise from businessmen and organizations from Philadelphia, Boston, Chicago, Detroit, St. Louis, Kansas City, and other cities are in the House Petition and Memorial File, Records of the United States House of Representatives, Record Group 233; and the Senate Petition and Memorial File, Records of the United States Senate, Record Group 46 (National Archives).

Index

Adams, Charles Francis, Jr., 11, 170, 179, 181
Adams, Henry, 19, 29–30, 173, 180, 181
Adams, John Quincy, 132
African Americans. 170. *See also* civil rights; emancipation; slavery
   American Anti-Slavery society on, 24–25
   as citizens, 3–4, 14, 16, 23, 54, 135–36, 142
   as Democrats, 102
   enfranchisement of, 16, 24, 25, 28, 54–55, 87, 142, 159, 163, 179
   equal rights and, xiii, 4, 15, 151, 170, 182
   factionalism and, 73, 74, 80, 86, 87
   middle-class, 80, 103
   as politicians and leaders, 80, 96–97, 103, 104, 105, 106, 169–70
   as Republicans, 102, 103–6
   Republicans and, ix, xiii, 3–4, 5, 6, 13–16, 19, 21, 23–26, 30, 128
   in Senate, 169–70
   state courts on, xi, 14
   suffrage for, 5, 16, 17–18, 19, 21, 23–25, 29, 30, 41, 50, 54, 55, 57–59, 86, 97, 116–17, 142–43, 159, 161, 162, 169, 182, 184
   voting, 104, 106, 158, 161, 178
   as workers, 102–3
Akerman, Amos, 49–51
Alabama, 40, 41, 76, 78, 80, 107, 153, 157–58, 165
Alcorn, James Lusk, 78
Alien and Sedition Acts, xi
Ames, Adelbert, 78, 95, 105–6, 154
amnesty, 52, 55, 73, 125, 127–28, 143, 144, 146, 147, 149
anthropologists, 68, 70, 74, 80
antimonopoly and regulatory legislation, 50, 53, 55
antislavery movement, 24–25, 54, 56, 61, 98, 112, 124, 127, 169, 182
   Salmon Portland Chase and, 129, 130–31, 132–38, 145–46
Anti-Slavery Standard, 26
aristocracy, 25, 104, 160, 161, 167, 171, 178, 179
Arkansas, 18, 40, 74, 101, 107, 153, 158, 159
Armstrong's Foundry case (*in re Armstrong's Foundry*), 149
army. *See* military
Atkinson, Edward, 126, 169, 171–72, 173, 175, 178, 179, 182

Badeau, Adam, 27
Bailey, F. G., 74
bankruptcy, 51, 53
banks and banking, 54, 55, 101, 130, 132, 145, 151, 177
Banks, Nathaniel, 30
Beale, Howard K., 23
Beecher, Henry Ward, ix
Berger, Raoul, 33, 34
Bigelow, John, 11
Bill of Rights, 134
Bingham, John, xi, 12–13, 15, 24, 35, 40, 43
Binney, John, 30
Birchard, Sardis, 30–31
Black, Charles, 32–33
blacks. *See* African Americans
Blaine, James G., 15, 24, 28, 30, 35, 40, 127–28, 191
Blair, Austin, 43, 78, 82
bloody-shirt issues, 51, 53, 122, 124, 128, 184
Blue, Frederick, 130, 131
Blyew v. U.S., 149
Bonadio, Felice, 79
Boston Advertiser, 25, 178–79, 180
Boutwell, George S., 10, 35, 41
Boynton, Henry Van Ness, 189, 190–91, 194, 195–96, 198–200, 202
Brandegee, Augustus, 15
Brandwein, Pamela, 6

Breckenridge, John C., 74
Bristow, Benjamin Helm, 190–91
Brock, William, 6, 7, 24
Broder, David S., 47–48
Bronson v. Rodes, 150
Brown, Joseph E., 96–97, 100, 104
Bryant, John M., 74
Buchanan, James, 74
Buckalew, Charles R., 161
Burger, Warren, 138
Burgess, John W., 6
Butler, Benjamin F., 24, 25, 28, 35, 86, 166, 172–73, 177, 178–79, 180

California, 28
Cameron, Simon, 27, 78, 83, 85, 170
Campbell, Tunis G., 80
capitalism, 126, 130, 175, 177, 186, 187, 193, 199
carpetbaggers, 74, 96, 101, 105, 106, 123, 125, 166, 183
Catholics and Catholicism, 54, 56, 94, 112, 127, 185
Chamberlain, Daniel, 152
Chandler, Zachariah, 27, 77, 78, 82, 124, 177, 191
Chase, Salmon Portland, 27, 28, 30
    ambition of, 61, 130, 131, 144
    antislavery movement and, 129, 130–31, 132–38, 145–46
    as chief justice, 26, 61, 129, 130, 138–41, 143–51
    constitutional politics and, 129–51
    Democrats and, 129, 130, 132–33, 137, 143, 144–47, 150–51
    family and social life of, 131–32
    Lincoln and, 73, 76, 129, 130, 136–37, 138, 140, 141, 147
    presidential nomination of, 61, 74, 76–77, 88, 129–30, 133, 136, 143, 144, 145–46, 151
    radicalism and, 26, 74, 85, 86, 130, 133, 137, 138, 139–40, 141, 142, 143
    Treasury Department and, 73, 129–30, 145, 150
Chicago Times, 29, 194
Chicago Tribune, 169, 180, 181
Cincinnati Commercial, 25, 179
citizens, ix, 47
    African Americans as, 3–4, 14, 16, 23, 54, 135–36, 142
    Civil Rights Act on, 21, 141–42, 149
    naturalized, 56
    rights of, xi, 5, 6, 8, 11, 12–13, 14–15, 20–21, 38, 39, 53, 56, 133, 135–36
    state v. national, 141–42
civil rights, x, 23, 52, 106, 184
    Democrats and, 50, 123–24
    legislation, 5, 6, 13, 34, 50, 52, 103, 118–19, 179
    Republicans and, 3–4, 5, 6, 13–15, 19–22, 50, 118–19, 123–24, 184
Civil Rights Act of 1866, 13–15, 141, 149
Civil Rights Act of 1875, 20–21
civil service, 65
    reform, 50, 53, 55, 73, 75, 76, 79, 82, 83, 84, 119, 173–74, 190–91
Civil War, x, xi, 34, 94, 119, 123, 190
    banking and financial policies, 62, 145, 150, 151, 174–75, 177
    complexity of, xiii
    constitutional transformation and, 3–4, 6, 7, 22
    "dead," fading issues after, 87, 125–26, 127, 128
    emancipation during, 88
    end of, ix, 38
    federal system and, x
    soldiers, xi–xii, 55, 76
    veterans, 82
    war powers and, 7–11, 13
class, 167
    black middle class, 80, 103
    capitalist, 126
    economic, 95, 183–84, 187
    exploitation, 155
    factionalism and, 70
    northern working, 4, 126, 169
    poor and illiterate, 99
    professional, 99
    property, 163
    tension and conflict, 126, 168–69
    white lower class, 179
    white upper class, 179
    working, 126
class legislation, 22, 106, 125, 126, 160, 162, 165, 166, 171, 183
Clayton, Powell, 81
Clemenceau, Georges, 30
Clientelism, 68, 69, 70, 71, 75, 79–82, 84
Clinton, Bill, 33–34
Cohen, Nancy, 169, 182
Colfax, Schuyler, 10, 54, 60
Colyar, Arthur S., 189

INDEX 305

Collector v. Day, 148–49
Commonwealth (Boston), 40–41
communism, 127, 152, 165, 172, 188
Confederacy, 34, 143
   currency, 138, 150
   debt, 142
   military, 38, 51
   pardoning and, 37, 149
   proscription and, 101–2
   surrender of, 54
Congress, xi, 12–13, 20, 23–24. *See also* House of Representatives; Senate
   elections, mid-nineteenth century, and, 47–66
   on impeachment, 32, 33, 34–39, 40, 43
   Military Government bill in, 15–16
   partisanship in, 48, 49–53, 56–66
   on southern states, 9–11, 12, 15–18, 21, 23
   voting patterns, 63–65
   war powers of, 7–11, 13
Conkling, Roscoe, 15, 18, 60, 78, 124
Connecticut, 28, 54, 58, 59
"conquered province" theory, 8–9
conservatism. *See* Democratic Party; Republican Party
constitutionalism
   emancipation and, 162, 164–65, 169
   freedmen and, 155, 158, 159, 161, 162, 163, 166
   laissez-faire, 160, 162, 163, 166, 169, 171, 172, 175
   popular, x
   problem of, 152–67
   Republican radicalism and, 155–56, 157, 161, 167
   revolutionary, 4, 22
   taxation and, 159, 162–66
constitutional liberty, xiii, 136, 152–53, 154, 159–60, 162, 166, 167, 193
constitutional politics, ix–xiii, x, 47, 129–51
constitutional transformation, Civil War and, 3, 6, 7, 22
Constitution, of People's Republic of China, 152
Constitution, of United States, ix–x. *See also* Fifteenth Amendment; Fourteenth Amendment; Thirteenth Amendment
   Declaration of Independence and, xiii, 3

   on Electoral College, 192
   equal rights and, ix, 24
   Fugitive Slave Clause in, 134–36
   impeachment and, 32–33, 35, 36–37, 38, 39, 41, 43
   presidential powers and, 35, 36–37, 39, 41–43
   proslavery, xi, 3, 6
   war powers and, 7–8, 10
constitutions, southern state, 99, 101, 104, 142–43, 152–59, 162, 167
Corporate subsidies, 51, 53
Correlation, election, 48, 64, 65, 116–17, 120–22, 126
Cox, Jacob Dolson, 10, 42
currency, 62, 141, 145, 150, 151, 174–75, 177, 179
   Confederate, 138, 150
   distribution, 101
   gold as, 150, 174, 175
   greenbacks as, 62, 150, 151, 174–75, 177
   in northern platform, 55
   shortage, 145
   stability, 84
Curtin, Andrew, 27, 78

Dana, Richard Henry, 10–11, 12, 16, 180, 181
"dangerous classes," 167, 172, 183
David, Paul T., 62–63
Davis, Jefferson, 127, 143, 146
debt, 150
   Confederate, 142
   "contingent," 164
   funding, 63
   national, 62, 175, 177
   state, 165, 189–90
Declaration of Independence, xiii, 3, 134
democracy, 34, 124, 136, 153, 156, 167, 169, 205
   equal rights v., 166
   as experiment, 173
   local, xiii
   majoritarian, 172
   northern, 27, 193, 195
   risks of, 160
   southern, 98
Democratic Party, 12
   African Americans in, 102
   Chase and, 129, 130, 132–33, 137, 143, 144–47, 150–51
   civil rights and, 50, 123–24

conservative, 73, 74, 81, 88
  in crisis of 1876–77, 77, 95–96, 186–209
  in elections of 1867, 24, 25, 26–29
  equal rights and, 55, 128, 145, 172
  factionalism and, 71, 72–73, 74, 75, 76, 77, 85, 86, 88
  Free Soil coalition and, 60, 74, 133, 134, 169
  impeachment and, 40, 41
  New Departure movement in, 54, 74, 123, 145, 189
  newspapers, 27, 29, 194
  partisanship, 47–49, 50–53, 55–56, 57–63, 65, 66
  platforms, 54–56
  race and, 55, 102, 123, 125, 128, 129, 145
  Reconstruction politics and, 93, 97, 98, 99, 100, 101, 102, 105, 106–7, 110–17, 121, 122–24, 125, 126, 127–28
  southern Democrats in, 125, 127, 128, 147, 186–209
  state rights oriented, x, 145
  voting patterns, 106–7, 110–17, 121
DeWitt, David Miller, 33
Richmond Dispatch, 122–23
Dodge, Grenville, 198, 199
Donald, David, 24, 187
Donnelly, Ignatius, 78, 83, 170
Douglass, Frederick, 80
Downs, Anthony, 66
Drake, Charles D., 35, 78
Dred Scott case (*Scott v. Sandford*), xii, 3
DuBois, W. E. B., 168, 188
Duer, William, 36
Dunning, William A., 6
Duverger, Maurice, 69, 83

economic issues, 55, 118–19. *See also* banks and banking; currency; debt; tariffs; taxation
  class and, 95, 183–84, 187
  inflation and, 55, 86–87, 144, 145–46, 151, 174–75, 178, 189, 190
  laissez-faire, 175
  science and, 170–71, 177
  slavery, emancipation, and, 97–99, 100, 102–4, 162
  of South, 97–99, 100–104, 106, 118–20, 142, 186–87, 189
Edmunds, George F., 17
education, 55, 98, 99–100, 161, 163. *See also* schools

election crisis of 1876–77, 77, 95–96, 186–209
  campaign strategies, 86–87
  Democrats and, 77, 95–96, 186–209
  electoral college and, 187–208
  filibuster in, 200–206, 209
  Rutherford B. Hayes in, 76, 122–23, 186–88, 189, 190–92, 194, 195–96, 197, 198–201, 205–6
  House of Representatives in, 192, 195–205, 206–9
  Supreme Court and, 192, 200
  Samuel J. Tilden in, 190, 193–95, 197–98, 199–200, 201, 205, 206, 208
  voting counts and patterns, 50, 51, 53, 63, 64, 65, 107, 122, 202–5
elections
  of 1866, 23, 27, 28–29, 63, 64, 65, 75, 121–22
  of 1867, 23–31, 58–59, 86, 95, 143
  of 1868, 26–28, 30–31, 49, 58–59, 107, 122, 189
  of 2000 and 2004, 47
  mid-nineteenth century, 47–66
  military and, 41–42
  state, 96–97
Electoral College, 29, 41
  in election crisis of 1876–77, 187–208
Eliot, Charles W., 169, 181
elites, 132, 169, 190
  economic, 95
  Redeemer, 167, 186, 190
  slaveholding, planter, 98, 99, 100, 102
  voting influence of, xii, 47–48, 94
emancipation, 80, 87
  during Civil War, 88
  constitutionalism and, 162, 164–65, 169
  economics of, 97–99, 100, 102–4, 162
  enforcing, 14
enfranchisement, 161
  of African Americans, 16, 24, 25, 28, 54–55, 87, 142, 159, 163, 179
  of southern males, 141
equal rights, 178
  for all, ix, 99, 144, 166
  African Americans and, xiii, 4, 15, 151, 170, 182
  Constitution and, ix, 24
  democracy v., 166
  Democrats and, 55, 128, 145, 172
  Republicans and, xiii, 55, 128, 169, 172

INDEX

socialism and, 179
Supreme Court on, 149, 151
ethnocultural issues, 54, 94, 96, 107–8, 112

factionalism, 71–89
African Americans and, 73, 74, 80, 86, 87
class and, 70
clientelism and, 68, 69, 70, 71, 75, 79–82, 84
custom house, 78, 81
Democrats and, 71, 72–73, 74, 75, 76, 77, 85, 86, 88
Horace Greeley and, 73, 76, 83, 85, 86
in Indiana, 75, 78, 83, 85, 86
Andrew Johnson and, 75, 76, 77, 88
literature of, historians on, 89
in New York, 73, 74, 76–77, 78, 79, 80, 83, 85, 87, 146, 172, 179
in Ohio, 74, 76–77, 79, 81, 85, 86, 87
partisanship and, 79–80, 84–85, 88
patronage and, 70, 71, 75–79, 80, 81, 82, 83, 84, 87, 88
in Pennsylvania, 78, 81, 83, 85
political structure and, 82–84
representation and, 84–88
Republicans and, 67, 69, 72–74, 75–77, 78, 79, 80, 81, 82–83, 84, 85–86, 87–88, 103–4, 188
South and, 67–69, 70, 71, 73–74, 78–79, 85, 88, 188
study of, 67–71
Fairman, Charles, 140
federalism, xiii, 4–8, 10, 20, 21, 138–39, 147, 148–49, 168
Federalist, 36
Fehrenbacher, Don E., 3
Fenton, Reuben E., 19, 20, 73, 76, 78, 85
Ferry, Thomas W., 192
Fessenden, William Pitt, 10, 12, 13–14, 18, 24, 35
Fifteenth Amendment, x, 4, 18–20, 21, 94, 112, 125, 182
filibuster, 200–206, 209
Fine, Sidney, 171
Fiscal policy, 51, 53
Fishback, William M., 158
Fitzgerald, Michael, 80
Foner, Eric, 4, 24, 93–94, 96, 126, 168–69
Force Act of 1871, 21, 49–51
Force Act of 1890, 128
"forfeit rights" theory, 8–9

Forney, John, 27–28
Fourteenth Amendment, x, xi, 4, 12–13, 20, 21, 23–24, 35, 139, 141, 149
John M. Bingham as author of, xi, 12–13
framing of, 12–13, 21
legal analysts on, 5–6
on officeholding, 101, 145, 150
ratification of, 23, 25
scope of, 222 n. 46
states and, 16, 20, 23–24
France, 11
Frankfurter, Felix, 138
fraud, 81–82, 153, 154, 158, 164, 167, 192
freedmen, 13, 34, 37–38, 130
constitutionalism and, 155, 158, 159, 161, 162, 163, 166
Reconstruction politics and, 94, 97, 100, 102–3, 104, 123–24, 125, 127–28
Reconstruction retreat and, 176, 179–80, 183, 184
Freedmen's Bureau, 13, 37–38, 40, 161
Free Soil, 60, 74, 133, 134, 135, 169
free trade, 171, 173, 175, 182
Fugitive Slave Act, 135–36
Fugitive Slave Clause, 134–36

Garfield, James A., 59, 60–62, 127, 169
Gathright, Thomas S., 163
Georgia, 20, 40, 74, 80, 81, 107, 153–54, 158, 196
German immigrants, 10, 54, 112–15, 179
gerrymandering, 78, 167
Gillem, Alvan C., 40
Gillette, William, 93, 94, 168
Godkin, Edwin L., 16, 124, 166, 169, 171, 176, 179, 180–81
gold, as currency, 150, 174, 175
Granger legislation, 125, 126
Grant, Ulysses S., 19, 21, 97, 98, 105, 107, 122, 125
corruption and, 123
Andrew Johnson and, 27, 42
military and, 26, 27, 127, 146
on Mississippi violence, 95–96, 127
nomination and election of, 26–28, 29, 30–31, 73, 76, 86, 130, 143, 151, 176, 182
grasp-of-war theory, 10–12, 16, 17, 19–20
Greeley, Horace, 26, 27, 125, 143, 146, 151, 164
factionalism and, 73, 76, 83, 85, 86

Grimes, James W., 7–8, 178
Guarantee Clause, 11–12, 17

Hamburg Massacre, 122–23
Hammarberg, Melvyn, 94
Hart, Bushnell, 139, 140
Hayes, Rutherford B., 29, 30, 60, 61, 76, 123, 184
  in crisis of 1876–77, 76, 122–23, 186–88, 189, 190–92, 194, 195–96, 197, 198–201, 205–6
Hewitt, Abram S., 197, 198, 199, 201
Hill, Benjamin H., 196, 197, 198
Hoadly, George, 139
Holden, William W., 96–97, 100, 104
Holman, William S., 204
Holmes, Oliver Wendell, 140, 181
Holt, Thomas, 80
House of Representatives
  in crisis of 1876–77, 192, 195–205, 206–9
  on impeachment, 32, 35
  legislation types proposed by, 118–19
  partisanship in, 40, 49, 50–51, 61, 62
  Reconstruction and, 8, 10, 11–12, 30, 153
Howard, Oliver Otis, 40, 161
Howells, William Dean, 60
Howe, Timothy Otis, 17
Hurlbut, Stephen A., xi
Hyman, Harold M., 7, 138

Illinois, 57, 63–64, 65, 75–76, 77, 112, 116, 121, 122, 136, 140
Immigrants, 56, 80, 112, 161, 172, 176. *See also* ethnocultural issues
  German, 10, 54, 112–15, 179
  northern, 104, 105
impeachment
  William J. Clinton and, 33–34
  Congress on, 32, 33, 34–39, 40, 43
  Constitution and, 32–33, 35, 36–37, 38, 39, 41, 43
  Democrats and, 40, 41
  English, 36
  House of Representatives on, 32, 35
  of Andrew Johnson, 25, 32–43, 139, 143–44, 146, 178
  Reconstruction and, 25, 32–43
  Republicans and, 33, 34–38, 39, 40, 41–43
  Senate on, 35, 36, 39, 42–43
  Watergate and Nixon and, 32, 33
Independent, 30, 40

Indiana, 54, 57, 75, 121, 191
  factionalism and, 75, 78, 83, 85, 86
Indian policy, 52
Inflation, 55, 86–87, 141, 144, 145–46, 151, 174–75, 178, 180, 189, 190
Iowa, 57, 58, 63–64, 65, 121
Italy, 67, 70, 80, 81

Jackson, Andrew, 132, 159, 172, 188
  Jackson Day and, 197, 199
Japan, 67, 81
Jeffersonian Republicans, x–xi, 160
Johnson, Andrew
  on black suffrage, 162
  factionalism and, 75, 76, 77, 88
  Ulysses S. Grant and, 27, 42
  impeachment of, 25, 32–43, 139, 143–44, 146, 178
  Andrew J. Kellar and, 189–90
  military and, 38–39, 40, 41–42, 142–43
  Republicans and, 8, 9, 15, 23, 25–26, 33, 34–38, 39, 40, 41–43, 62, 121, 156, 157, 177
  on southern states, 8, 9, 15, 23, 141, 142
Joint Committee on Reconstruction, 7–8, 10, 12
Julian, George W., 61–62, 74, 75, 78, 83, 85, 86

Kaczorowski, Robert J., 4, 217 n. 15
Kansas, 54–56, 58, 59, 121
Kellar, Andrew J., 189–90, 191, 195, 196, 198, 199–200, 202
Keller, Morton D., 83
Kelley, William H., 56–59, 177
Kellogg, William Pitt, 78
Kelly, Alfred, 6–7
Kennedy, John F., 33
Kent, James, 36
Kentucky, 11, 24, 28, 129, 149, 197
Keppel's Administrators v. Petersburg Rail Road Company, 150
Key, V. O., 67, 68, 69, 70, 71, 72, 78–79, 80
Kincaid, Larry G., 24
Kleppner, Paul, 94
Ku Klux Klan, 49, 105, 122, 154

labor, 38, 93, 100, 161, 177, 180, 185
  free, 94, 97, 98–99, 102–3, 126
  legislation, 82, 171, 172
  militancy, northern, 4, 126, 169
  shortage, 103

INDEX 309

Labovitz, John R., 33
laissez-faire constitutionalism, 160, 162, 163, 166, 169, 171, 172, 175
laissez-faire moralism, 126, 183, 185
Lamar, Lucius Q. C., 196, 197, 198
land
 confiscation and redistribution, 24–25, 26, 30, 37–38, 80, 102, 161, 163, 178–79
 General Land Office on, 81
 reform, 26, 37, 155
 for settlers, 55, 61–62
Lane County v. Oregon, 148–49
Larson, Bruce, 47
Lasswell, Harold, 70
Lawrence, William, 10
law and politics, relations between, ix–x
Legal Tender Act, 148, 150
Liberal Republicans. *See* Republican Party
Lieber, Francis, 7, 169, 173
Lincoln, Abraham, 34, 73, 76, 77
 Chase and, 73, 76, 129, 130, 136–37, 138, 140, 141, 147
Locke, David Ross, 62
Logan, John A., 75–76
Louisiana, 39, 78, 99, 107, 158, 159, 163, 165, 192, 200, 201, 205–6
 in electoral count roll calls, 207, 208
 overthrow in, 153, 154–55
Lowell, James Russell, 169, 173, 179, 180–81, 182–83

Mahone, William, 81
Marcus, Robert D., 67
Marshall, John, xi, 138
Maryland, 11, 24, 28
Massachusetts, 24, 28, 60, 63–64, 65, 81, 121, 179–80
Mayhew, David R., 48, 66
McCulloch, Hugh, 177, 178, 179, 182
McKitrick, Eric L., 6, 7, 23–24
McPherson, Edward, 54
McPherson, James, xi–xii
McWhorter family, 74
Meade, George, 40
Meredith, Solomon, 75
Michels, Robert, 69, 83
Michigan, 57, 58, 121
military
 appropriations, 52
 Confederate, 38, 51

control, of southern states, 15–16, 25, 38–39, 40, 157
 elections and, 41–42
 Ulysses S. Grant and, 26, 27, 127, 146
 Andrew Johnson and, 38–39, 40, 41–42, 142–43
Military Government bill, 15–16
Miller, Samuel F., 131, 141, 145
Mill, John Stuart, 170
Minnesota, 28, 58, 59, 78, 83, 117, 121, 122
Mississippi, 40, 78, 79, 95–96, 107, 127, 153, 154, 163, 165–66
levees, 100, 186, 189, 204, 206
modernization, 70, 71, 79–80
monopolies, 79, 171, 184
 legislation against, 50, 53, 55
Montgomery, David, 168
Morton, Oliver P., 75, 78, 86, 124, 191
Mosca, Gaetano, 69
Mugwumps, Republican Party, 82, 83

Nation, 16, 87, 102, 124, 166, 169, 179–80, 199
nativism, 54, 94, 112
New Departure movement, 54, 74, 123, 145, 189
New Jersey, 28, 54, 63–64, 65, 121
newspapers, xii, 25, 26, 75. *See also specific newspapers*
 Democratic, 27, 29, 194
 Republican, 18, 27, 30, 40, 73, 86, 98, 129, 191, 196, 205
 slanted reports in, 190
New York, 17, 27, 28, 29, 30, 58, 59, 60, 121
 factionalism, 73, 74, 76–77, 78, 79, 80, 83, 85, 87, 146, 172, 179
 Tammany Hall and, 80, 146, 172, 179
New York Herald, 27, 123, 146, 147
New York Times, 26, 27, 29, 98, 166, 184, 197
New York Tribune, 18, 73, 98, 129, 146
Niven, John, 130–31
Nixon, Richard M., 34
Nordhoff, Charles, 82–83, 169, 181
North Carolina, 96, 99, 104, 105, 107, 153, 154, 158, 159, 190, 194
North and northern states
 democracy and, 27, 193, 195
 racism of, 3, 4, 94, 118, 123, 128, 160, 166, 168, 169, 183
 working-class militancy in, 4, 126, 169

Ohio, 26, 28–29, 30, 42, 57, 58, 59, 63–64, 65, 121
  factionalism in, 74, 76–77, 79, 81, 85, 86, 87
Olmsted, Frederick Law, 97
Ord, Edward O. C., 40
Oregon, 58, 148–49, 207
Orr, James L., 162–63
Ostrogorski, Moisei, 69

Paris Commune, 172
Parrington, Vernon L., 160
partisanship
  in Congress, 48, 49–53, 56–66
  Democratic, 47–49, 50–53, 55–56, 57–63, 65, 66
  ethnocultural backgrounds in, 54
  factionalism and, 79–80, 84–85, 88
  in House of Representatives, 40, 49, 50–51, 61, 62
  median indices and, 49, 50–51, 52–53, 64–65
  party platforms and, 54–56
  personal ambition and, 56–66
  during Reconstruction, 47, 49–66
  Republican, 47–59, 61–64, 66
  rise in, 47–49
  in Senate, 49, 52, 60, 62
  in voting patterns, 54–55, 57–58
party system, xiii, 47–66, 49, 54, 78–79, 112. *See also* Democratic Party; elections; factionalism; Republican Party
patronage system, 38, 39, 65, 66, 69, 191
  factionalism and, 70, 71, 75–79, 80, 81, 82, 83, 84, 87, 88
  Senate and, 77–78
Pendleton, George H., 77, 144
Pennsylvania, 27, 28, 29, 54, 56–59, 63–64, 65, 121
  factionalism and, 78, 81, 83, 85
  Prigg v. Pennsylvania and, 135
Pension office, 82
Perman, Michael, 67, 85, 162
Peskin, Allan, 187, 198–99
Philadelphia Press, 27
Phillips, Wendell, ix, 24–25, 86, 98
Platt, Thomas C., 78
Polakoff, Keith Ian, 187, 205
Polsby, Nelson, 73
Pomeroy, John Norton, 37
Pope, John, 40

Potter, Clarkson, 193–94
presidency. *See also specific presidents*
  Constitution and, 35, 36–37, 39, 41–43
  terms for, 51
  voter turnout and, 120
Prigg v. Pennsylvania, 135
"Principles of '98," x–xi
proscriptive policies, 101–2
public works, 51, 53

race, xii, xiii, 24, 165, 172, 179. *See also* African Americans
  Democrats and, 55, 102, 123, 125, 128, 129, 145
  Reconstruction politics and, 55, 93, 94, 102, 103, 112, 123, 125, 128
  Republicans and, xiii, 55, 93, 94, 102, 103, 112, 118, 123, 125, 128, 155, 162, 165, 168–69, 170, 172, 183
  in voting patterns, 106–7, 116–17
racism, xiii, 96, 145
  northern, 3, 4, 94, 118, 123, 128, 160, 166, 168, 169, 183
  southern, 102, 112, 118, 155, 159, 160, 183
radicalism, Republican. *See* Republican Party, radicalism of
Railroads, 61–72, 81, 82, 186, 188–89, 200, 204, 206
  Reconstruction politics and, 95, 97, 98, 99, 100
Ramsey, Alexander, 78
Randall, Samuel J., 194, 201
Ranney, Austin, 72, 84
Rawle, William, 36
Rawlins, John A., 27
Reconciliation, with South, 35, 73, 104, 123, 128, 143, 149, 183
Reconstruction, 93–128
  Acts, 23–24, 25, 36, 38–39, 41, 99, 104, 142–43
  conservative basis of radical, 3–22
  constitutional politics and, ix–xiii, 47
  Democrats and, 93, 97, 98, 99, 100, 101, 102, 105, 106–7, 110–17, 121, 122–24, 125, 126, 127–28
  elections of 1867 and, 23–31
  failure and weakness of, xiii, 4–5, 17, 21–22, 168–69
  freedmen in, 94, 97, 100, 102–3, 104, 123–24, 125, 127–28
  grasp-of-war and, 10–12, 16, 17, 19–20
  historians on, 6–7, 23, 33, 54

Index

House of Representatives and, 8, 10, 11–12, 30, 153
Joint Committee on, 7–8, 10, 12
legislation, 4–5, 50–53, 55
partisanship during, 47, 49–66
race and, 55, 93, 94, 102, 103, 112, 123, 125, 128
Republican policy on, politics of, 93–128
Republican program of, first, ix, 3–15, 16, 21–22
Republican program of, second, 15–22
retreat from and end of, 19–22, 128, 168–85
Senate and, 10, 13–14, 17–18, 25, 30
tariffs and, 171, 175, 177–78, 179, 180, 183
Redeemers, 167, 186, 190
reformers, Republican. *See* Republican Party
religion, 55, 94, 170. *See also* Catholics and Catholicism; Protestants
representation
  factionalism and, 84–88
  taxation and, 162
Republican Party
  African Americans and, ix, xiii, 3–4, 5, 6, 13–16, 19, 21, 23–26, 30, 128
  African Americans in, 102, 103–6
  civil rights and, 3–4, 5, 6, 13–15, 19–22, 50, 118–19, 123–24, 184
  conservatism, 6–8, 9, 12–14, 15, 18, 21–22, 24, 25, 26–28
  elections of 1867 and, 23–31
  equal rights and, xiii, 55, 128, 169, 172
  factionalism and, 67, 69, 72–74, 75–77, 78, 79, 80, 81, 82–83, 84, 85–86, 87–88, 103–4, 188
  Jeffersonian, x–xi, 160
  Andrew Johnson and, 8, 9, 15, 23, 25–26, 33, 34–38, 39, 40, 41–43, 62, 121, 156, 157, 177
  liberal Republicans, 73–74, 75, 76, 99, 125, 136, 146, 151, 168, 169, 170, 176, 177
  moderation, 6, 23
  Mugwumps, 82, 83
  newspapers, 18, 27, 30, 40, 73, 86, 98, 129, 191, 196, 205
  partisanship, 47–59, 61–64, 66
  platforms, 54–56, 118–20
  public opinion and, xi
  race and, xiii, 55, 93, 94, 102, 103, 112, 118, 123, 125, 128, 155, 162, 165, 168–69, 170, 172, 183

Reconstruction policy, politics of, 93–128
Reconstruction program, first, ix, 3–15, 16, 21–22
Reconstruction program, second, 15–22
reformers, 82–84, 87–88, 94, 98, 99, 125–27, 168–85, 190–91, 199, 205–6
  in South, 25–26, 85, 96–107, 122–23, 157, 163–64, 183
  voting patterns, 107–9, 112–17, 121–22, 126
Republican Party, radicalism of
  Salmon Portland Chase and, 26, 74, 85, 86, 130, 133, 137, 138, 139–40, 141, 142, 143
  constitutionalism and, 155–56, 157, 161, 167
  impeachment of Johnson and, 33, 35–37, 38, 40, 41, 43
  irony and tragedy of, 167
  radicalism, conservative basis of, 3–22
  reformers and, 175–85
  rout of, 23–31
Reunion and Reaction (Woodward), 186–89, 195
"Revolution" of 1800, x–xi
Rhode Island, 28, 57, 116, 122
Rhodes, James Ford, 93, 140
Richardson, Heather Cox, 166, 168, 169

Sabato, Larry, 47
Sartori, Giovanni, 69, 70
schools, 24, 56, 97, 98, 99–100, 133, 183
Schuckers, James, 139
Schurz, Carl, 10, 13, 16, 19, 20, 42, 78, 165, 181, 206
Science and scientific ideas, 170–71, 174, 175, 177
Scott, John, 78
Scott, Thomas Alexander, 81, 94–95, 189, 198–200
Senate
  African Americans in, 169–70
  on impeachment, 35, 36, 39, 42–43
  partisanship in, 49, 52, 60, 62
  patronage and, 77–78
  Reconstruction and, 10, 13–14, 17–18, 25, 30
Seward, William H., 27, 76, 86, 129, 130, 142
Sheridan, Philip S., 39

Sherman, John, 15, 24, 30, 42, 190, 199
Sherman, William T., 42
Sickles, Daniel, 39
Silbey, Joel, 67, 85, 93, 95, 126
Simpson, Brooks, 21
Slaughterhouse Cases, 140, 149
slavery, ix. *See also* antislavery movement; African Americans; emancipation; freedmen
  "black codes" and, 34
  economics and, 97–99, 100, 102–4, 162
  elite control of, 98, 99, 100, 102
  Fugitive Slave Act on, 135–36
  Fugitive Slave Clause on, 134–36
  proslavery constitution and, xi, 3, 6
  proslavery southerners and, 74, 134, 139
Smith, Donnal V., 130
Smith, William Henry, 29, 76, 78, 189, 191, 195, 198, 200
socialism, 25, 166, 172, 179
social science, new, 176
soldiers, Civil War, xi–xii, 55, 76
South Carolina, 99, 107, 122–23, 153, 163, 207, 208
Southern Democrats, 125, 127, 128, 147, 186–209
South and southern states, 5, 8–9
  Bourbonism myth in, 186
  Congress on, 9–11, 12, 15–18, 21, 23
  constitutions of, 99, 101, 104, 142–43, 152–59, 162, 167
  democracy and, 98
  economic issues, 97–99, 100–104, 106, 118–20, 142, 186–87, 189
  factionalism in, 67–69, 70, 71, 73–74, 78–79, 85, 88, 188
  Andrew Johnson on, 8, 9, 15, 23, 141, 142
  Ku Klux Klan in, 49
  land confiscation and redistribution in, 24–25, 26, 30, 37–38, 80, 102, 161, 163, 178–79
  military control of, 15–16, 25, 38–39, 40, 157
  outrages in, 49, 123, 127, 128
  proslavery, 74, 134, 139
  racism of, 102, 112, 118, 155, 159, 160, 183
  reconciliation with, 35, 73, 104, 123, 128, 143, 149, 183
  Republicans in, 25–26, 85, 96–107, 122–23, 157, 163–64, 183–84
  Thaddeus Stevens on, 8, 9–10, 11, 15, 25, 155
  Union and, 8–9, 11, 13, 15, 16, 18, 19, 20, 23–24, 26, 41, 106, 125, 139, 142–43, 156, 157–58, 175–76, 182, 184
  voluntarism and, 10, 11, 12, 16, 135, 156
  whites in, 15, 23, 25–26, 38, 97, 98, 100, 101, 102, 103–4, 105, 122–23, 125–26, 154–55, 156, 157, 161–62, 165, 167, 179, 183, 205–6
Spalding, Rufus P., 177
Spencer, George S., 76, 78
Stampp, Kenneth M., 152
Stanbery, Henry, 25, 38–39
Stanton, Edwin M., 27, 39, 42
states. *See also* North and northern states; South and southern states
  "black codes" of, 34
  citizenship v. national, 141–42
  debt of, 165, 189–90
  elections in, 96–97
  Fourteenth Amendment and, 16, 20, 23–24
  rights of, x, xi, 4, 8, 16, 55, 134, 136–37, 142, 145, 147, 148, 189
  "state suicide" theory, 8–9
Stephens, Alexander H., 196, 197
Stevens, Thaddeus, xi, 24, 27, 35, 40, 51, 86, 161, 170, 177, 178
  on southern states, 8, 9–10, 11, 15, 25, 155
Stewart, William M., 17–18
Story, Joseph, 36
suffrage
  black, 5, 16, 17–18, 19, 21, 23–25, 29, 30, 41, 50, 54, 55, 57–59, 86, 97, 116–17, 142–43, 159, 161, 162, 169, 182, 184
  female, xi, 176
  Johnson on, 162
  male, 12, 16
  national law on impartial, 24–25
  universal, 98, 104
Sumner, Charles, xii, 8, 20, 24, 25, 35, 60, 177
Sumner, William, 172
Supreme Court, xi
  on *Armstrong's Foundry* case, 149
  on *Blyew v. U.S.*, 149
  on *Bronson v. Rodes*, 150
  Salmon Portland Chase as chief justice of, 26, 61, 129, 130, 138–41, 143–51
  on *Collector v. Day*, 148–49
  on *Dred Scott* case, xii, 3
  electoral crisis and, 192, 200

on equal rights, 149, 151
on *Keppel's Administrators v. Petersburg Rail Road Company*, 150
on *Lane County v. Oregon*, 148–49
John Marshall, as chief justice of, xi, 138
on *Prigg v. Pennsylvania*, 135
role of, x
on *The Slaughterhouse Cases*, 140, 149
on *Texas v. White*, 147–48
on *Veazie Bank v. Fenno*, 151
Swayne, Wager, 40

Tammany Hall faction, New York, 80, 146, 172, 179
Taney, Roger B., xi
tariffs, 50, 52, 54, 55, 73, 82, 87, 127, 160, 189
  retreat from Reconstruction and, 171, 175, 177–78, 179, 180, 183
taxation, 17, 55, 75, 81, 98, 99, 119, 120, 164, 183–84, 189, 190
  constitutionalism and, 159, 162–66
  representation and, 162
Taylor, Richard ("Dick"), 198–99
Tennessee, 15, 105, 107, 153, 159, 189, 190, 196
Tenure of Office Act, 39, 42, 77, 78, 124
Test Oath law, 38, 55
Texas, 100, 107, 147–48, 153, 165
Texas v. White, 147–48
Thirteenth Amendment, x, 3–4, 14, 142
Thomas, Dorsey, 189, 190
Thomas, Scott, 81, 94–95, 189, 198–99, 200
Tilden, Samuel J., 77, 87
  in crisis of 1876–77, 190, 193–95, 197–98, 199–200, 201, 205, 206, 208
Tilton, Theodore, 40
Toombs, Robert, 167
Tourgee, Albion W., 96
treason, 36, 143, 146, 155, 184, 201
Treasury Department, 38, 81, 177, 178, 179
  Salmon Portland Chase and, 73, 129–30, 145, 150
  Hugh McCulloch and, 177, 178, 179, 182
Trumbull, Lyman, 7, 13–14, 18, 25, 35, 75–76, 77, 83
Turpie, David, 60

Underwood, John C., 147
Union, 7, 34, 49, 147–48, 151
forces, 55, 149
southern states and, 8–9, 11, 13, 15, 16, 18, 19, 20, 23–24, 26, 41, 106, 125, 139, 142–43, 156, 157–58, 175–76, 182, 184
victory of, 123, 161

Vallandigham, Clement L., 74, 77
Veazie Bank v. Fenno, 151
Vermont, 121, 122, 208
Vinson, Fred M., 138
violence, 5, 95–96, 105, 106–7, 153, 154, 191, 192, 206
Virginia, 20, 79, 81, 104, 105, 107, 146–47, 158, 159
Voluntarism, 10, 11, 12, 16, 135, 156
Voting, 55. *See also* suffrage
  barring people from, 157
  African Americans, 104, 106, 158, 161, 178
  in crisis of 1876–77, 50, 51, 53, 63, 64, 65, 107, 122, 202–5
  elites' influence on, xii, 47–48, 94
  oaths, 38, 55
  property requirements for, 160
Voting patterns, xii, 88
  correlations and, 48, 64, 65, 116–17, 120–22, 126
  Democratic, 106–7, 110–17, 121
  ethnocultural variables in, 107–18
  gubernatorial, 57–59, 63–65, 107, 116–17, 120, 121
  partisanship in, 54–55, 57–58
  presidential, 63–65
  race in, 106–7, 116–17
  Republican, 107–9, 112–17, 121–22, 126
  roll-off and, 63
  white, 106–7

Wade, Benjamin F., 24, 26, 28–29, 30, 31, 76, 86, 177, 178, 180, 197, 207
Walker, Amasa, 169, 181
Ward, Durbin, 161
Warden, Robert, 131, 139, 145
War for Independence, 7
Warmoth, Henry Clay, 78, 102
Warner, Willard, 78
War powers
  of Congress, 7–11, 13
  Constitution and, 7–8, 10
  grasp-of-war and, 10–12, 16, 17, 19–20
Washburne, Elihu, 31, 40
Washington, Booker T., 80

Washington Chronicle, 27
Watergate scandal, 32, 33
Watson, Thomas Edward ("Tom"), 186
Watterson, Henry, 56, 197
Weed, Thurlow, 27, 86
Wells, David A., 169, 173, 177, 181
Whigs, 63–64, 76, 86, 97, 100, 112, 133, 145, 188–89
Whiskey Ring scandals, 81
White, Horace, 169, 180, 181, 183
whites
   lower- and upper-class, 179
   southern, 15, 23, 25–26, 38, 97, 98, 100, 101, 102, 103–4, 105, 122–23, 125–26, 154–55, 156, 157, 161–62, 165, 167, 179, 183, 205–6

   voting patterns of, 106–7
white supremacy, 4, 141, 163, 183
Whittington, Keith, 39
Williams, George H., 15
Wilson, Henry, 26, 161
Wilson, James, 35, 40, 43
Wirt, William, 131–32
Wisconsin, 57, 58, 59, 121
Woodward, C. Vann, 94, 186–89, 191, 195, 206
   Reunion and Reaction by, 186–89, 195
Wormley House Bargain, 206

Yates, Richard, 17

Zeller, Belle, 67–68

RECONSTRUCTING AMERICA SERIES
Paul A. Cimbala, series editor

1. Hans L. Trefousse
Impeachment of a President: Andrew Johnson, the Blacks, and Reconstruction

2. Richard Paul Fuke
Imperfect Equality: African Americans and the Confines of White Ideology in Post-Emancipation Maryland.

3. Ruth Currie-McDaniel
Carpetbagger of Conscience: A Biography of John Emory Bryant

4. Paul A. Cimbala and Randall M. Miller, eds.
The Freedmen's Bureau and Reconstruction: Reconsiderations

5. Herman Belz
A New Birth of Freedom: The Republican Party and Freedmen's Rights, 1861 to 1866

6. Robert Michael Goldman
"A Free Ballot and a Fair Count": The Department of Justice and the Enforcement of Voting Rights in the South, 1877–1893

7. Ruth Douglas Currie, ed.
Emma Spaulding Bryant: Civil War Bride, Carpetbagger's Wife, Ardent Feminist—Letters, 1860–1900

8. Robert Francis Engs
Freedom's First Generation: Black Hampton, Virginia, 1861–1890

9. Robert F. Kaczorowski
The Politics of Judicial Interpretation: The Federal Courts, Department of Justice and Civil Rights, 1866–1876

10. John Syrett
The Civil War Confiscation Acts: Failing to Reconstruct the South